Society and Politics in England,
1780–1960

SOCIETY AND POLITICS IN ENGLAND, 1780–1960

A Selection of Readings and Comments

edited by

J. F. C. HARRISON

Professor of History
University of Wisconsin

Harper & Row, Publishers
New York, Evanston, and London

Contents

Preface   *xi*

PART ONE.
OLD ENGLAND, 1780–1815

1. POPULATION AND SOCIAL STRUCTURE   3
   1 [A Map of Society], *by Patrick Colquhoun*   4
   2 An Essay on Civil Society, *by Adam Ferguson*   10
   3 Principles of Population, *by Arthur Young*   12
   4 Essay on Population, *by Thomas Robert Malthus*   14

2. THE FACE OF THE LAND   22
   5 [English Farming Practice], *by Arthur Young*   23
   6 [An Improving Landlord], *by Arthur Young*   25
   7 [Enclosure in Yorkshire], *by William Marshall*   27
   8 [Enclosure Proceedings], *from the* Journals of the House
     of Commons   32
   9 [The Condition of the Agricultural Workers], *by David
     Davies*   35
   10 [The Speenhamland System], *from* The Reading Mer-
     cury, *May 11, 1795*   42
   11 [The Old and the New Farmer], *by William Cobbett*   44
   12 The Diary of a Country Parson, *by James Woodforde*   46

3. THE PROGRESS OF INDUSTRIALISM   50
   13 [The Woolen Industry Around Halifax], *by Daniel
     Defoe*   51
   14 [A Handloom Weaver's Life], *by Samuel Bamford*   54
   15 [Change in the Cotton Industry], *by William Radcliffe*   58
   16 [The Industrial Revolution in Manchester], *by John Aikin*   62
   17 Observations on the Manufacturing System, *by Robert
     Owen*   66
   18 [A Protest Against Machinery], *by Yorkshire Cloth
     Workers*   70
   19 [Support for Machinery], *by the Leeds Cloth Merchants*   72

v

4. GOVERNMENT AND POLITICAL INSTITUTIONS   75
   20 [The British Constitution], *by William Paley*   76
   21 [The Role of a Member of Parliament], *by Edmund Burke*   84
   22 The State of the Representation, *by the Society of the Friends of the People*   86
   23 [Sinecures, Reversions, and Pensions], *by John Wade*   93

5. THE STATE OF RELIGION   99
   24 [The Case for an Established Church], *by William Paley*   101
   25 The People Called Methodists, *by John Wesley*   106
   26 True and Nominal Christianity, *by William Wilberforce*   109
   27 Practical Piety, *by Hannah More*   114

   Further Reading: General Works   118
   Further Reading: Part One   119

PART TWO.

THE FORCES OF CHANGE, 1815–1848

6. THE STRUGGLE FOR POPULAR DEMOCRACY   123
   28 [The Massacre of Peterloo], *by Samuel Bamford*   124
   29 England in 1819, *by Percy Bysshe Shelley*   129
   30 [Tory Opposition to Reform], *by the Duke of Wellington*   129
   31 [The 1832 Reform Bill], *by Thomas Babington Macaulay*   130
   32 [The £10 Householders], *by Edward Baines*   134

7. THE WORKSHOP OF THE WORLD   138
   33 The Principles of Political Economy, *by David Ricardo*   139
   34 The Philosophy of Manufactures, *by Andrew Ure*   144
   35 The 1834 Poor Law Report, *by His Majesty's Commissioners*   146
   36 [Child Labor in Factories], *Evidence Before Michael Thomas Sadler's Committee*   149
   37 The Sanitary Condition of the Labouring Population, *by Edwin Chadwick*   152

8. PROTEST AND REVOLT   157
   38 Initiation Ceremony of the Woolcomber's Union   157
   39 A New View of Society, *by Robert Owen*   162
   40 Labour's Wrongs and Labour's Remedy, *by John Francis Bray*   164

41 [Chartism in Halifax], *by Benjamin Wilson*   167
42 [Repeal of the Corn Laws], *by Richard Cobden*   170

9. CHURCH AND CHAPEL   173
43 [Rich and Poor in the Parish Church], *by Joseph Arch* 174
44 Tracts for the Times: No. 1, *by John Henry Newman*   177
45 [The State of the Church in Leeds], *by Walter Farquhar
   Hook*   181
46 [Methodist Class Meetings], *by Joseph Barker*   183
47 Piety Among the Peasantry, *by Henry Woodcock*   186

10. CULTURAL CHANGE   189
48 The Social, Educational and Religious State of the Manufacturing Districts, *by Edward Baines*   190
49 [The Education of the People], *by Joseph Lawson*   192
50 [Self-Education], *by Thomas Cooper*   195
51 The History of Ben the Soldier, *published by the Religious Tract Society*   197
52 The Philosophy of Drinking Usage, *by John Dunlop*   202

Further Reading: Part Two   206

PART THREE.
VICTORIAN PROSPERITY, 1848–1870

11. BOURGEOIS ENGLAND   209
53 [The Great Exhibition, 1851], *by the Prince Consort*   210
54 Self-Help, *by Samuel Smiles*   211
55 [A Successful Industrialist]: Sir Titus Salt, *by R. Balgarnie*   214
56 English Traits, *by Ralph Waldo Emerson*   217
57 [Domestic Servants], *by Isabella Beeton*   218

12. THE ATHENIAN AGE OF ENGLISH DEMOCRACY   224
58 The English Constitution, *by Walter Bagehot*   225
59 [The Extension of the Suffrage], *by John Stuart Mill* 230
60 [The Dangers of Democracy], *by Robert Lowe*   234
61 [The Demand for Parliamentary Reform], *by John Bright* 239

13. RELIGION AND SCIENCE   244
62 The Origin of Species, *by Thomas Henry Huxley*   245
63 [The Rejection of Darwinism], *by Samuel Wilberforce*   248

64 [Geology and Genesis], *by Edmund Gosse*   251
65 The Interpretation of Scripture, *by Benjamin Jowett*   255

14. CRITICS OF VICTORIAN CIVILIZATION   259
66 The Tyranny of the Majority, *by John Stuart Mill*   259
67 Barbarians, Philistines, Populace, *by Matthew Arnold*   263
68 Unto this Last, *by John Ruskin*   266
69 In a Manufacturing Town, *by Edward Carpenter*   272

Further Reading: Part Three   274

PART FOUR.
TOWARDS A MASS DEMOCRACY, 1870–1914

15. AGRICULTURAL AND INDUSTRIAL SOCIETY   277
70 [The Bases of English Society], *by Thomas Escott*   278
71 The Landed Interest, *by James Caird*   282
72 The Wheelwright's Shop, *by George Sturt*   287
73 [The Growth of Middlesbrough], *by Lady Bell*   293

16. THE RISE OF LABOR   300
74 [Pioneering Days in Yorkshire], *by Ben Turner*   301
75 [The Religion of Socialism], *by James Keir Hardie*   306
76 How I Became a Socialist, *by William Morris*   308
77 Merrie England, *by Robert Blatchford*   311
78 [The Fabian Society], *by George Bernard Shaw*   315
79 Program of the Independent Labour Party   321
80 Constitution of the Labour Party   324

17. SOME REPRESENTATIVE SOCIAL PATTERNS   328
81 Poverty, *by B. Seebohm Rowntree*   328
82 [An Early Board School], *by James Runciman*   331
83 [The Workers' Educational Association], *by Albert Mans-
    bridge*   334
84 [*The Daily Mail*], *by Henry Hamilton Fyfe*   340

18. CONSERVATIVES AND LIBERALS   346
85 England's Mission, *by William Ewart Gladstone*   347
86 [Home Rule for Ireland], *by William Ewart Gladstone*   351
87 [The Concept of Empire], *by Benjamin Disraeli*   357
88 Recessional, *by Rudyard Kipling*   359

89 [Tory Democracy], *by Randolph Churchill* 360
90 [The New Liberalism], *by David Lloyd George* 364

Further Reading: Part Four 367

PART FIVE.
BETWEEN THE WARS, 1914–1939

19. THE REVOLUTIONARY YEARS 371
    91 Labour and the New Social Order, *by the Labour Party* 372
    92 The Acquisitive Society, *by Richard Henry Tawney* 383
    93 [The General Strike], *by Henry Hamilton Fyfe* 389
    94 [The Decline of the Liberal Party], *by Herbert Henry Asquith* 397

20. CRISIS, 1929–1931 401
    95 [The Second Labour Government], by *Beatrice Webb* 401
    96 [The Formation of the National Government], *by Philip Snowden* 405

21. THE 1930s 410
    97 Men Without Work, *Pilgrim Trust Report* 411
    98 The Road to Wigan Pier, *by George Orwell* 415
    99 Forward from Liberalism, *by Stephen Spender* 420
    100 The General Theory of Employment, *by John Maynard Keynes* 423

Further Reading: Part Five 430

PART SIX.
THE WELFARE STATE, 1940–1960

22. WARTIME ORIGINS 433
    101 Their Finest Hour, *by Winston Spencer Churchill* 434
    102 The Beveridge Report, *by William Beveridge* 438
    103 The 1944 Education Act 445

23. THE LABOUR GOVERNMENT, 1945–1951 449
    104 Let us Face the Future, *by the Labour Party* 450
    105 [A Free Health Service], *by Aneurin Bevan* 453
    106 Socialism and the Welfare State, *by Kingsley Martin* 457
    107 The Right Road for Britain, *by the Conservative Party* 460

24. ENGLAND IN THE 1950s   465

  108 [The Decline of the Churches], *by B. Seebohm Rowntree and G. R. Lavers*   466

  109 Education 15 to 18, *by the Crowther Committee*   469

  110 ["Giving the Public What It Wants"], *by the Pilkington Committee*   476

Further Reading: Part Six   482

Preface

This book is based upon material used in courses on modern British history for university undergraduates and also for adults, in America and England. It is intended for use with standard histories of the period, such as Elie Halévy, *A History of the English People in the Nineteenth Century* (6 vols.), Asa Briggs, *The Age of Improvement,* and Charles Loch Mowat, *Britain between the Wars, 1918–1940.* The readings are not to be considered substitutes for, but rather introductions to the original works; they indicate some of the fascinating material that is available. At the same time it is hoped that they convey a little more of the flavor of English society and politics than it is normally possible to contain in a textbook.

The selection of the extracts is determined by an approach which emphasizes changes in the English economy, social structure and political framework. It is social history, though not in a trivial ("men-and-manners") or exclusive ("with-the-politics-left-out") sense. Local as well as national sources have been used, as regional variation is an important theme in the nineteenth century: English society and politics have to be set in the context of Manchester, Birmingham and Leeds, as well as Westminster. Religion, education, and workers' movements are important strands that were deeply woven into the texture of English life; and they are therefore more fully represented than is sometimes the case. The intent has been to depict English civilization as a whole, through a consideration of its various separate but related aspects.

Suggestions for further reading are given at the end of each part. These are not full bibliographies, which can be found in the general works listed on p. 118, and in particular in the two volumes of *English Historical Documents,* Vol. XI (1783–1832) and Vol. XII (1833–1874).

The readings are taken from the appropriate English editions, published in London unless otherwise stated.

J. F. C. HARRISON

Acknowledgements

Grateful acknowledgement is made to the following authors and owners of copyright material for permission to use extracts in these readings (in order of appearance).

Oxford University Press (James Woodforde, *Diary of a Country Parson, 1758–1802*, ed. John Beresford).

The Council, Thoresby Society, Leeds (*The Leeds Woollen Industry, 1780–1820*, ed. W. B. Crump).

Epworth Press, London (from *The Journal of John Wesley*, ed. Nehemiah Curnock).

William Heinemann, Ltd., and Charles Scribner's Sons (Reprinted with permission of Charles Scribner's Sons from *Father and Son* by Edmund Gosse. Copyright 1907 Charles Scribner's Sons; renewal copyright 1935 Philip Gosse).

George Allen & Unwin Ltd. (Edward Carpenter, *Towards Democracy;* H. Hamilton Fyfe, *Northcliffe; an Intimate Biography*).

Cassell & Co. Ltd. (T. H. S. Escott, *England: her People, Polity and Pursuits*).

Cambridge University Press (George Sturt, *The Wheelwright's Shop; Men without Work: a Report made to the Pilgrim Trust*).

Thomas Nelson & Sons Ltd. (Lady [Florence] Bell, *At the Works;* B. Seebohm Rowntree, *Poverty: a Study in Town Life*).

Mr. Emrys Hughes, M. P. (*Keir Hardie's Speeches and Writings*, ed. Emrys Hughes).

Fabian Society (George Bernard Shaw, *Tract No. 70. Report on Fabian Policy*).

National Administrative Council, Independent Labour Party (*Programme of the Independent Labour Party*).

The Labour Party (*Constitution of the Labour Party; Labour and the New Social Order; Let Us Face the Future*).

Chatto & Windus Ltd. (James Runciman, *Schools and Scholars*).

Longmans, Green & Co. Ltd. (Albert Mansbridge, *An Ad-*

venture in Working Class Education; Beatrice Webb's Diaries, 1924–1932, ed. Margaret Cole; B. Seebohm Rowntree & G. R. Lavers, *English Life and Leisure*).

Mrs. George Bambridge, Messrs. Methuen & Co. Ltd., the Macmillan Company of Canada Ltd., Doubleday & Co., Inc. (Rudyard Kipling, from *The Five Nations*).

Lord Beaverbrook (David Lloyd George, *Better Times*).

G. Bell & Sons, Ltd., Harcourt, Brace & World, Inc. (from *The Acquisitive Society* by R. H. Tawney, copyright, 1920, by Harcourt, Brace & World, Inc., renewed, 1948, by R. H. Tawney and reprinted by permissions of the publishers. Published by G. Bell & Sons, Ltd. London 1921).

Executors of the late Henry Hamilton Fyfe (H. Hamilton Fyfe, *Behind the Scenes of the Great Strike*).

Cassell & Co. Ltd., Little Brown & Co. (*Memoirs and Reflections 1852–1927* by Herbert Henry Asquith, published by Cassell & Company, Limited: London).

Mr. Arthur W. Pratt (Philip Viscount Snowden, *An Autobiography*).

A. M. Heath & Co. Ltd., Harcourt, Brace & World, Inc. (from *The Road to Wigan Pier* by George Orwell. Reprinted by permission of Harcourt, Brace & World, Inc.).

Mr. Stephen Spender (Stephen Spender, *Forward from Liberalism*).

Trustees of the estate of the late Lord Keynes, Macmillan & Co., Ltd., Harcourt Brace & World, Inc. (from *General Theory of Employment, Interest and Money* by J. M. Keynes. Reprinted by permission of Harcourt, Brace & World, Inc.

H. M. Stationery Office (*Hansard, Parliamentary Debates; Social Insurance and Allied Services: Report by Sir William Beveridge; Education Act, 1944; 15 to 18; Report of the Committee on Broadcasting*).

David Higham Associates Ltd. (Aneurin Bevan, *In Place of Fear*).

Mr. Kingsley Martin, and the Fabian Society (Kingsley Martin, *Tract No. 291. Socialism and the Welfare State*).

Conservative & Unionist Central Office (*The Right Road for Britain*).

Should any extracts from works still in copyright be included inadvertently without acknowledgement, the publishers should be notified so that such acknowledgement may be made in future editions.

PART ONE.
OLD ENGLAND,
1780-1815

Chapter 1.

Population and Social Structure

The pyramid of English society in the eighteenth century was made up of ranks and orders rather than classes. At the top were the king and the great proprietors of land, including the five degrees of nobility. This Whig oligarchy, numbering perhaps 150, reached its heyday in the third quarter of the eighteenth century. Below them were the substantial proprietors and the gentry, whose power and prestige were derived from their ownership of land. The yeomen (who owned their own land) and the tenant farmers (who rented from the substantial proprietors) came next in the rural hierarchy; and at the bottom were the cottagers and laborers. In the towns a small group of rich merchants constituted a ruling oligarchy which intermarried with the gentry. Tradesmen, domestic manufacturers, and professional men constituted the "middling sort" of people; while the rest of the community (craftsmen, artisans and laborers —of varying degrees of skill and remuneration) made up the "lower orders," the "common people," or simply "the poor."

Fundamentally this was a static concept of social order; each rank had its respective obligations and responsibilities as well as rights and privileges. But in practice the rigidity of the system was modified in several ways. Within each main group was an infinite number of subtle variations and nuances of social difference; and despite the small size of the country regional and local variations were significant. A strongly developed sense of social conscience among the "better orders" mitigated some of the harshness of life for their less fortunate neighbors. Above all, English society was relatively fluid. Distinctions of rank, although important, were not hard and fast, and the line between one group and the next was often blurred. For several centuries there had been a sufficient degree of social mobility to allow able or lucky individuals to "improve" themselves, and to prevent the development of anything resembling a caste system.

From the second half of the eighteenth century, however, contemporaries became increasingly concerned with certain developments which could not be accommodated within the accepted limits of social change. The rapid increase in population occasioned much speculation as to its origin and possible effects on the social and economic structure; but until the first census was taken in 1801 it was not possible to be sure of the magnitude of the problem—and indeed even then some writers like William Cobbett continued to assert that the population was declining. It is now generally accepted that the population of England and Wales increased from about 5½ million in 1700 to 6½ million in 1750 and nearly 9 million in 1801. The second half of the eighteenth century was thus characterized by a 40 percent increase in population, and the rate of increase was even greater in the succeeding decades of the nineteenth century. But though the facts of population increase are verifiable the interpretation of them is by no means agreed. In the main it seems probable that the increase was due to a fall in the death rate coupled with a steady but high birth rate. Explanations of why this should have been so are at present in the controversial stage, and the exact connections between population increase and economic growth remain obscure.

The first of the following extracts is a statistical analysis of English society; the other three provide representative reactions to the population problem.

1. [A MAP OF SOCIETY]

by PATRICK COLQUHOUN

After an early career in Glasgow, Patrick Colquhoun (1745–1820) became a stipendiary magistrate in London. His pioneer investigations of crime and poverty in the metropolis were followed by *A Treatise on the Wealth, Power, and Re-*

sources of the British Empire (1814). This work was a main source of statistical information for political economists, both orthodox and socialist, and was frequently quoted. The passages are from chap. IV, pp. 102–126.

AN ATTEMPT TO SHEW HOW THE NEW PROPERTY IN GREAT BRITAIN AND IRELAND, ARISING FROM AGRICULTURE, MINES AND MINERALS, MANUFACTURES, INLAND TRADE, FOREIGN COMMERCE AND SHIPPING, COASTING TRADE, FISHERIES, AND FOREIGN INCOME IS DISTRIBUTED AMONG THE DIFFERENT CLASSES OF THE COMMUNITY.

HAVING in the three preceding Chapters taken a general view of the population,—the estimated capital or wealth of the British Empire,—and the new property acquired annually by the land and labour; it becomes an interesting object to discover, as far as discovery is practicable, by approximating details, in what manner and in what proportions this property is divided among the various classes of society in Great Britain and Ireland.

With a view to this object [a] Table . . . has been constructed. It may be considered as a map of civil society, exhibiting in one view the proportions of created wealth which is allotted annually to every class of the community, from the Sovereign in regular gradation down to the pauper. Although all that is possible to attain after much labour and research *is approximating facts;* yet if these shall be found sufficient to assist the mind in forming conclusions, useful in moral and political views of a subject so extremely interesting, an object will be accomplished of great importance as it relates to the public weal. From this diagram more correct ideas may at once be formed of the state of civil society than can be attained by the labour of perusing many volumes.

It will, through this medium, be discovered, what classes of the community by their labour in different pursuits tend to increase the national capital, and what other classes diminish it, together with the degree of increase and diminution as applicable to each order or rank in society. This species of knowledge, drawn from approximating facts, is of great importance in the general affairs of government, more especially when they are presented to the minds of statesmen and politicians, in such a form as to bring the whole scheme of the national economy at once under the eye; exhibiting in one collected view the proportions of the land and labour of the country assigned to each class of the community for their immediate support, and for the exigencies of the state.

By the aid of political arithmetic, or, in other words, by the practice of reasoning by figures on matters relating to government in all the branches of its internal economy, much useful information is obtained, calculated to assist the mind with respect to the encouragements which may be afforded in promoting the prosperity of the country, and the blemishes in the existing system which call for a remedy, so as to effect those objects which shall tend in the greatest possible degree to improve the condition of the people, by a more general diffusion of productive industry and moral habits.

As the wealth of all nations arises from land and labour, great advantages may be derived from an accurate knowledge of the produce of this labour, and the manner in which it is distributed among the community, by suggesting measures of state policy, which shall give a right direction to this labour, and to the improvement of the morals of the people, than which nothing can tend more to the augmentation of the power and resources of the state, and to individual comfort and happiness.

The subject now to be discussed is placed in a point of view not less novel than interesting. It embraces the whole range of statistical economy connected with the existing population of the United Kingdom, divided into different classes.

It shews the distinction between the productive and unproductive labourers, according to their different pursuits in society. It discloses, by means of approximating facts, the share allotted to each class of the community of the disposable property or wealth annually created or obtained by land and labour, after reserving the capital employed in giving motion to this labour. It distinguishes the useful from the noxious members of the body politic, while it shews the relative degree of usefulness or noxious tendency, which applies to all the different ranks and degrees in society. . . .

The population of the United Kingdom of Great Britain and Ireland, including the army and navy, admits of the following division into classes, viz.

	Heads of Families.	Total persons, comprising their Families.
HIGHEST ORDERS		
1st. The Royal Family, the Lords Spiritual and Temporal, the Great Officers of State, and all above the degree of a Baronet, with their families	576	2,880
SECOND CLASS		
2d. Baronets, Knights, Country Gentlemen, and others having large incomes, with their families	46,861	234,305
THIRD CLASS		
3d. Dignified Clergy, Persons holding considerable employments in the State, elevated situations in the Law, eminent Practitioners in Physic, considerable Merchants, Manufacturers upon a large scale, and Bankers of the first order, with their families . .	12,200	61,000
Carried forward	59,637	298,185
FOURTH CLASS		
4th. Persons holding inferior situations in Church and State, respectable Clergymen of different persuasions, Practitioners in Law and Physic, Teachers of Youth of the superior order, respectable Freeholders, Ship Owners, Merchants and Manufacturers of the second class, Warehousemen and respectable Shopkeepers, Artists, respectable Builders, Mechanics, and Persons living on moderate incomes, with their families	233,650	1,168,250
FIFTH CLASS		
5th. Lesser Freeholders, Shopkeepers of the second order, Inn-keepers, Publicans, and Persons engaged in miscellaneous occupations or living on moderate incomes, with their families	564,799	2,798,475
SIXTH CLASS		
6th. Working Mechanics, Artisans, Handicrafts, Agricultural Labourers, and others who subsist by labour in various employments, with their families	2,126,095	8,792,800
Menial Servants	. . .	1,279,923

SEVENTH, OR LOWEST CLASS

7th. Paupers and their families, Vagrants, Gipsies, Rogues, Vagabonds, and idle and disorderly persons, supported by criminal delinquency	387,100	1,828,170
	3,371,281	16,165,803

THE ARMY AND NAVY

Officers of the Army, Navy, and Marines, including all Officers on half-pay and superannuated, with their families . . .	10,500	69,000
Non-commissioned Officers in the Army, Navy, and Marines, Soldiers, Seamen, and Marines, including Pensioners of the Army, Navy, &c. and their families	120,000	862,000
Total . .	3,501,781	17,096,803

. . . There is however another and, perhaps, a more interesting statistical view of this important and curious subject, as it relates to the productive and unproductive labourers in the United Kingdom, which it may be useful to explain,—as a means of more fully elucidating the state of society, which, in this country, differs in many respects from every other civilized nation, and will account for its superiority in arts and arms (when its population is considered) to every nation in the world.

It has been already shewn, that in this as indeed in all other kingdoms, states, and empires, the communities, of which they are composed, consist of *productive* and *unproductive* labourers. In the United Kingdom of Great Britain and Ireland, as far as approximating facts could be obtained, they seem to admit of the following classification.

Productive Labourers, by whose exertions a new
Property is created every year.

	Families.	Persons.	Income.
Agriculture, Mines, &c.	1,302,151	6,129,142	£107,246,795
Foreign Commerce, Shipping, Trade, Manufactures, Fisheries, &c.	1,506,774	7,071,989	183,908,352
Fine Arts	5,000	25,000	1,400,000
Total	2,813,925	13,226,131	£292,555,147

Unproductive Labourers, whose exertions do not create any new Property.

	Families.	Persons.	Income.
Royalty Nobility Gentry	47,437	416,835	£58,923,590
State and Revenue Army Navy Half-pay Pensioners	152,000	1,056,000	34,036,280
Clergy Law Physic	56,000	281,500	17,580,000
Universities Schools Miscellaneous	45,319	567,937	17,555,355
Paupers	387,100	1,548,400	9,871,000
Total	687,856	3,870,672	£137,966,225

Thus it would appear, that more than ⅕th part of the whole community are unproductive labourers, and that these labourers receive from the aggregate labour of the productive class about ⅓d part of the new property created annually. But it does not follow, as has been already observed, that a very great proportion of these unproductive labourers are not highly useful in their different stations in society. On the contrary, with a few exceptions, in addition to the benefits derived from personal exertions, they eminently tend to promote, invigorate, and render more productive the labour of the creating classes.

Such is the structure of civil society, that the classes, whose minds are enlarged and their intellects and faculties improved by a superior education, are indispensably necessary as master-springs in the great machine; not only for the purpose of giving energy to the efforts of the productive labourers by means of capital furnished by every member of the community possessing real or personal property, from which they derive an income, but from the skill and superior knowledge of those who give employment to the labouring classes in agriculture, manufactures, trade, commerce, and navigation, and other objects of productive industry. But this is not the only advantage resulting from the labour of the higher and middling classes of the community; particularly in the British dominions, where they are called upon as legislators, judges, magistrates, jurors, managers of the poor, and peace-officers, to execute the functions which are required for the purpose of preserving the harmony and order, which are necessary to the existence of civil society. . . .

2. AN ESSAY ON CIVIL SOCIETY

by ADAM FERGUSON

A sociological approach to the problems of population was brought by Adam Ferguson (1723–1816), one of a remarkable group of Scottish moral philosophers who in the second half of the eighteenth century conducted a searching enquiry into the nature of man and society. He was Professor of Natural Philosophy (1759), then of Pneumatics (i.e., psychology) and Moral Philosophy (1764–1785), and later of Mathematics at Edinburgh University. The following extracts are from "Of Population and Wealth," in *An Essay on the History of Civil Society* (1767), Part III, Section IV.

HOWEVER important the object of population may be held by mankind, it will be difficult to find, in the history of civil policy, any wise or effectual establishments, solely calculated to obtain it. The practice of rude or feeble nations is inadequate, or cannot surmount the obstacles which are found in their manner of life. The growth of industry, the endeavours of men to improve their arts, to extend their commerce, to secure their possessions, and to establish their rights, are indeed the most effectual means to promote population: but they arise from a different motive; they arise from regards to interest and personal safety. They are intended for the benefit of those who exist, not to procure the increase of their numbers.

It is, in the mean time, of importance to know, that where a people are fortunate in their political establishments, and successful in the pursuits of industry, their population is likely to grow in proportion. Most of the other devices thought of for this purpose, only serve to frustrate the expectations of mankind, or to mislead their attention.

In planting a colony, in striving to repair the occasional wastes of pestilence or war, the immediate contrivance of statesmen may be useful; but if, in reasoning on the increase of mankind in general, we overlook their freedom and their happiness, our aids to population become weak and ineffectual. They only lead us to work on the surface, or to pursue a shadow, while we neglect the substantial concern; and in a decaying state, make us tamper with palliatives, while the roots of an evil are suffered to remain. . . .

It is indeed happy for mankind, that this important object is not always dependent on the wisdom of sovereigns, or the policy of single men. A people intent on freedom, find for themselves a condition in which they may follow the propensities of nature with a more signal effect, than any which the councils of state could devise. When sovereigns, or projectors, are the supposed masters of this subject, the best they can do, is to be cautious of hurting an interest they cannot greatly promote, and of making breaches they cannot repair. . . .

Men will crowd where the situation is tempting, and, in a few generations, will people every country to the measure of its means of subsistence. They will even increase under circumstances that portend a decay. . . .

But even the increase of mankind which attends the accumulation of wealth, has its limits. The *necessary of life* is a vague and a relative term: it is one thing in the opinion of the savage; another in that of the polished citizen: it has a reference to the fancy, and to the habits of living. While arts improve, and riches increase; while the possessions of individuals, or their prospects of gain, come up to their opinion of what is required to settle a family, they enter on its cares with alacrity. But when the possession, however redundant, falls short of the standard, and a fortune supposed sufficient for marriage is attained with difficulty, population is checked, or begins to decline. The citizen, in his own apprehension, returns to the state of the savage; his children, he thinks, must perish for want; and he quits a scene overflowing with plenty, because he has not the fortune which his supposed rank, or his wishes, require. No ultimate remedy is applied to this evil, by merely accumulating wealth; for rare and costly materials, whatever these are, continue to be sought; and if silks and pearl are made common, men will begin to covet some new decorations, which the wealthy alone can procure. If they are indulged in their humour, their demands are repeated; for it is the continual increase of riches, not any measure attained, that keeps the craving imagination at ease.

Men are tempted to labour, and to practise lucrative arts, by motives of interest. Secure to the workman the fruit of his labour, give him the prospects of independence or freedom, the public has found a faithful minister in the acquisition of wealth, and a faithful steward in hoarding what he has gained. The statesman, in this, as in the case of population itself, can do little more than avoid doing mischief. It is well, if, in the beginnings of commerce, he knows how to repress the frauds to which it is subject. Commerce, if continued, is the branch in which men, committed to the effects of their own experience, are least apt to go wrong. . . .

If population be connected with national wealth, liberty and personal security is the great foundation of both: and if this foundation be laid in the state, nature has secured the increase and industry of its members; the one by desires the most ardent in the human frame, the other by a consideration the most uniform and constant of any that possesses the mind. The great object of policy, therefore, with respect to both, is, to secure to the family its means of subsistence and settlement; to protect the industrious in the pursuit of his occupation; to reconcile the restrictions of police, and the social affections of mankind, with their separate and interested pursuits.

In matters of particular profession, industry, and trade, the experienced practitioner is the master, and every general reasoner is a novice. The object in commerce is to make the individual rich; the more he gains for himself, the more he augments the wealth of his country. If a protection be required, it must be granted; if crimes and frauds be committed, they must be repressed; and government can pretend to no more. When the refined politician would lend an active hand, he only multiplies interruptions and grounds of complaint; when the merchant forgets his own interest to lay plans for his country, the period of vision and chimera is near, and the solid basis of commerce withdrawn. He might be told, that while he pursues his advantage, and gives no cause of complaint, the interest of commerce is safe. . . .

3. PRINCIPLES OF POPULATION

by ARTHUR YOUNG

Having made a name for himself as an agricultural journalist and advocate of scientific farming, Arthur Young (1741–1820) was appointed to the secretaryship of the new

Board of Agriculture in 1793. Before taking up the post he wrote to the prime minister, William Pitt: "It has been the employment of the last thirty years of my life to make myself as much a master of the practice and the political encouragement of agriculture as my talents would allow. I have examined every part of the kingdom, and have farming correspondents in all the counties." In the following passage from *Political Arithmetic* (1774), pp. 61–64, Young saw that there was some connection between economic activity and population growth, but his explanation was too simple to satisfy more acute observers.

THE national wealth increased the demand for labour, which had always the effect of raising the price; but this rise encouraged the production of the commodity, that is, of man or labour, call it which you will, and the consequent increase of the commodity sinks the price. Increasing the demand for a manufacture does not raise the price of the labour, it increases the number of labourers in that manufacture, as a greater quantum or regularity of employment, gives that additional value to the supply, which creates the new hands. Why have the inhabitants of *Birmingham* increased from 23,000 in 1750, to 30,000 in 1770? Certainly because a proportional increase of employment has taken place. Wherever there is a demand for hands, there they will abound: this demand is but another word for ease of subsistence, which operates in the same manner (the healthiness of one, and the unhealthiness of the other allowed for) as the plenty of land in the back country of *America*. Marriages abound there, because children are no burthen—they abound in *Birmingham* for the same reason, as every child as soon as it can use its hands, can maintain itself, and the father and mother need never to want employment, that is, income—land—support. Thus where employment increases, (*Birmingham*) the people increase: and where employment does not increase, (*Colchester*) the people do not increase. And if upon an average of the whole kingdom employment has for a century increased, most certainly the people have increased with it.

Go to the shipping of the kingdom, it will be found the same; our sailors have increased. Why? Because their employment has increased. As long as the demand for seamen increases, that demand will be answered, let it rise as high as it will. . . .

Go to the villages, the same truth will every where be apparent: if husbandry improves, it will demand more labour—that demand is the

encouragement of the production of the commodity demanded—and
it will be supplied. Who supposes that a county of warrens, heaths, and
farming slovens, converted to well tilled fields, does not occasion an
increased demand for hands?—And was it ever known that such a
demand existed without being supplied?

But the hands, it is said, leave certain villages and go to towns.
Why? Because there is not employment in one case, and there is in
another—their going to the town, proves that they go to employment
—they go to that very circumstance which is to increase their number.
They go, because they are demanded; that demand it is true takes, but
then it feeds them.

Let any person go to *Glasgow* and its neighbourhood, to *Birmingham,* to *Sheffield,* or to *Manchester,* according to some writers, every
cause of depopulation has acted powerfully against such places: how
then have they increased their people? Why, by emigrations from the
country. It would be very difficult for any person to shew me a depopulation in the country comparable to the increase of towns, not
to speak of counter tracts in the country that have doubled and trebled
their people: But why have not these emigrations been to other towns,
to *York,* to *Winchester,* to *Canterbury,* &c? Because employment does
not abound in those places—and therefore they do not increase. Does
not this prove that in every light you view it, it is employment which
creates population?

4. ESSAY ON POPULATION

by THOMAS ROBERT MALTHUS

A Church of England clergyman and Professor of History
and Political Economy at the East India College in Hert-
fordshire, Thomas Robert Malthus (1766–1834) published
An Essay on the Principle of Population in 1798, to express
his doubts about current ideas on the perfectibility of mankind and schemes for the improvement of society as propounded by reformers such as William Godwin. In subsequent editions Malthus elaborated further upon his original
"principle of population" (taken as a law of nature) and
applied it to immediate social problems, notably the poor
laws. The *Essay* made a deep impression on Malthus's generation and has remained at the center of population dis-

cussion ever since. These excerpts are from chaps. 1–2 of
the 4th ed. (1807), pp. 1–29.

BOOK I.

OF THE CHECKS TO POPULATION IN THE LESS CIVILISED PARTS OF
THE WORLD AND IN PAST TIMES.

CHAPTER I.

STATEMENT OF THE SUBJECT. RATIOS OF THE INCREASE OF
POPULATION AND FOOD.

IN an inquiry concerning the improvement of society, the mode of
conducting the subject which naturally presents itself, is—

1. To investigate the causes that have hitherto impeded the progress
of mankind towards happiness; and,

2. To examine the probability of the total or partial removal of these
causes in future.

To enter fully into this question, and to enumerate all the causes
that have hitherto influenced human improvement, would be much beyond the power of an individual. The principal object of the present
essay is to examine the effects of one great cause intimately united
with the very nature of man; which, though it has been constantly
and powerfully operating since the commencement of society, has been
little noticed by the writers who have treated this subject. The facts
which establish the existence of this cause have, indeed, been repeatedly stated and acknowledged; but its natural and necessary effects
have been almost totally overlooked; though probably among these
effects may be reckoned a very considerable portion of that vice and
misery, and of that unequal distribution of the bounties of nature,
which it has been the unceasing object of the enlightened philan-
thropist in all ages to correct.

The cause to which I allude, is the constant tendency in all animated
life to increase beyond the nourishment prepared for it.

It is observed by Dr. Franklin, that there is no bound to the prolific
nature of plants or animals but what is made by their crowding and
interfering with each other's means of subsistence. Were the face of
the earth, he says, vacant of other plants, it might be gradually sowed
and overspread with one kind only, as, for instance, with fennel: and
were it empty of other inhabitants, it might in a few ages be replenished from one nation only, as, for instance, with Englishmen.

This is incontrovertibly true. Throughout the animal and vegetable kingdoms Nature has scattered the seeds of life abroad with the most profuse and liberal hand; but has been comparatively sparing in the room and the nourishment necessary to rear them. The germs of existence contained in this earth, if they could freely develop themselves, would fill millions of worlds in the course of a few thousand years. Necessity, that imperious, all-pervading law of nature, restrains them within the prescribed bounds. The race of plants and the race of animals shrink under this great restrictive law; and man cannot by any efforts of reason escape from it.

In plants and irrational animals, the view of the subject is simple. They are all impelled by a powerful instinct to the increase of their species, and this instinct is interrupted by no doubts about providing for their offspring. Wherever, therefore, there is liberty, the power of increase is exerted, and the superabundant effects are repressed afterwards by want of room and nourishment.

The effects of this check on man are more complicated. Impelled to the increase of his species by an equally powerful instinct, reason interrupts his career, and asks him whether he may not bring beings into the world for whom he cannot provide the means of support. If he attend to this natural suggestion, the restriction too frequently produces vice. If he hear it not, the human race will be constantly endeavouring to increase beyond the means of subsistence. But as, by that law of our nature which makes food necessary to the life of man, population can never actually increase beyond the lowest nourishment capable of supporting it, a strong check on population, from the difficulty of acquiring food, must be constantly in operation. This difficulty must fall somewhere, and must necessarily be severely felt in some or other of the various forms of misery, or the fear of misery, by a large portion of mankind.

That population has this constant tendency to increase beyond the means of subsistence, and that it is kept to its necessary level by these causes, will sufficiently appear from a review of the different states of society in which man has existed. . . .

It may safely be pronounced . . . that population, when unchecked, goes on doubling itself every twenty-five years, or increases in a geometrical ratio.

It may be fairly pronounced . . . that, considering the present average state of the earth, the means of subsistence, under circumstances the most favourable to human industry, could not possibly be made to increase faster than in an arithmetical ratio.

The necessary effects of these two different rates of increase, when brought together, will be very striking. . . .

CHAPTER II.

OF THE GENERAL CHECKS TO POPULATION, AND THE MODE OF THEIR OPERATION.

The ultimate check to population appears then to be a want of food, arising necessarily from the different ratios according to which population and food increase. But this ultimate check is never the immediate check, except in cases of actual famine.

The immediate check may be stated to consist in all those customs, and all those diseases, which seem to be generated by a scarcity of the means of subsistence; and all those causes, independent of this scarcity, whether of a moral or physical nature, which tend prematurely to weaken and destroy the human frame.

These checks to population, which are constantly operating with more or less force in every society, and keep down the number to the level of the means of subsistence, may be classed under two general heads—the preventive and the positive checks.

The preventive check, as far as it is voluntary, is peculiar to man, and arises from that distinctive superiority in his reasoning faculties which enables him to calculate distant consequences. The checks to the indefinite increase of plants and irrational animals are all either positive or, if preventive, involuntary. But man cannot look around him, and see the distress which frequently presses upon those who have large families; he cannot contemplate his present possessions or earnings, which he now nearly consumes himself, and calculate the amount of each share, when with very little addition they must be divided, perhaps, among seven or eight, without feeling a doubt whether, if he follow the bent of his inclinations, he may be able to support the offspring which he will probably bring into the world. In a state of equality, if such can exist, this would be the simple question. In the present state of society other considerations occur. Will he not lower his rank in life, and be obliged to give up in great measure his former habits? Does any mode of employment present itself by which he may reasonably hope to maintain a family? Will he not at any rate subject himself to greater difficulties, and more severe labour, than in his single state? Will he not be unable to transmit to his children the same advantages of education and improvement that he had himself possessed? Does he even feel secure that, should he have a large family, his utmost exertions can save them from rags and squalid poverty, and their consequent degradation in the community? And may he not be reduced to the grating necessity of forfeiting his independence, and of being obliged to the sparing hand of charity for support?

These considerations are calculated to prevent, and certainly do prevent, a great number of persons in all civilised nations from pursuing the dictate of nature in an early attachment to one woman.

If this restraint do not produce vice, it is undoubtedly the least evil that can arise from the principle of population. Considered as a restraint on a strong natural inclination, it must be allowed to produce a certain degree of temporary unhappiness; but evidently slight, compared with the evils which result from any of the other checks to population; and merely of the same nature as many other sacrifices of temporary to permanent gratification, which it is the business of a moral agent continually to make.

When this restraint produces vice, the evils which follow are but too conspicuous. A promiscuous intercourse to such a degree as to prevent the birth of children, seems to lower, in the most marked manner, the dignity of human nature. It cannot be without its effect on men, and nothing can be more obvious than its tendency to degrade the female character, and to destroy all its most amiable and distinguishing characteristics. Add to which, that among those unfortunate females with which all great towns abound, more real distress and aggravated misery are, perhaps, to be found, than in any other department of human life.

When a general corruption of morals, with regard to the sex, pervades all the classes of society, its effects must necessarily be to poison the springs of domestic happiness, to weaken conjugal and parental affection, and to lessen the united exertions and ardour of parents in the care and education of their children;—effects which cannot take place without a decided diminution of the general happiness and virtue of society; particularly as the necessity of art in the accomplishment and conduct of intrigues, and in the concealment of their consequences, necessarily leads to many other vices.

The positive checks to population are extremely various, and include every cause, whether arising from vice or misery, which in any degree contribute to shorten the natural duration of human life. Under this head, therefore, may be enumerated all unwholesome occupations, severe labour and exposure to the seasons, extreme poverty, bad nursing of children, large towns, excesses of all kinds, the whole train of common diseases and epidemics, wars, plague, and famine.

On examining these obstacles to the increase of population which are classed under the heads of preventive and positive checks, it will appear that they are all resolvable into moral restraint, vice, and misery.

Of the preventive checks, the restraint from marriage which is not followed by irregular gratifications may properly be termed moral restraint.[1]

Promiscuous intercourse, unnatural passions, violations of the marriage bed, and improper arts to conceal the consequences of irregular connections, are preventive checks that clearly come under the head of vice.

Of the positive checks, those which appear to arise unavoidably from the laws of nature, may be called exclusively misery; and those which we obviously bring upon ourselves, such as wars, excesses, and many others which it would be in our power to avoid, are of a mixed nature. They are brought upon us by vice, and their consequences are misery.[2]

[1] It will be observed, that I here use the term *moral* in its most confined sense. By moral restraint I would be understood to mean a restraint from marriage from prudential motives, with a conduct strictly moral during the period of this restraint; and I have never intentionally deviated from this sense. When I have wished to consider the restraint from marriage unconnected with its consequences, I have either called it prudential restraint, or a part of the preventive check, of which indeed it forms the principal branch.

In my review of the different stages of society, I have been accused of not allowing sufficient weight in the prevention of population to moral restraint; but when the confined sense of the term, which I have here explained, is adverted to, I am fearful that I shall not be found to have erred much in this respect. I should be very glad to believe myself mistaken.

[2] As the general consequence of vice is misery, and as this consequence is the precise reason why an action is termed vicious, it may appear that the term *misery* alone would be here sufficient, and that it is superfluous to use both. But the rejection of the term *vice* would introduce a considerable confusion into our language and ideas. We want it particularly to distinguish those actions, the general tendency of which is to produce misery, and which are therefore prohibited by the commands of the Creator, and the precepts of the moralist, although, in their immediate or individual effects, they may produce perhaps exactly the contrary. The gratification of all our passions in its immediate effect is happiness, not misery; and, in individual instances, even the remote consequences (at least in this life) may possibly come under the same denomination. There may have been some irregular connections with women, which have added to the happiness of both parties, and have injured no one. These individual actions, therefore, cannot come

The sum of all these preventive and positive checks, taken together, forms the immediate check to population; and it is evident that, in every country where the whole of the procreative power cannot be called into action, the preventive and the positive checks must vary inversely as each other; that is, in countries either naturally unhealthy, or subject to a great mortality, from whatever cause it may arise, the preventive check will prevail very little. In those countries, on the contrary, which are naturally healthy, and where the preventive check is found to prevail with considerable force, the positive check will prevail very little, or the mortality be very small.

In every country some of these checks are, with more or less force, in constant operation; yet, notwithstanding their general prevalence, there are few states in which there is not a constant effort in the population to increase beyond the means of subsistence. This constant effort as constantly tends to subject the lower classes of society to distress, and to prevent any great permanent melioration of their condition.

These effects, in the present state of society, seem to be produced in the following manner. We will suppose the means of subsistence in any country just equal to the easy support of its inhabitants. The constant effort towards population, which is found to act even in the most vicious societies, increases the number of people before the means of subsistence are increased. The food, therefore, which before supported eleven millions, must now be divided among eleven millions and a half. The poor consequently must live much worse, and many of them be reduced to severe distress. The number of labourers also being above the proportion of work in the market, the price of labour must tend to fall, while the price of provisions would at the same time tend to rise. The labourer therefore must do more work to earn the same as he did before. During this season of distress, the discouragements to marriage and the difficulty of rearing a family are so great, that the progress of population is retarded. In the meantime, the cheapness of labour, the plenty of labourers, and the necessity of an increased industry among them, encourage cultivators to employ more labour upon their land, to turn up fresh soil, and to manure and improve more completely what is already in tillage, till ultimately the

---

under the head of misery. But they are still evidently vicious, because an action is so denominated which violates an express precept, founded upon its general tendency to produce misery, whatever may be its individual effect; and no person can doubt the general tendency of an illicit intercourse between the sexes to injure the happiness of society.

means of subsistence may become in the same proportion to the population as at the period from which we set out. The situation of the labourer being then again tolerably comfortable, the restraints to population are in some degree loosened; and, after a short period, the same retrograde and progressive movements with respect to happiness are repeated. . . .

But without attempting to establish . . . progressive and retrograde movements in different countries, which would evidently require more minute histories than we possess, and which the progress of civilisation naturally tends to counteract, the following propositions are intended to be proved:—

1. Population is necessarily limited by the means of subsistence.

2. Population invariably increases where the means of subsistence increase, unless prevented by some very powerful and obvious checks.

3. These checks, and the checks which repress the superior power of population, and keep its effects on a level with the means of subsistence, are all resolvable into moral restraint, vice, and misery.

The first of these propositions scarcely needs illustration. The second and third will be sufficiently established by a review of the immediate checks to population in the past and present state of society.

This review will be the subject of the following chapters.

Chapter 2.
The Face of the Land

England in the eighteenth century was a land of estates, of villages and small town communities, a society in which land was still the basis of status and power. The state of agriculture was everywhere regarded as the key to the nation's well-being; and rural interests and concerns were not the affair of a sectional minority but of the nation as a whole. Many industries were carried on in the countryside, and the people engaged in them led a rural type of life.

Since the Middle Ages much, though not all, of the land had been cultivated on the open-field system. The nucleated village, surrounded by great open "fields" divided into strips, together with the common (or "waste"), was a familiar sight throughout midland and parts of southern England. Within each village was a hierarchy derived originally from the feudal system of land holding, and constituting a tightly-knit community. Leadership in this society was provided by the squire (in his roles as the largest landowner and Justice of the Peace) and the parson, both of whom were normally resident in the village. The main business of farming was in the hands of tenant farmers; while below them were the cottagers and laborers, only a few of whom were entirely landless and without some customary rights.

Piecemeal changes within this system had been going on for centuries; but from 1760 agricultural change became greatly accelerated through the process of enclosure. The desire to consolidate the scattered strips in the open fields and to divide up the commons came mainly from the larger landowners, particularly those who wished to experiment with new farming methods. The "Norfolk" system of improved, scientific husbandry, which became fashionable under George III, was scarcely compatible with the custom-bound attitudes which dominated the typical open-field village. The needs of an expanding and increasingly urbanized population for more food were met by large-scale capitalist farming and a concentration of estates through the absorption of small holdings.

The result of these changes was to alter radically the outward appearance and the social composition of the English village. The modern English landscape of small, neat fields, each surrounded by a hedgerow, dates from the enclosures of the eighteenth and early nineteenth centuries. Within the village the changes produced social dislocation, and for many cottagers and squatters considerable distress. In particular the enclosure of the commons was a loss for the humbler villagers, and probably helped to swell the number of the class of landless agricultural laborers. But "Enclosure" became a slogan, and to it were attributed many rural ills for which it was not solely responsible.

5. [ENGLISH FARMING PRACTICE]

by A R T H U R   Y O U N G

This extract, from Arthur Young's *Six Month's Tour through the North of England* (1770), Vol. I, pp. 34–36, describes farming practice in Bedfordshire.

FROM *Wooburn* to *Newport Pagnell*, the soil has a great variety; for some miles it is quite a light sand, and then a gravel with some light loams: About *Wanden* the soil is chiefly sand, but few of their farms are very large, they run from 30*l.* to 200*l.* a year; their field land lets at an average for about 7*s.* 6*d.* an acre, and their inclosures from 10*s.* to 12*s.* Their course of crops is,

1. Fallow
2. Wheat or barley
3. Beans and pease

And 1. Fallow
2. Rye
3. Turnips
4. Barley

They plough four times for wheat, sow two bushels an acre, and reap on a medium three quarters. For barley they stir four times, sow four bushels, and get in return about three quarters. For oats they plough but once, sow four bushels, and reap at an average three quarters. For pease and beans mixed they likewise plough but once, sow four bushels, their crop not above 2½ quarters. They give but one tilth for beans alone, sow them broad-cast, never hoe them, but turn in sheep to feed off the weeds, and reckon three quarters a middling crop. For turnips they stir three or four times, hoe them twice, reckon the value at about 40*s.* an acre, and feed them off with sheep alone. They use four or five horses at length in their ploughs, and yet do no more than an acre a day: This miserable management cannot be too much condemned. The product of a cow they lay at near 4*l.* They let their dairies at 3*l.* a head. The particulars I gained of a farm are,

100	Acres
£.60	Rent
8	Horses
12	Cows
200	Sheep (a walk)
2	Servants
3	Labourers

Bread, ...	1¾*d.*
Cheese, ...	4
Butter, ...	7
Beef, ...	3½
Mutton, ...	4
Veal, ...	3
Pork, ...	3½
Candles, ...	7
Soap, ...	6½

Labourers house rent, *per annum,* 30*s.* to 50*s.*
Wear of their tools, 15*s.*
Their firing they get off the common.

LABOUR

In harvest, 35*s.* the month and board.
In hay time, 1*s* a day and victuals.
In winter, from 8*d.* to 1*s.* a day, and no beer,
Reaping wheat, 5*s.* 6*d.*
Mowing corn, 1*s.* 6*d.*
—Grass, 2*s.* and 2*s.* 6*d.*

6. [AN IMPROVING LANDLORD]

by ARTHUR YOUNG

From *Northern Tour,* Vol. I, pp. 307–317.

BUT the husbandry of the Marquis of *Rockingham* is much more worthy of attention than that of any palace; the effects which have and must continue to result from it are of the noblest and most truly national kind: A short sketch of his Lordship's operations, will convince you how much an extensive tract of country is obliged to this patriotic nobleman for introducing a cultivation unknown before.

Upon turning his attention to agriculture, his Lordship found the husbandry of the *West Riding* of *Yorkshire* extremely deficient in numerous particulars: It was disgusting to him to view so vast a property, cultivated in so slovenly a manner; eager to substitute better methods in the room of such unpleasing as well as unprofitable ones, he determined to exert himself with spirit in the attempt; and he executed the noble scheme in a manner that does honour to his penetration.—A very few particulars, among many of the common practice, will shew how much this country wanted a *Rockingham* to animate its cultivation.

1. Large tracts of land, both grass and arable, yielded but a trifling profit, for want of draining. In wet clays, the rushes and other aquatic rubbish usurped the place of corn and grass; the seasons of tilling were retarded, and even destroyed; and those pastures which ought to have fed an ox, scarcely maintained a sheep.

2. The pastures and meadows of this country were universally laid down in ridge and furrow, a practice highly destructive of profit, and detestable to the eye; and the manner of laying down such lands, was as miserable as their product denoted poverty; for after many years ploughing of numerous crops but insufficient fallows, when the soil was so exhausted as to disappoint the expectation of corn, a parcel of rubbish called hay-seeds was scattered over the surface, and the field left to time for improvement. A villainous custom, and too much practised in all parts of the kingdom.

3. The culture of turnips was become common, but in such a method

that their introduction was undoubtedly a real mischief; *viz.* without hoeing, so that the year of fallow, in the general management, was the most capital year of slovenliness and bad husbandry.

4. The implements used in agriculture through this tract were insufficient for a vigorous culture, and consequently the husbandman sustained a constant loss.

These circumstances, among others, shew how much the husbandry of this country wanted improvement. Let us, in the next place, examine the means taken by his Lordship to command that most beneficial purpose. He conducted himself from the beginning, upon the soundest of all principles, that of *practising* himself those methods which *reason* told him were the best;—well convinced that argument and persuasion would have little effect with the *John Trot* genius's of farming, he determined to set the example of good husbandry, as the only probable means of being successful.

In the pursuit of this end his Lordship's conduct was judicious and spirited. He has upwards of 2000 acres of land in his hands; and began their improvement with draining such as were wet, rightly considering this part of husbandry as the *sine qua non* of all others.—His method was the most perfect that experience has hitherto brought to light. That of *covered drains.* . . .

Secondly, His Lordship's management in laying down and keeping his grass lands, is worthy of universal imitation, as a spirit of culture has brought forth a fertility and richness of pasture beyond any thing I remember to have seen. The method of laying down is this: Oats are sown (under seeded) upon land that has been exceedingly well fallowed for a year and a half, by many ploughings, harrowings, &c. By which operations the surface is laid most completely level, so that not the least trace of a furrow is to be distinguished; with the corn, 12 lb. of white *Dutch* clover, and eight bushels of finely dressed hay-seeds are sown. At harvest the oats are reaped, and 6 lb. more of clover-seed sown over the stubble, which is then mown, and raked off, and consequently the seed pretty well buried in the ground; a very rich compost is immediately spread on the field, and well harrowed in, by which means the seed is completely covered; in this manner it is left the first winter. The crop is next year left until the seeds are ripe enough to shake in the mowing, and making, by which means the land gains a fresh sprinkling, and the whole surface ensured a total and thick covering. . . .

But Lord *Rockingham* in scarce any thing has acted with greater spirit, than the improvement of the turnip culture by hoeing; for the disgust he felt at seeing the common slovenly management of the farmers, in respect to this crop, made him determine to introduce the excellent practice of hoeing, common in many of the southern parts of the kingdom. . . .

Much does this neighbourhood owe to so patriotic a design, which was truly planned with judgment, and executed with spirit. Much more genuine fame ought to attend such an action, than the gaining a score of battles: The senseless rabble may praise the military hero; it belongs to *the few* to venerate the spirited cultivator. . . .

7. [ENCLOSURE IN YORKSHIRE]

by WILLIAM MARSHALL

In this extract from *The Rural Economy of Yorkshire* (1788), Vol. I, pp. 48–57, 97–100, William Marshall describes the enclosure movement in the Vale of Pickering, a fertile farming area of about 300 square miles lying between the Cleveland Hills to the north and the Yorkshire Wolds (low chalk uplands) to the south. Marshall (1745–1818), like Young, was an enthusiast for the new scientific agriculture and wrote voluminously on the subject.

THERE has no doubt been a time (and not perhaps many centuries past) when the entire country lay open; when common fields, common meadows, common pastures, open woods, and extensive forests and wastes, were the only division of lands in this kingdom. Even the demesne lands of the feudal lords appear to have once lain open with the lands of their tenants. . . .

In the present century, more especially within the last fifty years, inclosure has made a rapid progress; . . .

The garden is the highest state of cultivation; open fields and common pastures the lowest; separate inclosures a middle state which seems to be well adapted to the present population of this country.

Be this as it may, the spirit of inclosure continues to be such, that in half a century more an open field, or an undivided common may be rare, and the remembrance of them will of course soon wear away. This is therefore the proper time to register interesting facts relative to the subject, and *this* the proper place for adducing them.

In my own remembrance, more than half the Vale under observation lay open: now scarcely an open field or an undivided common remains. Besides, the largest parish in the Vale—one of the most extensive parishes in the kingdom—is now under inclosure; and the circumstances attending it are such as have seldom occurred: a suitable opportunity this for endeavouring to ascertain just ideas of a subject, which, though it has of late years been much agitated, appears to be, even yet, imperfectly understood.

In the beginning of the present century, the immediate township of PICKERING remained in its ancient uninclosed state.

Having been thought too large to be laid out conveniently as one township, it had been judiciously split into two divisions by a natural line, a considerable brook which runs through it.

On each side of the brook lay a suite of COMMON FIELDS; three in number; for the unvarying round of wheat, &c. beans, &c. fallow. These common fields were respectively divided into *oxgangs* evenly scattered over every field; so that each occupier might have an equal or similar share of good and bad, near and distant land; the houses being in this, as in every other common field township, placed in the town. Each field consisted of twenty-two oxgangs; each of which, on one side of the township, contained twenty-four acres—on the other twelve acres—consequently the six fields contained 2376 acres.

Each division had likewise its COMMON MEADOW.

Other portions of the township were laid out in STINTED PASTURES, wholly appendant to the common-field land; each oxgang of which having a right to a limited number of gaits for cows and working oxen.

The remainder of the township, containing many thousand acres, was COMMON.

During this century the common fields and common meadows have been gradually contracting by amicable *exchanges* and transfers, and are now in a manner wholly inclosed. The stinted pastures have, at different times, been inclosed *"by commission;"* namely, by the unanimous reference of the parties concerned, to certain arbitrators or commissioners appointed by themselves; without calling in the aid of parliament. The commons are now under inclosure, pursuant to a *bill* procured for that purpose.

This bill, and the circumstances attending the procurement of it, afford a striking picture of modern inclosures by act of parliament.

The lands to be appropriated in this case consisted of 3,700 acres of culturable soil, valued (by the commission under the inclosure) at 3s. to 50s. an acre rent; and of still greater quantity of heathy barren land, reaching to the center of the morelands, valued (by the same) from below 3s. down to 3d. an acre. The quantity of oxgang or common-field land (as above ascertained) 2376 acres; and the number of ancient common-right houses, or sites of such houses, two hundred and sixty.

To those 2376 acres, and these 260 houses or sites, the commons belonged; but in what proportion had not for ages perhaps been clearly understood. Within memory, it seems, an attempt was made to stint them; but the regulation lasted only one year. Before and since that time they have been, in the strictest sense of the word, *unstinted commons,* for all kinds of commonable stock; excepting sheep and working oxen, which last were, *by the by-laws of the township,* confined to the stinted pastures and the upland commons; and the former to the upland commons only.

It may be taken for granted, that the first mover to an inclosure is private interest, rather than public spirit. In the case of Pickering, the LAND-OWNERS in general were satisfied with the open state of the commons. Some of them who had inherited, or purchased, at an advanced price, lands which lay conveniently to the commons, were of course adverse to an inclosure; and the mere HOUSE-OWNERS were either apprehensive of the smallness of their claim, or their voices were too weak to be heard among those of the land-owners.

Under these circumstances the commons lay open, and would probably have continued in that state, had there been no other interest in the township than that of the owners of its LANDS and HOUSES.

But the *tithe* of three or four thousand acres of corn land was an object of too great magnitude to be overlooked by the lessee (for lives under the Dean of York); and, being seen, had charms in it too fascinating to be lost sight of.

Actuated thus powerfully, the *lessee of the tithes* applied to the LAND-OWNERS to join him in an application to parliament for an inclosure. The land-owners refused: their conduct, however, was impolitic and ill-judged; and a fair opportunity lost is not easily regained.

The lessee of the tithes acted under a restless impulse; and no matter the instruments he made use of, so they answered his purpose. He, therefore, applied to the HOUSE-OWNERS; who, seeing riches within their reach which till then they had never thought of, grew frantic with expectation.

A law-agent well suited to the design was pitched upon; and other agents, no less qualified, gave him their best assistance. An equal division of the commons among the houses only was the prize held out, and a bill, framed for the purpose of obtaining it, was sent up to Parliament.

A faint ill-conducted opposition was made by the land-owners; but a more powerful interest, well applied, having got there before them, their intentions of throwing out the bill were frustrated.

Parliament, however, seeing probably the iniquity of the bill, without being willing to enter into a minute investigation, or able at their distance to ascertain with conveniency sufficient facts, left a principal matter open to a trial at law; namely, whether the commons should be divided among the houses only; or whether one moiety of them should remain with "the lands of the township, which upon the first of January 1784, belonged to the owners of ancient common-right messuages, cottages or sites."

In consequence of this order of Parliament, the question was tried, on a feigned issue, at the assize for the county, in the summer of 1785.

The trial was conducted with the same exertions on the part of the promoters of the bill, and with the same tameness and ill-judged confidence on the part of its opposers, as had been evident in every stage of the business. These circumstances co-operating with the "uncertainty of the law," a verdict was obtained in favour of the houses.

Thus; by *manœuvre;* without even the shadow of *right* being offered; the owner of a mere cottage without a garden-place, or of a heap of stones which had long lain as ruins, and who could have no rightful advantage whatever from the commons in their open state, became entitled to an equal share, under the inclosure, with the largest landowner; who, perhaps, previous to the passing of this law, occupied rightfully some hundred acres.

It is true, many poor families may gain a temporary relief by this *inequitable* transaction; and so far the bill may have operated beneficially. But it must be evident to those who have a knowledge of the township, and who think impartially on the subject, that they might with equal propriety have been relieved out of the inclosed lands, or the personal property of the land-owners; and it could not be the intention of Parliament to be instrumental in transferring the property of one man to another without a sufficient cause: we may therefore safely conclude, that Parliament either in this case were imposed upon, or judged erroneously; or that they are in want of some general principles of inclosure. . . .

Before I take leave of this subject, I will note the effects of the three different means of Inclosure which have been, in different townships, made use of in this District: namely,

1. Inclosure by Exchanges, &c.
2. Inclosure by private commission.
3. Inclosure by Act of Parliament.

1. *Inclosure by Exchanges.* In the north-west division of the Vale, the common fields and common meadows have mostly been inclosed progressively, piece after piece; either in the original slips, singly; or more than one of them have been joined by purchase, or by private exchanges between the several proprietors: by which means the whole of the appropriated lands of the townships in which this species of Inclosure has taken place, have been, in process of time, inclosed and held in severalty.

This method of Inclosure is attended with at least one disagreeable consequence. The common field lands having lain principally in single ridges, some of them perhaps near a mile in length, the Inclosures are badly proportioned. They are either too long for their width, many of them resembling lanes rather than fields; or, if cut into lengths, there are no drift-ways to the inner divisions:—besides, much unnecessary fencing, with all its attendant evils, is by this mode of Inclosure incurred; and what is yet worse, each man's property is still, perhaps, scattered over the township.

2. *Inclosure by private commission.* Some entire townships (except perhaps the unstinted commons), and many stinted pastures, have been laid out by commissioners, chosen unanimously by the several interests concerned, without soliciting the assistance of Parliament.

By this means the distinct properties are laid together, in well-sized and well-proportioned Inclosures, with proper roads and driftways; and this without the expence, the inconveniency, or the *hazard* attending an application to Parliament.

3. *Inclosure by Act of Parliament.* By this expedient the advantages above-mentioned are obtained in their fullest extent; but they are unavoidably burdened with a train of attendant evils, which render this mode of Inclosure much less eligible than that of inclosing by *general consent.*

This, however, is frequently impracticable: obstinacy has its adherents in every township; and where various interests are concerned, as in the case of dividing unstinted commons, it is scarcely possible that every interest, and every individual of each interest should be of one mind. Therefore, without *some* exertion of legal authority, unstinted commons in general must continue to lie open.

8. [ENCLOSURE PROCEEDINGS]

from the JOURNALS OF THE HOUSE OF COMMONS

Although enclosure could be effected simply by mutual arrangement between the parties concerned, the normal method after 1760 was by Act of Parliament; and from that time the previous trickle of enclosure acts became a spate. The procedure is well illustrated by the case of the village of Stillington in the North Riding of Yorkshire, as recorded in the *Journals of the House of Commons*, Vol. XXX (1765–1766), pp. 459 ff. After the act was passed, commissioners were appointed to supervise the carrying out of the enclosure in the village.

JANUARY 17, 1766

A Petition of *Stephen Croft*, the Younger, Esquire, Lord of the Manor of *Stillington*, in the County of *York*, and Owner of several Estates, within the said Manor and Parish of *Stillington*, and also Impropriator of the Great Tythes there; of the Reverend *James Worsley*, Clerk, Prebendary of the Prebend of *Stillington* aforesaid, Patron of the Vicarage of *Stillington* aforesaid, of the Reverend *Lawrence Sterne*, Clerk, Vicar of the said Parish, and of *William Stainforth* Esquire, and of several other Persons, whose Names are thereunto subscribed, being also Owners of Copyhold Messuages, Cottages, Estates, and other Properties, within the said Parish; was presented to the House and read; Setting forth, That, within the said Manor and Parish, is a Common, or Waste, called *Stillington* Common, and also several Open Fields and Ings, which, in their present Situation, are incapable of Improvement; and that it would be of great Advantage to the several Persons interested in the said Common, Fields and Ings, if they were inclosed and divided into specific Allotments, and all Right of Common, and Average thereon, or upon any other Commonable Lands in the said Parish, were extinguished, or if the said Common was so inclosed, and a Power given to the several Proprietors and Owners of Estates, in the said Fields and Ings, to flat and inclose the same, first making Satisfaction to the Impropriator for the Tythes thereof; and after the flatting and inclosing the same, all Right of Common, or Average, was to cease: And therefore praying, that Leave may be given to bring in a Bill for the Purposes aforesaid, or any of them, in such Manner, and under such Regulations, as to the House shall seem meet.

Ordered, That Leave be given to bring in a Bill, pursuant to the Prayer of the said Petition: And that Mr. *Cholmley,* Sir *George Savile,* and Sir *Joseph Mawbey,* do prepare, and bring in, the same.

February 3, 1766

Mr. *Cholmley* presented to the House, according to Order, a Bill for inclosing and dividing the Common Waste Grounds, Open Fields, Open Meadows, Grounds, and Ings, within the Parish of *Stillington,* in the County of *York:* And the same was received; and read the First Time.

Resolved, That the Bill be read a Second Time.

February 10, 1766

A Bill for inclosing and dividing the Common Waste Grounds, Open Fields, Open Meadows, Grounds, and Ings, within the Parish of *Stillington,* in the County of *York,* was read a Second Time.

Resolved, That the Bill be committed to Mr. *Cholmley,* Mr. *Fonereau,* Sir *John Turner,* Mr. *Clive,* Mr. *Sullivan,* Mr. *De Grey,* Mr. *Norris,* Mr. *Edmonstone,* Mr. *Coventry,* Mr. *Tudway,* Mr. *Bootle,* Lord *Coleraine,* Sir *Edward Turner,* Sir *Jarrit Smith,* Mr. *Burrell,* Mr. *Calvert,* Sir *James Dashwood,* Lord *Grey,* Lord *George Cavendish,* Sir *John Delaval,* Lord *Garlies,* Mr. *Coutts,* Mr. *Shelley,* Mr. *Shiffner,* Mr. *Pennant,* Mr. *Paterson,* Sir *William Codrington,* Mr. *Ridley,* Mr. *Whichcot,* Mr. *Molesworth,* Mr. *Wood,* Mr. *Harris,* Mr. *Penton,* Mr. *Parker,* Mr. *Egerton,* Mr. *Willoughby;* and all the Members who serve for the Counties of *York, Nottingham, Northumberland,* and *Durham:* And they are to meet this Afternoon, at Five of the Clock, in the Speaker's Chamber.

February 27, 1766

Mr. *Cholmley* reported from the Committee, to whom the Bill for inclosing and dividing the Common Waste Grounds, Open Fields, Open Meadows, Grounds, and Ings, within the Parish of *Stillington*, in the County of *York*, was committed, That the Committee had examined the Allegations of the Bill; and found the same to be true; and that the Parties concerned had given their Consent to the Bill, to the Satisfaction of the Committee, except the Proprietors of Sixty Acres of Land, in the said Fields and Ings, who refused their Consent to the Inclosure, and the Proprietors of Twenty-seven Acres, who were not at Home when Application was made for their Consents; and that the whole of the said Fields and Ings contain Six hundred Acres, or thereabouts; and also, except the Proprietors of Eight Common Rights, who refused to consent, and the Proprietors of Seven Common Rights, who were from Home, when Application was made for their Consents; and that the whole Number of Common Rights are Eighty-nine; and that no Person appeared before the Committee to oppose the Bill; and that the Committee had gone through the Bill, and made several Amendments thereunto; which they had directed him to report to the House; and he read the Report in his Place; and afterwards delivered the Bill, with the Amendments, in at the Clerk's Table: Where the Amendments were Once read throughout; and then a Second Time, One by One; and, upon the Question severally put thereupon, were agreed to by the House; and several Amendments were made, by the House, to the Bill.

Ordered, That the Bill, with the Amendments, be ingrossed.

March 3, 1766

An ingrossed Bill for inclosing and dividing the Common Waste Grounds, Open Fields, Open Meadows, Grounds, and Ings, within the Parish of *Stillington,* in the County of *York,* was read the Third Time.

Resolved, That the Bill do pass: And that the Title be, An Act for inclosing and dividing the Common Waste Grounds, Open Fields, Open Meadows, Grounds, and Ings, within the Parish of *Stillington,* in the County of *York.*

Ordered, That Mr. *Cholmley* do carry the Bill to the Lords, and desire their Concurrence.

9. [THE CONDITION OF THE AGRICULTURAL WORKERS]

by DAVID DAVIES

In *The Case of Labourers in Husbandry,* 1795, the Rev. David Davies, Rector of Barkham in Berkshire, gathered together the results of his researches and reflections on the condition of the agricultural laborers, prompted by the increase in the poor rate. His account is based partly on his own observations in his parish, and partly on material supplied by correspondents in various parts of the country. The first extract gives a vivid picture of the realities of agricultural life through details of family budgets, and the second contains his views on the causes of an increase in rural poverty.

(A) A VIEW OF THE DISTRESSED CONDITION OF LABOURING FAMILIES
(pp. 7–8, 10–11, 110–112).

IN visiting the labouring families of my parish, as my duty led me, I could not but observe with concern their mean and distressed condition. I found them in general but indifferently fed; badly clothed; some children without shoes and stockings; very few put to school; and most families in debt to little shopkeepers. In short, there was scarcely any appearance of comfort about their dwellings, except that the children looked tolerably healthy. Yet I could not impute the wretchedness I saw either to sloth or wastefulness. For I knew that the farmers were careful that the men should not want employment; and had they been given to drinking, I am sure I should have heard enough of it. And I commonly found the women, when not working in the fields, well occupied at home; seldom indeed earning money; but baking their bread, washing and mending their garments, and rocking the cradle. . . .

These accounts of the earnings and expences of labouring families in my own parish, were collected about *Easter* 1787, when affairs relating to the poor were under the consideration of the Parliament and the public. From what loose information I could then gather near home, I saw sufficient reason to believe, that they presented but too faithful a view of the general distress of such families throughout this and the neighbouring counties. And the vast increase of the poor-rate, at that time every where a subject of complaint, rendered it very probable that the same misery had overspread the kingdom. . . .

Accounts of the Expences and Earnings of Six Labouring Families in the Parish of Barkham in the County of Berks, taken at Easter 1787.

No. I.

Weekly Expences of a Family, consisting of a Man and his Wife, and five children, the eldest eight years of age, the youngest an Infant.

	s.	d.
FLOUR: 7½ gallons, at 10d. *per* gallon	6	3
Yeast, to make it into bread, 2½d; and salt 1½d.	0	4
Bacon, 1 lb. boiled at two or three times with greens: the pot-liquor, with bread and potatoes, makes a *mess* for the children	0	8
Tea, 1 ounce, 2d.;—¾ lb. sugar, 6d.;—½ lb. butter or lard, 4d.	1	0
Soap, ¼ lb. at 9d. *per* lb.	0	2¼
Candles, ⅛ lb. one week with another at a medium, at 9d.	0	3
Thread, thrum, and worsted, for mending apparel, &c.	0	3
Total	8	11¼

Weekly Earnings of the Man and his Wife, viz.

	s.	d.
The man receives the common weekly wages 8 months in the year	7	0
By task work the remaining 4 months he earns something more: his *extra* earnings, if equally divided among the 52 weeks in the year, would increase the weekly wages about	1	0
The wife's common work is to bake bread for the family, to wash and mend ragged clothes, and to look after the children; but at bean-setting, hay-making, and harvest, she earns as much as comes one week with another to about	0	6
Total	8	6

	s.	d.
Weekly expenses of this family	8	11¼
Weekly earnings	8	6
Deficiency of earnings	0	5¼

Weekly Earnings of the Same Family, (*Easter, 1787*).

	£.	s.	d.
The husband receives 8s. per week, throughout the year	0	8	0
The eldest boy	0	2	6

The next boy	0	1	6

The *wife* was taught by her mother to *read* and *spin,* and she teaches her girls the same. Before she went into service, she used to spin a pair of coarse sheets every winter. When she sits closely to her wheel the whole day, she can spin 2 lbs. of coarse flax for ordinary sheeting and toweling, at 2½d. per lb.; therefore, supposing the business of the family to take up two days in the week, the 8 lbs. spun in the other four days comes to 0 1 8

The *eldest girl* can earn 2d. per day, spinning near 1 lb. of such flax; and supposing her also to lose two days in the week in going of errands, tending the infant, &c. her earnings will be 0 0 8

The *little girl,* aged five, can also spin adroitly; she goes to the wheel when her sister is otherwise employed, but is not kept closely to it, as that might hurt her health.

This family earns something extraordinary in harvest; and as the *man* does not scruple working over-hours occasionally, and looks after the stock on one of his employer's farms, they are allowed to live rent-free in the farm-house; all which together may be reckoned equal to 0 1 0

	0	15	4

Amount of *earnings* per annum	39	17	4
Amount of *expenses* per annum	39	14	4
Surplus of earnings	0	3	0

Weekly Expences of a Family [another case].

Consisting of a Man, his Wife, and Five Children; the eldest boy aged twelve years; the next a boy aged nine; the third and fourth, girls aged seven and five; the youngest, an infant.

(*This Account was taken at Easter* 1787.)

	£.	s.	d.
ONE bushel of flour, on an average, at 10d. per gallon . .	0	6	8
Yeast and salt	0	0	3½
A *fat hog* bought, weight about fourteen score, at 7s. 6d. per score, 5l. 5s.—And *bacon* bought beside, about six score, at 6½d. per lb. 3l. 5s.—Total 8l. 10s.—Per week . . .	0	3	3½
Tea, 1½ oz. 4d.—*Sugar,* ½ lb. 4d.—*Butter,* ½ lb. 4d. . .	0	1	0
Brews a *peck of malt* once a fortnight, cost 1s. 4d.—Buys 1½ gall. of *hopseed,* at 1s. 6d. which serves all the year; a handful of this put into the beer makes it keep well enough for that short time	0	0	8¼
Soap, Candles, Worsted, &c.	0	0	8
	£.0	12	7¼

The good woman reckons *small beer and bread* a better and cheaper supper, than *bread and cheese and water;* and says, that *cheese* is the dearest article that a poor family can use.

Her general account was this: that the earnings of her husband and the boys maintained the family in food; and that what she herself and the girls earnt by spinning, and in harvest, found them in clothes, linen, and other necessaries: with which the account of particulars agrees.

	£	s.	d.
Twelve shillings and seven-pence per week, is per annum .	32	14	4
Add for rent, fuel, clothing, &c.	7	0	0
Amount of *expences* per annum	£.39	14	4

(B) CIRCUMSTANCES WHICH HAVE DIRECTLY INCREASED THE NUMBER OF THE DEPENDENT POOR, AND BY CONSEQUENCE THE AMOUNT OF THE RATE (pp. 69–78).

I. *Our progressive population must have added to the Number of dependent poor:*—1st. *Directly*, the history of the poor laws shewing that an increase of population has been always accompanied in this country by an increased number of poor:—And, 2dly, It has perhaps added to it *indirectly* also, by increasing the demand for necessaries, and thereby causing an advance in their price; which of course has forced more and more persons to come for aid to their parishes. . . .

II. *Increased Number of Manufacturers.* Whatever opinion we may adopt as to the general population of the kingdom, all will acknowledge that *this* class of people is multiplied exceedingly. And depending upon their employers for their daily subsistence, they are in much the same situation with reduced farmers and impoverished labourers; that is, they are very liable to come to want. The caprice of fashion causes by fits and starts a great demand for one species of goods, and a cessation of demand for another: and thus workmen, who to-day are fully employed, may be to-morrow in the streets begging their bread. By living in towns, and associating at public-houses, they are habitually improvident, and mind nothing but present enjoyment; and when flung out of work, they are immediately in want. They are also from their sedentary occupations and habitual intemperance, more short-lived than day-labourers; and leaving families behind them unable wholly to maintain themselves, these, as the men die off, fall on their parishes. All this will account for the misery visible in manufacturing towns, in most of which the poor are numerous, and the rates higher than in other places. Manufacturers enjoy, however, one advantage over day-labourers, though they seldom make a right use of it. Several manufactories employ women and children, as well as men: and wherever this is the case, these families might earn a great deal more money, and live better, than labouring families do; but by contracting early the vices of towns, they commonly mis-spend those earnings, which, if used with frugality, would render their condition comfortable and themselves happy.

III. *The practice of enlarging and engrossing of farms, and especially that of depriving the peasantry of all landed property, have contributed greatly to increase the number of dependent poor.*

1st. The *land-owner,* to render his income adequate to the increased expence of living, unites several small farms into one, raises the rent to the utmost, and avoids the expence of repairs. The rich farmer also engrosses as many farms as he is able to stock; lives in more credit and comfort than he could otherwise do; and out of the profits of *several farms,* makes an ample provision for *one family.* Thus thousands of families, which formerly gained an independent livelihood on those separate farms, have been gradually reduced to the class of day-labourers. But day-labourers are sometimes in want of work, and are sometimes unable to work; and in either case their sole resource is the parish. It is a fact, that thousands of parishes have not now half the number of farmers which they had formerly. And in proportion as the number of farming families has decreased, the number of poor families has increased.

2dly. The depriving the peasantry of all landed property has beggared multitudes. It is plainly agreeable to sound policy, that as many individuals as possible in a state should possess an interest in the soil; because this attaches them strongly to the country and its constitution, and makes them zealous and resolute in defending them. But the gentry of this kingdom seem to have lost sight of this wise and salutary policy. Instead of giving to labouring people a valuable stake in the soil, the opposite measure has so long prevailed, that but few cottages, comparatively, have now *any* land about them. Formerly many of the lower sort of people occupied tenements of their own, with parcels of land about them, or they rented such of others. On these they raised for themselves a considerable part of their subsistence, without being obliged, as now, to buy all they want at shops. And this kept numbers from coming to the parish. But since those small parcels of ground have been swallowed up in the contiguous farms and inclosures, and the cottages themselves have been pulled down; the families which used to occupy them are crowded together in decayed farm-houses, with hardly ground enough about them for a cabbage garden: and being thus reduced to be *mere* hirelings, they are of course very liable to come to want. And not only the *men* occupying those tenements, but *their wives and children* too, could formerly, when they wanted work abroad, employ themselves profitably at home; whereas now, few of *these* are constantly employed, except in harvest; so that almost the whole burden of providing for their families rests upon the *men*. Add to this, that the former occupiers of small farms and tenements, though poor themselves, gave away something in alms to their poorer neighbours; a resource which is now much diminished.

Thus an amazing number of people have been reduced from a comfortable state of partial independence to the precarious condition of hirelings, who, when out of work, must immediately come to their parish. And the great plenty of working hands always to be had when wanted, having kept down the price of labour below its proper level, the consequence is universally felt in the increased number of dependent poor.

IV. *The Desertion of the Country by the rich Families during the greater Part of the Year has increased the Number of the Poor.—* Formerly, when the gentry resided constantly on their estates, the crumbs from their tables fed many families; their humanity comforted and relieved the poor under sickness and misfortune; and their influence and authority secured them from oppression and injustice. But of late, by the non-residence of the rich, the poor have lost that valuable support which they used to receive. When (as is too commonly the case) families of moderate fortunes have expended two-thirds of their income, in winter, upon the amusements and accomplishments in vogue in the capital; and have also dissipated a considerable part of the remainder at bathing and water-drinking places during some of the summer months; they have afterwards but little power to exercise hospitality, employ the industrious, and relieve the sick and needy, on their return to their mansions. And thus numbers of poor families are come to want parochial assistance, which, but for this change in the manners of the rich, might have made shift without it. This new mode of life has been the fruitful source of numerous evils: the worst of which perhaps is, that it has spread the vices of the capital over the whole kingdom, and infected even farm-houses and cottages.

V. *The Improvidence of the Lower Sort of People brings Multitudes of them very early to Poverty and Want.*—This carelessness about the future seems to have increased in proportion as the shame of applying for parish-relief has worn off. Few of them, strictly speaking, take any thought for the morrow. Seldom do we see any of them making provision for marriage, sickness, or old age; much less for the relief of infirm parents, or poor relations. Formerly it was not uncommon for young men and women to save in service twenty or thirty pounds in money, besides furnishing themselves with a decent stock of clothes, &c. But now young people are so unfrugal, that few of them have a decent suit to appear in even when they come to be married. And as for money, what in time past was wont to be laid by against a wet day, is all now thoughtlessly spent by the men in drink, and by the women in frippery. "What signifies saving?" say they; "is not the parish obliged to maintain us, when we come to want?" Though they see continually sad instances of coming to the parish, yet have they not the sense to ask themselves this short question, How shall *I* like to be reduced to this abject condition? The consequence of this inconsiderateness is, that, when married, they come soon to feel very severely the effects of that poverty, which, when single, they took no care to prevent. It is indeed some excuse for them, that the number of farmers being so much decreased, there are not now so many opportunities, as formerly, for putting out young persons servants in those families where these savings were chiefly made. Add to this, that these people having contracted the ruinous habit of frequenting ale-houses, seldom can they resolve to forsake it. A great part of their earnings received on Saturday night, is squandered away there on *Sunday*. The wife and children are abandoned to hunger and nakedness, or are left to supply their necessities as well as they can by following profligate courses!

VI. *Ale-houses* have undoubtedly brought many families to want, infamy, and ruin.—As the improvidence of the people encourages these houses, so do these houses encourage that improvidence. Ale-houses would not be so common as they are, if the keepers of them did not find their account in the improvidence of the people; nor would the people be so improvident as they are, if ale-houses did not every where tempt them to drown their senses, and waste their time and money in them. But the loss of sense, time, and money, is not the worst consequence of frequenting these places. There is good reason to believe, that the prevailing corruption of morals in the common people has been very much owing to what is heard, seen, and practised in them. It is in these houses that men, by falling into bad company, get the evil habits of idleness, blasphemy, and drunkenness; which prepare them for the worst crimes. The love of strong drink acquired here drives numbers upon unlawful ways of making money: among which, from the high request that *game* is held in, and from the little risk attending the trade, *poaching* is very generally followed. To be a clever poacher is deemed a reputable accomplishment in the country; and therefore parents take care to instruct their children betimes in this art; which brings them on gradually and regularly to pilfering and stealing. For poachers, in prowling about at night, if they miss of game, properly so called, are sometimes suspected of seizing on their neighbours' poultry, and such other things as they can find a vent for. By following these works of darkness, the loss of sleep and excessive drinking in time ruin their health. They get agues and other disorders, which disqualify them from either working or poaching; and then they and their families come on the parish. Every public-house, which is not absolutely necessary, is certainly a nuisance, and ought to be suppressed.

To the several causes and circumstances pointed out in this and the preceding section, we must, I apprehend, ascribe it, that multitudes of families, which about the middle of this century could with difficulty subsist without *any* help, do now require *some* help; and that multitudes of others, which then could not subsist without *some* help, do now require *more* help.

10. [THE SPEENHAMLAND SYSTEM]

from THE READING MERCURY, *May 11, 1795*

In a rural society, where the poor were taken for granted, the periodic need to help them beyond the extent of normal Christian charity created something of a dilemma. As Bernard Mandeville put it in his *Fable of the Bees* (1714), "the poor have nothing to stir them to labour but their wants, which it is wisdom to relieve but folly to cure." From Elizabethan times the responsibility of looking after its own poor was laid squarely upon each parish, under the direction of the Justices of the Peace. The Poor Law Act of 1601 provided Overseers of the Poor who were to levy a poor rate for the relief of the sick, aged, and unemployed. With the spread of enclosures after 1760 and the rise in food prices during the French Wars the numbers of poor to be relieved increased rapidly. To meet this situation the Justices of the Peace in the village of Speenhamland, Berkshire, decided in 1795 to grant relief on a scale determined by the price of bread and the size of the laborer's family. It was the intention of the Justices to help the poor by ensuring that each family had a minimum income sufficient for its needs; but the effect was to subsidize low wages out of poor rates. The system was adopted widely in the southern counties, and was held by the political economists to be largely responsible for rural pauperization.

AT a General Meeting of the Justices of this County, together with several discreet persons assembled by public advertisement, on Wednesday the 6th day of May, 1795, at the Pelican Inn in Speenhamland (in pursuance of an order of the last Court of General Quarter Sessions) for the purpose of rating Husbandry Wages, by the day or week, if then approved of, [names of those present] . . .

Resolved unanimously,

That the present state of the Poor does require further assistance than has been generally given them.

Resolved,

That it is not expedient for the Magistrates to grant that assistance by regulating the Wages of Day Labourers, according to the directions of the Statutes of the 5th Elizabeth and 1st James: But the Magistrates very earnestly recommend to the Farmers and others throughout the county, to increase the pay of their Labourers in proportion to the present price of provisions; and agreeable thereto, the Magistrates now present, have unanimously resolved that they will, in their several divisions, make the following calculations and allowances for relief of all poor and industrious men and their families, who to the satisfaction of the Justices of their Parish, shall endeavour (as far as they can) for their own support and maintenance.

That is to say,

When the Gallon Loaf of Second Flour, weighing 8lb. 11ozs. shall cost 1s.

Then every poor and industrious man shall have for his own support 3s. weekly, either produced by his own or his family's labour, or an allowance from the poor rates, and for the support of his wife and every other of his family, 1*s*. 6*d*.

When the Gallon Loaf shall cost 1*s*. 4*d*.

Then every poor and industrious man shall have 4*s*. weekly for his own, and 1*s*. and 10*d*. for the support of every other of his family.

And so in proportion, as the price of bread rise or falls (that is to say) 3*d*. to the man, and 1*d*. to every other of the family, on every 1*d*. which the loaf rise above 1*s*.

By order of the Meeting,

W. BUDD, Deputy Clerk of the Peace.

II. [THE OLD AND THE NEW FARMER]

by WILLIAM COBBETT

Few writers have written of the English countryside with more discernment and affection than William Cobbett (1763–1835). Throughout a life in which he was successively a sergeant-major in the army, a bookseller, an ultra patriot and apologist for the Tory government, and finally the greatest Radical journalist of the early nineteenth century, his constant love was for rural England. From 1806 he championed many radical causes and suffered imprisonment and persecution for doing so; but always he returned in his writings to the farmers and agricultural laborers. *Rural Rides,* 1830 (from which the following extract is taken) was originally a series of letters published from the fall of 1821 in his weekly periodical, *The Political Register,* and is probably the finest of Cobbett's works.

REIGATE.
Thursday Evening, October 20. [1825]

HAVING done my business at Hartswood to-day about eleven o'clock, I went to a sale at a farm, which the farmer is quitting. Here I had a view of what has long been going on all over the country. The farm, which belongs to *Christ's Hospital,* has been held by a man of the name of Charington, in whose family the lease has been, I hear, a great number of years. The house is hidden by trees. It stands in the Weald of Surrey, close by the *River Mole,* which is here a mere rivulet, though just below this house the rivulet supplies the very prettiest flour-mill I ever saw in my life.

Everything about this farm-house was formerly the scene of *plain manners* and *plentiful living.* Oak clothes-chests, oak bedsteads, oak chests of drawers, and oak tables to eat on, long, strong, and well supplied with joint stools. Some of the things were many hundreds of years old. But all appeared to be in a state of decay and nearly of *disuse.* There appeared to have been hardly any *family* in that house where formerly there were, in all probability, from ten to fifteen men, boys, and maids: and, which was the worst of all, there was a *parlour.* Aye, and a *carpet* and *bell-pull* too! One end of the front of this once plain and substantial house has been moulded into a *"parlour";* and there was the mahogany table, and the fine chairs, and the fine glass, and all as bare-faced upstart as any stock-jobber in the kingdom can boast of. And there were the decanters, the glasses, the "dinner-set" of crockery-ware, and all just in the true stock-jobber style. And I dare say it has been *'Squire* Charington and the *Miss* Charingtons; and not plain Master Charington, and his son Hodge, and his daughter Betty Charington, all of whom this accursed system has, in all likelihood, transmuted into a species of mock gentlefolks, while it has ground the labourers down into real slaves. Why do not farmers now *feed* and *lodge* their workpeople, as they did formerly? Because they cannot keep them *upon so little* as they give them in wages. This is the real cause of the change. There needs no more to prove that the lot of the working classes has become worse than it formerly was. This fact alone is quite sufficient to settle this point. All the world knows that a number of people, boarded in the same house, and at the same table, can, with as good food, be boarded much cheaper than those persons divided into twos, threes, or fours, can be boarded. This is a well-known truth: therefore, if the farmer now shuts his pantry against his labourers, and pays them wholly in money, is it not clear that he does it because he thereby gives them a living *cheaper* to him; that is to say, a *worse* living than formerly? Mind, he has a *house* for them; a kitchen for them to sit in, bedrooms for them to sleep in, tables, and stools, and benches, of everlasting duration. All these he has: all these *cost him nothing;* and yet so much does he gain by pinching them in wages that he lets all these things remain as of no use rather than feed labourers in the house. Judge, then, of the *change* that has taken place in the condition of these labourers! And be astonished, if you can, at the *pauperism* and the *crimes* that now disgrace this once happy and moral England.

The land produces, on an average, what it always produced, but there is a new distribution of the produce. This 'Squire Charington's father used, I dare say, to sit at the head of the oak table along with his men, say grace to them, and cut up the meat and the pudding. He might take a cup of *strong beer* to himself, when they had none; but that was pretty nearly all the difference in their manner of living. So that *all* lived well. But the *'squire* had many *wine-decanters* and *wine-glasses* and *"a dinner set,"* and a *"breakfast set,"* and *"dessert knives";* and these evidently imply carryings on and a consumption that must of necessity have greatly robbed the long oak table if it had remained fully tenanted. That long table could not share in the work of the decanters and the dinner set. Therefore it became almost untenanted; the labourers retreated to hovels, called cottages; and, instead of board and lodging, they got money; so little of it as to enable the employer to drink wine; but, then, that he might not reduce them to *quite starvation,* they were enabled to come to him, in the *king's name,* and demand food *as paupers.* And now, mind, that which a man received in the *king's name,* he knows well he has *by force;* and it is not in nature that he should *thank* anybody for it, and least of all the party *from whom it is forced.* Then, if this sort of force be insufficient to obtain enough to eat and to keep him warm, is it surprising if he think it no great offence against God (who created no man to starve) to use another sort of force more within his own control? Is it, in short, surprising, if he resort to *theft* and *robbery?*

12. THE DIARY OF A COUNTRY PARSON

by JAMES WOODFORDE

From December 1774 until his death the Rev. James Woodforde (1740–1803) lived an uneventful life in the quiet country parish of Weston Longeville, Norfolk, and were it not for the diary in which he vividly entered the events of his days he would be now unknown. The following extracts from *The Diary of a Country Parson, 1758–1802,* John Beresford, ed. (1949), depict the organization

of a parson's household, and his relationship with his neighbors, from the wealthy squire to the poor farmer.

OCTOBER 11, 1767 . . . Mr. Will Melliar sent me a note this morning, to desire me to be at the meeting of the Gentlemen etc., of this
County, at Bridgwater tomorrow, to put in nomination two proper
Persons to represent this County in Parliament, the ensuing Parliament; and it was so civil a note that I could not refuse him. . . . (p.
43)

April 5, 1786 . . . My tenants from Sandford Orcas came to me
this morning and paid me their rents in all 4.17.0. . . . I gave them
all a dinner; a loin of veal roasted and a good plumb pudding for
their prompt pay. . . . (pp. 48–49)

September 14, 1776 . . . Very busy all day with my Barley, did not
dine till near 5 in the afternoon, my Harvest Men dined here to-day,
gave them some Beef and some plumb Pudding and as much liquor
as they would drink. This evening finished my Harvest and all carried
into the Barn—8 acres. I had Mrs. Dunnell's Cart and Horses, and 2
men, yesterday and to-day. The men were her son Thomas and Robin
Buck. . . . (p. 125)

September 22, 1780 . . . My Squire called on me this morning to
desire me to come over in the afternoon and privately name his new
born son. I married one John Wont and Rose Branton this morning
by License at Weston Church—a compelled marriage. N.B. am owed
by Mr. Mann the Church Warden for marrying them, as I could not
change a Guinea—0. 10. 6. I took a ride in the afternoon to Mr.
Custance's of Ringland and privately named his child by name Edward. I stayed and drank a dish of Coffee with the Squire and one
Mr. Martineau of Norwich, a Doctor and Man Midwife. Recd. a
printed Letter from the Bishop to send him an account of the Roman
Catholics in my Parish—but I don't know of one in it. (pp. 164–165)

January 13, 1783 . . . This Evening paid all my Servants their Years
Wages—due January 6, 1783.

To my Head Maid, Betty Claxton pd.	5.15.6
To my Lower Maid, Lizzy Greaves pd.	2. 0.6
To my Man Will: Coleman pd.	4. 4.0
To Ditto for Grains pd.	17.0
To Ditto for dressing my Wiggs pd.	10.0

To Ditto what he owed me I gave	1. 1.0
To my Farming Man, Ben Leggatt pd.	10. 0.0
To my Boy, Jack Warton	10.6
Gave to him besides as a free gift	2.6 (p. 195)

June 16, 1783 . . . I walked to Forsters this morning between 11 and 12 and read Prayers and administered the H. Sacrament to Mrs. Forster who is something better to day—Her Mother was with her and received the Sacrament also with her. After I came down Stairs from Mrs. Forster I saw Forster and Herring of Ringland—Mr. Forster was very sorry for what he had said and if I would forgive him, he wd. beg my Pardon—which I did and he promised never to affront me more—so that all matters are made up. To Mr. Cary for things from Norwich &c. pd. 0.6.8. Of Ditto—for 7 Pints of Butter at 7d recd. 0.4.1. To Goody Doughty for 3 Lemons pd. 0.0.6. I privately baptised a Child of Billy Bidewells this morning at my House—by name William. Mr. Custance sent us some beans and a Colliflower this Even'. (p. 205).

November 5, 1788 . . . Soon after breakfast (young Rose called here and desired me to lend him my Greyhounds, having found a Hare sitting) Mr. Walker and self took a Walk with the Greyhounds and saw the Hare coursed which gave great Sport indeed, but was killed at last. I never saw a better Course. I let Mr. Rose have the Hare for a Friend of his. After we had killed that Hare we went after another and found one in about an Hour, but we had very little Diversion with her, the Greyhounds scarcely seeing her, She soon got of. Saw never another tho' we stayed out till 3 o'clock. Mr. Walker almost knocked up by walking so long, we were out from 11 till 3 in the Afternoon. Whilst we were out again this Morning, Mrs. Custance with 3 Children called at the Parsonage, and spent an Hour with my Niece and Betsy Davy. Mrs. Custance brought a brace of Partridges for us. After Tea again this Evening we got to Whist, Partners the same, Betsy mine, Nancy Mr. Walkers and we beat them again won 0.1.6. So that Nancy owes me now 0.17.0. Very fine Evening tho' cold for the Holkham Jubilee. (p. 334)

March 16, 1791, Wednesday . . . My Eye-lid is I think rather better than it was, I bathed it with warm milk and Water last Night. I took a little Rhubarb going to bed to night. My Eye-lid about Noon rather worse owing perhaps to the warm Milk and Water, therefore just before Dinner I washed it well with cold Water and in the Evening appeared much better for it. Recd. for Butter this Evening at 9d per Pint 0.2.7¼. Mr. Custance came (walking) to my House about six o'clock this Evening, he found us walking in the Garden, he drank Tea with us and left us about 7. o'clock. He gave me a Guinea to pay for the Inoculation of Harry Dunnells Children 6. in Number, which was extremely kind and good of him—The Parish refusing to pay for the same, tho' at the same time they agreed to the inoculating Case's Family and have had it done, tho' a Farmer and better off. All Mr. Custances Actions to the poor assimulate with the above, every one of them generous and charitable to the highest. Mrs. Custance just the same. Pray God! they may both long enjoy Health and Life, and blessings from above daily attend them. . . . (pp. 396–397)

December 22, 1800, Monday . . . We breakfasted, dined, &c. again at home. Yesterday being Sunday & St. Thomas's Day the Poor deferred going after their Christmas Gifts till this Morning, I had at my House fifty five, gave only to 53, the other two not living in the Parish. Gave in the Whole this Morn' at 6d each in Number 53.1.6.6. Dinner to day, boiled Beef & a rost Chicken. I was but poorly to day after dinner, giddy &c. Sitting too long to day at one time I think. The Poor to day behaved extremely well indeed tho' times were extremely hard for them—They all appeared very patient & submissive. Mr. Press Custance sent us a Pheasant this Even'. Very fine and open Weather for the Season. I cannot remember a finer day (I think) for St. Thomas's Day, than this Day proved. Pray God! make us all thankfull for the same. (p. 598)

Chapter 3.
The Progress of Industrialism

The term Industrial Revolution has been used by historians to describe the economic and social changes that occurred after 1760. In so far as it focuses attention on the rapidity, intensity, and cumulative effect of these changes as compared with any previous period, it is a useful label. Within the span of a single lifetime (such as that of Robert Owen, 1771–1858) England passed from a small, agrarian, aristocratic society to an expanding, urbanized, middle-class nation, the "workshop of the world." But if Industrial Revolution suggests that a series of inventions in the textile, iron, and engineering industries transformed the whole of English economic and social life as suddenly and as completely as political change was effected by the American or French Revolutions, it is somewhat misleading. While contemporaries who lived between 1760 and 1815 were constantly amazed at the pace of the changes going on around them, in fact the changes were largely confined to certain sectors of the economy, though these tended to be the pace setters for the rest.

By 1815 the process of industrial change had proceeded furthest in the cotton trade, in south Lancashire and Cheshire; with some notable developments also in the woolen and worsted industries of the West Riding of Yorkshire, and in iron production and engineering in the Midlands. The earlier forms of industry had been characterized by a rural location and a domestic organization. Cloth weaving, stocking knitting, nail making, for instance, were carried on in the homes of the people, using material supplied by a middle man (or "putter out") who also marketed the product; production was on a small scale, using only simple (usually wooden) hand machinery. The great inventions of the eighteenth century had the effect of revolutionizing the techniques and economic organization of first one and then another sector of an industry; and in all cases the result was ultimately away from the domestic system and towards the use of more elaborate machines, driven by water or steam power, in large "manufactories." With the expansion of the woolen industry in the West Riding came a decline in the older textile centers in East Anglia and the West Country. The development of the iron and engineering industries stimulated expansion in coal mining, especially in Northumberland and Durham. Industry became concentrated in the north and midlands, within easy distance of the coalfields.

Contemporary reactions, like those of later historians, to early industrialism varied according to whether the economic gains or the social dislocation appeared central. Moreover it was difficult to disentangle the effects of industrialism from population growth, agrarian changes, and the French wars. Many of the incidental developments, such as canal building, fast coaching services on the new turnpikes, and gas lighting, were of a spectacular nature, and helped to foster the idea of living in an epoch of change. Dr. Samuel Johnson spoke for many when he exclaimed, "the age is running mad after innovation; all the business of the world is to be done in a new way."

13. [THE WOOLEN INDUSTRY AROUND HALIFAX]

by DANIEL DEFOE

A Tour through the whole island of Great Britain (1724–1726) by Daniel Defoe (1659?–1731) provides a graphic journalistic account of English social and economic life before the coming of the machine age. His famous description of the woolen industry around Halifax in the West Riding of Yorkshire (Vol. III, letter VIII) was not entirely typical of the domestic system as found in other parts of the country. It provides nevertheless a valuable picture of an industrial society before the Industrial Revolution.

. . . THE nearer we came to Hallifax, we found the houses thicker, and the villages greater in every bottom; and not only so, but the

sides of the hills, which were very steep every way, were spread with
houses, and that very thick; for the land being divided into small
enclosures, that is to say, from two acres to six or seven acres each,
seldom more; every three or four pieces of land had a house belonging to it.

Then it was I began to perceive the reason and nature of the thing,
and found that this division of the land into small pieces, and scatter-
ing of the dwellings, was occasioned by, and done for the convenience
of the business which the people were generally employ'd in, and that,
as I said before, though we saw no people stirring without doors, yet
they were all full within; for, in short, this whole country, however
mountainous, and that no sooner we were down one hill but we
mounted another, is yet infinitely full of people; those people all full
of business; not a beggar, not an idle person to be seen, except here
and there an alms-house, where people antient, decrepid, and past
labour, might perhaps be found; for it is observable, that the people
here, however laborious, generally live to a great age, a certain testimony to the goodness and wholesomness of the country, which is,
without doubt, as healthy as any part of England; nor is the health
of the people lessen'd, but help'd and establish'd by their being constantly employ'd, and, as we call it, their working hard; so that they
find a double advantage by their being always in business.

This business is the clothing trade, for the convenience of which
the houses are thus scattered and spread upon the sides of the hills,
as above, even from the bottom to the top; the reason is this; such
has been the bounty of nature to this otherwise frightful country, that
two things essential to the business, as well as to the ease of the
people are found here, and that in a situation which I never saw the
like of in any part of England; and, I believe, the like is not to be
seen so contrived in any part of the world; I mean coals and running
water upon the tops of the highest hills: This seems to have been
directed by the wise hand of Providence for the very purpose which
is now served by it, namely, the manufactures, which otherwise could
not be carried on; neither indeed could one fifth part of the inhabitants be supported without them, for the land could not maintain
them. After we had mounted the third hill, we found the country, in
short, one continued village, tho' mountainous every way, as before;
hardly a house standing out of a speaking distance from another, and
(which soon told us their business) the day clearing up, and the sun
shining, we could see that almost at every house there was a tenter,

and almost on every tenter a piece of cloth, or kersie, or shalloon, for they are the three articles of that country's labour; from which the sun glancing, and, as I may say, shining (the white reflecting its rays) to us, I thought it was the most agreeable sight that I ever saw, for the hills, as I say, rising and falling so thick, and the vallies opening sometimes one way, sometimes another, so that sometimes we could see two or three miles this way, sometimes as far another; sometimes like the streets near St. Giles's, called the Seven Dials; we could see through the glades almost every way round us, yet look which way we would, high to the tops, and low to the bottoms, it was all the same; innumerable houses and tenters, and a white piece upon every tenter.

But to return to the reason of dispersing the houses, as above; I found, as our road pass'd among them, for indeed no road could do otherwise, wherever we pass'd any house we found a little rill or gutter of running water, if the house was above the road, it came from it, and cross'd the way to run to another; if the house was below us, it cross'd us from some other distant house above it, and at every considerable house was a manufactury or work-house, and as they could not do their business without water, the little streams were so parted and guided by gutters or pipes, and by turning and dividing the streams, that none of those houses were without a river, if I may call it so, running into and through their work-houses.

Again, as the dying-houses, scouring-shops and places where they used this water, emitted the water again, ting'd with the drugs of the dying vat, and with the oil, the soap, the tallow, and other ingredients used by the clothiers in dressing and scouring, &c. which then runs away thro' the lands to the next, the grounds are not only universally watered, how dry soever the season, but that water so ting'd and so fatten'd enriches the lands they run through, that 'tis hardly to be imagined how fertile and rich the soil is made by it.

Then, as every clothier must keep a horse, perhaps two, to fetch and carry for the use of his manufacture, (viz.) to fetch home his wooll and his provisions from the market, to carry his yarn to the spinners, his manufacture to the fulling mill, and, when finished, to the market to be sold, and the like; so every manufacturer generally keeps a cow or two, or more, for his family, and this employs the two, or three, or four pieces of enclosed land about his house, for they scarce sow corn enough for their cocks and hens; and this feeding their grounds still adds by the dung of the cattle, to enrich the soil.

. . . Among the manufacturers houses are likewise scattered an infinite number of cottages or small dwellings, in which dwell the workmen which are employed, the women and children of whom, are always busy carding, spinning, &c. so that no hands being unemploy'd, all can gain their bread, even from the youngest to the antient; hardly any thing above four years old, but its hands are sufficient to it self.

This is the reason also why we saw so few people without doors; but if we knock'd at the door of any of the master manufacturers, we presently saw a house full of lusty fellows, some at the dye-vat, some dressing the cloths, some in the loom, some one thing, some another, all hard at work, and full employed upon the manufacture, and all seeming to have sufficient business. . . .

14. [A HANDLOOM WEAVER'S LIFE]

by SAMUEL BAMFORD

The following passages describe the domestic system of industry in its last prosperous days around the turn of the century (the "golden age" to which William Radcliffe refers in Reading No. 15). Samuel Bamford (1788–1872) was a silk weaver from Middleton, Lancashire, and a leading radical in the area. His autobiography is in two volumes, *Passages in the life of a Radical* (1844) and *Early Days* (1849), and this account is from the latter, pp. 98–119.

THE row of houses in which my uncle lived faced the morning sun; a neatly paved footpath, and a causey for carts, lay in front of the houses from one end of the row to the other; and separated from the houses by the causey and footpath was a large green, used as a playground. My uncle's domicile, like all the others, consisted of one principal room called "the house"; on the same floor with this was a loom-shop capable of containing four looms, and in the rear of the house on the same floor, were a small kitchen and a buttery. Over the house and loom-shop were chambers; and over the kitchen and buttery was another small apartment, and a flight of stairs. The whole of the rooms were lighted by windows of small square panes, framed in lead, in good condition; those in the front being protected by shutters. The interior of this dwelling showed that cleanly and comfortable appearance which is always to be seen where a managing Englishwoman is present. There were a dozen good rush-bottomed chairs, the backs and rails bright with wax and rubbing; a handsome clock in mahogany case; a good chest of oaken drawers; a mahogany snap-table; a mahogany corner cupboard, all well polished; besides tables, weather-glass, cornice, and ornaments; pictures illustrative of Joseph and his Brethren, and various other articles indicative of a regard for convenience as well as ornament. And though last enumerated, not the least to be regarded by a hungry youth of my age, was a large bread-flake well stored with oaten cakes. . . .

The mode of living at my uncle's was of the simplest country style. At breakfast, a brown earthen dish being placed on a low beaufet° near the middle of the floor, a boiling of water porridge was poured into the dish, hot from the pan. A mess-pot of the same material as the dish was placed for each one about to partake of the breakfast, a quantity of milk and a spoon were placed in each pot, my uncle took a seat and asked a blessing, each of the children of the family standing around; we then took our several messes of milk, and helped ourselves to the steaming porridge as quickly as we chose, and mixing and eating in the manner we liked best, not a word being spoken all the time. The porridge being scraped up, which they† in general were rather quickly, each would take a piece of hard oaten cake and eat it to the remainder of his milk, after which a little butter, or a small piece of cheese, with more oaten bread, would finish the meal, and in a few minutes work was resumed. My aunt would shortly after make her appearance, her face red, and herself distressed with coughing; the kettle would then be set on for her, and when the asthmatic paroxysm had sufficiently abated she took her breakfast and sat down to her wheel. Our dinners consisted generally of butcher's meat and potatoes, or potato-pie, or meat and broth, or barn dumplings, or drink porridge, or hasty pudding, and in each case the food was partaken in the same primitive manner. When we had meat and potatoes each had an allowance of the meat on a piece of oat-cake, and the potatoes being poured into a dish placed on the beaufet as before, we all stood round, and with spoon or knife, as we chose, ate from the dish so long as the potatoes lasted, after which we stole out to play, eating our remnant of butcher's meat and cake the while. There

° A low three-legged stool, called in the north buffet-stool.
† Porridge used to be described in the plural number.

was not a word heard until we got out of doors, and then we were as noisy as others. . . . Our bagging, or afternoon lunch, consisted of half an oaten cake, with butter, treacle, cheese, or milk, as circumstances rendered most convenient, and our supper was generally the same as breakfast. On Sunday mornings we had mint or balm tea, sweetened with treacle, and oaten cake and butter; on Sunday afternoons we had tea of the same kind, and a slice of buttered loaf was added, which was an especial dainty.

. . . As I was getting rather too unmanageable for my aunt at the bobbin-wheel, fortunately in this respect for both her and myself, my brother went to reside at Manchester, and a vacancy thus occurring on one of the looms, I was transferred to it, and became a weaver. . . .

Having now become an active lad, and, from my good temper and willingness to perform any service, now that the abhorrent wheel was not in the way, had made some advances into the kindly feelings of my aunt and uncle, I was at times chosen to assist the latter when he took the work home to Manchester. The family were, at that time, chiefly employed by Messrs. Samuel and James Broadbent, of Cannon Street, and as the work was for the most part "pollicat" and "romoll" handkerchiefs, with a finer reed, occasionally, of silk and cotton "garments," or handkerchiefs, the "bearing-home wallet" was often both bulky and heavy; and when it happened to be too much so for one person to carry, a neighbour's wallet would be borrowed, the burden divided into two, and I would go with one part over my shoulder, behind or before my uncle. He being, as already stated, rather heavy in person would walk deliberately, with a stick in his hand, his green woollen apron twisted round his waist, his clean shirt showing at the open breast of his waistcoat, his brown silk handkerchief wrapped round his neck, a quid of tobacco in his mouth, and a broad and rather slouched hat on his head. So would he appear when setting out on a "bearing-home" journey; whilst I, with my smaller wallet, with my rough jacket, my knee breeches, my strong stockings and shoes, my open collared shirt, and pleasure and glee in my heart and countenance, footed the way as lightsomely as a young colt.

The warehouse of Messrs. Broadbent was nearly at the top of Cannon Street, on the right-hand side. We mounted some steps, went along a covered passage, and up a height or two of stairs, to a landing place, one side of which was railed off by the bannister, and the other furnished with a seat for weavers to rest upon when they arrived. Here we should probably find some half-dozen weavers and winders, waiting for their turn to deliver in their work and to receive fresh material; and the business betwixt workman and putter-out was generally done in an amicable, reasonable way. No captious fault-finding, no bullying, no arbitrary abatement, which have been too common since, were then practised. If the work were really faulty, the weaver was shown the fault, and if it were not a serious one he was only cautioned against repeating it; if the length or the weight was not what it should be, he was told of it, and would be expected to set it right, or account for it, at his next bearing-home, and if he were a frequent defaulter he was no longer employed. But very rarely indeed did it happen that any transaction bearing the appearance of an advantage being taken against the workman by the putter-out was heard of in those days.

It would sometimes happen that warp or weft would not be ready until after dinner, and on such occasions, my uncle having left his wallet in care of the putter-out, would go downstairs and get paid at the counting-house, and from thence go to the public-house where we lunched on bread and cheese, or cold meat and bread, with ale, to which my uncle added his ever-favourite pipe of tobacco. This house, which was the "Hope and Anchor," in the old churchyard, was also frequented by other weavers; the putter-out at Broadbents generally dined there in the parlour, and when he had dined he would come and take a glass of ale, smoke his pipe, and chat with the weavers, after which, my uncle would again go to the warehouse, and getting what material he wanted, would buy a few groceries and tobacco in the town, or probably, as we returned through the apple market, to go down Long Mill Gate, he would purchase a peck of apples, and giving them to me to carry, we wended towards home, I, by permission, making pretty free with the apples by the way. Before leaving the town my uncle would probably call at the "Queen Anne," in Long Mill Gate, to see if there were any suitable company going our way; if there were, we took a glass until all were ready, and then we walked on together. Another calling house was Schofield's, at Scotland Bridge, and the last in the town was the "Flower Pot," on Red Bank. In winter time, and especially when day was closing, the weavers preferred thus returning in groups, for the road was not altogether free of foot-pads any more than at present. In hot summer weather, the weavers would sometimes indulge themselves by a ride in a cart, or they would leave their heavy burdens at the "Three Crowns," in Cock Gates, to be forwarded by Abraham Lees, the Middleton carrier. When a party of weavers returned in company, they would generally make a halt at Blackley, either at the "White Lion," or at Travis's, the "Golden Lion," over the way. There the wallets, or "pokes" as they were mostly called, were piled in a heap, ale was ordered, seats drawn round the fire, pipes were soon lighted, news interchanged with the host or some of his company; half an hour, or sometimes more, was thus spent, when the shot being called and paid, the travellers took their wallets and climbing the Hill lane, were soon at home. Such was "a bearing-home day" to Manchester in those times.

15. [CHANGE IN THE COTTON INDUSTRY]

by WILLIAM RADCLIFFE

It was a characteristic of early industrialism that techno-logical change often proceeded unevenly in different branches of an industry, so that an invention in one sector might be in advance of parallel developments in the next. William Radcliffe, in his *Origin of the New System of Manufacture, commonly called Power Loom Weaving* (1828), pp. 9–10, 59–67, described the effects of machine spinning in the cotton industry on the handloom weavers, as he observed them in the township of Mellor, 14 miles from Manchester. The shortage of weavers to work up all the available yarn was remedied early in the new century by the rapid spread of power loom weaving in the cotton trade.

. . . THE principal estates being gone from the family, my father resorted to the common but never-failing resource for subsistence at that period, viz.—the loom for men, and the cards and hand-wheel for women and boys. He married a spinster, (in my etymology of the word) and my mother taught me (while too young to weave) to earn my bread by carding and spinning cotton, winding linen or cotton weft for my father and elder brothers at the loom, until I became of sufficient age and strength for my father to put me into a loom. After the practical experience of a few years, any young man who was industrious and careful, might then from his earnings as a weaver, lay by sufficient to set him up as a manufacturer, and though but few of the great body of weavers had the courage to embark in the attempt, I was one of those few. Availing myself of the improvements that came out while I was in my teens, by the time I was married, (at the age of 24, in 1785,) with my little savings, and a practical knowledge of every process from the cotton-bag to the piece of cloth, such as carding by hand or by the engine, spinning by the hand-wheel or jenny, winding, warping, sizing, looming the web, and weaving either by hand or fly-shuttle, I was ready to commence business for myself; and by the year 1789, I was well established, and employed many hands both in spinning and weaving, as a master manufacturer.

From 1789 to 1794, my chief business was the sale of muslin warps, sized and ready for the loom, (being the first who sold cotton twist in that state, chiefly to Mr Oldknow, the father of the muslin trade in our country.) Some warps I sent to Glasgow and Paisley. I also manufactured a few muslins myself, and had a warehouse in Manchester for my general business. . . .

In the year 1770, the land in our township was occupied by between fifty to sixty farmers; rents, to the best of my recollection, did not exceed 10s. per statute acre, and out of these fifty or sixty farmers, there were only six or seven who raised their rents directly from the produce of their farms; all the rest got their rent partly in some branch of trade, such as spinning and weaving woollen, linen, or cotton. The cottagers were employed entirely in this manner, except for a few weeks in the harvest. Being one of those cottagers, and intimately acquainted with all the rest, as well as every farmer, I am the better able to relate particularly how the change from the old system of hand-labour to the new one of machinery operated in raising the price of land in the sub-division I am speaking of. Cottage rents at that time, with convenient loom-shop and a small garden attached, were from one and a-half to two guineas per annum. The father of a family would earn from eight shillings to half a guinea at his loom, and his sons, if he had one, two, or three along side of him, six or eight shillings each per week; but the great sheet anchor of all cottages and small farms, was the labour attached to the hand-wheel, and when it is considered that it required six to eight hands to prepare and spin yarn, of any of the three materials I have mentioned, sufficient for the consumption of one weaver,—this shews clearly the inexhaustible source there was for labour for every person from the age of seven to eighty years (who retained their sight and could move their hands) to earn their bread, say one to three shillings per week without going to the parish. The better class of cottagers and even small farmers also helped to earn what might aid in making up their rents, and supporting their families respectably. . . .

From the year 1770 to 1788 a complete change had gradually been effected in the spinning of yarns,—that of wool had disappeared altogether, and that of linen was also nearly gone,—cotton, cotton, cotton, was become the almost universal material for employment, the hand-wheels, with the exception of one establishment were all thrown into lumber-rooms, the yarn was all spun on common jennies, the carding for all numbers, up to 40 hanks in the pound, was done on carding engines; but the finer numbers of 60 to 80 were still carded by hand, it being a general opinion at that time that machine-carding would never answer for fine numbers. In weaving no great alteration had taken place during these 18 years, save the introduction of the fly-shuttle, a change in the woollen looms to fustians and calico, and the linen nearly gone, except the few fabrics in which there was a mixture of cotton. To the best of my recollection there was no increase of looms during this period,—but rather a decrease. Although our family and some others in the neighbourhood during the latter half of the time, earned from three to four fold-wages to what the same families had heretofore done, yet, upon the whole, the district was not much benefited by the change; for what was gained by some families who had the advantage of machinery, might, in a great measure, be said to be lost to the others, who had been compelled to throw their old cards and hand-wheels aside as lumber.

One of the formidable consequences of this change now began to make its appearance, the poor's rate, which previous to this change had only been known in a comparatively nominal way by an annual meeting at Easter to appoint a new overseer, and the old one to make up his accounts which nobody thought it worth while to look into, as they only contained the expenses of his journey to a petty sessions at a distance, and a few cases of very old persons, 70 to 90 years of age, (whose eyes or hands failed them) having had a weekly allowance. Relief to persons who could not get employment, or bastardy, were alike unknown on their books,—this I state partly traditionally, and partly from many years under my own observance. There was no material advance in the rent of land or cottages during this period, but in the articles of butcher's meat, butter, cheese, and sundry necessaries of life, there had been some increase of price.

The next fifteen years, viz. from 1788 to 1803, which fifteen years I will call the golden age of this great trade, which has been ever since in a gradual decline. . . .

. . . I shall confine myself to the families in my own neighbourhood. These families, up to the time I have been speaking of, whether as cottagers or small farmers, had supported themselves by the different occupations I have mentioned in spinning and manufacturing, as their progenitors from the earliest institutions of society had done before them. But the mule-twist now coming into vogue, for the warp, as well as weft, added to the water-twist and common jenny yarns, with an increasing demand for every fabric the loom could produce, put all hands in request of every age and description. The fabrics made from wool or linen vanished, while the old loom-shops being insufficient, every lumber-room, even old barns, cart-houses, and outbuildings of any description were repaired, windows broke through the old blank walls, and all fitted up for loom-shops. This source of making room being at length exhausted, new weavers' cottages with loom-shops rose up in every direction; all immediately filled, and when in full work the weekly circulation of money as the price of labour only rose to five times the amount ever before experienced in this sub-division, every family bringing home weekly 40, 60, 80, 100, or even 120 shillings per week!!! . . .

. . . the operative weavers *on machine yarns,* both as cottagers and small farmers, even with three times their former rents, they might be truly said to be placed in a higher state of "wealth, peace, and godliness," by the great demand for, and high price of, their labour, than they had ever before experienced. Their dwellings and small gardens clean and neat,—all the family well clad,—the men with each a watch in his pocket, and the women dressed to their own fancy,—*the church crowded to excess every Sunday,*—every house well furnished with a clock in elegant mahogany or fancy case,—handsome tea services in Staffordshire ware, with silver or plated sugar-tongs and spoons,—Birmingham, Potteries, and Sheffield wares for necessary use and ornament, wherever a corner cupboard or shelf could be placed to *shew them off,*—many cottage families had their cow, paying so much for the summer's grass, and about a statute acre of land laid out for them in some croft or corner, which they dressed up as a meadow for hay in the winter.

16. [THE INDUSTRIAL REVOLUTION IN MANCHESTER]

by JOHN AIKIN

A Description of the Country from thirty to forty miles round Manchester (1795) is a typical eighteenth-century work on topography, written by John Aikin, a physician with literary interests. But as Aikin observed, "the centre we have chosen is that of the cotton manufacture; a branch of commerce, the rapid and prodigious increase of which is, perhaps, absolutely unparalleled in the annals of trading nations." Hence his book (pp. 167–184) provides a valuable contemporary account of the beginnings of the first industrial revolution.

. . . NO exertions of the masters or workmen could have answered the demands of trade without the introduction of *spinning machines*.

These were first used by the country people on a confined scale, twelve spindles being thought a great matter; while the awkward posture required to spin on them was discouraging to grown up people, who saw with surprise children from nine to twelve years of age manage them with dexterity, whereby plenty was brought into families formerly overburthened with children, and the poor weavers were delivered from the bondage in which they had lain from the insolence of spinners. . . .

The plenty of weft produced by this means gave uneasiness to the country people, and the weavers were afraid lest the manufacturers should demand finer weft woven at the former prices, which occasioned some risings, and the demolition of jennies in some places by the uninformed populace. At length Dorning Rasbotham, Esq. a worthy magistrate near Bolton, wrote and printed a sensible address to the weavers, in order to convince them of their own interest in encouraging these engines, which happily produced a general acquiescence in their use to a certain number of spindles. These were soon multiplied to three or four times the number; nor did the invention of mechanics rest here, for the demand for twist for warps was greater as weft grew more plentiful, whence engines were soon constructed for this purpose.

The improvements kept increasing, till the capital engines for twist were perfected, by which thousands of spindles are put in motion by a water wheel, and managed mostly by children, without confusion and with less waste of cotton than by the former methods. But the carding and slubbing preparatory to twisting required a greater range of invention. The first attempts were in carding engines, which are very curious, and now brought to a great degree of perfection; and an engine has been contrived for converting the carded wool to slubbing, by drawing it to about the thickness of candlewick preparatory to throwing it into twist. . . .

These machines exhibit in their construction an aggregate of clockmaker's work and machinery most wonderful to behold. The cotton to be spun is introduced through three sets of rollers, so governed by the clock-work, that the set which first receives the cotton makes so many more revolutions than the next in order, and these more than the last which feed the spindles, that it is drawn out considerably in passing through the rollers; being lastly received by spindles, which have every one on the bobbin a fly like that of a flax wheel; . . .

Upon these machines twist is made of any fineness proper for warps; but as it is drawn length way of the staple, it was not so proper for weft; wherefore on the introduction of fine callicoes and muslins, mules were invented, having a name expressive of their species, being a mixed machinery between jennies and the machines for twisting, and adapted to spin weft as fine as could be desired, by adding to the jennies such rollers, governed by clock-maker's work, as were described above, only with this difference, that when the threads are drawn out, the motion of the rollers is suspended by an ingenious contrivance, till the weft is hardened and wound up; in which operation the spindles are alternately drawn from and returned to the feeding rollers, being fixed on a moveable frame like those of the billies to make cardings into what are called rovings for the common jennies.

These mules carry often to a hundred and fifty spindles, and can be set to draw weft to an exact fineness up to 150 hanks in the pound, of which muslin has been made, which for a while had a prompt sale; but the flimsiness of its fabric has brought the finer sorts into discredit, and a stagnation of trade damped the sale of the rest. . . .

The prodigious extension of the several branches of the Manchester manufactures has likewise greatly increased the business of several trades and manufactures connected with or dependent upon them. The making of paper at mills in the vicinity has been brought to great perfection, and now includes all kinds, from the strongest parcelling paper to the finest writing sorts, and that on which banker's bills are printed. To the ironmongers shops, which are greatly increased of late, are generally annexed smithies, where many articles are made, even to nails. A considerable iron foundry is established in Salford, in which are cast most of the articles wanted in Manchester and its neighbourhood, consisting chiefly of large cast wheels for the cotton machines; cylinders, boilers, and pipes for steam engines; cast ovens, and grates of all sizes. This work belongs to Batemen and Sharrard, gen[tle]men every way qualified for so great an undertaking. Mr. Sharrard is a very ingenious and able engineer, who has improved upon and brought the steam engine to great perfection. Most of those that are used and set up in and about Manchester are of their make and fitting up. They are in general of a small size, very compact, stand in a small space, work smooth and easy, and are scarcely heard in the building where erected. They are now used in cotton mills, and for every purpose of the water wheel, where a stream is not to be got, and for winding up coals from a great depth in the coal pits, which is performed with a quickness and ease not to be conceived.

Some few are also erected in this neighbourhood by Messrs. Bolton and Watts of Birmingham, who have far excelled all others in their improvement of the steam engine, for which they have obtained a patent, that has been the source of great and deserved emolument. The boilers are generally of plate iron or copper; but some few for the smaller engines are of cast iron. . . .

The tin-plate workers have found additional employment in furnishing many articles for spinning machines; as have also the braziers in casting wheels for the motion-work of the rollers used in them; and the clock-makers in cutting them. Harness-makers have been much employed in making bands for carding engines, and large wheels for the first operation of drawing out the cardings, whereby the consumption of strong curried leather has been much increased. . . .

To this sketch of the progress of the *trade* of Manchester, it will be proper to subjoin some information respecting the condition and manners of its *tradesmen,* the gradual advances to opulence and luxury, and other circumstances of the domestic history of the place, which are in reality some of the most curious and useful subjects of speculation on human life. The following facts and observations have been communicated by an accurate and well-informed inquirer.

The trade of Manchester may be divided into four periods. The first is that, when the manufacturers worked hard merely for a livelihood, without having accumulated any capital. The second is that, when they had begun to acquire little fortunes, but worked as hard, and lived in as plain a manner as before, increasing their fortunes as well by economy as by moderate gains. The third is that, when luxury began to appear, and trade was pushed by sending out riders for orders to every market town in the kingdom. The fourth is the period in which expense and luxury had made a great progress, and was supported by a trade extended by means of riders and factors through every part of Europe.

It is not easy to ascertain when the second of these periods commenced; but it is probable that few or no capitals of 3000*l*. or 4000*l*. acquired by trade, existed here before 1690. However, towards the latter end of the last century and the beginning of the present, the traders had certainly got money beforehand, and began to build modern brick houses, in place of those of wood and plaster. For the first thirty years of the present century, the old established houses confined their trade to the wholesale dealers in London, Bristol, Norwich, Newcastle, and those who frequented Chester fair. The profits were thus divided between the manufacturer, the wholesale, and the retail, dealer; and those of the manufacturer were probably (though this is contrary to the received opinion) less per cent. upon the business they did, than in the present times. The improvement of their fortunes was chiefly owing to their economy in living, the expense of which was much below the interest of the capital employed. . . .

When the Manchester trade began to extend, the chapmen used to keep gangs of pack-horses, and accompany them to the principal towns with goods in packs, which they opened and sold to shopkeepers, lodging what was unsold in small stores at the inns. The pack-horses brought back sheep's wool, which was bought on the journey, and sold to the makers of worsted yarn at Manchester, or to the clothiers of Rochdale, Saddleworth, and the West-Riding of Yorkshire. On the improvement of turnpike roads waggons were set up, and the pack-horses discontinued; and the chapmen only rode out for orders, carrying with them patterns in their bags. It was during the forty years from 1730 to 1770 that trade was greatly pushed by the practice of sending these riders all over the kingdom, to those towns which before had been supplied from the wholesale dealers in the capital places before mentioned. As this was attended not only with more trouble, but with much more risk, some of the old traders withdrew from business, or confined themselves to as much as they could do on the old footing, which, by the competition of young adventurers, diminished yearly. In this period strangers flocked in from various quarters, which introduced a greater proportion of *young* men of some fortune into the town, with a consequent increase of luxury and gaiety. . . .

Within the last twenty or thirty years the vast increase of foreign trade has caused many of the Manchester manufacturers to travel abroad, and agents or partners to be fixed for a considerable time on the Continent, as well as foreigners to reside at Manchester. And the town has now in every respect assumed the style and manners of one of the commercial capitals of Europe. . . .

17. OBSERVATIONS ON THE MANUFACTURING SYSTEM

by R O B E R T   O W E N

Great as were the economic advantages of the industrial changes, the "moral" and social effects caused considerable concern from an early stage. Robert Owen (1771–1858) in his pamphlet, *Observations on the Effect of the Manufacturing System* (1815) wrote with all the authority of one of the most successful cotton spinners in the kingdom. His plea was for legislation to limit the length of the working day and the conditions of employment of children in mills. Later he extended his criticism of industrial society, and after 1824 he gave up his interest in the famous New Lanark mills and devoted the rest of his life to advocating the cause of cooperative socialism.

THOSE who were engaged in the trade, manufactures, and commerce of this country thirty or forty years ago formed but a very insignificant portion of the knowledge, wealth, influence, or population of the Empire.

Prior to that period, Britain was essentially agricultural. But, from that time to the present, the home and foreign trade have increased in a manner so rapid and extraordinary as to have raised commerce to an importance, which it never previously attained in any country possessing so much political power and influence. . . .

This change has been owing chiefly to the mechanical inventions which introduced the cotton trade into this country, and to the cultivation of the cotton tree in America. The wants which this trade created for the various materials requisite to forward its multiplied operations, caused an extraordinary demand for almost all the manufactures previously established, and, of course, for human labour. The numerous fanciful and useful fabrics manufactured from cotton soon became objects of desire in Europe and America: and the consequent extension of the British foreign trade was such as to astonish and confound the most enlightened statesmen both at home and abroad.

The immediate effects of this manufacturing phenomenon were a rapid increase of the wealth, industry, population, and political influence of the British Empire; and by the aid of which it has been enabled to contend for five-and-twenty years against the most formidable military and *immoral* power that the world perhaps ever contained.

These important results, however, great as they really are, have not been obtained without accompanying evils of such a magnitude as to raise a doubt whether the latter do not preponderate over the former.

Hitherto, legislators have appeared to regard manufactures only in one point of view, as a source of national wealth.

The other mighty consequences which proceed from extended manufactures *when left to their natural progress,* have never yet engaged the attention of any legislature. Yet the political and moral effects to which we allude, well deserve to occupy the best faculties of the greatest and the wisest statesmen.

The general diffusion of manufactures throughout a country generates a new character in its inhabitants; and as this character is formed upon a principle quite unfavourable to individual or general happiness, it will produce the most lamentable and permanent evils, unless its tendency be counteracted by legislative interference and direction.

The manufacturing system has already so far extended its influence over the British Empire, as to effect an essential change in the general character of the mass of the people. This alteration is still in rapid progress; and ere long, the comparatively happy simplicity of the agricultural peasant will be wholly lost amongst us. It is even now scarcely anywhere to be found without a mixture of those habits which are the offspring of trade, manufactures, and commerce.

The acquisition of wealth, and the desire which it naturally creates for a continued increase, have introduced a fondness for essentially injurious luxuries among a numerous class of individuals who formerly never thought of them, and they have also generated a disposition which strongly impels its possessors to sacrifice the best feelings of human nature to this love of accumulation. To succeed in this career, the industry of the lower orders, from whose labour this wealth is now drawn, has been carried by new competitors striving against those of longer standing, to a point of real oppression, reducing them by successive changes, as the spirit of competition increased and the ease of acquiring wealth diminished, to a state more wretched than can be imagined by those who have not attentively observed the changes as they have gradually occurred. In consequence, they are at present in a situation infinitely more degraded and miserable than they were before the introduction of these manufactories, upon the success of which their bare subsistence now depends. . . .

The inhabitants of every country are trained and formed by its great leading existing circumstances, and the character of the lower orders in Britain is now formed chiefly by circumstances arising from trade, manufactures, and commerce; and the governing principle of trade, manufactures, and commerce is immediate pecuniary gain, to which on the great scale every other is made to give way. All are sedulously trained to buy cheap and to sell dear; and to succeed in this art, the parties must be taught to acquire strong powers of deception; and thus a spirit is generated through every class of traders, destructive of that open, honest sincerity, without which man cannot make others happy, nor enjoy happiness himself.

Strictly speaking, however, this defect of character ought not to be attributed to the individuals possessing it, but to the overwhelming effect of the system under which they have been trained.

But the effects of this principle of gain, unrestrained, are still more lamentable on the working classes, those who are employed in the operative parts of the manufactures; for most of these branches are more or less unfavourable to the health and morals of adults. Yet parents do not hesitate to sacrifice the well-being of their children by putting them to occupations by which the constitution of their minds and bodies is rendered greatly inferior to what it might and ought to be under a system of common foresight and humanity. . . .

In the manufacturing districts it is common for parents to send their children of both sexes at seven or eight years of age, in winter as well as summer, at six o'clock in the morning, sometimes of course in the dark, and occasionally amidst frost and snow, to enter the manufactories, which are often heated to a high temperature, and contain an atmosphere far from being the most favourable to human life, and in which all those employed in them very frequently continue until twelve o'clock at noon, when an hour is allowed for dinner, after which they return to remain, in a majority of cases, till eight o'clock at night.

The children now find they must labour incessantly for their bare subsistence: they have not been used to innocent, healthy, and rational amusements; they are not permitted the requisite time, if they had been previously accustomed to enjoy them. They know not what relaxation means, except by the actual cessation from labour. They are surrounded by others similarly circumstanced with themselves; and thus passing on from childhood to youth, they become gradually initiated, the young men in particular, but often the young females also, in the seductive pleasures of the pot-house and inebriation: for which their daily hard labour, want of better habits, and the general vacuity of their minds, tend to prepare them.

Such a system of training cannot be expected to produce any other than a population weak in bodily and mental faculties, and with habits generally destructive of their own comforts, of the well-being of those around them, and strongly calculated to subdue all the social affections. Man so circumstanced sees all around him hurrying forward, at a mail-coach speed, to acquire individual wealth, regardless of him, his comforts, his wants, or even his sufferings, except by way of a *degrading parish charity*, fitted only to steel the heart of man against his fellows, or to form the tyrant and the slave. To-day he labours for one master, to-morrow for a second, then for a third, and a fourth, until all ties between employers and employed are frittered down to the consideration of what immediate gain each can derive from the other.

The employer regards the employed as mere instruments of gain, while these acquire a gross ferocity of character, which, if legislative measures shall not be judiciously devised to prevent its increase, and ameliorate the condition of this class, will sooner or later plunge the country into formidable and perhaps inextricable state of danger.

18. [A PROTEST AGAINST MACHINERY]

by YORKSHIRE CLOTH WORKERS

The introduction of new machines often threatened economic and social dislocation, which caused fear and protest. The scribbling machines referred to in this notice from the *Leeds Intelligencer* and *Leeds Mercury* of June 13, 1786, were used for teazing out the wool and straightening the fibers, preparatory to spinning.

TO the Merchants, Clothiers and all such as wish well to the Staple Manufactory of this Nation.

The Humble ADDRESS and PETITION of Thousands, who labour in the Cloth Manufactory.

SHEWETH, That the Scribbling-Machines have thrown thousands of your petitioners out of employ, whereby they are brought into great distress, and are not able to procure a maintenance for their families, and deprived them of the opportunity of bringing up their children to labour: We have therefore to request, that prejudice and self-interest may be laid aside, and that you may pay that attention to the following facts, which the nature of the case requires.

The number of Scribbling-Machines extending about seventeen miles south-west of LEEDS, exeed all belief, being no less than *one hundred and seventy!* and as each machine will do as much work in twelve hours, as ten men can in that time do by hand, (speaking within bounds) and they working night-and day, one machine will do as much work in one day as would otherwise employ twenty men.

As we do not mean to assert any thing but what we can prove to be true, we allow four men to be employed at each machine twelve hours, working night and day, will take eight men in twenty-four hours; so that, upon a moderate computation twelve men are thrown out of employ for every single machine used in scribbling; and as it may be supposed the number of machines in all the other quarters together, nearly equal those in the South-West, full four thousand men are left to shift for a living how they can, and must of course fall to the Parish, if not timely relieved. Allowing one boy to be bound apprentice from each family out of work, eight thousand hands are deprived of the opportunity of getting a livelihood.

We therefore hope, that the feelings of humanity will lead those who have it in their power to prevent the use of those machines, to give every discouragement they can to what has a tendency so prejudicial to their fellow-creatures.

This is not all; the injury to the Cloth is great, in so much that in Frizing, instead of leaving a nap upon the Cloth, the wool is drawn out, and the Cloth is left thread-bare.

Many more evils we could enumerate, but we would hope, that the sensible part of mankind, who are not biassed by interest, must see the dreadful tendancy of their continuance; a depopulation must be the consequence; trade being then lost, the landed interest will have no other satisfaction but that of being *last devoured*.

We wish to propose a few queries to those who would plead for the further continuance of these machines:

Men of common sense must know, that so many machines in use, take the work from the hands employed in Scribbling,—and who did that business before machines were invented.

How are those men, thus thrown out of employ to provide for their families;—and what are they to put their children apprentice to, that the rising generation may have something to keep them at work, in order that they may not be like vagabonds strolling about in idleness? Some say, Begin and learn some other business.—Suppose we do; who will maintain our families, whilst we undertake the arduous task; and when we have learned it, how do we know we shall be any better for all our pains; for by the time we have served our second apprenticeship, another machine may arise, which may take away that business also; so that our families, being half pined whilst we are learning how to provide them with bread, will be wholly so during the period of our third apprenticeship.

But what are our children to do; are they to be brought up in idleness? Indeed as things are, it is no wonder to hear of so many executions; for our parts, though we may be thought illiterate men, our conceptions are, that bringing children up to industry, and keeping them employed, is the way to keep them from falling into those crimes, which an idle habit naturally leads to.

These things impartially considered will we hope, be strong advocates in our favour; and we conceive that men of sense, religion and humanity, will be satisfied of the reasonableness, as well as necessity of this address, and that their own feelings will urge them to espouse the cause of us and our families—

Signed, in behalf of THOUSANDS, by

Joseph Hepworth	Thomas Lobley
Robert Wood	Thos. Blackburn.

19. [SUPPORT FOR MACHINERY]

by the LEEDS CLOTH MERCHANTS

This proclamation of the Leeds cloth merchants was issued as a broad-sheet in 1791, and is reprinted in W. B. Crump (ed.), *The Leeds Woollen Industry, 1780–1820* (1931), pp. 317–319.

THE CLOTH MERCHANTS OF LEEDS

BEING informed that various Kinds of MACHINERY, for the better and more expeditious DRESSING OF WOOLLEN-CLOTH, have been lately invented, that many such Machines are already made and set to work in different Parts of this County, and that great Numbers more are contracted for, to be used in the Dressing of Cloth in other Parts of Yorkshire, and in the Counties of Lancaster, Derby, Chester, Wilts and Gloucester, thought it necessary to meet together on the Eighteenth of October, to take into their most serious Consideration what Steps were needful to be taken, to prevent the Merchants and Cloth-Dressers in other Parts, from diminishing the Staple Trade of this Town, by the Enjoyment of superior Implements in their Business.

At the said Meeting, attended by almost every Merchant in the Town, the above Facts did clearly appear, and after a Discussion of the Merits of various Inventions, and the Improvement in Dressing likely to be derived from them, it appeared to them all, absolutely necessary that this Town should partake of the Benefit of all Sorts of Improvements that are, or can be made in the Dressing of their Cloths, to prevent the Decline of that Business, of which the Town of Leeds has for Ages had the greatest Share, and which from its local Advantages, we presume may be maintained and increased, provided the Merchants, and Dressers of Cloth, in Leeds, do not neglect to use the best Means in their Power, of performing their Work to the utmost Perfection.

In order that the Matter should be undertaken on a Plan to afford every possible Information, a Committee was then appointed for the Purpose of obtaining one of each of the different Machines now in Use, on the most approved Construction, and a Subscription was entered into for defraying the Expence thereof, and to enable them to obtain an eligible Situation for erecting and working them, for the Inspection of the Trade, previous to their being brought into general Use.

At a time when the People, engaged in every other Manufacture in the Kingdom, are exerting themselves to bring their Work to Market at reduced Prices, which can alone be effected by the Aid of Machinery, it certainly is not necessary that the Cloth Merchants of Leeds, who depend chiefly on a Foreign Demand, where they have for Competitors the Manufacturers of other Nations, whose Taxes are few, and whose manual Labour is only Half the Price it bears here, should have Occasion to defend a Conduct, which has for its Aim the Advantage of the Kingdom in general, and of the Cloth Trade in particular; yet anxious to prevent Misrepresentations, which have usually attended the Introduction of the most useful Machines, they wish to remind the Inhabitants of this Town, of the Advantages derived to every flourishing Manufacture from the Application of Machinery; they instance that of Cotton in particular, which in its internal and foreign Demand is nearly alike to our own, and has in a few Years by the Means of Machinery advanced to its present Importance, and is still increasing.

If then by the Use of Machines, the Manufacture of Cotton, an Article which we import, and are supplied with from other Countries, and which can every where be procured on equal Terms, has met with such amazing Success, may not greater Advantages be reasonably expected from cultivating to the utmost the Manufacture of Wool, the Produce of our own Island, an Article in Demand in all Countries, and almost the universal Cloathing of Mankind?

In the Manufacture of Woollens, the Scribbling Mill, the Spinning Frame, and the Fly Shuttle, have reduced manual Labour nearly Onethird, and each of them at its first Introduction carried an Alarm to the Work People, yet each has contributed to advance the Wages and to increase the Trade, so that if an Attempt was now made to deprive us of the Use of them, there is no Doubt, but every Person engaged in the Business, would exert himself to defend them.

From these Premises, we the undersigned Merchants, think it a Duty we owe to ourselves, to the Town of Leeds, and to the Nation at large, to declare that we will protect and support the free Use of the proposed Improvements in Cloth-Dressing, by every legal Means in our Power; and if after all, contrary to our Expectations, the Introduction of Machinery should for a Time occasion a Scarcity of Work in the Cloth Dressing Trade, we have unanimously agreed to give a Preference to such Workmen as are now settled Inhabitants of this Parish, and who give no Opposition to the present Scheme.

Appleby & Sawyer
Bernard Bischoff & Sons
[and 59 other names]

Chapter 4.

Government and Political Institutions

For most Englishmen in the eighteenth century "our matchless Constitution" was the beginning of all political wisdom. Through Sir William Blackstone's *Commentaries on the Laws of England* (1765–1769), J. de Lolme's *Constitution of England* (1777) and numerous lesser works was perpetuated an image of the constitution as the bulwark of liberty and the rule of law. Ever since the Glorious Revolution of 1688, it was argued, England had enjoyed a "mixed government," that is, a government in which the advantages of monarchy, aristocracy, and democracy were combined, without the disadvantages of any one. This happy state was maintained by a system of checks and balances between the several parts of government.

In reality England was, as the French historian Elie Halévy observed, "a museum of constitutional archaeology where the relics of past ages accumulated." The king still exercised power in the choice of ministers, and there were as yet no party machines nor even political parties in the later nineteenth century sense. By means of patronage the government of the day secured support in parliament, but was not thereby immune from the attacks of the opposition.

The House of Lords, which was held to constitute the "aristocratical" element in the constitution, was increased to 388 members by the Act of Union with Ireland in 1800. Usually the government could rely on a majority in the Lords provided that the king also gave his support, so that it was in the House of Commons that important issues were fought. The House of Commons, which since 1800 had 658 members, was in no sense a democratic body. Aristocratic influence within it was dominant, and it was the independent not the democratic nature of the Commons that most contemporaries stressed. Its members were grouped by "interest" and "connexion" rather than by party. The archaic nature of the franchise prevented the Commons from being a directly representative body, and it had to be defended on grounds of "virtual" representation. In the counties the suffrage was restricted to owners of freehold property worth 40 shillings a year: and in the boroughs to the possessors of various ancient franchises such as pot-walloping, burgage tenure, payment of scot and lot, freeman qualification, and membership of a municipal corporation. Almost everywhere "influence" was exercised through this system to control the election of members; indeed, only through patronage could the political system be made to work.

With such a relationship between parliament and the electorate the influence of public opinion was muted. But politicians were at pains to appeal to the state of feeling in the country—by which they usually meant the views of the propertied classes; and at times of crisis popular opinion could go even further in securing expression, as the events of 1831–1832 leading up to the reform bill were to show.

20. [THE BRITISH CONSTITUTION]

by WILLIAM PALEY

The following extracts are from *The Principles of Moral and Political Philosophy* (1785), pp. 385, 389–392, 394–398, 401–405, which was used as a standard textbook on ethics at Cambridge. The author, William Paley (1743–1805), was a fellow of Christ's College, Cambridge, and later (1782) Archdeacon of Carlisle. In 1794 he published his famous *View of the Evidences of Christianity*.

. . . THE constitution of England, like that of most countries in Europe, hath grown out of occasion and emergency; from the fluctuating policy of different ages; from the contentions, successes, interests, and opportunities of different orders and parties of men in the community. It resembles one of those old mansions, which, instead of being built all at once, after a regular plan, and according to the rules of architecture at present established, has been reared in different ages of the art, has been altered from time to time, and has been continually receiving additions and repairs suited to the taste, fortune, or conveniency of its successive proprietors. In such a building we look in vain for the elegance and proportion, for the just order and correspondence of parts, which we expect in a modern edifice; and which external symmetry, after all, contributes much more perhaps to the amusement of the beholder, than the accommodation of the inhabitant. . . .

The Government of England, which has been sometimes called a mixed government, sometimes a limited monarchy, is formed by a combination of the three regular species of government; the monarchy, residing in the King; the aristocracy, in the House of Lords; and the republic being represented by the House of Commons. The perfection intended by such a scheme of government is, to unite the advantages of the several simple forms, and to exclude the inconveniencies. To what degree this purpose is attained or attainable in the British constitution; wherein it is lost sight of or neglected; and by what means it may in any part be promoted with better success, the reader will be enabled to judge, by a separate recollection of these advantages and inconveniencies, as enumerated in the preceding chapter, and a distinct application of each to the political condition of this country. We will present our remarks upon the subject in a brief account of the expedients by which the British constitution provides,

1st, For the interest of its subjects.

2dly, For its own preservation.

The contrivances for the first of these purposes are the following:

In order to promote the establishment of salutary public laws, every citizen of the state is capable of becoming a member of the senate; and every senator possesses the right of propounding to the deliberation of the legislature whatever law he pleases.

Every district of the empire enjoys the privilege of choosing representatives, informed of the interests and circumstances and desires of their constituents, and entitled by their situation to communicate that information to the national council. The meanest subject has some one whom he can call upon to bring forward his complaints and requests to public attention.

By annexing the right of voting for members of the House of Commons to different qualifications in different places, each order and profession of men in the community become virtually represented; that is, men of all orders and professions, statesmen, courtiers, country gentlemen, lawyers, merchants, manufacturers, soldiers, sailors, interested in the prosperity, and experienced in the occupation of their respective professions, obtain seats in parliament.

The elections, at the same time, are so connected with the influence of landed property as to afford a certainty that a considerable number of men of great estates will be returned to parliament; and are also so modified, that men the most eminent and successful in their respective professions, are the most likely, by their riches, or the weight of their stations, to prevail in these competitions.

The number, fortune, and quality of the members; the variety of interests and characters amongst them; above all, the temporary duration of their power, and the change of men which every new election produces, are so many securities to the public, as well against the subjection of their judgments to any external dictation, as against the formation of a junto in their own body, sufficiently powerful to govern their decisions.

The representatives are so intermixed with the constituents, and the constituents with the rest of the people, that they cannot, without a partiality too flagrant to be endured, impose any burden upon the subject, in which they do not share themselves; nor scarcely can they adopt an advantageous regulation, in which their own interests will not participate of the advantage.

The proceedings and debates of parliament, and the parliamentary conduct of each representative, are known by the people at large.

The representative is so far dependent upon the constituent, and political importance upon public favour, that a member of parliament cannot more effectually recommend himself to eminence and advancement in the state, than by contriving and patronizing laws of public utility.

When intelligence of the condition, wants, and occasions of the people, is thus collected from every quarter, when such a variety of invention, and so many understandings are set at work upon the subject, it may be presumed, that the most eligible expedient, remedy or improvement, will occur to some one or other; and when a wise counsel, or beneficial regulation is once suggested, it may be expected, from the disposition of an assembly so constituted as the British House of Commons is, that it cannot fail of receiving the approbation of a majority.

To prevent those destructive contentions for the supreme power, which are sure to take place, where the members of the state do not live under an acknowledged head, and a known rule of succession; to preserve the people in tranquility at home, by a speedy and vigorous execution of the laws; to protect their interest abroad, by strength and energy in military operations, by those advantages of decision, secrecy and dispatch, which belong to the resolutions of monarchical councils;—for these purposes, the constitution has committed the executive government to the administration and limited authority of an hereditary King.

In the defence of the empire; in the maintenance of its power, dignity, and privileges, with foreign nations; in the advancement of its trade by treaties and conventions; and in the providing for the general administration of municipal justice, by a proper choice and appointment of magistrates, the inclination of the king and of the people usually coincide: in this part, therefore, of the regal office, the constitution entrusts the prerogative with ample powers. . . .

We proceed, in the second place, to inquire in what manner the constitution has provided for its own preservation; that is, in what manner each part of the legislature is secured in the exercise of the powers assigned to it, from the encroachment of the other parts. This security is sometimes called the *balance of the constitution;* and the political equilibrium, which this phrase denotes, consists in two contrivances,—a balance of power, and a balance of interest. By a balance of power is meant, that there is no power possessed by one part of the legislature, the abuse, or excess of which is not checked by some antagonist power, residing in another part. Thus the power of the two houses of parliament to frame laws is checked by the king's negative; that if laws subversive of regal government should obtain the consent of parliament, the reigning prince, by interposing his prerogative, may save the necessary rights and authority of his station. On the other hand, the arbitrary application of this negative is checked by the privilege which parliament possesses, of refusing supplies of money to the exigencies of the King's administration. The constitutional maxim, "that the king can do no wrong," is balanced by another maxim, not less constitutional, "that the illegal commands of the king do not justify those who assist, or concur, in carrying them into execution;" and by a second rule, subsidiary to this, "that the acts of the crown acquire not any legal force, until authenticated by the subscription of some of its great officers." The wisdom of this contrivance is worthy of observation. As the King could not be punished, without a civil war, the constitution exempts his person from trial or account;

but, lest this impunity should encourage a licentious exercise of dominion, various obstacles are opposed to the private will of the sovereign, when directed to illegal objects. The pleasure of the crown must be announced with certain solemnities, and attested by certain officers of state. In some cases, the royal order must be signified by a secretary of state; in others, it must pass under the privy seal, and in many, under the great seal. And when the king's command is regularly published, no mischief can be achieved by it, without the ministry and compliance of those to whom it is directed. Now all who either concur in an illegal order, by authenticating its publication with their seal or subscription, or who in any manner assist in carrying it into execution, subject themselves to prosecution and punishment, for the part they have taken; and are not permitted to plead or produce the command of the king, in justification of their obedience. But farther; the power of the crown to direct the military force of the kingdom, is balanced by the annual necessity of resorting to parliament for the maintenance and government of that force. The power of the king to declare war, is checked by the privilege of the house of commons, to grant or withhold the supplies by which the war must be carried on. The king's choice of his ministers is controlled by the obligation he is under of appointing those men to offices in the state, who are found capable of managing the affairs of his government, with the two houses of parliament. Which consideration imposes such a necessity upon the crown, as hath in a great measure subdued the influence of favouritism; insomuch, that it is become no uncommon spectacle in this country, to see men promoted by the king to the highest offices, and richest preferments, which he has in his power to bestow, who have been distinguished by their opposition to his personal inclinations.

By the *balance of interest*, which accompanies and gives efficacy to the *balance of power*, is meant this, that the respective interests of the three estates of the empire are so disposed and adjusted, that whichever of the three shall attempt any encroachment, the other two will unite in resisting it. If the king should endeavour to extend his authority, by contracting the power and privileges of the commons, the house of lords would see their own dignity endangered by every advance which the crown made to independency upon the resolutions of parliament. The admission of arbitrary power is no less formidable to the grandeur of the aristocracy, than it is fatal to the liberty of the republic; that is, it would reduce the nobility from the hereditary share they possess in the national councils, in which their real greatness consists, to the being made a part of the empty pageantry of a despotic court. On the other hand, if the house of commons should intrench upon the distinct province, or usurp the established prerogative of the crown, the house of lords would receive an instant alarm from every new stretch of popular power. In every contest in which the king may be engaged with the representative body, in defence of his established share of authority, he will find a sure ally in the collective power of the nobility. An attachment to the monarchy, from which they derive their own distinction; the allurements of a court, in the habits and with the sentiments of which they have been brought up; their hatred of equality, and of all levelling pretensions, which may ultimately affect the privileges, or even the existence of their order; in short, every principle and every prejudice which are wont to actuate human conduct, will determine their choice, to the side and support of the crown. Lastly, if the nobles themselves should attempt to revive the superiorities, which their ancestors exercised under the feudal constitution, the king and the people would alike remember, how the one had been insulted, and the other enslaved, by that barbarous tyranny. They would forget the natural opposition of their views and inclinations, when they saw themselves threatened with the return of a domination, which was odious and intolerable to both. . . .

There is nothing, in the British constitution, so remarkable, as the irregularity of the popular representation. The house of commons consists of five hundred and forty eight members, of whom, two hundred are elected by seven thousand constituents: so that a majority of these seven thousand, with[out] any reasonable title to superior weight or influence in the state, may, under certain circumstances decide a question against the opinion of as many millions. Or, to place the same object in another point of view: if my estate be situated in one county of the kingdom, I possess the ten thousandth part of a single representative; if in another, the thousandth; if in a particular district, I may be one in twenty who choose two representatives; if in a still more favoured spot, I may enjoy the right of appointing two myself. If I have been born, or dwell, or have served an apprenticeship in one town, I am represented in the national assembly by two deputies, in the choice of whom, I exercise an actual and sensible share of power; if accident has thrown my birth or habitation, or service into another town, I have no representative at all, nor more power or concern in the election of those who make the laws, by which I am governed, than if I was a subject of the Grand Signior—and this partiality subsists without any pretence whatever of merit or of propriety to justify the preference of one place to another. Or, thirdly, to describe the state of national representation as it exists in reality, it may be affirmed, I believe, with truth, that about one half of the house of commons obtain their seats in that assembly by the election of the people, the other half by purchase, or by the nomination of single proprietors of great estates.

This is a flagrant incongruity in the constitution; but it is one of those objections which strike most forcibly at first sight. The effect of all reasoning upon the subject is to diminish the first impression: on which account it deserves the more attentive examination, that we may be assured, before we adventure upon a reformation, that the magnitude of the evil justifies the danger of the experiment. In the few remarks that follow, we would be understood, in the first place, to decline all conference with those who wish to alter the form of government of these kingdoms. The reformers with whom we have to do, are they, who, whilst they change this part of the system, would retain the rest. If any Englishman expect more happiness to his country under a republic, he may very consistently recommend a new modelling of elections to parliament; because, if the king and house of lords were laid aside, the present disproportionate representation would produce nothing but a confused and ill-digested oligarchy. In like manner we wave a controversy with those writers who insist upon representation as a *natural* right: we consider it so far only as a right at all, as it conduces to public utility; that is, as it contributes to the establishment of good laws, or as it secures to the people the just administration of these laws. These effects depend upon the disposition and abilities of the national counsellors. Wherefore, if men the most likely by their qualifications to know and to promote the public interest, be actually returned to parliament, it signifies little who return them. If the properest persons be elected, what matters it by whom they are elected? At least, no prudent statesman would subvert long established or even settled rules of representation, without a prospect of procuring wiser or better representatives. This then being well observed, let us, before we seek to obtain any thing more, consider duly what we already have. We *have* a house of commons composed of five hundred and forty-eight members, in which number are found, the most considerable landholders and merchants of the kingdom; the heads of the army, the navy, and the law; the occupiers of great offices in the state; together with many private individuals, eminent by their knowledge, eloquence, or activity. Now, if the country be not safe in such hands, in whose may it confide its interests? If such a number of such men be liable to the influence of corrupt motives, what assembly of men will be secure from the same danger? Does any new scheme of representation promise to collect together more wisdom, or to produce firmer integrity? In this view of the subject, and attending not to ideas of order and proportion (of which many minds are much enamoured), but to effects alone, we may discover just excuses for those parts of the present representation, which appear to a hasty observer most exceptionable and absurd. It should be remembered as a maxim extremely applicable to this subject, that no order or assembly of men whatever can long maintain their place and authority in a mixed government, of which the members do not individually possess a respectable share of personal importance. Now, whatever may be the defects of the present arrangement, it infallibly secures a great weight of property to the house of commons, by rendering many seats in that house accessible to men of large fortunes, and to such men alone. By which means those characters are engaged in the defence of the separate rights and interests of this branch of the legislature, that are best able to support its claims. The constitution of most of the small boroughs, especially the burgage tenure, contributes, though undesignedly, to the same effect; for the appointment of the representatives we find commonly annexed to certain great inheritances. Elections purely popular are in this respect uncertain: in times of tranquility, the natural ascendancy of wealth will prevail; but when the minds of men are inflamed by political dissensions, this influence often yields to more impetuous motives.—The variety of tenures and qualifications, upon which the right of voting is founded, appears to me a recommendation of the mode which now subsists, as it tends to introduce into parliament a corresponding mixture of characters and professions. It has been long observed that conspicuous abilities are most frequently found with the representatives of small boroughs. And this is nothing more than what the laws of human conduct might teach us to expect: when such boroughs are set to sale, those men are likely to become purchasers who are enabled by their talents to make the best of their bargain: when a seat is not sold, but given by the opulent proprietor of a burgage tenure, the patron finds his own interest consulted, by the reputation and abilities of the member whom he nominates. If certain of the nobility hold the appointment of some part of the house of com-

mons, it serves to maintain that alliance between the two branches of
the legislature, which no good citizen would wish to see dissevered:
it helps to keep the government of the country in the house of commons, in which, it would not perhaps long continue to reside, if so
powerful and wealthy a part of the nation as the peerage compose,
were excluded from all share and interest in its constitution. If there
be a few boroughs so circumstanced as to lie at the disposal of the
crown, whilst the number of such is known and small, they may be
tolerated with little danger. For where would be the impropriety, or
the inconveniency, if the king at once should nominate a limited number of his servants to seats in parliament; or, what is the same thing,
if seats in parliament were annexed to the possession of certain of the
most efficient and responsible offices in the state? The present representation, after all these deductions, and under the confusion in which
it confessedly lies, is still in such a degree popular; or rather the
representatives are so connected with the mass of the community, by
a society of interests and passions, that the will of the people, when it
is determined, permanent, and general, almost always at length prevails.

21. [THE ROLE OF A MEMBER OF PARLIAMENT]

by EDMUND BURKE

The English constitution and the conservative philosophy
of government were never more brilliantly defended than
by Edmund Burke (1729–1797) during the period of the
American and French Revolutions. In his *Speech to the
Electors of Bristol* (1774) he stated in classic form the relationship between a member of the House of Commons
and the electorate. *Works* (1st American ed., 1806), Vol.
II, pp. 13–15.

CERTAINLY, gentlemen, it ought to be the happiness and glory of
a representative to live in the strictest union, the closest correspondence, and the most unreserved communication with his constituents.

Their wishes ought to have great weight with him; their opinions high respect; their business unremitted attention. . . . But his unbiassed opinion, his mature judgment, his enlightened conscience, he ought not to sacrifice to you, or to any set of men living. These he does not derive from your pleasure; no, nor from the Law and the constitution. They are a trust from Providence, for the abuse of which he is deeply answerable. Your representative owes you, not his industry alone, but his judgment; and he betrays, instead of serving you, if he sacrifices it to your opinion.

My worthy colleague says his will ought to be subservient to yours. If that be all, the thing is innocent. If government were a matter of will upon any side, yours, without question, ought to be superior. But government and legislation are matters of reason and judgment, and not of inclination; and what sort of reason is that, in which the determination precedes the discussion; in which one set of men deliberate and another decide; and where those who form the conclusion are perhaps three hundred miles distant from those who hear the arguments?

To deliver an opinion is the right of all men; that of constituents is a weighty and respectable opinion, which a representative ought always to rejoice to hear; and which he ought always most seriously to consider. But *authoritative* instructions, *mandates* issued, which the member is bound blindly and implicitly to obey, to vote, or to argue for, though contrary to the clearest conviction of his judgment and conscience—these are things utterly unknown to the laws of this land, and which arise from a fundamental mistake of the whole order and tenor of our constitution.

Parliament is not a *congress* of ambassadors from different and hostile interests . . . but parliament is a *deliberative* assembly of *one* nation, with *one* interest, that of the whole; where not local purposes, not local prejudices, ought to guide, but the general good, resulting from the general reason of the whole. You choose a member indeed; but when you have chosen him, he is not member of Bristol, but he is a member of *parliament.*

22. THE STATE OF THE REPRESENTATION

by the SOCIETY OF THE FRIENDS OF THE PEOPLE

The anomalies of the old representative system were most clearly brought out by those who sought to change them. Under the impact of the American war a movement for parliamentary reform developed and in 1785 Pitt raised the issue in the House of Commons but was defeated. The reform movement of the 1780s was marked by the development of extraparliamentary associations, of which one of the most important was the Yorkshire Association. Its chairman was the Reverend Christopher Wyvill (1740–1822) from whose *Political Papers,* 6 vols. (1794–1802), Vol. III, App. pp. 194–250 this reading is taken. The Society of the Friends of the People was formed in 1792 and continued the struggle for parliamentary reform; their *Report on the State of the Representation* was dated February 9, 1793.

. . . YOUR committee have found it impracticable to obtain any accurate account of the total number of electors in England, but they conceive that the necessity for such an account is essentially obviated by the one which they are enabled to lay before you. The following statement . . . is conclusive to prove, that, by the partial and unequal manner in which the mass of electors is divided, such a proportion of the 513 representatives [of England and Wales] is returned to Parliament by a few, as renders it of little consequence by how many the remainder is elected. . . .

Your committee find that *256 members,* being a *majority* of the Commons of England, are elected by 11,075 voters; or in other words by little more than the 170th part of the people to be represented, even supposing them to be only two millions. . . .

A statement of the proportions in which the elective franchise is distributed among that body of electors who return the majority of the 513 members for England and Wales.

Places where the right of voting is in burgage and other tenures of a similar description.

Number of voters		Number of voters	
Appleby	220	Knaresborough	110
Ashburton	200	Malton	200
Great Bedwin	80	Midhurst	100
Beeralston	100	Northallerton	200
Bletchingly	90	Petersfield	154
Boroughbridge	74	Richmond	270
Bramber	36	Ripon	186
Clitheroe	102	Reigate	200
Cockermouth	260	Saltash	38
Downton	20	Old Sarum	7
East Grinstead	36	Thirsk	50
Heytesbury	50	Weobley	45
Horsham	60	Westbury	50

Electors 2938
return 52 members.

Places where the number of voters does not exceed 50.

Aldeburgh (Suffolk)	35	Hastings	12
Andover	15	Launceston	20
Banbury	19	Liskeard	50
Bath	32	Lostwithiel	24
Beaumaris	24	Lyme Regis	31
Bewdley	14	Lymington	18
Bishop's Castle	50	Malmesbury	13
Bodmin	36	Marlborough	7
Bossiney	20	St. Mawes	36
Brackley	33	St. Michael	42
Buckingham	13	Newport (I.o.W.)	24
Calne	34	Newton (Lancs.)	50
Camelford	19	Newtown (I.o.W.)	36
Castle Rising	50	Orford	20
Christchurch	40	Romney	13
Corfe Castle	20	Rye	15
Devizes	30	Scarborough	44
Droitwich	14	Tavistock	50
Dunwich	40	Thetford	31
East Looe	20	Tiverton	26
Bury St. Edmunds	36	Truro	26
Gatton	10	Wilton	50
St. Germans	20	Winchelsea	9
Grampound	50	Wycombe	48
Harwich	31	Yarmouth (I.o.W.)	13
Helston	36		

Electors 1449
return 100 members.

Places where the number of voters does not exceed 100.

Amersham	70	Okehampton	96
Aldborough (Yorks.)	57	Poole	100
Callington	62	Portsmouth	60
Dartmouth	98	Salisbury	54
West Looe	70	Seaford	82
Fowey	63	Steyning	100
Great Grimsby	75	Stockbridge	102
Haslemere	60	Totnes	80
Higham Ferrers	84	Tregony	60
Hythe	96	Wenlock	100
Montgomery	80	Whitchurch	70
Newport (Cornwall)	62		

Electors 1781
return 44 members.

Places where the number of voters does not exceed 200.

Arundel	190	Minehead	160
Boston	200	Milborne Port	114
Bridport	180	Morpeth	200
Chippenham	140	Penryn	140
Cambridge	200	Plymouth	160
Dorchester	200	Plympton	104
Eye	200	Queenborough	131
Guildford	120	Retford	112
Heydon	190	Wallingford	140
Hindon	200	Wareham	150
Huntingdon	200	Wendover	120
Ilchester	150	Woodstock	200
St. Ives	180	Wootton Bassett	160
Ludgershall	110	Winchester	110

Electors 4461
return 56 members.

Places where the number of voters does not exceed 300:

Marlow   216   Bridgewater   230   [Electors] 446 return 4 members.

Abstract: 2,938 elect 52; 1,449 elect 100; 1,781 elect 44; 4,461 elect 56; 446 elect 4:[Total] 11,075 return 256.

Your commitee will now call your attention to the various rights of voting which are exercised in the different places returning members to Parliament.

They find that the members for the 52 Counties are all elected by one uniform right. Every man throughout England, possessed of 40 shillings per annum freehold . . . is entitled to a vote for the County in which such freehold is situated.

With respect to the different cities, towns, and boroughs, they exercise a variety of separate and distinct rights, scarcely capable of being classed in any methodical order, and still less of being ascertained by the application of any fixed principle. In the greater part of them indeed the right of voting appears to be vested in the freemen of bodies corporate, but, under this general description, an infinite diversity of peculiar customs is to be found. In some places the number of voters is limited to a select body not exceeding 30 or 40; in others it is extended to 8, or 10,000. In some places the freeman must be a resident inhabitant to entitle him to vote; in others his presence is only required at an election. The right to the freedom is also different in different boroughs, and may, according to the peculiar usage, be obtained by birth, servitude, marriage, redemption, &c. &c.

The remaining rights of voting are of a still more complicated description. Burgageholds, leaseholds, and freeholds,—scot and lot, inhabitants householders, inhabitants at large, potwallopers, and commonalty, each in different boroughs prevail, and create endless misunderstandings and litigation, from the difficulty which is daily found to arise in defining and settling the legal import of those numerous distinctions, which, in some places, commit the choice of two members to as many inhabitants as every house can contain; in others, to the possessor of a spot of ground where neither houses nor inhabitants have been seen for years. . . .

A man possessed of £1000 per annum, or any greater sum, arising from copyhold, leasehold for 99 years, trade, property in the national funds, or even freehold in the City of London, and many other cities and towns having peculiar jurisdictions, is not thereby entitled to vote.

Religious opinions create an incapacity to exercise the elective franchise. All Catholics are excluded generally, and by the operation of the Test laws, Protestant Dissenters are deprived of a voice in the election of representatives in about 30 boroughs, where the right of voting is confined to the corporate officers alone.

A man paying taxes to any amount, how great soever, for his domestic establishment, does not obtain a right to vote unless his residence is in some borough where that right is vested in the inhabitants. . . .

ON THE MODE OF CONDUCTING ELECTIONS.

. . . The first defect in the system . . . is, that the poll, whether the voters consist of 10, or 10,000 . . . is only taken in one fixed place. A freeholder of Cornwall, living in Northumberland, must forego the exercise of his franchise, or travel to Lostwithiel; and a freeman of Berwick, residing at Falmouth, can only be heard as an elector after a journey of 400 miles. . . .

In County elections, it frequently happens that the freeholder, living in the County itself, must go 40, 50, or 60 miles before he can be admitted to poll; but these are trifling journeys compared to what must be taken by those who, being freemen of one city or town, reside in another. Your committee have thought they could not furnish better information respecting this inconvenience, than by consulting and making extracts from a certain number of . . . poll books. . . . From these it appears that, at the following places, the proportion at the last contests stood thus:

	Residents	From London	From the Country	Total
Canterbury	832	153	354	1339
Coventry	1891	356	278	2525
Bedford	919	187	332	1438
Lincoln	428	126	406	960
Newcastle on Tyne	1148	208	889	2245
Bristol	3957	663	1429	6049
Colchester	528	227	525	1280
Lancaster	657	144	1481	2182

ESTIMATE OF THE LEAST EXPENSE OF CONVEYING A VOTER FROM THE PLACE OF HIS RESIDENCE TO THE PLACE OF THE POLL.

6d. per mile—cost of conveyance. 7s. 6d. per day—cost of maintenance. 10s. 6d. per day—for loss of time and trouble. . . .

According to this estimate it appears, that a voter taken 50 miles to poll, will cost, For conveyance out and home, £2 10 0; For three days maintenance, £1 2 6; For three days loss of time and trouble, £1 11 6 [total] £5 4 0.

A voter taken 250 miles to poll, will cost, For conveyance out and home, £12 10 0; For seven days maintenance, £2 12 6; For seven days loss of time and trouble, £3 13 6 [total] £18 16 0. . . .

At Colchester the voters resident in London, being 227, to be brought 50 miles to poll, must, if absent 3 days, cost at least £5. 4s. each, or all together, £1180. At Coventry the voters resident in London, being 356, to be brought 90 miles, supposing them only to be out 3 days, cost £7. 4s. each, or all together, £2563. At Newcastle-upon-Tyne the voters resident in London, being 208, to be brought 274 miles, must, supposing them to be absent from home 7 days, cost at least £20 each, or all together, £4160. At Bristol the voters resident in London being 663, to be brought 120 miles, even supposing them only to be out 4 days, must cost at least £9. 12s. each, or all together, £6364. . . .

This evil of the voters residing at a place distant from the poll has also another effect, namely, the rendering nugatory an Act passed *to prevent giving meat and liquor at elections.* Custom has sanctioned the propriety of opening public houses for the reception of voters from the country, and it may easily be conceived how impossible it must be, during the tumult of an election, to distinguish one description of electors from another; the consequence is, that the resident freemen are equally with the non-residents admitted to participate in the distribution of liquor, and that the whole town is a scene of drunkenness and confusion, to the great inconvenience of the inhabitants, and the intolerable expense of the candidates. . . .

OF PRIVATE PATRONAGE, AND THE INFLUENCE POSSESSED BY PEERS AND COMMONERS.

. . . Your committee report, that the gross defects and abuses which . . . they have proved to exist in the present mode of representation, have established a system of private patronage, which renders the condition of the House of Commons practically as follows.

71 Peers and the Treasury nominate	92
Procure the return of	77
	—
Patronage of 71 peers and the Treasury	169
91 Commoners nominate	82
Procure the return of	57
	—
Patronage of 91 commoners	139
162 return	308 out of 513 members. . . .

The patronage your committee have divided under two heads—

nomination, and *influence;* and attributed it to distinct persons, under the description of *Peers* and *Commoners.*

. . . Your committee desire to have it understood that, by a *nomination,* they would describe that *absolute authority in a borough which enables the patron to command the return.* The number of places set down in this class might, your committee have every reason to believe, be with strict propriety considerably increased, but from a wish to avoid all cavil, they have confined themselves to such boroughs as are under undoubted control. These, in general, are the private property of the patrons, or have the right of voting vested in a small corporate body, the majority of whom are his immediate dependents.

By *influence,* your committee would describe *that degree of weight acquired in a particular county, city, or borough, which accustoms the electors on all vacancies to expect the recommendation of a candidate by the patron, and induces them, either from fear, from private interest, or from incapacity to oppose, because he is so recommended, to adopt him.* . . .

County elections may be said to be, in general, contested, either *by two political parties,* or *by two great families,* or *by a great family and the gentry.* In all these cases the expedient usually had recourse to, to prevent the consequences of a struggle, is *for each of the contending interests to name one member.* . . .

With respect to the influence of the Treasury, your committee apprehend that it will occasion much surprise to find it apparently so limited, but it must be observed, that this is not a species of influence subject to any direct proof, and therefore your committee have, wherever they could, avoided the mention of it, by inserting the name of the ostensible patron, even where he openly holds a place during pleasure under Government. . . .

The following boroughs, *viz.* Stockbridge, Hedon and Barnstaple, though under the management of no particular patron, must not however be passed over in silence. The number of voters in them all does not amount to 500; and though your Committee do not think it prudent to state the sort of influence which they are informed has most weight in these places, they conceive it right to mention their names separately, and others may determine how far the Members they contribute, might with propriety be added to the list of those, with whose return to Parliament the unbiassed suffrages of the people have little or no concern. . . .

The following is a list of the places compromised by political parties: Newcastle upon Tyne-Bristol-Cheshire-Essex-York-Westminster-Leicester - Maldon - Lancashire - Gloucester - Preston - Cumberland-Herefordshire, and Sussex.

23. SINECURES, REVERSIONS, AND PENSIONS

by JOHN WADE

The working of the political system in the eighteenth and early nineteenth centuries was dependent to a considerable extent on public patronage. Places, pensions and honors were used by the government to control parliamentary support, in the absence of party machines. Such patronage was a natural target for reformers, and in his indictment in *The Black Book* (first published anonymously in 1820) John Wade (1788–1875) provided details of the system in Church and state. This is a typical passage from the 1832 ed., pp. 484–493.

SINECURES are offices without employment! . . . Let us shortly inquire into the origin and present state of these corruptions.

Sinecures have mostly originated from changes in the usages of society, from alterations in the management of the revenue, the administration of justice, and partly from the unions of the three kingdoms. They ought all to have ceased with the duties attached to them; but have been kept up for sake of patronage. Of the first description of sinecures, the office of master of the hawks, in the royal household, held, with a salary of £1,392, by the Duke of St. Albans, is an example. The chief-justices in Eyre, with salaries amounting to £4,566, have been kept up for centuries, after such a mode of administering the laws had terminated. In Scotland and Ireland is a host of offices of which the holders, without employment or responsibility, have only to receive their salaries and emoluments. Of this class are the offices of Vice-admiral of Scotland, held by *general* Lord Cathcart; the Keeper of the Privy Seal of Scotland, held by the late first Lord of the Admiralty, Lord Melville; the offices of Keeper of the Signet and Register of Sasines, held by the brother of Lord Melville: the office of Chancellor of Scotland, held by lieutenant-general the Earl of Rosslyn; and the office of Justice-general of Scotland, held by the late Lord Chamberlain, the Duke of Montrose. All these are absolute sinecures, with salaries varying from £1500 to £5000 per annum. The offices of Chief Justices-in-Eyre, now held by Lord Clarendon and the Right Hon. T. Grenville, are to cease with *existing interests;* but when that will be no one can tell, since many of these lucrative appointments have been made *hereditary* in particular families, or patent offices granted for a long term of years.

Next to absolute sinecures are offices of which the salaries are vastly disproportioned to the employment, and of which the duties are discharged wholly by *deputy.* This forms a very numerous class. As specimens may be mentioned, the Auditorship of the Exchequer, held by Lord Grenville, with a salary of £4000; the Registrarship of the Admiralty, held by Lord Arden, with an income, during the war, of £10,500; the four Tellerships of the Exchequer, each with salaries of £2700; and the four Clerkships of the Pells, with salaries of £1500, held by the Bathursts, Dundasses, and Percevals. In the departments of the Army, the Navy, and Revenue, are numerous sinecures, which ought to have been long since extinguished.

But the COURTS OF JUSTICE present the most rank and unweeded garden of lucrative offices without employment, or of which the employment is executed by deputy. Among the foremost of these is Lord Ellenborough, who is clerk in the Court of King's Bench, with an income of £9,625; he is also *custos brevium* of the same court. This pompous man threw out an insolent threat, last session, on some comment being made on the heavy contributions levied by legal sinecurists on suitors for justice. Lord Kenyon is joint *custos brevium* with Lord Ellenborough, with an income of £2,696; and his lordship's brother, the Hon. Thomas Kenyon, is filazer and clerk of outlawries, with emoluments averaging £7,000 a year. Next, is the Duke of Grafton, sealer in the King's Bench, £2,888, though we dare say his grace never sealed a writ in his life, nor ever once entered the dark and dirty hole in Inner Temple Lane, where that function is performed by his representative. Charles Short, clerk of the rules and orders of the King's Bench, receives *from fees,* £5,172 per annum. What can be the grave and responsible duties of Mr. Short to entitle him to this enormous tribute, we cannot precisely state. Again; there is John Waters, clerk to the chief justice, *from fees*, £2,169. Lord Tenterden receives £10,000 a year as chief judge of this court; but his lordship's office is no sinecure, whatever may be the offices held by his son and nephew, who receive, respectively, £2,985, and £1,000 per annum. . . .

We pass on to another description of sinecures, under the titles of governors, lieutenant-governors, town-adjutants, town-majors, constables, gunners, wardens, lord-wardens, and God knows what beside, of the cities, towns, forts, castles, garrisons, &c. of Great Britain and Ireland. Berwick-on-Tweed, Chester, Hull, Blackness-Castle, Dover-Castle, Edinburgh-Castle, Walmer-Castle, and Tilbury-Fort, are examples of these appointments, and which cost the country upwards of £35,000 per annum. Numerous commissioners of revenue, comptrollers, inspectors of taxes, and distributors of stamps, are little more than sinecurists, the duties, where any exist, being discharged by deputies. But the chief *nidus* of sinecures is in the Colonies. The duties of nearly all offices in the West Indies, civil or judicial, are discharged by *deputy*, while the principal resides in England. They form an immense branch of patronage to the crown. It is impossible to estimate correctly their total value, the incomes being paid in fees, received by the deputy, who stipulates to pay a fixed annual sum to the principal. The total value of colonial sinecures, exclusive of those at the Cape of Good Hope, the Isle of France, and Malta, has been estimated at £76,546. . . .

Having spoken of Sinecures, we come next to their natural off-spring—REVERSIONS. It was very natural that the holders of situations, to which large emoluments and no duties were attached, should not only wish to preserve them during their lives, but also, if possible, transmit them to their relatives and friends after death: hence originated grants in reversion. Another reason, however, may be assigned; ministers not having situations in sufficient abundance to satisfy all their adherents, endeavoured to satisfy them by anticipation. Those for whom they could not immediately provide, they satisfied by obtaining grants from the king, making them the *heirs* of places at the death of the present possessors. Sometimes these reversions were granted to two or three persons at once; first to one, and if *he* or *she* should die, to *another;* and if he or she should die, to another; in this way have been granted most of the places on the Irish establishment for sixty or seventy years to come, and many of the most valuable legal sinecures in England. . . .

From the large emoluments of Sinecures, and the granting them in reversion, have originated some ludicrous incongruities. Many noble lords and their sons, right honourable and honourable gentlemen, fill the offices of clerks, tide-waiters, harbour-masters, searchers, gaugers, packers, craners, wharfingers, prothonotaries, and other degrading situations. Some of these offices are filled by women and some by children. The *Countess* of Mansfield receives £1000 a year from the Barbadoes planters; and the *duchess dowager* of Manchester £2928 a-year, as late collector of the customs outwards! Not long since a right honourable lady, a baroness, was *sweeper* of the Mall in the Park; another lady was *chief usher* in the Court of Exchequer; and the Honourable Louisa Browning and Lady B. Martny were *custos brevium:* some of these offices, we see, from the *Law List,* have been recently merged in and executed by the husbands and children of these *high-born* dames. Then of noble Lords; the Beresfords hold the appropriate offices of *wine-tasters, storekeepers, packers, and craners,* in Ireland; the Duke of Grafton, and Lords Ellenborough and Kenyon, with deputies to help, are clerks, sealers, and keepers of writs. Lord Henley is master in chancery; the late lord Walsingham was in the petty office of comptroller of first fruits in the Court of Exchequer; and Lord Wm. Bentinck, now located in India as governor-general of Bengal, is clerk of the pipe, part of whose office it is to attend or assist the man who holds up Lord Chancellor Brougham's train!

We could enumerate a great many more, but they will be noticed in our *List;* we shall pass on to PENSIONS.

As nearly as can be collected from the various official returns submitted to Parliament, it would appear there are upwards of fifteen hundred pensioners, who receive about £805,022 per annum. This is exclusive of colonial pensions, and of all grants, allowances, half-pay, and superannuations for civil, military, and naval services. . . .

First on the list is Lord Sidmouth, £3000 a year for life: his lordship, besides, has Richmond-park Lodge, and for many years has been receiving, as deputy-ranger, from £1000 to £2000 per annum, out of the rents and profits of the crown lands. The sinecure of clerk of the pells was many years held by his son; and there are several other Addingtons in the church, and on foreign missions. Altogether £5000 a year may be put down as the reward of the famous circular, the memorable *letter of thanks,* to the Manchester magistrates, for the massacre of the 16th of August, and other high and efficient public services of Henry Viscount Sidmouth.

The next is the honourable Robert Ward £1000, late auditor of the civil list, we believe, and who has run through various ranks and degrees as clerk of the Ordnance, M.P. for Haslemere, &c. This gentleman is only to receive half his pension, if he hold office of less annual value than twice its amount.

The right honourable Henry Goulbourn £2000, the Duke's luminous and most efficient chancellor of the Exchequer. Then follows a Mr. Hamilton £1000, of whom we know nothing, unless he be a late consul or clerk of the Treasury. Afterwards we have Thomas Peregrine Courtenay, M.P. for Totness, colonial agent for the Cape of Good Hope, and late secretary of the India Board. This is the "family man," with a wife and fourteen children, for whom Canning once made so melting an appeal to the guardians of the public purse;—they must be provided for. Mr. Courtenay is the cousin of a peer—let him be put down for £1000, and his sons have the first vacancies in the Mint, the Treasury, or Exchequer!

Now, right honourable John Wilson Croker, come forth; don't be ashamed; who can begrudge any thing to the paymaster of the widows' charity, and a twenty-one years' secretary of the Admiralty, with £3000 per annum. Put John down for £1500 a year for life—but stop; do not let him receive his pension, any more than his brother pamphleteer, Peregrine Courtenay, if he hold offices yielding £3000 a year.

Joseph Planta, Esq. we congratulate you; enrolled among the high and efficient public men; a secretary of the Treasury, with £3500 a year, and a pension for life of £1000 a year. Mr. Planta, you are a happy man; your calling and election are sure, and you are now placed beyond the risk of accident, by "flood or field." Next to Castor and Pollux, whom you have so good a right to follow, you have been one of the most humble and industrious labourers in the borough vineyard.

We pass over Canning and Huskisson; at the time of their death, each was down for £3000; they were amongst the most greedy and audacious of corruptionists; but they are gone to their audit elsewhere;—not, however, without leaving long trails of calamities behind, of which more hereafter.

Next is a Hobhouse £1000; but we pass over him also to come to the last and greatest of our "high and efficient public men," the right honourable Lord Bexley. How ought a statesman like this to be rewarded: the great Sieur Vansittart, the steadfast coadjutor of the

"Thunderer," the astounding financier, the man of infinite resource, who, in the period of our greatest tribulations, did, by the mere force of native genius, make a pound note and a shilling equal to a guinea, when the former was depreciated thirty per cent. Put Nicholas down for £3000 a year for life, and make him a LORD!

Chapter 5.
The State of Religion

The Church of England "as by law established" was a peculiar mixture of Catholic and Protestant elements. The Reformation, while sweeping away many late-Medieval usages and repudiating the headship of Rome, had left the Church in England basically Catholic in organization, liturgy, and sacraments. By the eighteenth century however this was overlaid by a thick blanket of Protestantism, and the Erastian position established in the sixteenth century had reduced the Church in many respects to a department of state. The archbishops and bishops were nominated by the crown, and the parochial clergy were for the most part nominees not of the bishops but of the crown or lay patrons. The Convocations of York and Canterbury (the highest assemblies of the Church) had not met since 1717. In the parishes the "parson" was commonly regarded as a gentleman first and priest second, though benefices varied considerably from those which could provide a comfortable living for the rector and his family to others cared for by a poor curate. Harmful as were obvious abuses, such as nonresidence of clergy, and pluralism, an equally severe limitation on the religous effectiveness of the Church was its close identification with the interests of the dominant social order.

It had been the hope of the framers of the Elizabethan settlement that the established Church would be broad enough to contain all but the most extreme reformers and supporters of Rome. But in fact this hope was never realized, and from the beginning the national Church was faced by groups of "nonconformists" (i.e., those who refused to conform to the practices of the established Church) or "dissenters" (so called because they dissented from the doctrines of Anglicanism) and "papists" (Catholics who continued to acknowledge the authority of the Pope of Rome). The Roman Catholics were soon reduced to a tiny minority (except in Ireland) and played virtually no part in English national life; but the dissenters flourished, and from the seventeenth century the Presbyterians, Baptists, Independents (Congregationalists), and Quakers continually challenged the claims and exclusive position of the Church of England. Under the Test and Corporation Acts they were barred from all national or municipal offices; and even though by the end of the eighteenth century they had secured a considerable degree of practical toleration they were still denied full civil equality.

All religious bodies—Anglican and nonconformist—reflected the general temper of the eighteenth century, which was not conducive to very profound spirituality. Christianity was commonly regarded as a set of beliefs which could be "proved" by rational argument, and its supernatural elements were pushed into the background. "Enthusiasm" in religious matters was to be deprecated, and missionary zeal for the saving of souls was not in good taste.

From these comfortable and deep slumbers the religious world was awakened by the impact of "vital" Christianity. John Wesley, an ordained minister of the Church of England, founded Methodist societies to recall England to a stricter and more devout observance of Christian precepts. It was not Wesley's intention to break away from the established Church but the opposition which he met within the Church of England drove him into unorthodox paths. From 1784 the "people called Methodists" became virtually another nonconformist sect, and after Wesley's death in 1791 they soon broke away from the Church of England completely. Methodism was essentially a popular movement and drew its support from the middle and working classes. The extension of vital religion to the upper classes was the work of a small group of "Evangelicals" within the Church of England, centered particularly in Cambridge and Clapham (south London). Their influence in modifying the morality of the age was out of all proportion to their numbers; and the "Saints," as they were nicknamed, began in earnest to reform the Anglican Church from within.

24. [THE CASE FOR AN ESTABLISHED CHURCH]

by WILLIAM PALEY

This latitudinarian view of the established Church is from William Paley's *Principles of Moral and Political Philosophy* (1785), pp. 456, 457–459, 460–464, 466. (For Paley see also Reading No. 20.)

A RELIGIOUS establishment is no part of Christianity, it is only the means of inculcating it. . . . It cannot be proved that any form of church government was laid down in the Christian, as it had been in the Jewish scriptures, with a view of fixing a constitution for succeeding ages; and which constitution, consequently, the disciples of Christianity would, every where, and at all times, by the very law of their religion, be obliged to adopt. Certainly no command for this purpose was delivered by Christ himself. . . .

The authority therefore of a church establishment is founded in its utility: and whenever, upon this principle, we deliberate concerning the form, propriety, or comparative excellency of different establishments, the single view, under which we ought to consider any of them, is that of "a scheme of instruction;" the single end we ought to propose by them is, "the preservation and communication of religious knowledge." Every other idea, and every other end that have been mixed with this, as the making of the church an engine, or even *an ally* of the state; converting it into the means of strengthening or of diffusing influence; or regarding it as a support of regal in opposition to popular forms of government, have served only to debase the institution, and to introduce into it numerous corruptions and abuses.

The notion of a religious establishment comprehends three things; a clergy, or an order of men secluded from other professions to attend upon the offices of religion; a legal provision for the maintenance of the clergy; and the confining of that provision to the teachers of a particular sect of Christianity. If any one of these three things be wanting; if there be no clergy, as amongst the quakers; or, if the clergy have no other provision than what they derive from the voluntary contribution of their hearers; or, if the provision which the laws assign to the support of religion be extended to various sects and denominations of Christians, there exists no national religion or established church, according to the sense which these terms are usually made to convey. He, therefore, who would defend ecclesiastical establishments, must show the separate utility of these three essential parts of the constitution.

1. The question first in order upon the subject, as well as the most fundamental in its importance, is, whether the knowledge and profession of Christianity can be maintained in a country, without a class of men set apart by public authority to the study and teaching of religion, and to the conducting of public worship; and for these purposes secluded from other employments. I add this last circumstance, because in it consists, as I take it, the substance of the controversy. Now it must be remembered that Christianity is an historical religion, founded in facts which are related to have passed, upon discourses which were held, and letters which were written, in a remote age, and distant country of the world, as well as under a state of life and manners, and during the prevalency of opinions, customs and institutions, very unlike any which are found amongst mankind at present. Moreover, this religion, having been first published in the country of Judea, and being built upon the more ancient religion of the Jews, is necessarily and intimately connected with the sacred writings, with the history and polity of that singular people: to which must be added, that the records of both revelations are preserved in languages which have long ceased to be spoken in any part of the world. Books which come down to us from times so remote, and under so many causes of unavoidable obscurity, cannot, it is evident, be understood without study and preparation. The languages must be learnt. The various writings which these volumes contain must be carefully compared with one another, and with themselves. What remains of contemporary authors, or of authors connected with the age, the country, or the subject of our scriptures, must be perused and consulted, in order to interpret doubtful forms of speech, and to explain allusions which refer to objects or usages that no longer exist. Above all the modes of expression, the habits of reasoning and argumentation, which were then in use, and to which the discourses even of inspired teachers were necessarily adapted, must be sufficiently known, and can only be known at all, by a due acquaintance with ancient literature. And, lastly, to establish the genuineness and integrity of the canonical scriptures themselves, a

series of testimony, recognizing the notoriety and reception of these books, must be deduced from times near to those of their first publication, down the succession of ages through which they have been transmitted to us. The qualifications necessary for such researches demand, it is confessed, a degree of leisure, and a kind of education, inconsistent with the exercise of any other profession; . . . We contend, therefore, that an order of clergy is necessary to perpetuate the evidences of revelation, and to interpret the obscurities of these ancient writings, in which the religion is contained. . . .

2. If then an order of clergy be necessary, if it be necessary also to seclude them from the employments and profits of other professions, it is evident they ought to be enabled to derive a maintenance from their own. Now this maintenance must either depend upon the voluntary contributions of their hearers, or arise from revenues assigned by authority of law. To the scheme of voluntary contribution there exists this insurmountable objection, that few would ultimately contribute any thing at all. However the zeal of a sect, or the novelty of a change, might support such an experiment for a while, no reliance could be placed upon it as a general and permanent provision. It is at all times a bad constitution which presents temptations of interest in opposition to the duties of religion; or which makes the offices of religion expensive to those who attend upon them; or which allows pretences of conscience to be an excuse for not sharing in a public burthen. If, by declining to frequent religious assemblies, men could save their money, at the same time that they indulged their indolence, and their disinclination to exercises of seriousness and reflection; or if, by dissenting from the national religion, they could be excused from contributing to the support of the ministers of religion, it is to be feared that many would take advantage of the option which was thus imprudently left open to them, and that this liberty might finally operate to the decay of virtue, and an irrecoverable forgetfulness of all religion in the country. Is there not too much reason to fear, that, if it were referred to the discretion of each neighbourhood, whether they would maintain amongst them a teacher of religion or not, many districts would remain unprovided with any; that with the difficulties which incumber every measure, requiring the co-operation of numbers, and where each individual of the number has an interest secretly pleading against the success of the measure itself, associations for the support of Christian worship and instruction would neither be numerous nor long continued? The devout and pious might lament in vain the want or the

distance of a religious assembly: they could not form or maintain one, without the concurrence of neighbours who felt neither their zeal nor their liberality.

From the difficulty with which congregations would be established and upheld upon the *voluntary* plan, let us carry our thoughts to the condition of those who are to officiate in them. Preaching, in time, would become a mode of begging. With what sincerity, or with what dignity, can a preacher dispense the truths of Christianity, whose thoughts are perpetually solicited to the reflection how he may increase his subscription? His eloquence, if he possess any, resembles rather the exhibition of a player who is computing the profits of his theatre, than the simplicity of a man, who, feeling himself the awful expectations of religion, is seeking to bring others to such a sense and understanding of their duty as may save their souls. Moreover, a little experience of the disposition of the common people will in every country inform us, that it is one thing to edify them in Christian knowledge, and another to gratify their taste for vehement impassioned oratory; that he, not only whose success, but whose subsistence depends upon collecting and pleasing a crowd, must resort to other arts than the acquirement and communication of sober and profitable instruction. For a preacher to be thus at the mercy of his audience, to be obliged to adapt his doctrines to the pleasure of a capricious multitude, to be continually affecting a style and manner neither natural to him, nor agreeable to his judgment, to live in constant bondage to tyrannical and insolent directors, are circumstances so mortifying, not only to the pride of the human heart, but to the virtuous love of independency, that they are rarely submitted to without a sacrifice of principle, and a depravation of character—at least it may be pronounced, that a ministry so degraded would soon fall into the lowest hands; for it would be found impossible to engage men of worth and ability, in so precarious and humiliating a profession.

If in deference then to these reasons it be admitted, that a legal provision for the clergy, compulsory upon those who contribute to it, is expedient; the next question will be, whether this provision should be confined to one sect of Christianity, or extended indifferently to all. Now it should be observed, that this question never *can* offer itself where the people are agreed in their religious opinions; and that it never *ought* to arise, where a system may be framed of doctrines and worship wide enough to comprehend their disagreement; and which might satisfy all by uniting all in the articles of their common faith, and in a mode of divine worship, that omits every subject of controversy or offence. Where such a comprehension is practicable, the comprehending religion ought to be made that of the state. But if this be despaired of; if religious opinions exist, not only so various, but so contradictory, as to render it impossible to reconcile them to each other, or to any one confession of faith, rule of discipline, or form of worship; if consequently, separate congregations and different sects must unavoidably continue in the country: under such circumstances, whether the laws ought to establish one sect in preference to the rest, that is, whether they ought to confer the provision assigned to the maintenance of religion upon the teachers of one system of doctrines alone, becomes a question of necessary discussion and of great importance. And whatever we may determine concerning speculative rights and abstract proprieties, when we set about the framing of an ecclesiastical constitution adapted to real life, and to the actual state of religion in the country, we shall find this question very nearly related to, and principally indeed dependent upon another; namely, "in what way, or by whom ought the ministers of religion to be *appointed?*" If the species of patronage be retained to which we are accustomed in this country, and which allows private individuals to nominate teachers of religion for districts and congregations to which they are absolute strangers; without some test proposed to the persons nominated, the utmost discordancy of religious opinions might arise between the several teachers and their respective congregations. A popish patron might appoint a priest to say mass to a congregation of protestants; an episcopal clergyman be sent to officiate in a parish of presbyterians; or a presbyterian divine to inveigh against the errors of popery before an audience of papists. The requisition then of subscription, or any other test by which the national religion is guarded, may be considered merely as a restriction upon the exercise of private patronage. . . .

The argument, then, by which ecclesiastical establishments are defended, proceeds by these steps. The knowledge and profession of Christianity cannot be upheld without a clergy; a clergy cannot be supported without a legal provision: a legal provision for the clergy cannot be constituted without the preference of one sect of Christians to the rest: and the conclusion will be satisfactory in the degree in which the truth of these several propositions can be made out.

25. THE PEOPLE CALLED METHODISTS

by JOHN WESLEY

After his conversion in 1738, John Wesley (1703–1791) knew that his divinely inspired task was "to promote as far as I am able vital practical religion and by the grace of God to beget, preserve and increase the life of God in the souls of men." His *Journal* is a magnificent record of over 50 years of evangelization, in the course of which he rode 250,000 miles on horseback and preached thousands of sermons. These typical entries are taken from Vol. I, pp. 475–477, and Vol. VII, pp. 3–7, 179–182, 486 of the standard edition, Nehemiah Curnock, ed. (1960 ed.).

WEDNESDAY, May 24, 1738 . . . In the evening I went very unwillingly to a society in Aldersgate Street, where one was reading Luther's preface to the *Epistle to the Romans*. About a quarter before nine, while he was describing the change which God works in the heart through faith in Christ, I felt my heart strangely warmed. I felt I did trust in Christ, Christ alone for salvation; and an assurance was given me that He had taken away *my* sins, even *mine*, and saved *me* from the law of sin and death.

I began to pray with all my might for those who had in a more especial manner despitefully used me and persecuted me. I then testified openly to all there what I now first felt in my heart. But it was not long before the enemy suggested, 'This cannot be faith; for where is thy joy?' Then was I taught that peace and victory over sin are essential to faith in the Captain of our salvation; but that, as to the transports of joy that usually attend the beginning of it, especially in those who have mourned deeply, God sometimes giveth, sometimes withholdeth them, according to the counsels of His own will.

After my return home, I was much buffeted with temptations; but cried out, and they fled away. They returned again and again. I as often lifted up my eyes, and He 'sent me help from His holy place.' And herein I found the difference between this and my former state chiefly consisted. I was striving, yea, fighting with all my might under the law, as well as under grace. But then I was sometimes, if not often, conquered; now, I was always conqueror. . . .

Sunday, July 18, 1784 . . . I preached, morning and afternoon, in Bingley church; but it would not near contain the congregation. Before service I stepped into the Sunday school, which contains two hundred and forty children taught every Sunday by several masters, and superintended by the curate. So many children in one parish are restrained from open sin, and taught a little good manners, at least, as well as to read the Bible. I find these schools springing up wherever I go. Perhaps God may have a deeper end therein than men are aware of. Who knows but some of these schools may become nurseries for Christians?

Tuesday, July 20 . . . Though it rained all day, in the morning we had a good congregation at five.

Wednesday, July 21 . . . I met the society, and found but one or two of the original members, most of them being gone to Abraham's bosom. I was a little surprised to find that only two or three of the rest had stood fast in the glorious liberty. But, indeed, most of them recovered their loss four years ago.

Thursday, July 22 . . . Although it rained, yet I met the congregation in the morning, and most of them were athirst for full salvation.

Friday, July 23 . . . Abundance of people were present at five in the morning, and such a company of children as I have hardly seen in England.

Saturday, July 24 . . . In the evening I went to Hanging Heaton, a little village near Dewsbury. Some months since, an uncommon work of God broke out here. The whole town was in a flame. There are now about two hundred in the society, and very few that do not know God. I was obliged to preach abroad, by the multitude that flocked together; and many of them found that God was there, to their unspeakable comfort.

Sunday, July 25 . . . I preached to several thousands at Birstall, and to at least as many at Leeds.

Tuesday, July 27 . . . Our Conference began, at which four of our brethren, after long debate (in which Mr. Fletcher took much pains), acknowledged their fault, and all that was past was forgotten.

Thursday the 29th being the public Thanksgiving Day, as there was not room for us in the old church, I read prayers, as well as preached, at our room. I admired the whole Service for the day. The prayers, scriptures, and every part of it, pointed at one thing: 'Beloved, if

God so loved us, we ought also to love one another.' Having five clergymen to assist me, we administered the Lord's Supper, as was supposed, to sixteen or seventeen hundred persons.

Sunday, August 1 . . . We were fifteen clergymen at the old church.

Tuesday, August 3 . . . Our Conference concluded in much love, to the great disappointment of all. This evening I went as far as Halifax, and the next day to Manchester. . . .

Thursday, June 29, 1786 . . . I took a cheerful leave of my affectionate friends at Epworth, leaving them much more alive than I found them. About one I preached at Thorne, now one of the liveliest places in the circuit, to a numerous congregation, and in the evening at Doncaster. I know not that ever I saw this preaching-house filled before; and many of them seemed to feel as well as hear. It may be some will bring forth fruit with patience.

Friday, June 30 . . . I turned aside to Barnsley, formerly famous for all manner of wickedness. They were then ready to tear any Methodist preacher in pieces. Now not a dog wagged his tongue. I preached near the market-place to a very large congregation; and I believe the word sunk into many hearts; they seemed to drink in every word. Surely God will have a people in this place.

Saturday, July 1 . . . I went on to Bramley, about four miles from Sheffield, where a gentleman has built a neat preaching-house for the poor people, at his own expense. As the notice was short, I had no need to preach abroad. The congregation was deeply serious, while I explained what it was to build upon a rock, and what to build upon the sand. In the evening I spoke very plain to a crowded audience at Sheffield on 'Now it is high time to awake out of sleep.' One of the hearers wrote me a nameless letter upon it. But he could remember nothing of the sermon, but only that 'the rising early was good for the nerves!'

Sunday, July 2 . . . I read prayers, preached, and administered the sacrament to six or seven hundred hearers; it was a solemn season. I preached soon after five in the evening on 'There is joy in heaven over one sinner that repenteth.' Afterwards I gave an account of the rise of Methodism (that is, old scriptural Christianity) to the whole congregation; as truth will bear the light, and loves to appear in the face of the sun.

Monday, July 3 . . . We had our Quarterly Meeting, followed by a lovefeast, at which many spoke without reserve, and several of them admirably well; showing that with the fear of the Lord is under-standing.

Tuesday, July 4 . . . I met the select society, most of them walking in glorious liberty. Afterwards I went to Wentworth House, the splendid seat of the late Marquis of Rockingham. He lately had forty thousand a year in England, and fifteen or tweny thousand in Ireland. And what has he now? Six foot of earth. . . .

April 12 (Easter Day) 1789 . . . We had a solemn assembly indeed; many hundred communicants in the morning, and in the afternoon far more hearers than our room would contain, though it is now con-siderably enlarged. Afterwards I met the society, and explained to them at large the original design of the Methodists, viz. not to be a distinct party, but to stir up all parties, Christians or heathens, to worship God in spirit and in truth; but the Church of England in particular, to which they belonged from the beginning. With this view, I have uniformly gone on for fifty years, never varying from the doctrine of the Church at all, nor from her discipline, of choice, but of necessity. So, in a course of years, necessity was laid upon me (as I have proved elsewhere), (1) to preach in the open air; (2) to pray extempore; (3) to form societies; (4) to accept of the assistance of lay preachers; and, in a few other instances, to use such means as occurred, to prevent or remove evils that we either felt or feared.

26. TRUE AND NOMINAL CHRISTIANITY

by WILLIAM WILBERFORCE

The revival of spiritual life within the Church of England which began in the 1780s was the work of a small group of Evangelicals. From 1785, when he was converted from "nominal" to "vital" or "true" Christianity, William Wilber-force (1759–1833) was their acknowledged leader. He came of a rich Hull family and was a Member of Parlia-ment and close friend of the prime minister, William Pitt. His long struggle against the slave trade is probably the best known of his many activities for moral reform. In 1797 he published his widely-read *Practical View of the*

Prevailing Religious System of Professed Christians, from
which the following passages are taken (pp. 148–150, 154–
156, 171–173, 182–183, 331, 389, 434–435).

IT seems in our days to be the commonly received opinion, that provided a man admit in general terms the truth of Christianity, though
he neither know nor consider much concerning the particulars of the
system; and if he be not habitually guilty of any of the grosser vices
against his fellow-creatures, we have no great reason to be dissatisfied
with him, or to question the validity of his claim to the name and
privileges of a Christian. The title implies no more than a sort of
formal, general assent to Christianity in the gross, and a degree of
morality in practice, little if at all superior to that for which we look
in a good Deist, Mussulman, or Hindoo.

Should any one be disposed to deny that this is a fair representation of the religion of the bulk of the Christian world, he might be
asked, whether if it were proved to them beyond dispute that Christianity is a mere forgery, would this occasion any great change in
their conduct or habits of mind? Would any alteration be made in
consequence of this discovery, except in a few of their speculative
opinions, which, when distinct from practice, it is a part of their own
system, to think of little consequence; and with regard to public worship, (knowing the good effects of religion upon the lower orders of
the people) they might still think it better to attend occasionally for
example's sake? Would not a regard for their character, their health,
their domestic and social comforts, still continue to restrain them
from vicious excesses, and prompt them to persist in the discharge, according to their present measure, of the various duties of their stations? Would they find themselves dispossessed of what had been to
them hitherto the repository of counsel and instruction, the rule of
their conduct, their habitual source of peace, and hope, and consolation?

It were needless to put these questions. They are answered in fact
already by the lives of many known unbelievers, between whom and
these professed Christians, even the familiar associates of both, though
men of discernment and observation, would discover little difference
either in conduct or temper of mind. How little then does Christianity
deserve that title to novelty and superiority which has been almost
universally admitted; that pre-eminence, as a practical code, over all
other systems of ethics! How unmerited are the praises which have

been lavished upon it by its friends; praises, in which even its enemies (not in general disposed to make concessions in its favour) have so often been unwarily drawn in to acquiesce!

Was it then for this, that the Son of God condescended to become our instructor and our pattern, leaving us an example that we might tread in his steps? Was it for this that the apostles of Christ voluntarily submitted to hunger and nakedness and pain, and ignominy and death, when forewarned too by their Master that such would be their treatment? That, after all, their disciples should attain to no higher a strain of virtue than those who rejecting their Divine authority, should still adhere to the old philosophy? . . .

I apprehend the essential practical characteristic of true Christians to be this; that relying on the promises to repenting sinners of acceptance through the Redeemer, they have renounced and abjured all other masters, and have cordially and unreservedly devoted themselves to God. This is indeed the very figure which baptism daily represents to us: like the father of Hannibal, we there bring our infant to the altar, we consecrate him to the service of *his proper owner,* and vow *in his name* eternal hostilities against all the enemies of his salvation. After the same manner Christians are become the sworn enemies of sin; they will henceforth hold no parley with it, they will allow it in no shape, they will admit it to no composition; the war which they have denounced against it, is cordial, universal, irreconcilable.

But this is not all—It is now their determined purpose to yield themselves without reserve to the reasonable service of their rightful sovereign. "They are not their own:"—their bodily and mental faculties, their natural and acquired endowments, their substance, their authority, their time, their influence; all these, they consider as belonging to them, not for their own gratification, but as so many instruments to be consecrated to the honour of God and employed in his service. This is the master principle to which every other must be subordinate. Whatever may have been hitherto their ruling passion; whatever hitherto their leading pursuit; whether sensual, or intellectual, of science, of taste, of fancy, or of feeling, it must now possess but a secondary place; or rather (to speak more correctly) it must exist only at the pleasure of its true and legitimate superior, and be put altogether under its direction and controul.

. . . But the notion of Religion entertained by many among us seems altogether different. They begin indeed, in submission to her clear prohibitions, by fencing off from the field of human action, a certain district, which, though it in many parts bear fruits on which they cast a longing eye, they cannot but confess to be forbidden ground. They next assign to Religion a portion, larger or smaller according to whatever may be their circumstances and views, in which however she is to possess merely a qualified jurisdiction, and having so done, they conceive that without let or hindrance they have a right to range at will over the spacious remainder. Religion can claim only a stated proportion of their thoughts, their time, their fortune, and influence; and of these, or perhaps of any of them, if they make her any thing of a liberal allowance, she may well be satisfied: the rest is now their own to do what they will with; they have paid their tythes, say rather their composition, the demands of the Church are satisfied, and they may surely be permitted to enjoy what she has left without molestation or interference.

It is scarcely possible to state too strongly the mischief which results from this fundamental error. At the same time its consequences are so natural and obvious, that one would think it scarcely possible not to foresee that they must infallibly follow. The greatest part of human actions is considered as indifferent. If men are not chargeable with actual vices, and are decent in the discharge of their religious duties; if they do not stray into the forbidden ground, if they respect the rights of the conceded allotment, what more can be expected from them? Instead of keeping at a distance from *all sin,* in which alone consists our safety, they will be apt not to care how near they approach what they conceive to be the boundary line; if they have not actually passed it, there is no harm done, it is no trespass. Thus the free and active spirit of Religion is "cribbed and hemmed in;" she is checked in her disposition to expand her territory, and enlarge the circle of her influence. She must keep to her prescribed confines, and every attempt to extend them will be resisted as an encroachment. . . .

Meanwhile Religion seldom comes in our way, scarcely occurs to our thoughts; and when some secret misgivings begin to be felt on this head, company soon drowns, amusements dissipate, or habitual occupations insensibly displace or smother the rising apprehension. Professional and commercial men perhaps, especially when they happen to be persons of more than ordinary reflection, or of early habits of piety not quite worn away, easily quiet their consciences by the plea, that necessary attention to their business leaves them no time to think on these serious subjects at present. "Men of leisure they confess should consider them; they themselves will do it hereafter when they retire; meanwhile they are usefully or at least innocently employed." Thus business and pleasure fill up our time, and the "one thing needful," is forgotten. Respected by others, and secretly applauding ourselves (perhaps congratulating ourselves that we are not like such an one who is a spendthrift or a mere man of pleasure, or such another who is a notorious miser) the true principle of action is no less wanting in us, and personal advancement, or the acquisition of wealth, is the object of our supreme desires and predominant pursuit. . . .

But the grand radical defect in the practical system of these nominal Christians, is their forgetfulness of all the peculiar doctrines of the Religion which they profess—the corruption of human nature—the atonement of the Saviour—and the sanctifying influence of the Holy Spirit.

Here then we come again to the grand distinction, between the Religion of Christ and that of the bulk of nominal Christians in the present day.

. . . The preceding chapters have pointed out, among those who believe themselves to be orthodox Christians, a deplorable ignorance of the Religion they profess, an utter forgetfulness of the peculiar doctrines by which it is characterized, a disposition to regard it as a mere system of ethics, and, what might seem an inconsistency, at the same time a most inadequate idea of the nature and strictness of its practical principles. This declension of Christianity into a mere system of ethics, may partly be accounted for, as has been lately suggested, by considering the corruption of our nature, what Christianity is, and in what circumstances she has been placed in this country.

Thus have we endeavoured to trace the chief defects of the religious system of the bulk of professed Christians in this country. We have pointed out their low idea of the importance of Christianity in general; their inadequate conceptions of all its leading doctrines, and the effect hereby naturally produced in relaxing the strictness of its practical system; more than all, we have remarked their grand fundamental misconception of its genius and essential nature. Let not therefore the difference between them and true believers be considered as a trifling difference; as a question of forms or opinions. The question is of the very substance of Religion; the difference is of the most serious and momentous amount. We must speak out. *Their Christianity is not Christianity.* It wants the radical principle. It is mainly defective in all the grand constituents. Let them no longer then be deceived by names in a matter of infinite importance: but with humble prayer to the Source of all wisdom, that he would enlighten their understandings, and clear their hearts from prejudice; let them seriously examine by the Scripture standard their real belief and allowed practice, and they will become sensible of the shallowness of their scanty system.

27. PRACTICAL PIETY

by HANNAH MORE

One of the most widely read of the Evangelical propagandists was Hannah More (1745–1833), a blue-stocking who turned from an early life in London literary circles to "true" religion. In 1787 she became acquainted with the leaders of the Evangelical movement; and two years later, after a visit to the villages in the Mendip Hills of Somerset with William Wilberforce, she decided to try to improve the condition of the people there. This letter to Wilberforce, written in 1791, describes her work in the village of Cheddar. From her experiences in this philanthropic work she was encouraged shortly afterwards to write a series of *Cheap Repository Tracts* to counteract the influence of popular radical publications. The letter is reprinted in William Roberts' *Memoirs of the Life and Correspondence of Mrs Hannah More* (1834), Vol. II, pp. 300–306.

. . . AFTER the discoveries made of the deplorable state of that place [Cheddar], my sister and I went and took a lodging at a little public house there, to see what we could do, for we were utterly at a loss how to begin. We found more than two thousand people in the parish, almost all very poor; no gentry, a dozen wealthy farmers, hard, brutal, and ignorant. We visited them all, picking up at one house, (like fortune-tellers) the name and character of the next. We told them we intended to set up a school for their poor. They did not like it. We assured them we did not desire a shilling from them, but wished for their concurrence, as we knew they could influence their workmen. One of the farmers seemed pleased and civil; he was rich, but covetous, a hard drinker, and his wife a woman of loose morals, but good natural sense; she became our friend, sooner than some of the decent and the formal, and let us a house, the only one in the parish, at £7. per annum, with a good garden. Adjoining to it was a large ox-house; this we roofed and floored; and by putting in a couple of windows, it made a good school-room. While this was doing, we went to every house in the place, and found every house a scene of the greatest ignorance and vice. We saw but one Bible in all the parish, and that was used to prop a flower-pot. No clergyman had resided in it for forty years. One rode over, three miles from Wells, to preach once on a Sunday, but no weekly duty was done, or sick persons visited; and children were often buried without any funeral service. Eight people in the morning, and twenty in the afternoon, was a good congregation. We spent our whole time in getting at the characters of all the people, the employment, wages, and number of every family; and this we have done in our other nine parishes. On a fixed day, of which we gave notice in the church, all the women, with all their children above six years old, met us. We took an exact list from their account, and engaged one hundred and twenty to attend on the following Sunday. A great many refused to send their children, unless we should pay them for it! and not a few refused, because they were not sure of my intentions, being apprehensive that at the end of seven years, if they attended so long, I should acquire a power over them, and send them beyond sea. I must have heard this myself in order to have believed that so much ignorance existed out of Africa. While this was going on, we had set every engine to work to find proper teachers. On this every thing depended. I had the happiness to find a woman of excellent natural sense, great knowledge of the human heart, activity, zeal, and uncommon piety. She had had a good fortune for one in middling life, but a wicked son had much reduced it. She had, however, still an estate of £40. a year, or very nearly. She brought with her a daughter, twenty-five years old, quite equal to herself in all other points: in capacity superior.

It was winter, and we all met at the school on Sunday morning at nine o'clock, having invited many parents to be present at the opening. We had drawn up some rules, which were read; then some suitable portions of Scripture; part of the 34th Psalm; then a hymn sung; and then a prayer read, composed for the occasion.

For the first year, these excellent women had to struggle with every kind of opposition, so that they were frequently tempted to give up their laborious employ. They well entitled themselves to £30. per annum salary, and some little presents. We established a Weekly School of thirty girls, to learn reading, sewing, knitting, and spinning. The latter, though I tried three sorts, and went myself to almost every clothing town in the county, did not answer,—partly from the exactions of the manufacturer, and partly from its not suiting the genius of the place. They preferred knitting after the school hours on weekdays. The mother or daughter visited the sick, chiefly with a view to their spiritual concerns; but we concealed the true motive at first; and in order to procure them access to the houses and hearts of the people, they were furnished, not only with medicine, but with a little money, which they administered with great prudence. They soon gained their confidence, read and prayed to them, and in all respects did just what a good clergyman does in other parishes.

At the end of a year we perceived that much ground had been gained among the poor; but the success was attended with no small persecution from the rich, though some of them grew more favourable. I now ventured to have a sermon read after school on a Sunday evening, inviting a few of the parents, and keeping the grown-up children; the sermons were of the most awakening sort, and soon produced sensible effect. It was at first thought a very methodistical measure, and we got a few broken windows; but quiet perseverance, and the great prudence with which the zeal of our good mistresses was regulated, carried us through. Many reprobates were, by the blessing of God, awakened, and many swearers and sabbath-breakers reclaimed. The numbers both of young and old scholars increased, and the daily life and conversation of many, seemed to keep pace with their religious profession on the Sunday.

We now began to distribute Bibles, Prayer Books, and other good books, but never at random, and only to those who had given some evidence of their loving and deserving them. They are always made the reward of superior learning, or some other merit, as we can have no other proof that they will be read. Those who manifest the greatest diligence, get the books of most importance. During my absence in the winter, a great many will learn twenty or thirty chapters, psalms, and hymns. At the end of three years, during the winter the more serious of the parents began to attend on a Wednesday night; and on Tuesday nights, twenty or thirty young people of superior piety met at the school to read the Scriptures, and hear them explained.

Finding the wants and distresses of these poor people uncommonly great, (for their wages are but 1s. per day,) and fearing to abuse the bounty of my friends, by too indiscriminate liberality, it occurred to me that I could make what I had to bestow go much further by instituting clubs, or societies for the women, as is done for men in other places. It was no small trouble to accomplish this; for though the subscription was only three half-pence a week, it was more than they could always raise; yet the object appeared so important, that I found it would be good economy privately to give widows and other very poor women money to pay their club. After combating many prejudices, we carried this point, which we took care to involve in the general system, by making it subservient to the schools, the rules of the club restraining the women to such and such points of conduct respecting the schools. In some parishes we have one hundred and fifty poor women thus associated; you may guess who are the patronesses.

We have an anniversary feast of tea, and I get some of the clergy, and a few of the better sort of people to come to it. We wait on the women, who sit and enjoy their dignity. The journal and state of affairs is read after church; and we collect all the facts we can as to the conduct of the villagers; whether the church has been more attended, fewer or more frauds, less or more swearing, scolding, or sabbath-breaking. All this is produced for or against them, in battle array, in a little sort of sermon made up of praise, censure, and exhortation, as they may be found to have merited.

One rule is, that any girl bred in the school, who continues when grown up to attend its instructions, and has married in the past year with a fair character, is presented on this day with five shillings, a pair of white stockings, and a new Bible; and several very good girls have received this public testimony to their virtuous conduct. Out of this club, (to which we find it cheaper to contribute a few guineas, than to give at random,) a sick woman receives 3s. a week, 7s. 6d. for a lying-in, &c. &c.

We are now in our sixth year at Cheddar, and two hundred children and above two hundred old people constantly attend. God has blessed the work beyond all my hopes. The farmer's wife, (our landlady,) is become one of the most eminent Christians I know; and though we had last year the great misfortune to lose our elder mistress, her truly christian death was made the means of confirming many in piety; and the daughter proceeds in the work with great ability. She has many teachers under her, who are paid 1s. a Sunday. Once a year each young person receives some articles of dress; but having so many other schools to run away with our money, we cannot do quite so much for any as I could wish. I should add, that we have about twenty young men, apprentices, servants, &c. who attend the whole Sunday with the humility of little children; and these, as they try hard to get a few clothes, we think it right to help with a small present. Amongst the collateral advantages resulting from the clubs, one is that the women who used to plead that they could not go to church, because they had no clothes, now come. The necessity of going to church in procession with us on the anniversary, raises an honest ambition to get something decent to wear, and the churches on Sunday are now filled with very clean-looking women. . . .

FURTHER READING: General Works

Ashworth, William, *An Economic History of England, 1870–1939* (1960).

Briggs, Asa, *The Age of Improvement* (1959).

Clapham, J. H., *An Economic History of Modern Britain*, 3 vols. (1930–1938 ed.).

Cole, G. D. H., and R. W. Postgate, *The British Common People* (1946 ed.).

Court, W. H. B., *Concise Economic History of Britain from 1760* (1954).

Ensor, R. C. K., *England, 1870–1914*, (1936).

Fay, C. R., *Great Britain from Adam Smith to the Present Day* (1950 ed.).

Gregg, Pauline, *A Social and Economic History of Britain, 1760–1950* (1956 ed.).

Halévy Elie, *A History of the English People in the Nineteenth Century*, 6 vols. (1961 ed.).

Havighurst, Alfred F., *Twentieth Century Britain* (1962).

Jones, G. P., and A. G. Pool, *A Hundred Years of Economic Development in Great Britain* (1940).

Keir, D. L., *Constitutional History of Modern Britain* (1953 ed.).

Marshall, Dorothy, *Eighteenth Century England* (1962).

Mowat, Charles Loch, *Britain Between the Wars, 1918–1940* (1955).

Pelling, Henry, *Modern Britain, 1885–1955* (1960).

Plumb, J. H., *England in the Eighteenth Century* (1950).

Thomson, David, *England in the Nineteenth Century* (1950).

Watson, J. Steven, *The Reign of George III, 1760–1815* (1960).

Williams, Raymond, *Culture and Society, 1780–1950* (1959).

Williams, Raymond, *The Long Revolution* (1961).

Woodward, E. L., *The Age of Reform, 1815–1870* (1938).

Part One

Ashton, T. S., *The Industrial Revolution, 1760–1830* (1950 ed.).

Aspinall, A., and E. Anthony Smith, *English Historical Documents, 1783–1832* (1959).

Brown, Ford K., *Fathers of the Victorians* (1961).

Carpenter, S. C., *Church and People, 1789–1889* (1959 ed.).

Cole, G. D. H., *Life of William Cobbett* (1947 ed.).

Edwards, Maldwyn, *After Wesley* (1935).

Edwards, Maldwyn, *John Wesley and the Eighteenth Century* (1955).

Eversley, D. E. C., *Social Theories of Fertility and the Malthusian Debate* (1959).

Gayer, Arthur D., W. W. Rostow, and Anna J. Schwartz, *Growth and Fluctuations of the British Economy, 1790–1850*, 2 vols. (1953).

George, Dorothy, *England in Transition* (1953 ed.).

Glass, D. V. (ed.), *Introduction to Malthus* (1953).

Hammond, J. L., and Barbara Hammond, *The Town Labourer, 1760–1832* (1949 ed.).

Hammond, J. L., and Barbara Hammond, *The Village Labourer* (1948 ed.).

Lampard, Eric E., *Industrial Revolution: Interpretations and Perspectives* (1957).

Mantoux, Paul, *The Industrial Revolution in the Eighteenth Century* (1961 ed.).

Mingay, Gordon E., *English Landed Society in the Eighteenth Century* (1963).

Namier, Sir Lewis, *The Structure of Politics at the Accession of George III* (1957 ed.).

Namier, Sir Lewis, *England in the Age of the American Revolution* (1961 ed.).

Polanyi, Karl, *The Great Transformation* (1944).

Prothero, R. E. (Lord Ernle), *English Farming, Past and Present* (1961 ed.).

Rostow, W. W., *The Stages of Economic Growth* (1960).

Smelser, Neil J., *Social Change in the Industrial Revolution* (1959).

Taylor, Philip A. M. (ed.), *The Industrial Revolution in Britain* (1958).

Townsend, W. J., H. B. Workman, and George Eayrs, *A New History of Methodism*, 2 vols. (1909).

Wagner, A. R., *English Ancestry* (1961).

PART TWO.
THE FORCES OF CHANGE, 1815-1848

Chapter 6.
The Struggle for Popular Democracy

The movement for parliamentary reform in the 1780s was followed after the French Revolution by working-class agitation of a much more democratic character. This was ruthlessly suppressed after 1795 and for a time the movement died down. But from 1812, and especially after the Napoleonic Wars, it revived more strongly than before. In the main provincial cities the radical reformers organized themselves in Hampden Clubs, Union Societies, and radical associations. With the support of a vigorous press, led by Cobbett's *Political Register,* and under the leadership of popular figures such as Henry ("Orator") Hunt and William Cobbett, the radicals' propaganda for parliamentary reform soon reached very large proportions. Their main demands were for universal suffrage, annual parliaments, and repeal of the corn laws. The Tory government reacted to this with repressive legislation, suspending Habeas Corpus and suppressing seditious meetings in 1817, and (after the climax of the reform demonstrations at Peterloo in August 1819) enacting the Six Acts to prevent armed insurrection and to restrict the radical press.

From 1820 to 1825 the extra-parliamentary reform movement made little headway, and working-class energies were directed into other channels. Within parliament however the case for some degree of reform gradually began to gain support, though the crucial preliminary step of overcoming Tory resistance was achieved on religious not political issues: in 1828 the Test and Corporation Acts barring dissenters from office were repealed, and in 1829 Catholic emancipation was passed by Wellington's Tory government. The solid front of Tory opposition to all reform was now broken and when the Whigs were returned to power in 1830 the country awaited eagerly the long-delayed reform bill.

The Reform Act was not passed until 1832, and then only after prolonged debate in parliament, a constitutional crisis over the House of Lords, and revolutionary ferment in the provinces led by the radical Political Unions which had come to life again in 1829. The bill, as finally passed, enfranchised only the middle classes, for the Whig government was basically conservative in its attitude towards reform. The rotten boroughs were swept away and seats redistributed to the new large towns of the north and midlands. In the towns the vote was given to the £10 householders and in the counties was extended to include £50 tenants. The result was to increase the total electorate by about a half, but the vote was still restricted in England to one man in five. As the old radical, Francis Place, commented, "The Reform Bills are in themselves of little value, but as a commencement of the breaking up of the old rotten system they are invaluable."

28. [THE MASSACRE OF PETERLOO]

by SAMUEL BAMFORD

The great demonstration in St. Peter's Fields, Manchester, on August 16, 1819, climaxed the movement for parliamentary reform which had revived after 1815. Eleven people were killed and over 400 wounded by the yeomanry and regular cavalry in their attempt to disperse the peaceful meeting. The "massacre" was dubbed "Peterloo," and its memory was enshrined in the writings and speeches and on the banners of succeeding generations of reformers. Samuel Bamford (see Reading No. 14) took part in the demonstration, and this account is from his *Passages in the Life of a Radical* (1844), Vol. I, pp. 176–177, 197, 200, 206–210.

AMONGST the meetings for reform held in the early part of the summer of 1819 were the one which took place on Spa Fields, London, at which Mr. Hunt was chairman, and another held at Birmingham, at which Major Cartwright and Sir Charles Wolseley were elected to act as legislatorial attornies for that town in Parliament.

It would seem that these movements in the country induced our friends at Manchester to adopt a course similar to that at Birmingham, and it was accordingly arranged that a meeting for that purpose should be held on St. Peter's Field on the 9th of August. But the object of that meeting having been declared illegal by the authorities, it was countermanded, and another was appointed to be held on the 16th of the same month.

It was deemed expedient that this meeting should be as morally effective as possible, and that it should exhibit a spectacle such as had never before been witnessed in England. We had frequently been taunted by the press with our ragged, dirty appearance at these assemblages; with the confusion of our proceedings, and the mob-like crowds in which our numbers were mustered; and we determined that, for once at least, these reflections should not be deserved—that we would disarm the bitterness of our political opponents by a display of cleanliness, sobriety, and decorum, such as we never before had exhibited. In short, we would deserve their respect by showing that we respected ourselves, and knew how to exercise our rights of meeting, as it were well Englishmen always should do, in a spirit of sober thoughtfulness, respectful, at the same time, to the opinions of others.

"Cleanliness," "sobriety," "order," were the first injunctions issued by the committee, to which, on the suggestion of Mr. Hunt, was subsequently added that of "peace." The fulfilment of the two first was left to the good sense of those who intended to join our procession to this "grand meeting"; the observance of the third and of the last injunctions—order, peace—were provided for by general regulations. Order in our movements was obtained by drilling; and peace, on our parts, was secured by a prohibition of all weapons of offence or defence, and by the strictest discipline, of silence, steadiness, and obedience to the directions of the conductors. Thus our arrangements, by constant practice and an alert willingness, were soon rendered perfect, and ten thousand men moved with the regularity of ten score. . . .

By eight o'clock on the morning of Monday, the 16th of August, 1819, the whole town of Middleton might be said to be on the alert: some to go to the meeting, and others to see the procession, the like of which, for such a purpose, had never before taken place in that neighborhood. . . .

Our whole column, with the Rochdale people, would probably consist of six thousand men. At our head were a hundred or two of women, mostly young wives, and mine own was amongst them. A hundred or two of our handsomest girls, sweethearts to the lads who were with us, danced to the music, or sung snatches of popular songs; a score or two of children were sent back, though some went forward; whilst on each side of our line walked some thousands of stragglers. And thus, accompanied by our friends and our dearest and most tender connections, we went slowly towards Manchester.

. . . The meeting was indeed a tremendous one. [Hunt] mounted the hustings; the music ceased . . . Mr. Hunt, stepping towards the front of the stage, took off his white hat, and addressed the people.

Whilst he was doing so, I proposed to an acquaintance that, as the speeches and resolutions were not likely to contain anything new to us, and as we could see them in the papers, we should retire awhile and get some refreshment, of which I stood much in need, being not in very robust health. He assented, and we had got to nearly the outside of the crowd, when a noise and strange murmur arose towards the church. Some persons said it was the Blackburn people coming, and I stood on tip-toe and looked in the direction whence the noise proceeded, and saw a party of cavalry in blue and white uniform come trotting, sword in hand, round the corner of a garden-wall, and to the front of a row of new houses, where they reined up in a line.

"The soldiers are here," I said; "we must go back and see what this means." "Oh," some one made reply, "they are only come to be ready if there should be any disturbance in the meeting." "Well, let us go back," I said, and we forced our way towards the colours.

On the cavalry drawing up they were received with a shout of good-will, as I understood it. They shouted again, waving their sabres over their heads; and then, slackening rein, and striking spur into their steeds, they dashed forward and began cutting the people.

"Stand fast," I said, "they are riding upon us; stand fast." And there was a general cry in our quarter of "Stand fast." The cavalry were in confusion: they evidently could not, with all the weight of man and horse, penetrate that compact mass of human beings; and their sabres were plied to hew a way through naked held-up hands and defenceless heads; and then chopped limbs and wound-gaping skulls were seen; and groans and cries were mingled with the din of that horrid confusion. "Ah! ah!" "for shame! for shame!" was shouted. Then,

"Break! break! they are killing them in front, and they cannot get away;" and there was a general cry of "break! break." For a moment the crowd held back as in a pause; then was a rush, heavy and resistless as a headlong sea, and a sound like low thunder, with screams, prayers, and imprecations from the crowd-moiled and sabre-doomed who could not escape.

By this time Hunt and his companions had disappeared from the hustings, and some of the yeomanry, perhaps less sanguinarily disposed than others, were busied in cutting down the flag-staves and demolishing the flags at the hustings.

On the breaking of the crowd the yeomanry wheeled, and, dashing whenever there was an opening, they followed, pressing and wounding. Many females appeared as the crowd opened; and striplings or mere youths also were found. Their cries were piteous and heart-rending, and would, one might have supposed, have disarmed any human resentment: but here their appeals were in vain. Women, white-vested maids, and tender youths, were indiscriminately sabred or trampled; and we have reason for believing that few were the instances in which that forbearance was vouchsafed which they so earnestly implored.

In ten minutes from the commencement of the havoc the field was an open and almost deserted space. The sun looked down through a sultry and motionless air. The curtains and blinds of the windows within view were all closed. A gentleman or two might occasionally be seen looking out from one of the new houses before mentioned, near the door of which a group of persons (special constables) were collected, and apparently in conversation; others were assisting the wounded or carrying off the dead. The hustings remained, with a few broken and hewed flag-staves erect, and a torn and gashed banner or two dropping; whilst over the whole field were strewed caps, bonnets, hats, shawls, and shoes, and other parts of male and female dress, trampled, torn, and bloody. The yeomanry had dismounted—some were easing their horses' girths, others adjusting their accoutrements, and some were wiping their sabres. Several mounds of human beings still remained where they had fallen, crushed down and smothered. Some of these still groaning, others with staring eyes, were gasping for breath, and others would never breathe more. All was silent save those low sounds, and the occasional snorting and pawing of steeds. Persons might sometimes be noticed peeping from attics and over the tall ridgings of houses, but they quickly withdrew, as if fearful of being observed, or unable to sustain the full gaze of a scene so hideous and abhorrent.

Besides the Manchester yeomanry, who, as I have already shown, did "the duty of the day," there came upon the ground soon after the attack the 15th Hussars and the Cheshire yeomanry; and the latter, as if emulous of the Manchester corps, intercepted the flying masses, and inflicted some severe sabre wounds. The hussars, we have reason for supposing, gave but few wounds, and I am not aware that it has been shown, that one of those brave soldiers dishonoured his sword by using the edge of it. In addition to the cavalry, a strong body of the 88th Foot was stationed at the lower corner of Dickinson Street: with their bayonets at the charge, they wounded several persons, and greatly impeded the escape of the fugitives by that outlet. Almost simultaneously with the hussars, four pieces of Horse artillery appeared from Deansgate, and about two hundred special constables were also in attendance; so that force for a thorough massacre was ready, had it been wanted.

On the first rush of the crowd I called to our men to break their flag-staves and secure their banners, but probably I was not heard or understood, all being then inextricable confusion. He with the blue banner saved it, the cap of liberty was dropped and left behind—indeed, woe to him who stopped, he would never have risen again; and Thomas Redford, who carried the green banner, held it aloft until the staff was cut in his hand, and his shoulder was divided by the sabre of one of the Manchester yeomanry.

A number of our people were driven to some timber which lay at the foot of the wall of the Quakers' meeting house. Being pressed by the yeomanry, a number sprung over the balks and defended themselves with stones which they found there. It was not without difficulty, and after several were wounded, that they were driven out. A heroine, a young married woman of our party, with her face all bloody, her hair streaming about her, her bonnet hanging by the string, and her apron weighed with stones, kept her assailant at bay until she fell backwards and was near being taken; but she got away covered with severe bruises. It was near this place and about this time that one of the yeomanry was dangerously wounded and unhorsed by a blow from a fragment of a brick; and it was supposed to have been flung by this woman.

29. ENGLAND IN 1819

by PERCY BYSSHE SHELLEY

Peterloo roused the reformers to a frenzied pitch of excitement and bitter denunciations of the government, which replied with repressive legislation (the Six Acts). The poet Shelley (1792–1822) was not present at Peterloo but wrote from Italy his famous poem *The Mask of Anarchy—written on the occasion of the massacre at Manchester*. Something of the feeling of radicals towards the events of this period is conveyed in his *Sonnet: England in 1819*.

An old, mad, blind, despised, and dying king,—
Princes, the dregs of their dull race, who flow
Through public scorn,—mud from a muddy spring,—
Rulers who neither see, nor feel, nor know,
But leech-like to their fainting country cling,
Till they drop, blind in blood, without a blow,—
A people starved and stabbed in the untilled field,—
An army, which liberticide and prey
Makes as a two-edged sword to all who wield,—
Golden and sanguine laws which tempt and slay;
Religion Christless, Godless—a book sealed;
A Senate,—Time's worst statute unrepealed,—
Are graves, from which a glorious Phantom may
Burst, to illumine our tempestuous day.

30. [TORY OPPOSITION TO REFORM]

by THE DUKE OF WELLINGTON

The rising tide of demand for parliamentary reform was strengthened by the 1830 July Revolution in France, and when parliament met in November 1830 it was hoped that the Tory government would introduce a moderate reform bill. But the Duke of Wellington (1769–1852), who had

been prime minister since 1828, and who enjoyed great
national esteem as the victor at Waterloo, decided against
any reform whatsoever and in his speech in the House of
Lords on November 2, 1830 made his position clear. The
report is from Hansard, *Parliamentary Debates*, 3rd series,
1830, Vol. I, p. 53.

THE noble earl has been candid enough to acknowledge that he is
not prepared with any measure of Reform, and I can have no scruple
in saying that his Majesty's Government is as totally unprepared with
any plan as the noble lord. Nay, I on my own part will go further,
and say that I have never read or heard of any measure up to the
present moment which can in any degree satisfy my mind that the
state of representation can be improved . . . I will go further and say
that the legislature and the system of representation possesses the full
and entire confidence of the country . . . I will go still further and
say that, if at the present moment I had imposed on me the duty of
forming a legislature for any country, and particularly for a country
like this, in possession of great property of various descriptions, I do
not mean to assert that I could form such a legislature as you possess
now, for the nature of man is incapable of reaching such excellence
at once; but my great endeavour would be to form some description
of legislature which would produce the same results . . . I am not
only not prepared to bring in any measure of the description alluded
to by the noble lord, but I will at once declare that, as far as I am
concerned, as long as I hold any station in the Government of the
country, I shall always feel it my duty to resist such measures when
proposed by others.

31. [THE 1832 REFORM BILL]

by THOMAS BABINGTON MACAULAY

The fall of Wellington's Tory government in November
1830 was followed by the return of a Whig government
under the leadership of Lord Grey and pledged to bring in
a measure of parliamentary reform. The Whigs calculated
that reform was the wisest policy to maintain themselves,
and their reform bill was concerned to do only what was

necessary to that end, and no more. Thomas Babington
Macaulay (1800–1859), the historian, expressed this clearly
in his speech supporting the reform bill in the House of
Commons on March 2, 1831. Macaulay's father, a London
merchant, had been a leading member of the Clapham
Sect (of Evangelicals); and Macaulay, after his education
at Cambridge and a short career as a lawyer, entered
parliament as the member for Calne. This speech is reprinted in his *Miscellaneous Writings and Speeches* (1889
ed.), pp. 483–492.

IT is a circumstance, Sir, of happy augury for the motion before the
House, that almost all those who have opposed it have declared themselves hostile on principle to parliamentary reform. . . .

I consider this, Sir, as a practical question. I rest my opinion on no
general theory of government. I distrust all general theories of government. I will not positively say, that there is any form of polity
which may not, in some conceivable circumstances, be the best possible. I believe that there are societies in which every man may safely
be admitted to vote. Gentlemen may cheer, but such is my opinion. I
say, Sir, that there are countries in which the condition of the laboring classes is such that they may safely be entrusted with the right of
electing Members of the Legislature. If the laborers of England were
in that state in which I, from my soul, wish to see them, if employment were always plentiful, wages always high, food always cheap,
if a large family were considered not as an encumbrance but as a
blessing, the principal objections to Universal Suffrage would, I think,
be removed. Universal Suffrage exists in the United States without
producing any very frightful consequences; and I do not believe that
the people of those States, or of any part of the world, are in any
good quality naturally superior to our own countrymen. But, unhappily, the laboring classes in England, and in all old countries, are occasionally in a state of great distress. Some of the causes of this distress are, I fear, beyond the control of the government. We know
what effect distress produces, even on people more intelligent than the
great body of the laboring classes can possibly be. We know that it
makes even wise men irritable, unreasonable, credulous, eager for
immediate relief, heedless of remote consequences. There is no quack-
ery in medicine, religion, or politics, which may not impose even on a
powerful mind, when that mind has been disordered by pain or fear.

It is therefore no reflection on the poorer class of Englishmen, who are not, and who cannot in the nature of things be, highly educated, to say that distress produces on them its natural effects, those effects which it would produce on the Americans, or on any other people, that it blinds their judgment, that it inflames their passions, that it makes them prone to believe those who flatter them, and to distrust those who would serve them. For the sake, therefore, of the whole society, for the sake of the laboring classes themselves, I hold it to be clearly expedient that, in a country like this, the right of suffrage should depend on a pecuniary qualification.

But, Sir, every argument which would induce me to oppose Universal Suffrage induces me to support the plan which is now before us. I am opposed to Universal Suffrage, because I think that it would produce a destructive revolution. I support this plan, because I am sure that it is our best security against a revolution.

. . . I support this bill because it will improve our institutions; but I support it also because it tends to preserve them. That we may exclude those whom it is necessary to exclude, we must admit those whom it may be safe to admit. At present we oppose the schemes of revolutionists with only one half, with only one quarter of our proper force. We say, and we say justly, that it is not by mere numbers, but by property and intelligence, that the nation ought to be governed. Yet, saying this, we exclude from all share in the government great masses of property and intelligence, great numbers of those who are most interested in preserving tranquillity, and who know best how to preserve it. We do more. We drive over to the side of revolution those whom we shut out from power.

. . . All history is full of revolutions, produced by causes similar to those which are now operating in England. A portion of the community which had been of no account expands and becomes strong. It demands a place in the system, suited, not to its former weakness, but to its present power. If this is granted, all is well. If this is refused, then comes the struggle between the young energy of one class and the ancient privileges of another. Such was the struggle between the Plebeians and the Patricians of Rome. Such was the struggle of the Italian allies for admission to the full rights of Roman citizens. Such was the struggle of our North American colonies against the mother country. Such was the struggle which the Third Estate of France maintained against the aristocracy of birth. Such was the struggle which the Roman Catholics of Ireland maintained against the aristoc-

racy of creed. Such is the struggle which the free people of color in
Jamaica are now maintaining against the aristocracy of skin. Such,
finally, is the struggle which the middle classes in England are maintaining against an aristocracy of mere locality, against an aristocracy
the principle of which is to invest a hundred drunken pot-wallopers in
one place, or the owner of a ruined hovel in another, with powers
which are withheld from cities renowned to the furthest ends of the
earth for the marvels of their wealth and of their industry.

. . . The question of Parliamentary Reform is still behind. But
signs, of which it is impossible to misconceive the import, do most
clearly indicate that, unless that question also be speedily settled,
property, and order, and all the institutions of this great monarchy,
will be exposed to fearful peril. Is it possible that gentlemen long
versed in high political affairs cannot read these signs? Is it possible
that they can really believe that the representative system of England,
such as it now is, will last till the year 1860? If not, for what would
they have us wait? Would they have us wait merely that we may
show to all the world how little we have profited by our own recent
experience? Would they have us wait, that we may once again hit
the exact point where we can neither refuse with authority, nor concede with grace? Would they have us wait, that the numbers of the
discontented party may become larger, its demands higher, its feelings
more acrimonious, its organization more complete? Would they have
us wait till the whole tragi-comedy of 1827 has been acted over again;
till they have been brought into office by a cry of "No Reform," to
be reformers, as they were once before brought into office by a cry of
"No Popery," to be emancipators? Have they obliterated from their
minds—gladly, perhaps, would some among them obliterate from their
minds—the transactions of that year? And have they forgotten all the
transactions of the succeeding year? Have they forgotten how the
spirit of liberty in Ireland, debarred from its natural outlet, found a
vent by forbidden passages? Have they forgotten how we were forced
to indulge the Catholics in all the license of rebels, merely because we
chose to withhold from them the liberties of subjects? Do they wait for
associations more formidable than that of the Corn Exchange, for contributions larger than the Rent, for agitators more violent than those
who, three years ago, divided with the King and the Parliament the
sovereignty of Ireland? Do they wait for that last and most dreadful
paroxysm of popular rage, for that last and most cruel test of military
fidelity? Let them wait, if their past experience shall induce them to

think that any high honor or any exquisite pleasure is to be obtained by a policy like this. Let them wait, if this strange and fearful infatuation be indeed upon them, that they should not see with their eyes, or hear with their ears, or understand with their heart. But let us know our interest and our duty better. Turn where we may, within, around, the voice of great events is proclaiming to us, Reform, that you may preserve. Now therefore while everything at home and abroad forebodes ruin to those who persist in a hopeless struggle against the spirit of the age, now, while the crash of the proudest throne of the Continent is still resounding in our ears, now, while the roof of a British palace affords an ignominious shelter to the exiled heir of forty kings, now, while we see on every side ancient institutions subverted, and great societies dissolved, now, while the heart of England is still sound, now, while old feelings and old associations retain a power and a charm which may too soon pass away, now, in this your accepted time, now, in this your day of salvation, take counsel, not of prejudice, not of party spirit, not of the ignominious pride of a fatal consistency, but of history, of reason, of the ages which are past, of the signs of this most portentous time. Pronounce in a manner worthy of the expectation with which this great debate has been anticipated, and of the long remembrance which it will leave behind. Renew the youth of the state. Save property, divided against itself. Save the multitude, endangered by its own ungovernable passions. Save the aristocracy, endangered by its own unpopular power. Save the greatest, and fairest, and most highly civilized community that ever existed, from calamities which may in a few days sweep away all the rich heritage of so many ages of wisdom and glory. The danger is terrible. The time is short. If this bill should be rejected, I pray to God that none of those who concur in rejecting it may ever remember their votes with unavailing remorse, amidst the wreck of laws, the confusion of ranks, the spoliation of property, and the dissolution of social order.

32. [THE £10 HOUSEHOLDERS]

by EDWARD BAINES

The dilemma which faced the Whigs when they sought to carry through parliamentary reform was how to en-franchise sufficient numbers of the middle class to ensure adequate support for the Whig cause, without at the same time widening the suffrage until it introduced the dangers of democracy. This reduced itself to an argument about the exact amount of property which was to be the basis of the franchise, as the following letter to Lord John Russell shows. The letter was from Edward Baines (1774–1848), editor and proprietor of the *Leeds Mercury* and a leader of the Whig-Liberal interests in Yorkshire. It is from the *Life of Edward Baines,* by his son, Edward Baines, Jr. (2nd ed., 1859), pp. 129–131.

TO THE RIGHT HON. LORD JOHN RUSSELL.

Leeds Mercury Office, November 7th, 1831.

MY Lord,

I am honoured by your Lordship's letter of the 3rd inst., asking if I possess any information concerning the numbers and respectability of the £10 householders in Leeds.

In order to enable me to give this information with the greatest correctness, I immediately convened a meeting of the principal Reformers in Leeds, to the number of forty or fifty, including the individuals who a few weeks ago canvassed the borough in favour of the two Liberal Candidates, Mr. John Marshall, Jun., and Mr. T. B. Macaulay. These canvassers were from twenty to thirty in number, and they were men of good judgment and respectable character and station in life.

At the meeting the following questions were put to the canvassers individually:—

1st. Does the result of your canvass lead you to conclude that the limitation of the elective franchise to householders renting £10 houses admits to the exercise of the franchise any considerable number of persons who are not fitted by their station, intelligence, and stake in society, to vote for members?

2nd. Does the £10 qualification *exclude* any considerable number of persons who are thus suitable to vote?

3rd. Does the stipulation with respect to payment of rates and taxes exclude any considerable number of £10 householders?

4th. What is the proportion which the £10 householders bear to the population of the district?

In answer to the first question the canvassers stated *unanimously,* that the £10 qualification did not admit to the exercise of the elective franchise a single person who might not safely and wisely be enfranchised; that they were surprised to find how few comparatively would be allowed to vote.

To the second question they replied with equal unanimity, that the £10 qualification *did exclude* a great number of persons who they thought might be entrusted with the franchise with safety and advantage to the public.

The third question caused some difference of opinion. It appeared that in some quarters of the town the practice prevails of the landlord paying the rates and taxes for houses as high as £15 or £20 rent, and thus a very considerable number of respectable tenants would be deprived of a vote. In the majority of instances, however, comparatively few £10 householders would be excluded by the obligation to pay rates and taxes. The general opinion of the canvassers was that the obligation to pay rates, &c., might with perfect safety and with advantage be removed.

The answers to the fourth question of course varied according as the different divisions of the town were occupied principally by the working classes or by tradespeople. It appeared that in the parts occupied chiefly by the working classes, not one householder in fifty would have a vote. In the streets principally occupied by shops, almost every householder had a vote. In those parts chiefly devoted to dwelling-houses, a great number of deductions were made for female tenants. In the township of Holbeck, containing 11,000 inhabitants, chiefly of the working classes, but containing several mills, dye-houses, public-houses, and respectable dwellings, there are only 150 voters. If the qualification was raised to £15 house-rent, there would only be about 50 voters. Out of 140 householders, heads of families, working in the mill of Messrs. Marshall and Co., there are *only two* who will have votes. The details of these facts have been sent by Mr. John Marshall to Lord Althorp a few days since. Out of 160 or 170 householders in the mill of Messrs. O. Willans and Sons, Holbeck, there is *not one* vote. Out of about 100 householders in the employment of Messrs. Taylor and Wordsworth, machine-makers,—the highest class of mechanics,—*only one* has a vote. It appeared that of the working classes not more than one in fifty would be enfranchised by the Bill. In some districts there are many more 40s. freeholders than £10 householders—even four times as many in one instance.

According to a Parliamentary Paper entitled 'Copies of further information touching the amount of population, and the number and value of houses,' &c., there will be in the borough of Leeds, the population of which is 124,000, the number of 6,683 voters. Making the deductions for female householders and uninhabited houses, and persons disqualified by the obligation to pay rates and taxes, I should think the number of voters will be reduced to less than 5,000.

The general opinion of the canvassers was, that the £10 qualification was rather too high than too low.

The cases of mills above selected are not taken for effect; they are fair specimens of the proportion of the working classes who will be entitled to vote under the Bill.

I may be permitted to mention to your Lordship a fact which I heard from the son of a gentleman who is candidate for one of the towns in the West Riding of Yorkshire, namely, that the obligation to pay rates and taxes will cut off 250 out of 800 voters for that town.

I need not remark to your Lordship, that if the proportion of voters is comparatively so small in such a town as Leeds, it must be still smaller in less populous places.

I have only, my Lord, in conclusion, to express my strong conviction, from what I have seen in this town, that the raising of the qualification for voting in boroughs above £10 house-rent, would make the Reform Bill nearly as unpopular as it has ever been popular, and that it would greatly diminish the blessing which that measure confers upon the people.

Allow me to offer to your Lordship my humble but hearty acknowledgments for the noble and patriotic measure which you submitted to Parliament, and for the wisdom and firmness which your Lordship and the rest of his Majesty's Ministers have displayed in supporting it.

I have the honour to subscribe myself,
My Lord,
Your Lordship's most obedient humble Servant,
EDWD. BAINES.

Chapter 7.

The Workshop
of the World

In 1836 when the economist G. R. Porter published his
Progress of the Nation he explained that his country and
generation had "made the greatest advances in civilization
that can be found recorded in the annals of mankind." The
constituents of this progress, as he described it, consisted
of rapid growth in population, production, consumption,
capital investment, commerce, public expenditure, and
"moral progress." England was now entering the second
phase of her Industrial Revolution; after her self-generated
take-off in the eighteenth century she was now driving
forward with sustained economic growth. From the development of intensive industrialism in the 1820s until the
Great Depression beginning in 1873 Britain could claim
to be "the workshop of the world."

While most contemporaries in the 1830s and 1840s rejoiced in the economic and technological marvels of the
age, they were at the same time concerned at the social
price which industrialism seemed to demand. The "condition of England question," as Thomas Carlyle described
it in 1839, seemed to present a baffling complex of problems arising out of the factory system, urbanization, and
population growth. Great as were the economic changes,
they were uneven and spasmodic; with the result that the
distress and exploitation of some sections of the community
could alternate or coexist with the prosperity of others.
There was no blueprint for building the world's first industrial society; and the "hungry forties" were a grim re-
minder of this.

33. THE PRINCIPLES OF POLITICAL ECONOMY

by DAVID RICARDO

The new industrial society of the nineteenth century was in the grip of one of the most persuasive ideologies hitherto known—Political Economy, or "the dismal science," as its critics termed it. From the teachings of Adam Smith, Thomas R. Malthus, and David Ricardo was elaborated a theory to justify industrial capitalism in all its aspects, and to sanctify it with all the force of scientific inevitability. By appeal to "natural laws" of economic development the doctrines of laissez faire, competition and the wage fund theory were underwritten; and by every means of popularization available they were disseminated widely throughout society.

David Ricardo (1772–1823), the son of a Dutch-Jewish banker, made a fortune on the London Exchange, and published his *Principles of Political Economy and Taxation* in 1817. The following section from chap. 5 deals with one of the most important tenets of orthodox political economy, namely the determination of wages (2nd ed., 1819, pp. 83–88, 90–94, 95–98, 103–104).

Chapter V
ON WAGES

LABOUR, like all other things which are purchased and sold, and which may be increased or diminished in quantity, has its natural and its market price. The natural price of labour is that price which is necessary to enable the labourers, one with another, to subsist and to perpetuate their race, without either increase or diminution.

The power of the labourer to support himself, and the family which may be necessary to keep up the number of labourers, does not depend on the quantity of money which he may receive for wages, but on the quantity of food, necessaries, and conveniences become essential to him from habit which that money will purchase. The natural price of labour, therefore, depends on the price of the food, necessaries, and conveniences required for the support of the labourer and his family. With a rise in the price of food and necessaries, the natural price of labour will rise; with the fall in their price, the natural price of labour will fall.

With the progress of society the natural price of labour has always a tendency to rise, because one of the principal commodities by which its natural price is regulated has a tendency to become dearer from the greater difficulty of producing it. As, however, the improvements in agriculture, the discovery of new markets, whence provisions may be imported, may for a time counteract the tendency to a rise in the price of necessaries, and may even occasion their natural price to fall, so will the same causes produce the correspondent effects on the natural price of labour.

The natural price of all commodities, excepting raw produce and labour, has a tendency to fall in the progress of wealth and population; for though, on one hand, they are enhanced in real value, from the rise in the natural price of the raw material of which they are made, this is more than counterbalanced by the improvements in machinery, by the better division and distribution of labour, and by the increasing skill, both in science and art, of the producers.

The market price of labour is the price which is really paid for it, from the natural operation of the proportion of the supply to the demand; labour is dear when it is scarce and cheap when it is plentiful. However much the market price of labour may deviate from its natural price, it has, like commodities, a tendency to conform to it.

It is when the market price of labour exceeds its natural price that the condition of the labourer is flourishing and happy, that he has it in his power to command a greater proportion of the necessaries and enjoyments of life, and therefore to rear a healthy and numerous family. When, however, by the encouragement which high wages give to the increase of population, the number of labourers is increased, wages again fall to their natural price, and indeed from a reaction sometimes fall below it.

When the market price of labour is below its natural price, the condition of the labourers is most wretched: then poverty deprives them of those comforts which custom renders absolute necessaries. It is only after their privations have reduced their number, or the demand for labour has increased, that the market price of labour will rise to its natural price, and that the labourer will have the moderate comforts which the natural rate of wages will afford. . . .

It is not to be understood that the natural price of labour, estimated even in food and necessaries, is absolutely fixed and constant. It varies at different times in the same country, and very materially differs in different countries. It essentially depends on the habits and customs of the people. An English labourer would consider his wages under their natural rate, and too scanty to support a family, if they enabled him to purchase no other food than potatoes, and to live in no better habitation than a mud cabin; yet these moderate demands of nature are often deemed sufficient in countries where "man's life is cheap" and his wants easily satisfied. Many of the conveniences now enjoyed in an English cottage would have been thought luxuries at an earlier period of our history.

From manufactured commodities always falling and raw produce always rising, with the progress of society, such a disproportion in their relative value is at length created, that in rich countries a labourer, by the sacrifice of a very small quantity only of his food, is able to provide liberally for all his other wants.

Independently of the variations in the value of money, which necessarily affect money wages, but which we have here supposed to have no operation, as we have considered money to be uniformly of the same value, it appears then that wages are subject to a rise or fall from two causes:—

First, the supply and demand of labourers.

Secondly, the price of the commodities on which the wages of labour are expended.

In different stages of society, the accumulation of capital, or of the means of employing labour, is more or less rapid, and must in all cases depend on the productive powers of labour. The productive powers of labour are generally greatest when there is an abundance of fertile land: at such periods accumulation is often so rapid that labourers cannot be supplied with the same rapidity as capital.

It has been calculated that under favourable circumstances population may be doubled in twenty-five years; but under the same favourable circumstances the whole capital of a country might possibly be doubled in a shorter period. In that case, wages during the whole period would have a tendency to rise, because the demand for labour would increase still faster than the supply.

In new settlements, where the arts and knowledge of countries far advanced in refinement are introduced, it is probable that capital has a tendency to increase faster than mankind; and if the deficiency of labourers were not supplied by more populous countries, this tendency would very much raise the price of labour. In proportion as these countries become populous, and land of a worse quality is taken into cultivation, the tendency to an increase of capital diminishes; for the surplus produce remaining, after satisfying the wants of the existing population, must necessarily be in proportion to the facility of production, viz. to the smaller number of persons employed in production. Although, then, it is probable that, under the most favourable circumstances, the power of production is still greater than that of population, it will not long continue so; for the land being limited in quantity, and differing in quality, with every increased portion of capital employed on it there will be a decreased rate of production, whilst the power of population continues always the same. . . .

With a population pressing against the means of subsistence, the only remedies are either a reduction of people or a more rapid accumulation of capital. In rich countries, where all the fertile land is already cultivated, the latter remedy is neither very practicable nor very desirable, because its effect would be, if pushed very far, to render all classes equally poor. But in poor countries, where there are abundant means of production in store, from fertile land not yet brought into cultivation, it is the only safe and efficacious means of removing the evil, particularly as its effect would be to elevate all classes of the people.

The friends of humanity cannot but wish that in all countries the labouring classes should have a taste for comforts and enjoyments, and that they should be stimulated by all legal means in their exertions to procure them. There cannot be a better security against a super-abundant population. In those countries where the labouring classes have the fewest wants, and are contented with the cheapest food, the people are exposed to the greatest vicissitudes and miseries. They have no place of refuge from calamity; they cannot seek safety in a lower station; they are already so low that they can fall no lower. On any deficiency of the chief article of their subsistence there are few substitutes of which they can avail themselves and dearth to them is attended with almost all the evils of famine.

In the natural advance of society, the wages of labour will have a tendency to fall, as far as they are regulated by supply and demand; for the supply of labourers will continue to increase at the same rate, whilst the demand for them will increase at a slower rate. . . . I say that, under these circumstances, wages would fall if they were regulated only by the supply and demand of labourers; but we must not forget that wages are also regulated by the prices of the commodities on which they are expended.

As population increases, these necessaries will be constantly rising in price, because more labour will be necessary to produce them. If, then, the money wages of labour should fall, whilst every commodity on which the wages of labour were expended rose, the labourer would be doubly affected, and would be soon totally deprived of subsistence. Instead, therefore, of the money wages of labour falling, they would rise; but they would not rise sufficiently to enable the labourer to purchase as many comforts and necessaries as he did before the rise in the price of those commodities. . . .

Notwithstanding, then, that the labourer would be really worse paid, yet this increase in his wages would necessarily diminish the profits of the manufacturer; for his goods would sell at no higher price, and yet the expense of producing them would be increased. This, however, will be considered in our examination into the principles which regulate profits.

It appears, then, that the same cause which raises rent, namely, the increasing difficulty of providing an additional quantity of food with the same proportional quantity of labour, will also raise wages; and therefore, if money be of an unvarying value, both rent and wages will have a tendency to rise with the progress of wealth and population.

But there is this essential difference between the rise of rent and the rise of wages. The rise in the money value of rent is accompanied by an increased share of the produce; not only is the landlord's money rent greater, but his corn rent also; he will have more corn, and each defined measure of that corn will exchange for a greater quantity of all other goods which have not been raised in value. The fate of the labourer will be less happy; he will receive more money wages, it is true, but his corn wages will be reduced; and not only his command of corn, but his general condition will be deteriorated, by his finding it more difficult to maintain the market rate of wages above their natural rate. While the price of corn rises 10 per cent., wages will always rise less than 10 per cent., but rent will always rise more; the condition of the labourer will generally decline, and that of the landlord will always be improved. . . .

These, then, are the laws by which wages are regulated, and by which the happiness of far the greatest part of every community is governed. Like all other contracts, wages should be left to the fair and free competition of the market, and should never be controlled by the interference of the legislature.

The clear and direct tendency of the poor laws is in direct opposition to these obvious principles: it is not, as the legislature benevolently intended, to amend the condition of the poor, but to deteriorate the condition of both poor and rich; instead of making the poor rich, they are calculated to make the rich poor; and whilst the present laws are in force, it is quite in the natural order of things that the fund for the maintenance of the poor should progressively increase till it has absorbed all the net revenue of the country, or at least so much of it as the state shall leave to us, after satisfying its own never-failing demands for the public expenditure.

34. THE PHILOSOPHY OF MANUFACTURES

by ANDREW URE

No apologist of the new industrialism waxed more eloquent than Dr. Andrew Ure (1778–1857), a Scottish professor at Anderson's Institution in Glasgow, who later (1830) became a scientific consultant in London. He published several works on applied science and industry, but it was *The Philosophy of Manufactures* (1835) which gained him notoriety, including the sarcasm of Friedrich Engels in *The Condition of the Working Class in England in 1844*. These typical passages are from pp. 5–7, 23, 301, of Dr. Ure's book.

THIS island is pre-eminent among civilized nations for the prodigious development of its factory wealth, and has been therefore long viewed with a jealous admiration by foreign powers. This very pre-eminence, however, has been contemplated in a very different light by many influential members of our own community, and has been even denounced by them as the certain origin of innumerable evils to the people, and of revolutionary convulsions to the state. If the affairs of the kingdom be wisely administered, I believe such allegations and fears will prove to be groundless, and to proceed more from the envy of one ancient and powerful order of the commonwealth, towards another suddenly grown into political importance, than from the nature of things. . . .

The blessings which physico-mechanical science has bestowed on society, and the means it has still in store for ameliorating the lot of mankind, have been too little dwelt upon; while, on the other hand, it has been accused of lending itself to the rich capitalists as an instrument for harassing the poor, and of exacting from the operative an accelerated rate of work. It has been said, for example, that the steam-engine now drives the power-looms with such velocity as to urge on their attendant weavers at the same rapid pace; but that the hand-weaver, not being subjected to this restless agent, can throw his shuttle and move his treddles at his convenience. There is, however, this difference in the two cases, that in the factory, every member of the loom is so adjusted, that the driving force leaves the attendant nearly nothing at all to do, certainly no muscular fatigue to sustain, while it procures for him good, unfailing wages, besides a healthy workshop *gratis:* whereas the non-factory weaver, having everything to execute by muscular exertion, finds the labour irksome, makes in consequence innumerable short pauses, separately of little account, but great when added together; earns therefore proportionally low wages, while he loses his health by poor diet and the dampness of his hovel. . . .

It is, in fact, the constant aim and tendency of every improvement in machinery to supersede human labour altogether, or to diminish its cost, by substituting the industry of women and children for that of men; or that of ordinary labourers for trained artisans. In most of the water-twist, or throstle cotton-mills, the spinning is entirely managed by females of sixteen years and upwards. The effect of substituting the self-acting mule for the common mule, is to discharge the greater part of the men spinners, and to retain adolescents and children. The proprietor of a factory near Stockport states, in evidence to the commissioners, that, by such substitution, he would save 50*l.* a week in wages, in consequence of dispensing with nearly forty male spinners, at about 25*s.* of wages each. This tendency to employ merely children with watchful eyes and nimble fingers, instead of journeymen of long experience, shows how the scholastic dogma of the division of labour into degrees of skill has been exploded by our enlightened manufacturers.

. . . I have visited many factories, both in Manchester and in the surrounding districts, during a period of several months, entering the spinning rooms, unexpectedly, and often alone, at different times of the day, and I never saw a single instance of corporal chastisement inflicted on a child, nor indeed did I ever see children in ill-humour. They seemed to be always cheerful and alert, taking pleasure in the light play of their muscles,—enjoying the mobility natural to their age. The scene of industry, so far from exciting sad emotions in my mind, was always exhilarating. It was delightful to observe the nimbleness with which they pieced the broken ends, as the mule-carriage began to recede from the fixed roller-beam, and to see them at leisure, after a few seconds' exercise of their tiny fingers, to amuse themselves in any attitude they chose, till the stretch and winding-on were once more completed. The work of these lively elves seemed to resemble a sport, in which habit gave them a pleasing dexterity. Conscious of their skill, they were delighted to show it off to any stranger. As to exhaustion by the day's work, they evinced no trace of it on emerging from the mill in the evening; for they immediately began to skip about any neighbouring play-ground, and to commence their little amusements with the same alacrity as boys issuing from a school. It is moreover my firm conviction, that if children are not ill-used by bad parents or guardians, but receive in food and raiment the full benefit of what they earn, they would thrive better when employed in our modern factories, than if left at home in apartments too often ill-aired, damp, and cold.

35. THE 1834 POOR LAW REPORT

by HIS MAJESTY'S COMMISSIONERS

The New Poor Law of 1834, based upon the *Report from His Majesty's Commissioners for inquiring into the Administration and Practical Operation of the Poor Laws* (1834), marked a crucial stage in the development of English social policy. The Commissioners were exponents of the new philosophy of scientific Utilitarianism and Political Economy, and they were determined to do away with the old Elizabethan system of poor relief which the new age had inherited from the eighteenth century. For over 40 years the problem of how to reduce the growing burden of

poor rates had been debated, without any conclusive result. But by 1834 the pressure to create a free labor market
in accordance with Malthusian and Ricardian principles
was sufficiently strong to overcome working-class radical
and Tory opposition. The two basic principles of the *Report*, which were embodied in the 1834 Act,—the work-
house test and "less eligibility"—are set out in the following passages from pp. 227–228, 261–262, 297.

THE most pressing of the evils which we have described are those
connected with the relief of the Able-bodied. They are the evils,
therefore, for which we shall first propose remedies.

If we believe the evils stated in the previous part of the Report,
or evils resembling, or even approaching them, to be necessarily incidental to the compulsory relief of the able-bodied, we should not
hesitate in recommending its entire abolition. But we do not believe
these evils to be its necessary consequences. We believe that, under
strict regulations, adequately enforced, such relief may be afforded
safely, and even beneficially.

In all extensive communities, circumstances will occur in which an
individual, by the failure of his means of subsistence, will be exposed
to the danger of perishing. To refuse relief, and at the same time to
punish mendicity when it cannot be proved that the offender could
have obtained subsistence by labour, is repugnant to the common
sentiments of mankind; it is repugnant to them to punish even dep-
redation, apparently committed as the only resource against want.

In all extensive civilised communities, therefore, the occurrence of
extreme necessity is prevented by alms-giving, by public institutions
supported by endowments or voluntary contributions, or by a provision
partly voluntary and partly compulsory, or by a provision entirely
compulsory, which may exclude the pretext of mendicancy.

But in no part of Europe except England has it been thought fit
that the provision, whether compulsory or voluntary, should be applied to more than the relief of *indigence*, the state of a person unable to labour, or unable to obtain, in return for his labour, the means
of subsistence. It has never been deemed expedient that the provision
should extend to the relief of *poverty;* that is the state of one, who, in
order to obtain a mere subsistence, is forced to have recourse to
labour.

From the evidence collected under this Commission, we are induced to believe that a compulsory provision for the relief of the indigent can be generally administered on a sound and well-defined principle; and that under the operation of this principle, the assurance that no one need perish from want may be rendered more complete than at present, and the mendicant and vagrant repressed by disarming them of their weapon—the plea of impending starvation.

It may be assumed, that in the administration of relief, the public is warranted in imposing such conditions on the individual relieved, as are conducive to the benefit either of the individual himself, or of the country at large, at whose expense he is to be relieved.

The first and most essential of all conditions, a principle which we find universally admitted, even by those whose practice is at variance with it, is, that his situation on the whole shall not be made really or apparently as eligible as the situation of the independent labourer of the lowest class. Throughout the evidence it is shown, that in proportion as the condition of any pauper class is elevated above the condition of independent labourers, the condition of the independent class is depressed; their industry is impaired, their employment becomes unsteady, and its remuneration in wages is diminished. Such persons, therefore, are under the strongest inducements to quit the less eligible class of labourers, and enter the more eligible class of paupers. The converse is the effect when the pauper class is placed in its proper position, below the condition of the independent labourer. Every penny bestowed, that tends to render the position of the pauper more eligible than that of the independent labourer, is a bounty on indolence and vice. We have found, that as the poor's-rates are at present administered, they operate as bounties of this description, to the amount of several millions annually. . . .

The chief specific measures which we recommend . . . are—

First, that except as to medical attendance, and subject to the exception respecting apprenticeship herein-after stated, all relief whatever to able-bodied persons or to their families, otherwise than in well-regulated workhouses (*i.e.* places where they may be set to work according to the spirit and intention of the 43rd. of Elizabeth) shall be declared unlawful, and shall cease, in manner and at periods hereafter specified; and that all relief afforded in respect of children under the age of 16 shall be considered as afforded to their parents. . . .

We recommend . . . the appointment of a Central Board to control the administration of the Poor-Laws, with such Assistant Commissioners as may be found requisite; and that the Commissioners be empowered and directed to frame and enforce regulations for the government of workhouses, and as to the nature and amount of the relief to be given and the labour to be exacted in them, and that such regulations shall, as far as may be practicable, be uniform throughout the country. . . .

36. [CHILD LABOR IN FACTORIES]

Evidence before MICHAEL THOMAS SADLER'S COMMITTEE

The employment of children in factories in the early days of the Industrial Revolution had been occasioned partly by a shortage of labor; but was continued thereafter because of its cheapness and the nature of the jobs which machine production necessitated. The system was a standing temptation to rapacity by the mill owners, and it was only too easy to exploit such helpless labor as child workers. A movement of protest (known as the Short Time or Factory movement) grew rapidly after 1830 under the leadership of Richard Oastler, a Tory-Radical from Yorkshire. In parliament attempts were made to introduce a Ten Hours bill, to limit the conditions of employment of children and young persons in factories, and in this connection a Select Committee was appointed to enquire into the matter. The chairman of this committee was Michael Thomas Sadler (1780–1835), the Tory M.P. who had championed the Ten Hours bill in the Commons. Although the witnesses were carefully selected and leading questions were often put to them, the *Report of the Select Committee on Factory Children's Labour,* Vol. XV, 1831–1832, presented a vivid picture of cruelty in the textile mills which was never effectively disproved. The following evidence was corroborated by many other witnesses.

EVIDENCE OF SAMUEL COULSON

5047. AT what time in the morning, in the brisk time, did those girls go to the mills?

In the brisk time, for about six weeks, they have gone at 3 o'clock in the morning, and ended at 10, or nearly half past at night.

5049. What intervals were allowed for rest or refreshment during those nineteen hours of labour?

Breakfast a quarter of an hour, and dinner half an hour, and drinking a quarter of an hour.

5051. Was any of that time taken up in cleaning the machinery?

They generally had to do what they call dry down; sometimes this took the whole of the time at breakfast or drinking, and they were to get their dinner or breakfast as they could; if not, it was brought home.

5054. Had you not great difficulty in awakening your children to this excessive labour?

Yes, in the early time we had them to take up asleep and shake them, when we got them on the floor to dress them, before we could get them off to their work; but not so in the common hours.

5056. Supposing they had been a little too late, what would have been the consequence during the long hours?

They were quartered in the longest hours, the same as in the shortest time.

5057. What do you mean by quartering?

A quarter was taken off.

5058. If they had been how much too late?

Five minutes.

5059. What was the length of time they could be in bed during those long hours?

It was near 11 o'clock before we could get them into bed after getting a little victuals, and then at morning my mistress used to stop up all night, for fear that we could not get them ready for the time; sometimes we have gone to bed, and one of us generally awoke.

5060. What time did you get them up in the morning?

In general me or my mistress got up at 2 o'clock to dress them.

5061. So that they had not above four hours' sleep at this time?

No, they had not.

5062. For how long together was it?

About six weeks it held; it was only done when the throng was very much on; it was not often that.

5063. The common hours of labour were from 6 in the morning till half-past eight at night?

Yes.

5064. With the same intervals for food?

Yes, just the same.

5065. Were the children excessively fatigued by this labour?

Many times; we have cried often when we have given them the little victualling we had to give them; we had to shake them, and they have fallen to sleep with the victuals in their mouths many a time.

5066. Had any of them any accident in consequence of this labour?

Yes, my eldest daughter when she went first there; she had been about five weeks, and used to fettle the frames when they were running, and my eldest girl agreed with one of the others to fettle hers that time, that she would do her work; while she was learning more about the work, the overlooker came by and said, "Ann, what are you doing there?" she said, "I am doing it for my companion, in order that I may know more about it," he said, "Let go, drop it this minute," and the cog caught her forefinger nail, and screwed it off below the knuckle, and she was five weeks in Leeds Infirmary.

5067. Has she lost that finger?

It is cut off at the second joint.

5068. Were her wages paid during that time?

As soon as the accident happened the wages were totally stopped; indeed, I did not know which way to get her cured, and I do not know how it would have been cured but for the Infirmary.

5069. Were the wages stopped at the half-day?

She was stopped a quarter of a day; it was done about four o'clock.

5072. Did this excessive term of labour occasion much cruelty also?

Yes, with being so very much fatigued the strap was very frequently used.

5073. Have any of your children been strapped?

Yes, every one; the eldest daughter; I was up in Lancashire a fortnight, and when I got home I saw her shoulders, and I said, "Ann, what is the matter?" she said, "The overlooker has strapped me; but," she said, "do not go to the overlooker, for if you do we shall lose our work"; I said I would not if she would tell me the truth as to what caused it. "Well," she said, "I will tell you, father." She says, "I was fettling the waste, and the girl I had learning had got so perfect she could keep the side up till I could fettle the waste; the overlooker came round, and said, "What are you doing?" I said, "I am fettling while the other girl keeps the upper end up"; he said, "Drop it this minute;" she said, "No, I must go on with this"; and because she did not do it, he took a strap, and beat her between the shoulders. My wife was out at the time, and when she came in she said her back was beat nearly to a jelly; and the rest of the girls encouraged her to go to Mrs. Varley, and she went to her, and she rubbed it with a part of a glass of rum, and gave her an old silk handkerchief to cover the place with till it got well.

5080. What was the wages in the short hours?

Three shillings a week each.

5081. When they wrought those very long hours what did they get?

Three shillings and sevenpence halfpenny.

5082. For all that additional labour they had only 7½d. a week additional?

No more.

5083. Could you dispose of their wages, when they had received them, as you wished: did you understand that?

They never said anything to me; but the children have said, "If we do not bring some little from the shop I am afraid we shall lose our work." And sometimes they used to bring a bit of sugar or some little oddment, generally of their own head.

5084. That is, they were expected to lay out part of their wages under the truck system?

Yes.

5086. Had your children any opportunity of sitting during those long days of labour?

No; they were in general, whether there was work for them to do or not, to move backwards and forwards till something came to their hands.

5118. At the time they worked those long hours, would it have been in their power to work a shorter number of hours, taking the 3*s.*?

They must either go on at the long hours, or else be turned off.

37. THE SANITARY CONDITION OF THE LABOURING POPULATION

by EDWIN CHADWICK

The high price of early industrialism in terms of social misery was fully documented in investigations of housing and public health in the 1830s and 1840s. Squalid dwellings, unpaved and unsewered streets, typhus and cholera epidemics, were the outward manifestations of what amounted to an almost complete breakdown in the techniques of urban living. This passage is from the famous *Report on the Sanitary Condition of the Labouring Population* (1842), pp. 3, 39–41, which was written by Edwin Chadwick (1800–1890) and sponsored by the Poor Law Commission. Chadwick was a model Benthamite reformer-administrator, and had already played a leading role in framing the 1834 Poor Law Report.

A CONCEPTION may be formed of the aggregate effects of the several causes of mortality from the fact, that of the deaths caused during one year in England and Wales by epidemic, endemic, and contagious diseases, including fever, typhus, and scarlatina, amounting to 56,461, the great proportion of which are proved to be preventible, it may be said that the effect is as if the whole county of Westmoreland, now containing 56,469 souls, or the whole county of Huntingdonshire, or any other equivalent district, were entirely depopulated annually, and were only occupied again by the growth of a new and feeble population living under the fears of a similar visitation. The annual slaughter in England and Wales from preventible causes of typhus which attacks persons in the vigour of life, appears to be double the amount of what was suffered by the Allied Armies in the battle of Waterloo. . . .

Mr. Baker in his report on the sanitary condition of the residences of the labouring classes in Leeds, thus describes their external condition:—

"The river Aire, which courses about a mile and a half through the town, is liable suddenly to overflow from violent or continued rains, or from the sudden thawing of heavy falls of snow. The lower parts and dwellings, both in its vicinity and in that of the becks, are not unfrequently therefore inundated; and as the depth of the cellars is below the means of drainage, the water has to be pumped out by hand-pumps on to the surface of the streets. In those parts of the town, and particularly where the humbler classes reside, during these inundations, and where there are small sewers, the water rises through them into the cellars, creating miasmatic exhalations, and leaving offensive refuse, exceedingly prejudicial to the health as well as to the comfort of the inhabitants. It was stated, on the authority of one of the registrars, that during a season remarkable for an unprecedented continuation of hot weather, that in one of these localities, the deaths were as three to two, while in other parts of the town, at the same period, they were as two to three. The condition of the Timble Bridge beck is doubtless much worse for drainage purposes than formerly, for the bottom has been raised by continual deposits, until the oldest water-wheel upon it has had to be removed as useless and inoperative; and stepping-stones, once the means of passage over it, are at this moment said to be buried under the accumulation of years, as much as one or two feet in depth. It is quite clear, therefore, that that which was once the main receptacle for the drainage of an entire district is, in its present state, no longer capable of fulfilling that purpose; and that though a considerable amount of drainage might still be effected by it, yet, unless emptied of its superfluous matter, it cannot now be made available for the wants of the entire population on its course.

"In an inundation about the period of 1838 or 1839, which happened in the night, this beck overflowed its boundaries so greatly, and regurgitated so powerfully into petty drains communicating with houses 100 yards distant from its line, that many of the inhabitants were floated in their beds, and fever to a large amount occurred from the damp and exhalations which it occasioned. Of the 586 streets of Leeds, 68 only are paved by the town, *i.e.*, by the local authorities; the remainder are either paved by owners, or are partly paved, or are totally unpaved, with the surfaces broken in every direction, and ashes and filth of every description accumulated upon many of them. In the manufacturing towns of England, most of which have enlarged with great rapidity, the additions have been made without regard to either the personal comfort of the inhabitants or the necessities which congregation requires. To build the largest number of cottages on the smallest allowable space seems to have been the original view of the speculators, and the having the houses up and tenanted, the *ne plus ultra* of their desires. Thus neighbourhoods have arisen in which there is neither water nor out-offices, nor any conveniences for the absolute domestic wants of the occupiers. But more than this, the land has been disposed of in so many small lots, to petty proprietors, who have subsequently built at pleasure, both as to outward form and inward ideas, that the streets present all sorts of incongruities in the architecture; causeways dangerous on account of steps, cellar windows without protection, here and there posts and rails, and everywhere clothes-lines intersecting them, by which repeated accidents have been occasioned. During the collection of the statistical information by the Town Council, many cases of broken legs by these unprotected cellars, and of horsemen dismounted by neglected clothes-lines hanging across the streets, were recorded.

"It might be imagined that at least the streets over which the town surveyors have a legal right to exercise control would be sewered. But this is not the case; of the 68 streets which they superintend, 19 are not sewered at all, and 10 are only partly so; nay, it is only within the three or four years past that a sewer has been completed through the main street for two of the most populous wards of the town, embracing together a population of 30,540 persons, by which to carry off the surface and drainage water of an elevation of 150 feet, where, indeed, there could be no excuse for want of sufficient fall. I have seen, in the neighbourhood to which I now refer, an attempt made to drain the cottage houses into a small drain passing under the causeway, and which afterwards had to be continued through a small sewer, and through private property, by a circuitous route, in order to reach its natural outlet, and the water from the surveyors' drain regurgitate into the cutting from the dwellings. It only needs to be pointed out that the sewer which has subsequently been made, and is most effective, is an evidence of the previous practicability of a work so essential to the welfare of the people; but, I may add, that many of the inhabitants of districts a little further distant from the town, where fever is always rife, are yet obliged to use cesspools which are constructed under their very doors, for the want of the continuation of this desirable measure.

"Along the line of these two wards, and down the street which divides them, and where this sewer has been recently made, numbers of streets have been formed and houses erected without pavement, and hence without surface drainage—without sewers—or if under drainage can be called sewers, then with such as, becoming choked in a few months, are even worse than if they were altogether without. The surface of these streets is considerably elevated by accumulated ashes and filth, untouched by any scavenger; they form nuclei of disease exhaled from a thousand sources. Here and there stagnant water, and channels so offensive that they have been declared to be unbearable, lie under the doorways of the uncomplaining poor; and privies so laden with ashes and excrementitious matter as to be unuseable prevail, till the streets themselves become offensive from deposits of this description; in short, there is generally pervading these localities a want of the common conveniences of life.

"The courts and *culs-de-sac* exist everywhere. The building of houses back to back occasions this in a great measure. It is in fact part of the economy of buildings that are to pay a good per centage. In one *cul-de-sac*, in the town of Leeds, there are 34 houses, and in ordinary times, there dwell in these houses 340 persons, or ten to every house; but as these houses are many of them receiving houses for itinerant labourers, during the periods of hay-time and harvest and the fairs, at least twice that number are then here congregated. The name of this place is the Boot and Shoe-yard, in Kirkgate, a location from whence the Commissioners removed, in the days of the cholera, 75 cart-loads of manure, which had been untouched for years, and where there now exists a surface of human excrement of very considerable extent, to which these impure and unventilated dwellings are additionally exposed. This property is said to pay the best annual interest of any cottage property in the borough."

Chapter 8.
Protest and Revolt

Within the new industrial society there had developed by the 1840s a strong tradition of popular protest and revolt. This working-class movement was an intricate complex of organizations and purposes, with differing forms and emphases in each region. Trade unions, Short Time Committees for factory reform, the struggle for an unstamped (free) press, anti-Poor Law agitation, Chartism, Owenite socialism, land schemes, cooperative stores, and the extension of the franchise—all claimed the support of working men. These movements were not so much rivals competing for support, nor even complementary parts of a greater national movement, as different expressions of a general discontent on the part of the people with their lot under the new conditions of industrialism, and a reaching out to a more equitable organization of society. The movements tended to fade into one another, and the new cause with the more urgent dynamic absorbed the energies that had previously gone into an earlier movement.

In sharp contrast to the indifferent success of most of these working-class endeavors to better their condition were the middle-class protest movements, directed against the interests and privileges of traditional, aristocratic England. The Anti-Corn Law League, like its contemporary, Chartism, was an extra-parliamentary movement; but whereas the Chartists failed to get universal suffrage the Corn Laws were repealed in 1846.

38. INITIATION CEREMONY

of the WOOLCOMBERS' UNION

Institutionally, labor unions developed from the trade clubs of the eighteenth century, and were often indistinguishable from friendly societies. Between 1799 and 1824 unions were illegal, and even after the repeal of the Combination Acts in 1824 they continued to organize in secret because of the employers' opposition. The text of this ceremony, enacted on the reception of new members into the woolcombers' union, is taken from a hostile source, *The Character, Object and Effects of Trades Unions* (1834), written by Edward Carlton Tufnell, a factory and poor law inspector. The pamphlet explains that "the scene is usually the first floor of a tavern, which is doubly planked throughout, and the interstices filled with wood shavings in order to prevent anyone overhearing the ceremonies. The time is 8 or 9 o'clock in the evening, at which hour the above-named *dramatis personae* with the exception of the principal conductor, and those who are about to enter the Union, are supposed to be collected together for the performance of the following drama. On one side of the apartment is a skeleton, above which is drawn sword and a battle-axe, and in front stands a table upon which lies a Bible. The principal officers of the Union are clothed in surplices."

DRAMATIS PERSONAE

OUTSIDE TILER, a member of the Union who keeps guard on the outside of the room in which the members are assembled.

INSIDE TILER, ditto, on the inside.

PRINCIPAL CONDUCTOR, the person who conducts to the Lodge those who are to be initiated into the mysteries of the Union.

PRESIDENT, VICE-PRESIDENT, WARDEN, SECRETARY, MEMBERS OF THE UNION, WORKMEN ABOUT TO BE MADE MEMBERS.

Members say the following prayer:

O God, who art the author of peace and lover of concord, defend us in this our undertaking, that we may not fear the power of our adversaries, through the merits of Jesus Christ, our Lord. Amen.

Outside Tiler knocks at the door

INSIDE TILER: Who comes here to disturb the peace and harmony of this our most worthy and honourable order?

PRINCIPAL CONDUCTOR (*from without*):   I am not come here to disturb the peace and harmony of this your most worthy and honourable order. I am a brother, with strangers who wish to be admitted into your most worthy and honourable order.

INSIDE TILER: Most worthy President, Vice-, Secretary, and brothers all, a brother stands at the door with strangers, who wish to be admitted into this your most worthy and honourable order.

PRESIDENT: In the name of the Lord, admit him.

Enter Principal Conductor followed by the strangers with their eyes bandaged. Members salute, and then sing a hymn

PRINCIPAL CONDUCTOR: Strangers, within our secret walls we have admitted you,

Hoping you will prove honest, faithful, just and true,

If you cannot keep the secrets we require,

Go hence, you are at liberty to retire.

Are your motives pure?

STRANGERS: Yes.

PRINCIPAL CONDUCTOR: Do you declare they are?

STRANGERS: Yes.

PRINCIPAL CONDUCTOR: Then, brethren, to initiate these strangers we will now proceed, And our most worthy master may proceed to read.

Members sing a hymn

WARDEN: Stand, ye presumptuous mortals, strangers' steps I hear,

And I must know your trade and business here.

By my great power, there's nothing can from vengeance stay us,

If you come here intending to betray us.

PRESIDENT: Most worthy guardian of our sacred laws,

They're woolcombers, and wishful to protect the united cause.

WARDEN: Then all is well.

VICE-PRESIDENT: Strangers, you're welcome, and if you prove sincere,

You'll not repent your pains and labour here.

We have one common interest, and one common soul,

Which should by virtue guide and actuate the whole.

Our trade requires protection, by experience sad we know;

Our duty is to prevent recurrence of our former woe.

Our commonwealth was like some savage land,

Where the weaker slaves, and stronger bear command,

Where tyrants rule with uncontrolled sway,

And degraded subjects do their will obey.

Such was our domestic lot, our suffering and our care

Enraged our minds with sadness and despair.

And when we'd united and our rights obtained,

We found that only half our point was gained,

Our interests were so many and so various,

The tenure of our rights so frail and so precarious,
That had we not invented Lodges our protection to ensure,
All, all would have come to nought, as it had done before.
Strangers, the design of all our Lodges is love and unity,
With self-protection founded on the laws of equity,
And when you have our mystic rights gone through,
Our secrets all will be disclosed to you.
We deem you worthy our friendship, trust and confidence to share,
See that you make the prosperity of our cause your constant care.
Let your tongue be always faithful, your heart conceal its trust,
Woe, woe and dishonour attend the faithless and unjust.
Guards, give the strangers sight.

> *The bandages are removed from the eyes of the strangers, and they are placed opposite the skeleton*

PRESIDENT (pointing to the skeleton):
   Strangers, mark well this shadow, which you see,
It is a faithful emblem of man's destiny.
Behold that head, once filled with pregnant wit,
These hollow holes once sparkling eyes did fit;
This empty mouth nor lips nor tongue contains,
Of a once well furnished head, see all that now remains.
Behold this breast, where a generous heart once moved,
Filled with affection, loving and beloved,
Mark well these bones, the flesh hath left its place;
These arms could once a tender wife embrace.
These legs in gay activity could roam,
But, alas! the spirit's dead, the life is gone.
O death! O death! Thy terrors strike us with dismay.
Only the spirit just, which hath left its empty clay,
Can set thee at defiance and in triumph say,
O death, where is thy sting? O grave, where is thy victory?
The sting of death is sin—are we not sinners all?
Then upon us one day the heavy stroke of death must fall.
VICE-PRESIDENT: Strangers, hear me; and mark well what I say,
Be faithful to your trust, or you may rue this day.
You are now within our secret walls, and I must know if you can keep a secret.
STRANGERS: Yes.
VICE-PRESIDENT: And will you do it?
STRANGERS: Yes.

VICE-PRESIDENT: Then amongst us, you will shortly be entitled to the endearing name of brother,

And what you hear or see here done, you must not disclose to any other;

We are uniting to cultivate friendship as well as to protect our trade,

And due respect must to all our laws be paid.

Hoping you will prove faithful, and all encroachments on our rights withstand,

As a token of your alliance,—give me your hand.

And now, shouldst thou ever prove deceitful, remember thy end, remember. Guards, put these strangers into darkness, and conduct them to our most worthy master, to be further instructed in this our most worthy and honourable order.

The eyes of the strangers are again bandaged, and they are then made to walk several times round the room, while the members stamp on the floor with their feet. They are then led to the table, upon which the Bible is placed; the right hand of each is placed upon the sacred volume: the bandages are then removed from their eyes, and they take the following oath:

I, A. B., woolcomber, being in the awful presence of Almighty God, do voluntarily declare that I will persevere in endeavouring to support a brotherhood, known by the name of the Friendly Society of Operative Stuff Manufacturers, and other Industrious Operatives, and I solemnly declare and promise that I will never act in opposition to the brotherhood in any of their attempts to support wages, but will, to the utmost of my power, assist them in all lawful and just occasions, to obtain a fair remuneration for our labour. And I call upon God to witness this my most solemn declaration, that neither hopes, fears, rewards, punishments, nor even death itself, shall ever induce me directly or indirectly, to give any information respecting any thing contained in this Lodge, or any similar Lodge connected with the Society; and I will neither write nor cause to be written, upon paper, wood, sand, stone, or any thing else, whereby it may be known, unless allowed to do so by the proper authorities of the Society. And I will never give my consent to have any money belonging to the Society divided or appropriated to any other purpose than the use of the Society and support of the trade, so help me God, and keep me steadfast in this my most solemn obligation; and if ever I reveal either part or parts of this my most solemn obligation, may all the Society I am about to belong to, and all that is just, disgrace me so long as I live;

and may what is now before me plunge my soul into the everlasting pit of misery. Amen.

VICE-PRESIDENT: Guards, put these strangers into darkness. Rise and stand. (*To the strangers.*)

> *The strangers having been blindfolded, the members sing a hymn, and then salute. The strangers are then led out. Members then say the following prayer:*

O God, who art the author of peace, etc. (*same as at the commencement*).

PRESIDENT: In the name of King Edward the Third, I declare this Lodge to be now duly closed, and so it is.

God save our noble King,
William the Fourth let's sing.

Brethren, 'ere we depart, let us join hand and heart
In this our cause;

May our next meeting be blest with sweet harmony,
Honour, and secrecy in the Mechanic's cause.

Exeunt

39. A NEW VIEW OF SOCIETY

by ROBERT OWEN

In opposition to the dominant orthodoxy of laissez-faire society there developed a school of early English socialism. Drawing upon ideas of natural law, utilitarianism, and anticapitalist economics, the socialists sought a solution to the problems of early industrialism by means of some "social system," as opposed to the prevailing emphasis on individualism. The idea of communitarianism and the practical experiments in establishing "villages of cooperation" as a means of radically transforming society, stemmed from Robert Owen (for whom see also Reading No. 17), whose views were widely disseminated by periodicals, pamphlets, lectures, debates, and local Owenite societies in the 1830s and 1840s. Fundamental to Owen's theory of cooperative socialism was the doctrine of the paramount influence of environment on men's character and ideas, as set forth in the following passage from his *New View of Society* (1813–1814), 3rd essay, pp. 14–17.

HITHERTO, indeed, in all ages and in all countries, man seems to have blindly conspired against the happiness of man, and to have remained as ignorant of himself as he was of the solar system prior to the days of Copernicus and Galileo.

Many of the learned and wise among our ancestors were conscious of this ignorance, and deeply lamented its effects; and some of them recommended the partial adoption of those principles which can alone relieve the world from the miserable effects of ignorance.

The time, however, for the emancipation of the human mind had not then arrived: the world was not prepared to receive it. The history of humanity shows it to be an undeviating law of nature, that man shall not prematurely break the shell of ignorance; that he must patiently wait until the principle of knowledge has pervaded the whole mass of the interior, to give it life and strength sufficient to bear the light of day.

Those who have duly reflected on the nature and extent of the mental movements of the world for the last half-century, must be conscious that great changes are in progress; that man is about to advance another important step towards that degree of intelligence which his natural powers seem capable of attaining. Observe the transactions of the passing hours; see the whole mass of mind in full motion; behold it momentarily increasing in vigour, and preparing ere long to burst its confinement. But what is to be the nature of this change? A due attention to the facts around us, and to those transmitted by the invention of printing from former ages, will afford a satisfactory reply.

From the earliest ages it has been the practice of the world to act on the supposition that each individual man forms his own character, and that therefore he is accountable for all his sentiments and habits, and consequently merits reward for some and punishment for others. Every system which has been established among men has been founded on these erroneous principles. When, however, they shall be brought to the test of fair examination, they will be found not only unsupported, but in direct opposition to all experience, and to the evidence of our senses.

This is not a slight mistake, which involves only trivial consequences; it is a fundamental error of the highest possible magnitude; it enters into all our proceedings regarding man from his infancy; and it will be found to be the true and sole origin of evil. It generates and perpetuates ignorance, hatred, and revenge, where, without such error, only intelligence, confidence, and kindness would exist. It has hitherto been the Evil Genius of the world. It severs man from man throughout the various regions of the earth; and makes enemies of those who, but for this gross error, would have enjoyed each other's kind offices and sincere friendship. It is, in short, an error which carries misery in all its consequences.

This error cannot much longer exist; for every day will make it more and more evident *that the character of man is, without a single exception, always formed for him; that it may be, and is, chiefly, created by his predecessors; that they give him, or may give him, his ideas and habits, which are the powers that govern and direct his conduct. Man, therefore, never did, nor is it possible he ever can, form his own character.*

The knowledge of this important fact has not been derived from any of the wild and heated speculations of an ardent and ungoverned imagination; on the contrary, it proceeds from a long and patient study of the theory and practice of human nature, under many varied circumstances; it will be found to be a deduction drawn from such a multiplicity of facts, as to afford the most complete demonstration.

40. LABOUR'S WRONGS AND LABOUR'S REMEDY

by JOHN FRANCIS BRAY

Central to most early English socialist thought was the doctrine of the labor theory of value. From Ricardo the socialists obtained the idea of labor as the source or measure of value, and from this they developed a detailed criticism of the capitalist system, which they claimed denied to the worker his right to the whole produce of his labor. John Francis Bray (1809–1897), a journeyman printer of Leeds, expressed these views in terms of "the principle of unequal exchanges," which is here taken from his book, *Labour's Wrongs and Labour's Remedy, or the Age of Might and the Age of Right* (Leeds, 1839), pp. 48–50. Bray left Leeds for America in 1842, reappearing in the 1870s as a veteran socialist in the American labor movement.

THE subject of exchanges is one on which too much attention cannot be bestowed by the productive classes; for it is more by the infraction of this third condition by the capitalist, than by all other causes united, that inequality of condition is produced and maintained, and the working man offered up, bound hand and foot, a sacrifice upon the altar of Mammon.

From the very nature of labour and exchange, strict justice not only requires that all exchangers should be *mutually*, but that they should likewise be *equally*, benefited. Men have only two things which they can exchange with each other, namely, labour, and the produce of labour; therefore, let them exchange as they will, they merely give, as it were, labour for labour. If a just system of exchanges were acted upon, the value of all articles would be determined by the entire cost of production; *and equal values should always exchange for equal values.* If, for instance, it take a hatter one day to make a hat, and a shoemaker the same time to make a pair of shoes—supposing the material used by each to be of the same value—and they exchange these articles with each other, they are not only mutually but equally benefited: the advantage derived by either party cannot be a disadvantage to the other, as each has given the same amount of labour, and the materials made use of by each were of equal value. But if the hatter should obtain *two* pair of shoes for *one* hat—time and value of material being as before—the exchange would clearly be an unjust one. The hatter would defraud the shoemaker of one day's labour; and were the former to act thus in all his exchanges, he would receive, for the labour of *half a year*, the product of some other person's *whole year;* therefore the gain of the first would necessarily be a loss to the last.

We have heretofore acted upon no other than this most unjust system of exchanges—the workmen have given the capitalist the labour of a whole year, in exchange for the value of only half a year—and from this, and not from the assumed inequality of bodily and mental powers in individuals, has arisen the inequality of wealth and power which at present exists around us. It is an inevitable condition of inequality of exchanges—of buying at one price and selling at another—that capitalists shall continue to be capitalists, and working men be working men—the one a class of tyrants and the other a class of slaves—to eternity. By equality of exchanges, however, no able-bodied individual can exist, as thousands now do, unless he fulfill that condition of the economist, "that there shall be labour;" nor can one class appropriate the produce of the labour of another class, as the capitalists now appropriate and enjoy the wealth which the powers of the working man daily call into existence. It is inequality of exchanges which enables one class to live in luxury and idleness, and dooms another to incessant toil.

By the present unjust and iniquitous system, exchanges are not only *not* mutually beneficial to all parties, as the political economists have asserted, but it is plain, from the very nature of an exchange, that there is, in most transactions between the capitalist and the producer, *after the first remove*, no *exchange* whatever. An exchange implies the giving of one thing for another. But what is it that the capitalist, whether he be manufacturer or landed proprietor, gives in exchange for the labour of the working man? The capitalist gives no labour, for he does not work—he gives no capital, for his store of wealth is being perpetually augmented. It is certain that the capitalist can have only his labour or his capital to exchange against the labour of the working man; and if, as we daily see, the capitalist gives no labour, and his original stock of capital does not decrease, he cannot in the nature of things make an exchange with anything that belongs to himself. The whole transaction, therefore, plainly shews that the capitalists and proprietors do no more than give the working man, for his labour of one week, a part of the wealth which they obtained from him the week before!—which just amounts to giving him *nothing* for *something*—and is a method of doing business which, however consonant with the established usages of the present system, is by no means compatible with a working man's ideas of justice. The wealth which the capitalist appears to give in exchange for the workman's labour was generated neither by the labour nor the riches of the capitalist, but it was originally obtained by the labour of the workman; and it is still daily taken from him, by a fraudulent system of unequal exchanges. The whole transaction, therefore, between the producer and the capitalist, is a palpable deception, a mere farce: it is, in fact, in thousands of instances, no other than a barefaced though legalised robbery, by means of which the capitalists and proprietors contrive to fasten themselves upon the productive classes, and suck from them their whole substance.

41. [CHARTISM IN HALIFAX]

by BENJAMIN WILSON

Of all the early movements of protest and revolt Chartism had the widest appeal. It took its name from the Charter, a six-point program headed by the demand for universal manhood suffrage. For some years after its launching in 1837 it overshadowed all other working-class movements, and even after its last great manifestation in 1848 it lingered on in the industrial areas until 1853. As a national organization Chartism was never very effective. The strength of the movement was in the localities, where it produced vigorous and able leaders like Benjamin Wilson of Halifax. These extracts are from his reminiscences, *The Struggles of an Old Chartist* (Halifax, 1887), pp. 3, 13–14, 22–23.

JOSEPH WILSON, my uncle, was a small piece-maker in the village and it was about this time that I went to help him in the warehouse, and wind bobbins. My aunt was a famous politician, a Chartist, and a great admirer of Fergus O'Connor. It was whilst there that I first became acquainted with the Chartist movement. The delegates to the convention broke up at Whitsuntide, and forthwith addressed meetings throughout the country. On Whit-Monday, 1839, a great meeting was held at Peep Green, which I attended along with Samuel Jackson, a neighbour; we joined the procession in Halifax, which was a very large one headed by a band of music, and marched by Godley Lane and Hipperholme, at which place the Queensbury procession joined us; on reaching the top of the hill above Bailiffe Bridge we met the Bradford procession, headed by Peter Bussey, on horseback, and wearing a green sash. On our arrival at the place of meeting some thousands of people had already assembled, and for almost an hour we witnessed the continuous arrival of processions from different directions, with bands playing and flags and banners flying, a great many of them far superior to any that I have seen in our late demonstrations. At the commencement of the meeting I had never seen anything to compare with it in numbers, and scarcely ever since have I seen anything to equal it. The proceedings opened with prayer by Mr. William Thornton, at the close of which Fergus O'Connor put his hand on his shoulder and said "Well done, Thornton, when we get the People's Charter I will see that you are made the Archbishop of York." Thornton I knew well, for he lived at Skircoat Green; he was a fine speaker; I had heard him lecture in the Wesleyan School in the village. He was very popular in the Chartist movement, but very soon after went to America in order, it was said, to avoid imprisonment. This was my first meeting in the Chartist movement.

Fergus O'Connor's paper *"The Northern Star,"* was the recognised organ of the Chartist movement, and was doing great service on its behalf; it had a large circulation in Halifax and neighbourhood, and its total issue was reputed to be 60,000 per week. . . .

[In 1848] A great many people in these districts were arming themselves with guns or pikes, and drilling on the moors. Bill Cockroft, one of the leaders of the physical force party in Halifax, wished me to join the movement, I consented, and purchased a gun, although I knew it to be a serious thing for a chartist to have a gun or pike in his possession. I had had several years practice in shooting, as the farmer for whom I worked supplied me with gun, powder, and shot for the purpose of shooting birds in summer. I saw Cockroft who gave me instructions how to proceed until wanted, which did not occur as the scheme was abandoned. It might now be said we were fools, but I answer young people now have no idea of what we had to endure. Tom Brown's Schooldays would have had no charm for me, as I had never been to a day school in my life; when very young I had to begin working, and was pulled out of bed between 4 and 5 o'clock in the morning in summer time to go with a donkey 1½ miles away, and then take part in milking a number of cows; and in the evening had again to go with milk and it would be 8 o'clock before I had done. I went to a card shop afterwards and there had to set 1500 card teeth for a ½d. From 1842 to 1848 I should not average 9/- per week wages; out-door labour was bad to get then and wages were very low. I have been a woollen weaver, a comber, a navvy on the railway, and a barer in the delph that I claim to know some little of the state of the working classes. I well remember only a few years ago having some talk with a friend who told me he was moulding bullets in the cellar in 1848; he had a wife and five children dependent upon him, but was unable to get work, trade being so bad. Since then, however, under the blessings of free trade and by dint of perseverance he has succeeded in saving a considerable sum, and is now living retired from business. Many a time in winter have I known what it was to be short of the commonest of food, and thousands in this parish were in the same condition. A great many tales of sorrow could be told, but enough has been said to shew that those were times to make men desperate, for life then was not so valuable as now. Many persons were arrested and imprisoned, and several had narrow escapes of being caught with arms in their possession, whilst many who had arms were getting rid of them as fast as possible. The Chartists were called ugly names, the swinish multitude unwashed and levellers. I never knew levelling advocated amongst the Chartists, neither in public or private, for they did not believe in it, nor have I known a case of plunder in the town, though thousands have marched through its streets to meetings in various places. What they wanted was a voice in making the laws they were called upon to obey; they believed that taxation without representation was tyranny, and ought to be resisted; they took a leading part in agitating in favour of the ten hours question, the repeal of the taxes on knowledge, education, co-operation, civil and religious liberty and the land question, for they were the true pioneers in all the great movements of their time. . . .

The death of Benjamin Rushton occurred on the 19th June, 1853, at his residence at Friendly, in Ovenden, in his 68th year. He was highly respected by the Chartists of Yorkshire and Lancashire, and was looked upon in this town and neighbourhood as the "grand old man;" he had been a reformer before such as myself were born, and a leader amongst the Chartists since its commencement. He had been the chairman of some of the greatest demonstrations of his time; was a good speaker, although using rather broad language, but never failed to make an impression upon an audience. He died poor, as many other reformers have done, and it was decided by the Chartists of Halifax that his funeral expenses should be borne by them, and his funeral to take place on Sunday, June 26th, and be a public one. It was arranged that six of the oldest Chartists should bear him to the grave, and twelve of the younger be conductors, with wands crape-tipped. We met at Nicholl's Hotel, and marched from there, with Ernest Jones and Mr. Gammage, to the Northgate Hotel fields, which had been engaged purposely, and mounted the platform. Mr. Jones wished the people to join in the procession. The field at an early hour presented a dense mass of human beings, through which it was almost impossible to force a way; we had not much difficulty in forming the procession, as all appeared willing to obey the orders given here. It was led by Ernest Jones and R. Gammage, after them came the public walking six abreast; the hearse, a modern one, was drawn by two horses. At the entrance of the village the Odd-fellows were waiting at their lodge to the number of 140, and walked in advance. On approaching the house of the deceased patriot they opened out in double line. The sight was magnificent, and whilst waiting the notes of a band of music were heard, and soon came in sight the Bradford procession, led by Chartist veterans, including our old friend, Joseph Alderson. The coffin—a double one, covered with black cloth, and very elegant—was borne from the house at twelve o'clock.

> Chartists weep, and let your grief be true,
> A nobler patriot country never knew.

The coffin was carried by six veteran Chartists, and the splendid pall by six Odd-fellows. The return to Halifax was then commenced, the distance from the Cemetery being about two miles, and from one end of the route to the other the people lined the streets, particularly in the heart of the town, where the processionists had scarcely room to walk, whilst at the Cemetery the gates were closed after the corpse had entered to prevent the crush of the people. The wish of the departed patriot was that no paid priest should officiate at his funeral. Mr. Gammage spoke at the grave side, and after him a member of the Odd-fellows said a few words, and then Mr. Ernest Jones delivered a long address . . . One of the local papers, I believe it was the *Guardian,* gave the numbers marching in the procession from 6,000 to 10,000, and it took an hour and half to pass through the town. I will not give any numbers myself, but I will say that I saw more people in Halifax that day than I had ever seen before or since, and the public funerals that I have seen in this town have been a mere nothing in comparison to this.

42. [REPEAL OF THE CORN LAWS]

by RICHARD COBDEN

It was not only the working classes who felt they had economic and political grievances in the 1840s. The rising middle classes, although they had secured the franchise in

1832, were conscious of an antagonism towards the aristocratic and landed interests which had remained strongly entrenched. The corn laws (a system of protective tariffs for agriculture instituted in 1815) became a symbol of the predominance of the landed interest, and the attack on them became an assertion of middle-class power. From Manchester the Anti-Corn Law League in 1838 began its campaign, parallel to its contemporary, the Chartist movement. Typical of the League arguments are the following extracts from a speech by Richard Cobden (1804–1865) in London on July 3, 1844. (*Speeches* [1870], Vol. I, pp. 187–208). Cobden was a Manchester manufacturer, and the acknowledged leader of the Anti-Corn Law League.

IN the first place, we want free trade in corn, because we think it just; we ask for the abolition of all restriction upon that article, exclusively, simply because we believe that, if we obtain that, we shall get rid of all other monopolies without any trouble. We do not seek free trade in corn primarily for the purpose of purchasing it at a cheaper money-rate; we require it at the natural price of the world's market, whether it becomes dearer with a free trade—as wool seems to be getting up now, after the abolition of the 1d. a pound—or whether it is cheaper, it matters not to us, provided the people of this country have it at its natural price, and every source of supply is freely opened, as nature and nature's God intended it to be;—then, and then only, shall we be satisfied. If they come to motives, we state that we do not believe that free trade in corn will injure the farmer; we are convinced that it will benefit the tenant-farmer as much as any trader or manufacturer in the community.

Neither do we believe it will injure the farm-labourer; we think it will enlarge the market for his labour, and give him an opportunity of finding employment, not only on the soil by the improvements which agriculturists must adopt, but that there will also be a general rise in wages from the increased demand for employment in the neighbouring towns, which will give young peasants an opportunity of choosing between the labour of the field and that of the towns. We do not expect that it will injure the land-owner, provided he looks merely to his pecuniary interest in the matter; we have no doubt it will interfere with his political despotism—that political union which now exists in the House of Commons, and to a certain extent also, though terribly shattered, in the counties of this country. We believe it might interfere with that; and that with free trade in corn men must look for political power rather by honest means—to the intelligence and love of their fellow-countrymen—than by the aid of this monopoly, which binds some men together by depressing and injuring their fellow-citizens.

We are satisfied that those landowners who choose to adopt the improvement of their estates, and surrender mere political power by granting long leases to the farmers—who are content to eschew some of their feudal privileges connected with vert and venison—I mean the feudal privileges of the chase—if they will increase the productiveness of their estates—if they choose to attend to their own business —then, I say, free trade in corn does not necessarily involve pecuniary injury to the landlords themselves. . . .

We believe that free trade will increase the demand for labour of every kind, not merely of the mechanical classes and those engaged in laborious bodily occupations, but for clerks, shopmen and warehousemen, giving employment to all those youths whom you are so desirous of setting out in the world. . . . Finally, we believe that Free Trade will not diminish, but, on the contrary, increase the Queen's revenue.

Chapter 9.

Church and Chapel

The Victorian era was essentially a religious age, at least as measured by the extent of outward religious observance. Strict sabbatarianism and regular church- or chapel-going were the effects of that evangelicalism which spread beyond all sects and creeds and gradually permeated every aspect of Victorian life. The census of religious worship carried out by Horace Mann in 1851 showed that more than half of the people attended some place of worship on Sunday—a high figure when account is taken of those who for various reasons were unable to attend. Church and chapel were closely woven into the texture of English social life, and helped to provide something of that social cement which was so conspicuously lacking in the new urban industrial civilization. From the pulpit came social as well as religious leadership, and a powerful means of molding public opinion.

Within the Church of England the spirit of the eighteenth century lingered long, and the original saintliness of the earlier Evangelicals was lost when Evangelicalism became respectable and fashionable. But from 1836 signs of change within the Church became apparent, and by 1850 evidence of new life was abundant in many quarters. There was a veritable spate of repairing old churches and building new ones. The building of schools, the formation of guilds, sisterhoods, and charities, were indicative of a new fervor in parochial work. The repercussions of the Oxford Movement were felt in a more devout attitude towards the liturgy and ceremonial of the Church, and in the observation of Holy Days and Seasons. A new and more vital conception of the role of the Church in the community began to appear, especially in the industrial areas, where Anglican champions of social reform stood by the side of Chartists and radicals.

The Church of England, however, was hampered by its conservative traditions and the difficulty of bridging the

gulf between the vicarage and the cottage. The Nonconformists had similar problems. But in the towns their large
and prosperous chapels—Congregational, Unitarian, Bap-
tist, Presbyterian, and Quaker—became fashionable centers
of middle-class influence, from which civic leadership and
support for national Liberal policies emanated.

The Methodists after the death of Wesley in 1791 were
plagued by schism, and successive break-aways from the
main body resulted in the establishment of a number of
different Methodist "connexions." Wesleyan Methodism
became increasingly conservative and respectable, reflecting the social outlook of its prosperous middle-class membership. But the new connexions were democratic and
liberal in spirit and reached down deep into the working
classes. From their chapels came many of the self-educated
leaders of popular movements.

43. [RICH AND POOR IN THE PARISH CHURCH]

by JOSEPH ARCH

In rural England the Established Church was most closely
identified with political Toryism and the maintenance of
the social hierarchy. Incidents such as the following go far
to explain the success of Methodism in attracting many of
the finest elements in the working classes. Joseph Arch
(1826–1919) was a Warwickshire agricultural laborer and
Methodist local preacher, who organised the National
Agricultural Labourers' Union in 1872 and later entered
parliament. The extracts are from his autobiography,
Joseph Arch: the story of his life, Countess of Warwick ed.
(1898), pp. 16–22, and refer to his boyhood in the village
of Barford, Warwickshire, in the 1830s.

. . . IN the parish church the poor man and his wife were shown
pretty plainly where they came among their fellow-creatures and
fellow-worshippers—men and women of the same flesh and blood, and
of like passions with themselves, however superior they might seem
to be in the eyes of the world because they were rich and high-placed.

In the parish church the poor were apportioned their lowly places, and taught that they must sit in them Sunday after Sunday all their lives long. They must sit meekly and never dare to mingle with their betters in the social scale. In was an object lesson repeated week after week, one which no one could mistake, and it sank deep into my mind.

I remember a thing which made my mother very angry. The parson's wife issued a decree, that the labourers should sit on one side of the church and their wives on the other. When my mother heard of it she said, "No, 'those whom God hath joined together let no man put asunder,' and certainly no woman shall!"

I can also remember the time when the parson's wife used to sit in state in her pew in the chancel, and the poor women used to walk up the church and make a curtsey to her before taking the seats set apart for them. They were taught in this way that they had to pay homage and respect to those "put in authority over them," and made to understand that they must "honour the powers that be," as represented in the rector's wife. You may be pretty certain that many of these women did not relish the curtsey-scraping and other humiliations they had to put up with, but they were afraid to speak out. They had their families to think of, children to feed and clothe somehow; and when so many could not earn a living wage, but only a half-starving one, when very often a labouring man was out of work for weeks at a stretch,—why, the wives and mothers learned to take thankfully whatever was doled out to them at the parsonage or elsewhere, and drop the curtsey expected of them, without making a wry face. A smooth face and a smooth tongue was what their benefactors required of them, and they got both. . . .

I can remember when the squire and the other local magnates used to sit in state in the centre of the aisle. They did not, if you please, like the look of the agricultural labourers. Hodge sat too near them, and even in his Sunday best he was an offence to their eyes. They also objected to Hodge looking at them, so they had curtains put up to hide them from the vulgar gaze. And yet, while all this was going on, while the poor had to bear with such high-handed dealings, people wondered why the Church had lost its hold, and continued to lose its hold, on the labourers in the country districts! It never had any hold on me—in that, I was my mother's son also. I never took the Communion in the parish church in my life. When I was seven years old I saw something which prevented me once for all. One Sunday my father was going to stop to take the Communion, and I, being a boy, had of course to go out before it began. I may here mention that the church door opened then in a direct line with the chancel and the main aisle, so that anybody looking through the keyhole could easily see what was going on inside. The door is now more to the side of the church, and out of direct line with the chancel. I was a little bit of a fellow, and curious. I said to myself, "What does father stop behind for? What is it they do? I'll see." So I went out of church, closed the door, placed my eye at the keyhole and peeped through, and what I saw will be engraved on my mind until the last day of my life. That sight caused a wound which has never been healed. My proud little spirit smarted and burned when I saw what happened at that Communion service.

First, up walked the squire to the communion rails; the farmers went up next; then up went the tradesmen, the shopkeepers, the wheelwright, and the blacksmith; and then, the very last of all, went the poor agricultural labourers in their smock frocks. They walked up by themselves; nobody else knelt with them; it was as if they were unclean—and at that sight the iron entered straight into my poor little heart and remained fast embedded there. I said to myself, "If that's what goes on—never for me!" I ran home and told my mother what I had seen, and I wanted to know why my father was not as good in the eyes of God as the squire, and why the poor should be forced to come up last of all to the table of the Lord. . . .

There was no chapel in our village, but when I was about fourteen years of age some dissenters began to come over from Wellsbourne. They used to hold meetings in a back lane. When the parson got wind of it, he and his supporters, the farmers, dared the labourers to go near these unorthodox Christians. If we did, then good-bye to all the charities; no more soup and coals should we have. And it was no idle threat. . . . I well remember going with my mother to listen to these dissenters. They used to preach under an old barn in the back lane. Rough and ready men were they, dressed in their fustian coats, earnest and devoted to the truth as they saw it, good men all—they have gone home now. God rest them!

44. TRACTS FOR THE TIMES: NO. I

by JOHN HENRY NEWMAN

The low spiritual state of the Church of England in the 1820s on the one hand, and the apprehension caused by the 1832 Reform Bill and the suppression of ten Irish bishoprics on the other, led to the launching of the Oxford (or Tractarian) Movement in 1833. It emphasized the Catholic elements in the Church of England (the creeds, sacraments, liturgy, apostolic succession) and looked back to the teachings of the High Church Anglican divines of the seventeenth century. The leaders of the movement were three Oxford scholars—John Keble (1792–1866), Dr. Edward Bouverie Pusey (1800–1882), and John Henry Newman (1801–1890)—and they soon gained influential supporters. They aimed at spreading their views through a series of *Tracts for the Times,* the first of which, by Newman, appeared in 1833 and is printed below. The first phase of the movement came to an end in 1845 when Newman and several other leading Tractarians went over to Rome. But the majority remained in the Church of England, and despite the hostility of most of the bishops, the movement was largely responsible for revitalizing the worship of the Church in the second half of the nineteenth century.

TO MY BRETHREN IN THE SACRED MINISTRY, THE PRESBYTERS AND DEACONS OF THE CHURCH OF CHRIST IN ENGLAND, ORDAINED THEREUNTO BY THE HOLY GHOST AND THE IMPOSITION OF HANDS.

FELLOW-LABOURERS,—I am but one of yourselves—a Presbyter; and therefore I conceal my name, lest I should take too much on myself by speaking in my own person. Yet speak I must; for the times are very evil, yet no one speaks against them.

Is not this so? Do not we "look one upon another," yet perform nothing? Do we not all confess the peril into which the Church is come, yet sit still each in his own retirement, as if mountains and seas cut off brother from brother? Therefore suffer me, while I try to draw you forth from those pleasant retreats, which it has been our blessedness hitherto to enjoy, to contemplate the condition and prospects of our Holy Mother in a practical way; so that one and all may unlearn that idle habit, which has grown upon us, of owning the state of things to be bad, yet doing nothing to remedy it.

Consider a moment. Is it fair, is it dutiful, to suffer our bishops to stand the brunt of the battle without doing our part to support them? Upon them comes "the care of all the Churches." This cannot be helped; indeed it is their glory. Not one of us would wish in the least to deprive them of the duties, the toils, the responsibilities of their high office. And, black event as it would be for the country, yet (as far as they are concerned) we could not wish them a more blessed termination of their course than the spoiling of their goods and martyrdom.

To them then we willingly and affectionately relinquish their high privileges and honours; we encroach not upon the rights of the SUCCESSORS OF THE APOSTLES; we touch not their sword and crozier. Yet surely we may be their shield-bearers in the battle without offence; and by our voice and deeds be to them what Luke and Timothy were to St. Paul.

Now then let me come at once to the subject which leads me to address you. Should the Government and the Country so far forget their God as to cast off the Church, to deprive it of its temporal honours and substance, *on what* will you rest the claim of respect and attention which you make upon your flocks? Hitherto you have been upheld by your birth, your education, your wealth, your connexions; should these secular advantages cease, on what must Christ's Ministers depend? Is not this a serious practical question? We know how miserable is the state of religious bodies not supported by the State. Look at the Dissenters on all sides of you, and you will see at once that their Ministers, depending simply upon the people, become the *creatures* of the people. Are you content that this should be your case? Alas! can a greater evil befall Christians, than for their teachers to be guided by them, instead of guiding? How can we "hold fast the form of sound words," and "keep that which is committed to our trust," if our influence is to depend simply on our popularity? Is it not our very office to *oppose* the world? Can we then allow ourselves to *court* it? to preach smooth things and prophesy deceits? to make the way of life easy to the rich and indolent, and to bribe the humbler classes by excitements and strong intoxicating doctrine? Surely it must not be so;—and the question recurs, *on what* are we to rest our authority when the State deserts us?

Christ has not left His Church without claim of its own upon the attention of men. Surely not. Hard Master He cannot be, to bid us oppose the world, yet give us no credentials for so doing. There are some who rest their divine mission on their own unsupported assertion; others, who rest it upon their popularity; others, on their success; and others, who rest it upon their temporal distinctions. This last case has, perhaps, been too much our own; I fear we have neglected the real ground on which our authority is built—OUR APOSTOLICAL DESCENT.

We have been born, not of blood, nor of the will of the flesh, nor of the will of man, but of God. The Lord Jesus Christ gave His Spirit to His Apostles; they in turn laid their hands on those who should succeed them; and these again on others; and so the sacred gift has been handed down to our present bishops, who have appointed us as their assistants, and in some sense representatives.

Now every one of us believes this. I know that some will at first deny they do; still they do believe it. Only, it is not sufficiently, practically impressed on their minds. They *do* believe it; for it is the doctrine of the Ordination Service, which they have recognised as truth in the most solemn season of their lives. In order, then, not to prove, but to remind and impress, I entreat your attention to the words used when you were made ministers of Christ's Church.

The office of Deacon was thus committed to you: "Take thou authority to execute the office of a Deacon in the Church of God committed unto thee: In the name, etc."

And the Priesthood thus:

"Receive the Holy Ghost, for the office and work of a Priest, in the Church of God, now committed unto thee by the imposition of our hands. Whose sins thou dost forgive, they are forgiven; and whose sins thou dost retain, they are retained. And be thou a faithful dispenser of the Word of God, and of His Holy Sacraments: In the name, etc."

These, I say, were words spoken to us, and received by us, when we were brought nearer to God than at any other time of our lives. I know the grace of ordination is contained in the laying on of hands, not in any form of words;—yet in our own case (as has ever been usual in the Church) words of blessing have accompanied the act. Thus we have confessed before God our belief that the bishop who ordained us gave us the Holy Ghost, gave us the power to bind and

to loose, to administer the Sacraments, and to preach. Now *how* is
he able to give these great gifts? *Whence* is his right? Are these words
idle (which would be taking God's name in vain), or do they express
merely a wish (which surely is very far below their meaning), or do
they not rather indicate that the speaker is conveying a gift? Surely
they can mean nothing short of this. But whence, I ask, his right to
do so? Has he any right, except as having received the power from
those who consecrated him to be a bishop? He could not give what
he had never received. It is plain then that he but *transmits;* and that
the Christian Ministry is a *succession.* And if we trace back the power
of ordination from hand to hand, of course we shall come to the
Apostles at last. We know we do, as a plain historical fact; and therefore all we, who have been ordained clergy, in the very form of our
ordination acknowledged the doctrine of the APOSTOLICAL SUCCES-
SION. . . .

Therefore, my dear brethren, act up to your professions. Let it not
be said that you have neglected a gift; for if you have the Spirit of
the Apostles on you, surely this *is* a great gift. "Stir up the gift of
God which is in you." Make much of it. Show your value of it. Keep
it before your minds as an honourable badge, far higher than that
secular respectability, or cultivation, or polish, or learning, or rank,
which gives you a hearing with the many. Tell *them* of your gift.
The times will soon drive you to do this, if you mean to be still anything. But wait not for the times. Do not be compelled, by the world's
forsaking you, to recur as if unwillingly to the high source of your
authority. Speak out now, before you are forced, both as glorying in
your privilege and to insure your rightful honour from your people.
A notion has gone abroad that they can take away your power. They
think they have given and can take it away. They think it lies in the
Church property, and they know that they have politically the power
to confiscate that property. They have been deluded into a notion
that present palpable usefulness, produceable results, acceptableness
to your flocks, that these and such like are the tests of your divine
commission. Enlighten them in this matter. Exalt our Holy Fathers
the bishops, as the representatives of the Apostles, and the Angels of
the Churches; and magnify your office, as being ordained by them to
take part in their Ministry.

But, if you will not adopt my view of the subject, which I offer to
you, not doubtingly, yet (I hope) respectfully, at all events, CHOOSE

YOUR SIDE. To remain neuter much longer will be itself to take a part. *Choose* your side; since side you shortly must, with one or other party, even though you do nothing. Fear to be of those whose line is decided for them by chance circumstances, and who may perchance find themselves with the enemies of Christ, while they think but to remove themselves from worldly politics. Such abstinence is impossible in troublous times. HE THAT IS NOT WITH ME IS AGAINST ME, AND HE THAT GATHERETH NOT WITH ME SCATTERETH ABROAD.

45. [THE STATE OF THE CHURCH IN LEEDS]

by WALTER FARQUHAR HOOK

The revival within the Church of England after 1836 is admirably illustrated by the work of Dr. Walter Farquhar Hook (1798–1875) as vicar of Leeds between 1837 and 1859. When he began his ministry the fortunes of the Church of England in Leeds were at a low ebb; although the parish was as large as a small diocese there were scarcely 50 communicants, and those mostly elderly women. In a strongly evangelical community he asserted his High Church principles and succeeded in rehabilitating the Church of England in the eyes of the middle classes, and won the respect and even the affection of many of the working classes. These letters describe his impressions of the Church of England in this large industrial northern city shortly after his arrival in 1837, and are from the *Life and Letters of Walter Farquhar Hook,* by his son-in-law, W. R. W. Stephens (7th ed., 1885), pp. 240–243.

Vicarage, Leeds: July 1837.

. . . I DO not oppose Dissenters by disputations and wrangling, but I seek to exhibit to the world the Church in her beauty; let the services of the Church be properly performed, and right-minded people will soon learn to love her. But here, all that is thought of is preaching; partly, without doubt, because the church is so arranged that to perform the services well and properly is almost impossible. I am much annoyed on Sundays by persons coming to hear me preach; but they will soon find out that I am not that most detestable of all characters, a popular preacher. And then I shall get my regular flock around me, and I am longing to preach a course of sermons on the Liturgy, which will, I think, surprise the Leedites, as they imagine that there can be only two subjects for sermons—Justification and Sanctification. The real fact is, that the established religion in Leeds is Methodism, and it is Methodism that all the most pious among the Churchmen unconsciously talk. If you ask a poor person the ground of his hope, he will immediately say that he feels that he is saved, however great a sinner he may be . . .

August 21, 1837.

. . . As to religion, the traditional or established religion in Leeds is Methodism; and consequently, as is natural, since we breathe a Methodistic atmosphere, everything has a Methodistic tendency. A pious Churchman here means a person who likes an establishment, and consequently supports the Church; but then the Church is not sufficient to supply his wants; so that he probably institutes two or three prayer-meetings in some large house or warehouse on the week-days, where he can indulge in extemporaneous prayer and Methodistic rant. Nor do the people venture to entertain a notion that the Church is *right;* their mode of defence is to show that it is not so *very wrong* that it is sinful to belong to it; they *do* therefore belong to it, looking forward to the day when it will be reformed—i.e. brought down to the state of some Methodistic sect. Even many of the clergy, without knowing it, shape their doctrines and style of preaching according to the Methodistic system; and those who are not humdrum, labour not to instruct, but to excite. I am stirring up the clergy by insisting upon the strictest rubrical observance in all the occasional services—baptisms, marriages, and funerals. Nobody here seems to have a notion that baptism is anything more than a form of registration; I think it my duty therefore to have it always administered with peculiar solemnity. They do stare sometimes when I tell them that before administering the Sacrament, I require them to attend the prayers of the Church, and pray with me: they think by the Sacrament I must needs mean the Lord's Supper.

46. [METHODIST CLASS MEETINGS]

by JOSEPH BARKER

The weekly class meeting for "fellowship in Christian experience" was the germ cell of early Methodism. This critical account is by Joseph Barker (1806–1875), a weaver of Bramley (Leeds). After educating himself he became a local preacher for the Wesleyans, but after a time joined the Methodist New Connexion, becoming first a travelling preacher and later a chapel minister. In 1841 he was expelled from that Connexion, taking with him a number of followers (Barkerites). He subsequently progressed through various religious positions, engaged in radical politics and journalism, and finally emigrated to America. The following passage is from his *Life of Joseph Barker,* John Thomas Barker ed. (1880), pp. 44–52.

THE class-meetings are held weekly. The classes ought, according to rule, to consist of ten or twelve members; but they sometimes contain as many as thirty, forty, or fifty, and at other times not more than three or four. Each member kneels down as soon as he enters, to pray a little by himself. The leader then begins the meeting by giving out a hymn, and the members stand up to sing. Then the leader prays, gives out another hymn, and then tells his experience. Sometimes he tells what trials he has met with, and what deliverances he has experienced through the week, what joys and sorrows he has had, how he felt at the love-feast, the prayer-meeting, or the fellowship-meeting, what liberty he had in secret prayer, how he felt while reading the Scriptures, or hearing sermons, or while busy at his work, what passages have come to his mind, or what promises have been applied to his soul. At other times he simply tells how he feels at that moment; while at other times he says nothing about his experience or feelings, but just gives thanks to God for what He has done for him, in a general way, or offers a few words of exhortation or preaching to the members. He then asks each member in turn the state of his mind. A very common form of the question is, "Well, brother, or well, sister, how do you feel the state of your mind to-night?" At other times it will be, "Well, brother, will you tell us what the Lord is doing for you?" Different leaders have different ways of proposing the question, and the same leader varies it at times. When the question is put, the member answers. Some of the members tell a long and flaming story; others say little, or next to nothing. Some speak loud, and even shout; others speak so low that they cannot be heard, either by the leaders or the rest of the members. Some are always happy, according to their story; others are always doubtful and fearful, and can never say much either about their feelings or performances. One tells you he has been on the sunny side of the hill all the week; another says he has been on the mount of transfiguration, and that he could say with one of old, "Master, it is good to be here." Another has been with Moses on the top of Pisgah, and got a view of the promised land. Another felt that he was like the beloved disciple in the Isle of Patmos, in the spirit on the Lord's day, and that he had not lost the blessing he received under the Sunday morning's sermon all the week through. It frequently happens that when the first has told a good experience, the rest follow the example; while when the first tells of troubles and trials, the rest generally speak of having had the same kind of trials, or something similar. . . .

I may observe that in most class-meetings, as well as in love-feasts, fellowship-meetings, and band-meetings, a happy experience is accounted creditable, while a low and desponding experience is accounted rather discreditable. As it is generally considered an honour in the world to be rich and well dressed, inasmuch as the rich and well dressed are, in the language of the world, called *respectable;* so it is generally considered respectable or creditable in the Methodist world to be rich in religious consolations or experience. And as it commonly happens in the world that the *appearance* of wealth secures the same respect as wealth itself, so does it commonly happen in the Methodist world, that the appearance of religious wealth, the profession of rich consolations and plentiful supplies of spiritual blessings, secures the same respect and reverence that real religious excellence alone deserves. . . .

It is customary in many classes for the leader to ask one of the members occasionally to lead the class, or a part of the class, partly perhaps for the purpose of exercising the member's gifts, and thus preparing him for after usefulness, and partly to encourage and please the member, and engage him more thoroughly in the cause. Most members like to be honoured, and it is generally considered an honour to be employed in any work, especially in the work of leading a class or preaching. It is astonishing how such honours are prized in the Methodist societies, and how much the careful or skilful distribution of such honours tends to perpetuate the strength and increase the resources of the body. Men that had not a word to say for Methodism or Methodist preachers yesterday, will talk for hours in their praise to-day, because the preacher called upon them by name to pray in the class last night, or because the leader employed them in leading a portion of the class. Men that never thought of giving above a penny a week and a shilling a quarter till lately, will now give three-pence a week and half-a-crown a quarter, because they are appointed leaders or assistant leaders. Persons that never used to give more than copper at a collection, will give silver or gold now, because they were invited to sit on the platform lately at a missionary meeting, or were appointed collectors at the late chapel anniversary. This love of honour appears to be universal in the Methodist society; it is felt all through the body, from the class and the prayer-leaders' meeting, to the district meeting and the conference.

There is little instruction given in the classes. The talk both of the members and the leaders is generally formal and commonplace; seldom or never such as is calculated to make people truly great and good.

It was to one of those classes I went. The leader was a draper of Bramley, called G—— B——. He was a ready talker and a zealous Methodist. He was loud in his praying, rather bold in his manner, but very ignorant; and willing, for anything I could ever see, to remain so. He was a great preacher's man, and fond of little honours, and would do anything to be well thought of or favoured by the preachers. He knew, too, that to be on good terms with the preachers was the way to get customers to his shop; and he was very fond of gain. He had no scruples against laying up treasure on earth, though he read over Wesley's rules to us every quarter. He was a great respecter of persons; and though he seemed to have sense enough to know that it was wrong, he had not virtue or shame enough to keep him from practising it even in the face of the whole class. He had abundance of respect for the richer members of his class, or at least he was abundantly ready to show respect to them; but with the poorer members he could use as much freedom as you like. He would tell the poorer members to speak up; but he never told the richer ones to do so, though the richer ones were generally most prone to speak low. The rich members used generally to get into one corner by themselves, while the poor ones sat anywhere about the room. When he came to the rich members' corner, and found that scarce one of them could speak loud enough to be heard, either by himself or us, he used to feel rather at a loss sometimes what to do, especially when he had just before been urging some of the poorer members to speak; but he durst not complain, not he. Then how did he do? He did just like himself. When he knew that some would be thinking, Why does he not ask them to speak up? he would exclaim, "Glory be to God! They are as happy as queens here in the corner." I wonder how we could bear with such a shallow, worthless person for a leader; but we knew no better, I suppose, then.

47. PIETY AMONG THE PEASANTRY

by HENRY WOODCOCK

The Primitive Methodist Connexion was formed in 1811 by Hugh Bourne and William Clowes, whose camp-meeting forms of evangelism and assertion of democratic powers by the laity were not approved by the official Wesleyan body. From their beginning the Primitive Methodists were rooted in the working classes, both in the industrial areas and also in some rural districts. This extract is a description by a Primitive Methodist minister of some aspects of Primitive Methodism in the 1840s in the Wolds, an agricultural area of low uplands in East Yorkshire. It is from Henry Woodcock, *Piety among the Peasantry: being Sketches of Primitive Methodism on the Yorkshire Wolds* (1889), pp. 222, 229–230, 262.

WE have sometimes been asked by strangers to Methodism, 'How do you manage to maintain the spiritual life, growth, and power of your village churches?' We could give but one answer: 'By the efficient labours of 34,000 local preachers.' . . .

The language of some of these preachers was sometimes strangely provincial, and their grammar very imperfect: they often misplaced their aspirates, as all uneducated people do, whether on the Wolds or elsewhere, but they knew how to preach the three R.'s—Ruin, Redemption, Regeneration. Indeed, nowhere are the peculiar doctrines of Methodism more clearly understood or more urgently taught than by the local preachers on the Wolds. For seventy years they have proclaimed with unabated breath and unfaltering voice, the three great Universalities: *God loves all; Christ died for all; The Holy Spirit is shed forth upon all.* Their sermons, filled with Gospel truth, enlivened by homely wit and racy anecdotes, freshened by details of their own personal experience, winged by common-sense and Christian sympathy, and accompanied by the Holy Ghost, sent down from heaven—their preaching was neither 'waterish, bleak, or thin,' but went home to the hearts of the people.

Some of these locals possessed warm hearts and gifted brains, and reminded us of the three S.'s—Shortness, Sense, and Salt. Their sentences, rough hewn and roughly expressed, were, like the pebbles from the brook, thrown by a master slinger, and went whistling into the hearts of men who could not be well reached by any more polished weapons.

Crooked sticks are not straightened at once. You cannot turn a tap-room sinner into a drawing-room saint in a moment. Grace, like lightning, when it strikes a man, generally follows the grain. The mannerisms of these locals often betrayed their personal dispositions and their daily avocations.

During the making of the Hull and Scarbro' Railway (1844) many navvies came to work along these Wolds. They got drunk on Saturdays, and then had a big fight. The Sabbath was known as the hair-cutting and dog-washing day. One of these men got converted, and became a local preacher, and whenever he wanted to give emphasis to a sentence he clasped his hands and then gave the Bible a whack as if driving his spade into the ground. Another was an expert mower, and, when very excited, would swing his right arm like the sweep of a scythe, as if he were cutting corn in the field. A third was a blacksmith, and, when he wanted to break the rocky hearts in pieces, he startled the people by striking the hand-rail, as if he were striking the anvil. A fourth was a woodman, and when he assayed 'to cut down the stout-hearted sinners' with 'the sword of the Spirit, which is the Word of God,' he stood erect for a moment; then retreated a step (till he nearly pitched the writer out of the waggon); then, swinging his brawny arm round and round, as if, with sure aim and resounding blows, he was cutting down trees in the wood, he repeated his text; 'The axe is laid at the root of the tree;' then glanced at the crowd below, as if expecting to see sinners fall under the Word, as the trees of the wood fell before his successful blows. He was disappointed, tho' he took a sure aim, and was a workman that had no need to be ashamed of his work. . . .

Thousands who had sunk to a level of dull monotony, unbroken from year to year, except by fairs, races, foxhunting, &c., found, in our oft-recurring means of grace—soul-stirring preaching services, fervent prayer-meetings, lively class-meetings and hearty singing—a life, a freedom, and a joy to which they had been strangers. Existing wrongs, injustices and estrangements between families and neighbours were corrected, and there was created and fostered a neighbourly solidarity which changed the spirit of whole villages. Indeed, Methodist chapels have long been the centres around which the religious life of these villagers has revolved. They feel at home *there* as they do not at the Parish Church.

Chapter 10.
Cultural Change

Early industrial society, to a far greater extent than any previous age, was based on the written word. The socializing functions of print were recognized, and used as agents to shape the new society. Print served to destroy earlier attitudes to work and substitute new norms and goals. Traditional social habits and customs seldom fitted into the new pattern of industrial life, and they had therefore to be discredited as hindrances to Progress. In the manufacturing towns a large working-class population, with its roots in the popular culture of the countryside effectively severed, and disciplined to the routine of mill life, gradually acclimatized itself to the new ethos. The breakup of the old popular culture and its supersession by formal, literary "instruction" based on the three Rs, was the conscious aim of middle-class educationists.

The schools were not primarily the people's institutions, but rather instruments for shaping society according to dominant middle-class patterns. Several types of institution provided a modicum of instruction for working-class children—the private day school (including the dame school), the Sunday school, the factory school, the charity school, and (for a fortunate minority) the ancient endowed grammar school. Changes in this system came mainly through the work of voluntary religious bodies, organized in two societies—the British and Foreign School Society (founded in 1807) and the National Society (1811). The Nonconformists supported the former, the Anglicans the latter, and between them provided a skeleton system of elementary schools, organized at first largely on the Bell and Lancaster (monitorial) system. In 1833 the first modest state grant of £20,000 was made to the two societies; and this important precedent was followed in 1839 by an increased grant and the establishment of school inspectors and a regular administrative machinery. However, the reliance upon the religious bodies introduced Anglican-Nonconformist antagonisms which soon proved to be the biggest single stumbling block to the creation of a complete public educational system.

Beyond the schools was a whole series of adult educational agencies which attempted to remedy the deficiencies of formal educational provision. Mechanics' Institutes, Adult Schools, mutual improvement societies, and night schools helped to reduce the illiteracy figures, which were variously estimated at between a quarter and a third of the working-class population in the 1830s and 1840s. The idea that education of the poor would make them discontented or that it was an unnecessary luxury died hard in conservative quarters; and conversely the faith in education as the way to social and political emancipation became firmly rooted in the minds of many intelligent working-class leaders.

For the upper middle classes the development of a system of (exclusive) Public Schools, modeled on the work of Thomas Arnold at Rugby (1827–1842), provided the means of assimilation into a pattern of governing-class education. Higher education, as provided in the ancient universities of Oxford and Cambridge, remained steeped in medieval forms and eighteenth-century lethargy, and not until after the 1850 Commission of Inquiry into the Universities did they make a serious effort to adjust to contemporary national needs. In the meantime London University had been created in 1836, and its constituent colleges offered a more liberal, intellectual, and less exclusive type of university education.

48. THE SOCIAL, EDUCATIONAL AND RELIGIOUS STATE OF THE MANUFACTURING DISTRICTS

by EDWARD BAINES

During the campaign for the factory acts, evidence before commissions of inquiry and in parliamentary debates suggested that the educational, religious, and moral condition of the industrial areas was worse than in other parts of the country. This was fiercely repudiated by industrialists; and

Edward Baines (see Reading No. 32) conducted a survey in Yorkshire and Lancashire to show the extent of Church, chapel, Sunday school, and day school provision. The summary of his findings is reprinted from *The Social, Educational and Religious State of the Manufacturing Districts* (1843), pp. 27–28, 62.

[THE returns made to our committee] establish the following important CONCLUSIONS, namely:

1st. That in these Manufacturing Districts there is *Church and Chapel room for 45 per cent. of the entire population;* and, deducting the Catholics, who fill their chapels several times in the day, the Church and Chapel room for Protestants cannot fall greatly short of 50 *per cent.*

2d. That that provision for the religious instruction of the community has been made, and is still supported, almost wholly by the *voluntary zeal and liberality of the inhabitants,*—no less than 682,795 sittings in Churches and Chapels having been provided within the present century, of which only 70,611 are in Parliamentary churches.

3d. That the provision for religious instruction is *far more abundant, in proportion to the population, now than it was at the beginning of the century.* The Church and Chapel accommodation has been increased 219 per cent., whilst the population has only increased 127 per cent.

4th. That *Sunday Schools* have been provided, and are supported and taught, by the voluntary zeal of the inhabitants, in which *one in every 5⅖ of the population* are enrolled on the books,—which must include an immense proportion of all the children of the working classes.

5th. That 55⅖ *per cent.* of the children in Sunday Schools are *able* to read, and are *actually reading, the Holy Scriptures.*

6. That *sixty-six thousand teachers* are gratuitously engaged in the benevolent and pious duty of Sunday School instruction.

7th. That *one in every ten of the population* are taught in *Day Schools,* of whom only a small proportion in Dame and Factory Schools.

8th. That the proportions of the Established Church and other religious bodies, so far as the sittings in Churches and Chapels would indicate, are as follows, viz.:—Established Church, 377,104 sittings, —other Religious Denominations, 617,479: but probably the proportion actually attending the Churches would be less than this, in comparison with the other sects.

9th. That the proportions of Sunday Scholars taught are as follow, viz.;—in the Schools of the Established Church, 123,451,—in the Schools of all other Denominations, 285,080. . . .

I might dwell upon the many institutions and associations for the diffusion of knowledge, and for the dispensing of every kind of good, which have arisen within the present or the last generation, and which flourish most in the Manufacturing towns and villages;—such as Mechanics' Institutes, Literary Societies, Circulating Libraries, Youths' Guardian Societies, Friendly Societies, Temperance Societies, Medical Charities, Clothing Societies, Benevolent and District Visiting Societies, &c.,—forty-nine fiftieths of which are of quite recent origin. The moral, intellectual, and physical good done by these associations is beyond calculation; and their existence is one of the most decisive proofs possible of the growth and commanding influence of true Christian principle in the communities where they have been formed.

49. [THE EDUCATION OF THE PEOPLE]

by JOSEPH LAWSON

To many older people in the 1880s it was apparent that great changes in educational and cultural opportunities had occurred during their lifetime. The "low state of education" as he remembered it in the 1820s and 1830s is described by Joseph Lawson in his reminiscences, *Progress in Pudsey* (Stanningley, 1887), pp. 39–42. Similar conditions pertained in the neighboring towns and villages of the industrial area of the West Riding of Yorkshire.

THERE were very few schools, and many of the teachers could not have passed our present Board Schools' sixth standard. Some taught nothing but reading and spelling, or knitting and sewing; others only reading and writing from printed copies (not being able to write themselves so well). A few taught arithmetic as well, but a grammar, geography, or history were scarcely ever seen in a school in those days. A few of the sons of the middle class learnt writing and arithmetic, but very few others learnt anything but reading. Large numbers never entered the door of a schoolhouse—having to work at something when they arrived at school age, or were allowed to run about all day, as if they were mere animals, and not capable of cultivation, or did not possess faculties waiting for, and needing, development. Writing was looked upon by many parents as a mere luxury for the rich only, and never likely to be wanted by their sons and daughters. A person who was a good reader of the newspaper, and could talk about various wars, battles, and sieges, was looked up to by the people, and said to be a "great scholar" and "a far-learned man." There were few school books, and those were of a poor kind—the tax or duty on paper, and the small demand, causing them to be very high in price. Sunday schools were in their infancy, and there was considerable prejudice against them at first, especially if writing was taught. Many of the teachers were very unfit for their position, and knew less than some of their pupils, and were appointed as teachers because older than the rest. Besides, the great or prime object of Sunday schools with many was not so much to teach children to read, as to make the school a kind of nursery which should supply the church or chapel with adherents to its particular faith or creed, and thus replenish it by adding to the church membership. It was quite common for some of the little ones when they returned from Sunday school to talk to their parents about the many errors of the teachers; but even that state of things was better than having no school. Very few attempted to teach writing in a Sunday school—that being looked upon as a desecration of the Sabbath. . . .

Newspapers were scarce and dear; very few could read them. There was a blacksmith's shop where several met to hear and read the newspaper, subscribed for amongst them weekly, and costing twenty times as much as the same matter would cost now. One of them read for the rest, and explained. He was looked upon as a very learned man, and so he was for the times in which he lived. There was one slight drawback, viz., he had considerable self-conceit, and thought he knew more than he really did, though very few of the many blunders he made were ever detected in those days, and if he was contradicted by any other knowing one, who might happen to drop in during the readings or conversations, his old pupils mostly voted him in the right.

After all, this reader and expounder of the newspaper, from fifty to sixty years ago, was far ahead of the bulk of the middle class at that time, though he made many serious blunders, as we have said, not on mere matters of opinion, but on matters of fact, relating to history and geography. Others, who had a desire to know what was going on in the world, went to the inns, where a weekly paper was taken in, and where someone would read for the company. A barber's shop, where people went once each week to get a shave, was a kind of rendezvous for that day's literature. We said barber's shop, but the man did not make a living by shaving alone. He worked at some other business during the remainder of the week, and was a barber on Saturday. At that time it gave a kind of authenticity to any rumour to say: "I heard it at such an one's, where I went to be shaved." As for hair-cutting, people mostly cut each other's. . . .

There were no libraries for the people, who had no access even to the few books there were; and the house that had a family Bible, hymn-book, prayer-book, or catechism, the Pilgrim's Progress, or News from the Invisible World, together with a sheet almanack nailed against the wall, was considered well furnished with literature. Others would be content with a sheet of Christmas hymns, sheet songs, and a number of the "last dying words and confessions" of culprits hung at York; or perhaps some little books on such matters as "Jack and his eleven Brothers," "Jack and the Beanstalk," "Little Cock Robin," &c. A house that had a sampler done by one of the family framed and hung up, was considered a somewhat superior house for a working man—even if the needlework was not done to perfection. There was not as much waste paper thrown or blown about as we see now. No, waste paper meant something then, and was not as now—almost given away.

One great institution relied upon very much in those days, was "street news"—men shouting or singing news through the village. As already mentioned, the hanging of a murderer, got up in a sensational way, and frequently written before the event took place, as facts proved, was a great attraction. The inhabitants would stand at their doors and listen, or crowd around the man with amazement. Much of the news, true and false, was circulated in this way. . . .

50. [SELF-EDUCATION]

by THOMAS COOPER

In a society which offered only meagre opportunities for popular education, self-help was virtually the only recourse to which intelligent working men could turn. There developed therefore a remarkable minority tradition of exceptional artisans who were prepared to pay almost any price to educate themselves in the fullest sense of the term. Nearly all of the famous working-class leaders of the early nineteenth century (and indeed later) belonged to this tradition. Thomas Cooper (1805–1892), a leader of the Leicester Chartists, was typical; and these passages from his autobiographical *Life of Thomas Cooper* (1872), pp. 55–61, refer to his life as a poor shoemaker in Gainsborough (Lincolnshire) between 1824 and 1828.

ONE of the greatest incentives I had to solid study was the reading, in Drew's "Imperial Magazine," an account of the life of Dr. Samuel Lee, Professor of Hebrew in the University of Cambridge, and a scholar, it was said, in more than a dozen languages. He had been apprenticed to a carpenter at eleven years old, had bought Ruddiman's Latin Rudiments on an old book-stall for a trifle, and learnt the whole book by heart; and had stepped on, from Corderius's Colloquies to Caesar, and from Caesar to Virgil, and so on; and had learnt to read Greek, Hebrew, and Syriac, all from self-tuition, by the time he was five or six and twenty. Yet he was ignorant of English Grammar and Arithmetic!

I said in my heart, if one man can teach himself a language, another can. But there seemed such a wealth of means of learning now around me, that I felt as if I must attempt to accomplish a broader triumph of self-education than Lee accomplished. I must try if I could not combine the study of languages with that of mathematics; complete a full course of reading in ancient and modern history, and get an accurate and ample acquaintance with the literature of the day. . . .

I thought it possible that by the time I reached the age of twenty-four I might be able to master the elements of Latin, Greek, Hebrew, and French; might get well through Euclid, and through a course of Algebra; might commit the entire "Paradise Lost," and seven of the best plays of Shakespeare, to memory; and might read a large and solid course of history, and of religous evidences; and be well acquainted also with the current literature of the day.

I failed considerably, but I sped on joyfully while health and strength lasted. I was between nineteen and twenty when I began to commit Ruddiman's Rudiments to memory—thinking it was better to begin to learn Latin with the book that Lee used—though I found afterwards I might have done better. I committed almost the entire volume to memory—notes and all. Afterwards, I found Israel Lyon's small Hebrew Grammar, on a stall, bought it for a shilling, and practised Hebrew *writing* as the surest means of beginning to learn, every Sunday evening. I got hold of a Greek Grammar about a year after; but did not master it earnestly, because I thought it better to keep close to the Latin for some time. I also picked up a small French Grammar; but *that* seemed so easy, that I thought I could master it without care or trouble.

On Sunday mornings, whether I walked, or had to stay indoors on account of the weather, my first task was to commit a portion of the "Paradise Lost" to memory. I usually spent the remainder of Sunday, save the evening, whether I walked or remained at home, in reading something that bore on the Evidences. Thus I not only read through the well-known "Natural Theology" and "Horæ Paulinæ," and "Evidences" of Paley, and the equally popular "Apologies for the Bible and Christianity" of Bishop Watson, Soame Jenyns' "Internal Evidences," Lord Lyttelton's "Conversion of St. Paul," and Sherlock's "Trial of the Witnesses,"—but I diligently read books that required deeper thinking, and some that were filled with profound learning—such as Butler's "Analogy," Bentley's "Folly of Atheism," Dr. Samuel Clarke's "Demonstrations of the Being and Attributes of God," Stillingfleet's "Origines Sacræ," and Warburton's "Divine Legation of Moses."

Historical reading, or the grammar of some language, or translation, was my first employment on week-day mornings, whether I rose at three or four, until seven o'clock, when I sat down to the stall.

A book or a periodical in my hand while I breakfasted, gave me another half-hour's reading. I had another half-hour, and sometimes an hour's reading, or study of language, at from one to two o'clock, the time of dinner—usually eating my food with a spoon, after I had cut it in pieces, and having my eyes on a book all the time.

I sat at work till eight, and sometimes nine, at night; and, then, either read, or walked about our little room and committed "Hamlet" to memory, or the rhymes of some modern poet, until compelled to go to bed from sheer exhaustion—for it must be remembered that I was repeating something, audibly, as I sat at work, the greater part of the day—either declensions and conjugations, or rules of syntax, or propositions of Euclid, or the "Paradise Lost," or "Hamlet," or poetry of some modern or living author. . . .

I was seldom later in bed than three or four in the morning; and when, in the coldness of winter, we could not afford to have a fire till my mother rose, I used to put a lamp on a stool, which I placed on a little round table, and, standing before it, wrapped up in my mother's old red cloak, I read on till seven, or studied a grammar, or my Euclid, and frequently kept my feet moving to secure warmth, or prevent myself from falling asleep.

In the finer seasons of the year I was invariably on the hills, or in the lanes or woods, or by the Trent, by sunrise, or before; and thus often strolled several miles with my book in my hand, before I sat down in the corner to work, at seven o'clock. . . .

51. THE HISTORY OF BEN THE SOLDIER

published by the RELIGIOUS TRACT SOCIETY

Almost without exception the autobiographies and reminiscences of working men referred to the serious lack of suitable reading matter which they encountered during the first 30 years of the nineteenth century. To fill this gap was the object of various popular publishing ventures, whether sponsored by political radicals, religious evangelicals, or the exponents of the "diffusion of useful knowledge." This anonymous tract, *The History and Adventures of Ben the Soldier* (c. 1816) is representative of a large class of such literature distributed (usually free) by the different tract societies of the churches. The Religious Tract Society was founded in 1799 as a missionary agency of the Evangelicals.

IN a pleasant village, about 100 miles from London, situated on the banks of a small river, and at the bottom of a high hill, dwelt an honest hard-working old couple, named Timothy and Deborah Clay. Timothy was a ploughman, and worked for Farmer Hayfield; and Deborah used to work in the fields, and do other odd jobs, but was now past hard labor, and employed herself in spinning worsted, and knitting stockings for her husband and grandson. They had only one daughter, who died when Benjamin, her child, was an infant, as did her husband soon afterwards of a violent fever; upon which the old couple took the little orphan, and brought him up with the greatest care and tenderness they were capable of.

As they had some difficulty to make both ends meet, they could not afford to send him to school, but put him to work as soon as he was able to do any thing, so that when he was nine years old, he did not know a letter of the alphabet, and as there was no church in the village, he knew nothing about God and his Son Jesus Christ, but was as ignorant of his Bible as a Heathen or a Hottentot.

About this time some good people hired a room at old Dame Motherly's and opened a Sunday School, where they instructed the poor ignorant children to read their Bibles, (and on Thursday evenings to write,) and the young men who attended it, Mr. Paul Christian, and Mr. Barnabas Lovesoul, took great care to catechize them, and explain to them the meaning of what they read. To this school was Benjamin regularly sent.

When he was thirteen years of age his grandmother died, and his grandfather departed this life the year following. Farmer Hayfield's lease expired at the same time, and Mr. Nabal Squeezepoor, a rich overgrown farmer, took the farm. Mr. Squeezepoor, whose name expressed his nature, would not give Ben sufficient wages to keep body and soul together, so that the poor boy was obliged to leave his service, and seek for a better master.

Benjamin remembered he had read in his Bible at the Sunday School, "That God provideth food for the ravens," and says, "Call upon me in the day of trouble, I will deliver thee, and thou shalt glorify me;" he therefore fell down upon his knees, and prayed to God, for Jesus Christ's sake, not to let him starve, but to provide for him in some way or other. The Bible speaks of God as a God hearing and answering prayer, and Ben found him to be so, for God provided for him by means of Mr. Christian, who recommended him to Mr. Lancet, an eminent apothecary at Wedgely, a market town about 11 miles off, who wanted a stout active lad to carry out his medicines; at the same time earnestly exhorting him to keep the Sabbath-day holy, to study his Bible, to pray to God regularly and fervently, and to avoid loose and idle company.

He acquitted himself in his new place highly to the satisfaction of his employer, and attended public worship as often as he had opportunity. But alas! for poor Ben, Dr. Lancet was little better than an infidel, and cared neither for his own soul, nor for the souls of his servants: The maids in the kitchen, and the young men in the shop, were perpetually sneering at him as a Methodist, so that between the one and the other he had but a sorry life of it. The clergyman of the parish, however, observing he was a serious steady boy, took notice of him, and frequently gave him good advice, and put some religious books and tracts into his hands.

In this way he went on for more than nine months. If he had lived in a better family, perhaps, he might have been a truly pious youth; and if it had not been for the kind care of the minister, and his old schoolmasters, he had probably been led away from every thing that is good. It is a great blessing indeed for a young person to live in a holy Christian family.

One afternoon Bob Buck, Dr. Lancet's apprentice, and Fuddle, the shopman, prevailed upon Benjamin to go with them to a neighbouring fair, as he was a sober and moral lad, to make him drunk; and as he was not used to liquor, a small quantity overcame him; while they continued plying him with more, till he was quite intoxicated. In this situation a recruiting serjeant got hold of him, slipped a shilling into his hand, and enlisted him.

The next morning Ben found himself much indisposed in body, and still more so in mind. His reflections were of the most painful sort. Alas! exclaimed he, what have I done? I have committed the worse than beastly sin of drunkenness, and sold my liberty. Ah! how often has my dear Mr. Christian, and Mr. Lovesoul, cautioned me against fairs and such wicked places, and to beware of bad company. A sin is soon committed; but I find by sad experience that the bitter effects of it are not soon over. The pleasures of sin are short, but the punishment of it is lasting. "God be merciful to me a vile sinner!"

A day or two afterwards he was marched to London; and as he was an awkward clumsy lad, he could not easily acquire the air and gait of a soldier. Many a chuck under the chin did he get, to make him hold his head up, and many a knock of the shins to make him turn his toes out.

He continued in England for about four years, during which time he experienced the truth of the Apostle's remark, "Evil communications corrupt good manners." By degrees he forgot the good things he had learned at the Sunday-school, and at the Church. His conscience indeed would not suffer him to swear, and sin so shamefully as many of his comrades did, yet he was awfully altered for the worse. Though not one of the most notorious sinners, he was far from being a holy character, as every Christian should be, whatever station of life he may be in.

He was then sent abroad to the continent to fight the French. The scenes of blood and slaughter which he saw shocked him: and conscience, which had been pretty quiet for some time, now began to disturb him exceedingly; and a thousand times did he lament that he had gone into temptation, "And thereby fallen into evil."

They lay under arms during the whole of one night, expecting to be attacked every minute. Ben was much alarmed and distressed, for he feared, lest in case of his being killed, that holy God against whom he had sinned, would assuredly cast him into hell. He mentioned his apprehensions to a serious elderly man who was next to him, who replied, "You see, young man, that a guilty conscience makes a coward. Many people make shift to live without religion, but it is hard to die without it." "Religion," exclaimed a profane wretch with a sneer, "it's all my eye." "Fools make a mock at sin," replied the old soldier; you have imbibed the horrid sentiments of Tom Paine. Ay! said the other, and I am not to be hummed with your cant. God be praised, said Ben, though I am a vile sinner, I am not an Infidel. But are you a Christian? replied the old soldier. I hope I am, returned Ben. Have you reason to believe that you are washed in the blood of Christ, and born again of the Holy Ghost? inquired the pious veteran. Benjamin paused, and replied with a trembling voice, I fear not. Would that I was. Ah! young man, said the old soldier, what a melancholy thing it is when people neglect religion, till danger and death stare them in the face. It is dangerous trusting to a death-bed repentance, for those who live in sin commonly die in sin. It is not enough to be born and baptized in a Christian country; much more is necessary. Jesus Christ died upon the cross to make atonement for sin, yet we shall not be saved unless we believe in him according to the gospel. I have been a follower of Christ for more than twenty years, and I would not part with my hope for a thousand worlds. I am not afraid of dying, for I can say, "O death! Where is thy sting? O grave! Where is thy victory?" It is more than I can, said Ben, with a deep sigh. People, added the old soldier, have very low notions of Christianity. Christians are holy people, for God makes them so. They are dead to sin, and alive to God. Christ did not shed his precious blood, that men might live in sin, without fear of Hell, but that he might redeem them from all iniquity, and purify to himself a peculiar people, zealous of good works.—At this moment the French attacked them. About 20 of the English fell at the first fire, and a musket-ball knocked off the cap of the profane scoffer at religion. Terrified, he exclaimed, "The Lord have mercy upon me; if I am killed I shall be damned; Oh! if I get out of the battle alive, I will be a Christian." But, alas! God, whom he had despised, now despised him; at the next volley, another ball went through his head, carrying away his foreteeth, and the back part of his skull. (It is a fearful thing to fall into the hands of the living God) and another wounded Ben in the Knee. The French, after some sharp fighting, were repulsed.

In consequence of his wound, Ben received his discharge, and was sent back to England. During his confinement in the hospital, he thought much of former times; and of the religious instructions he then received, and felt the importance of them; and determined to give himself up to God, to serve him in holiness and righteousness all the days of his life; trusting his soul to the Lord Jesus Christ, to save him from eternal misery. He was sensible that his own goodness could not save him, and therefore esteemed it a great mercy that God would save him through the righteousness of Jesus Christ.

When he arrived at Wedgley, the pious Clergyman, and his other friends, were rejoiced to find that God had dealt so graciously with him, and made him a Christian in reality, as well as in name. They got him the place of foreman to a neighbouring farmer, who being frequently troubled with the rheumatism, could not always work at his farm. Sally Rosebud, his pretty cherry-cheeked daughter, soon conceived a sneaking kindness for Benjamin, who thought he discovered in her every thing he could wish for in a woman. The good old farmer presently perceived it, and wisely considering that a pious husband would make his pious daughter happier than a rich one, cheerfully gave his consent, and Benjamin Gracious and Sally Rosebud were accordingly married. Mrs. Gracious has produced her husband several fine children, and they live happily together, "walking in all the commandments and ordinances of the Lord blameless."

52. THE PHILOSOPHY OF DRINKING USAGE

by JOHN DUNLOP

To the middle classes the necessity of destroying many aspects of the old popular culture was nowhere more clearly demonstrated than in the temperance question. The traditional customs of the people were condemned as "the pastimes of village buffoonery and rudeness"; and the customary drinking usages which were deeply woven into many aspects of the people's life at work, in the home, and at festivals were to be deplored. The temperance movement has to be interpreted not only as a compassionate concern for the moral and religious state of the working classes but as part of a wider effort to assimilate the industrial population to new norms of work and social conduct. These passages from John Dunlop's *Philosophy of Artificial and Compulsory Drinking Usage in Great Britain and Ireland* (6th ed., 1839), pp. 3, 6–8, 246–252, give some hint of the magnitude of the problem. Dunlop (1789–1868) was president of the General Temperance Union of Scotland.

THE system of rule and regulation, as to times and occasions of drinking, pervades all branches of society in Great Britain—at meals, markets, fairs, baptisms, and funerals; and almost every trade and profession has its own code of strict and well-observed laws on this subject. There are numerous occasions when general custom makes the offer and reception of liquor as imperative as the law of the land. Most other countries have, on the whole, only *one general motive* to use liquor—viz. natural thirst, or desire for it; but in Great Britain there exists a large plurality of motives, derived from etiquette and rule. . . .

Scarcely has the stripling commenced his apprenticeship, in some towns, *to the business of the joiner or cabinet-maker,* than he is informed that the custom of the shop is to pay a sum as *an entry,* or footing, to be disposed of in drink by the workmen. He receives charge of the fire in the premises; and at every failure of kindling, mending, or extinguishing at night, he is fined in a small sum, to be expended in whisky: failure in putting out candles at the proper time, or in watching the work at meal-hours, and a number of other petty offences, are met by small amercements for the same purpose. At the ceremony of brothering, ten or twelve shillings are sacrificed in this way; the first wages of a journeyman also are consecrated to the same unhallowed purpose, being in many cases the commencement of a course of inebriation that ends only with poverty and death. If one leaves the shop, his station at a particular bench is *rouped,* i.e. auctioned by the men who remain, and the price spent in drink: sometimes six shillings are thus obtained. When furniture is carried to a customer's house, at moving, packing, &c. the employer generally bestows a glass or two. When winter commences, and candles begin to be used, masters give their operatives a *treat* of spirits; and whenever the smallest sum is raised by a fine, the men greedily add to it, and thus a nucleus is easily formed, and drinking perpetuated. The penalties for nonconformity to the usages are so various, ingenious, and severe, that it is nearly impossible, as we shall find in the sequel, for an operative to stand out against them, and be able to continue in his business. On refusal to comply, men are sent to Coventry; refused assistance and cooperation, which is sometimes essential to carry on work; ridiculed, affronted, maltreated in a variety of ways. A journeyman carpenter, in a town north of the Forth, having declined to pay the customary drink-money, found one morning his tools removed. He received no satisfaction, but in about three months they were found in the side of a dunghill, which was being taken away for agricultural purposes.

In the course of apprenticeship to other occupations, a sum, varying from one to five shillings, is at intervals levied: among *plumbers,* for instance, when the apprentice casts his first sheet of lead. In manufacturing districts, when a *blockcutter* cuts his first printing-block, he is bound to pay twenty shillings for the purpose of treating his fellow-workmen with drink. Among *cloth-lappers,* and some other trades, the apprentice not only gives his entry drink, but at successive stages of learning the business, he has to pay drinking usage-money; to all which payments the other workmen contribute a smaller sum, and often a debauch follows. *Entries,* either at admission of apprentices, or new workmen coming to a shop, are general among *founders, coopers, tin-smiths,* and others; and drinking never stops with the occasion of its commencement, but always proceeds in an augmented ratio. A respectable man, having a family, going lately to work at a *blacksmith's* shop, refused to pay *entry;* he was maltreated, and finally knocked down and wounded: on the aggressors being summoned, they actually pleaded, in bar of judgment, before a magistrate, the *custom* of the shop having been infringed.

AGRICULTURAL CLASSES.—In some of the central counties in the South of England, and in the corn trade, on the farmer receiving the money for his grain, the corn-dealer deducts a shilling from the sum due, and presents a glass of spirits and water in its stead; sometimes several glasses are added to the first. This practice has been represented to me as mischievous in a high degree, for a farmer will in one day do business with several dealers. And on the whole, the drinking at bargains and sales, has a most pernicious effect, so far as I can learn, on the habits, morals, families and dependents of the agricultural class. At auctions in the district above-mentioned, and I presume very generally throughout the country, the auctioneer is supplied with beer, strong ale, cider, and spirits; in many cases, the spirits and beer are mixed together, and bidders are most liberally plied with the liquor. An informant seeing two drunken men attempting to lead a horse, was told that they had been at a sale of stock in the neighbourhood, where they had got beer and spirits.

In Wales, servant men and women are permitted after milking-time to go to fairs, often remaining in the public-house till the next morning; and it is a common practice for farm servants to be hired at a fair or market, amid scenes of drinking and inebriation. I have found, also, in the central counties of England, that farm servants are hired in towns, on which occasions it is usual to give them money to drink.

Farriers are expected to come round at Christmas to their employers, whose horses they shoe, and receive money to drink.

Liquor is often given at sheep washing and shearing; and at reaping, and other rural occasions; but as this is intended as diet, and not as a piece of courtesy, we shall pass it over.

In some places, farmers usually sell their produce within a public-house, instead of making the bargain in the market-place. I have heard it complained of, also, that in some districts markets are held too late in the day, so as greatly to promote intemperance, and the practice of selling in public-houses.

FRIENDLY CLUBS.—It constitutes a great national calamity that, in the large majority of instances, the meetings of these are held in public-houses. I have noticed this frequently already, in treating of trade clubs and unions. They would deserve well of this country who should be privileged to make a clean end of this most vicious system. The facility with which a room is thus obtained for the transaction of business, and the difficulty of procuring any convenient place for that purpose unconnected with the retail of liquor, are the immediate obstacles in the way of a general reformation on this subject. . . .

WOOLLEN TRADE.—. . . In the present state of the trade no apprentices are taken by master manufacturers. When a young man enters a factory for the purpose of learning the business, he must pay 5s., to which 6d. or 1s. is added, and expended in drink. A single man entering a factory to work pays 3s. 6d., a married man, 2s. 6d., to which is added 3d. or 6d. If a man be under age while learning the business, he pays when twenty-one years of age, what is called his *colting,* which is 1l. if he remains in the establishment, and 10s. 6d. if he leaves it: to this sum 2s. 6d. or more is added by the others and drunk. The first time any young man in the shop is seen by his shopmates walking with a young woman, he has to pay 1s., this is called the bull shilling; 2d. or 3d. each is added to this by the others.

When a man gets married, he has 5s. to pay, to which 6d. or 1s. each is added by the rest. For every child born, 1s., to which 3d. is added by each; this is called washing the child's head, and the story is that its hair will not grow unless this ceremony is performed. If a married man stop from his house all night on 'a spree,' he is fined 1s., to which other sums are added and drunk. In the dressing department a master has to pay 1l. for every 500 pieces of cloth received to be dressed; this is called a 'flocker,' and the workmen frequently mortgage a flocker, so that they will sometimes be 6l. or 8l. indebted to one of their more careful shopmates, who takes care of his money, and allows them sums to drink on the faith of a subsequent flocker.

There are several annual fairs; at each of these the workmen of an establishment send one of their comrades to all their master's customers for a fairing, which generally amounts to 1s. or 1s. 6d. from each person. In anticipation of these occasions, they will put up the next fairing, and sell it by auction, and the buyer has to supply the sum for which it sells, and take the risk whether or not he shall procure the amount by begging fairings at the next fair. To this sum others are added, all of which are drunk.

A workman who changes from one room to another, pays 1s. A spinner who changes from one loom to another, pays 2s. 6d. A weaver,

1s. Any body in the factory driving a nail, pays 1s. When the factory is first lighted in autumn, the master gives to each hand 1s. 6d., and they all have a supper together, and drink afterwards as much as they can guzzle; and the extra expense over the 1s. 6d. is equally divided.

In the manufactories the workmen have always three or four or more barrels of beer kept in the cellars, which are replenished as regularly as if they were at inns. From this supply all the hands get a pint every day, for which they pay 2d. each. The man who attends to collect the money and supply the beer, is called tapster. Any person who refuses to pay his footing is subjected to all kinds of petty annoyances and persecutions; his hat or coat taken and secreted, and often pledged for the sum of his fine.

FURTHER READING: Part Two

Barnard, H. C., *A Short History of English Education, 1760–1944* (1959 ed.).

Beer, Max, *A History of British Socialism* (1940 ed.).

Briggs, Asa (ed.), *Chartist Studies* (1959).

Butler, J. R. M., *The Passing of the Great Reform Bill* (1914).

Chambers, J. D., *The Workshop of the World* (1961).

Church, R. W., *The Oxford Movement* (1892 ed.).

Clark, George Kitson, *The Making of Victorian England* (1962).

Cole, G. D. H., *A Short History of the British Working Class Movement, 1789–1947* (1948 ed.).

Driver, Cecil, *Tory Radical: the Life of Richard Oastler* (1946).

Finer, S. E., *Life and Times of Sir Edwin Chadwick* (1952).

Gash, Norman, *Politics in the Age of Peel* (1953).

Harrison, John F. C., *Learning and Living, 1790–1960* (1961).

Hovell, Mark, *The Chartist Movement* (1950 ed.).

McCord, Norman, *The Anti-Corn Law League, 1838–1845* (1958).

Podmore, Frank, *Robert Owen: a Biography*, 2 vols. (1906).

Seymour, C., *Electoral Reform in England and Wales* (1915).

Thompson, F. M. L., *English Landed Society in the Nineteenth Century* (1963).

Wearmouth, Robert F., *Methodism and the Working-Class Movements of England, 1800–1850* (1937).

Webb, Robert K., *The British Working Class Reader, 1790–1848* (1955).

Webb, Sidney and Beatrice, *The History of Trade Unionism* (1920 ed.).

White, R. J., *Waterloo to Peterloo* (1957).

Young, G. M., and W. D. Handcock, *English Historical Documents, 1833–1874* (1956).

PART THREE.
VICTORIAN PROSPERITY, 1848-1870

Chapter 11.
Bourgeois England

The pay-off for the hungry forties came in the third quarter of the nineteenth century, which was a period of unprecedented prosperity. The "workshop of the world" had a long lead on all other nations and the British economy had a dynamic quality which was new and distinctive. Belief in Progress was almost universal and helped to sustain the mood of confidence which was so typical of mid-Victorian writers. In fact, the prosperity was not nearly so widespread as many contemporaries assumed; but enough of it trickled down to the upper strata of the working classes to justify hopes of increasing betterment in the future.

The lion's share of Victorian prosperity went not to the aristocracy, nor to the working classes, but to the middle classes. It was they who increased so markedly in numbers, affluence, and confidence. Victorianism was essentially a bourgeois civilization, tempered by the strength of gentlemanly traditions and checked by fear of the "lower orders." In the generation before 1848 life for a majority of the middle classes was a rather serious, drab affair; the rewards were great for those who succeeded in the economic struggle, but left little opportunity for leisure and cultural refinement. By the 1860s a pattern of middle-class living had become established which included considerable amenities and a relatively high degree of domestic comfort.

The middle-class achievement in setting the general social climate of the nation can be measured by comparing England in 1860 with the aristocratic degeneracy of the Regency only 30 years earlier. Now even the royal family provided an image of happy bourgeois domesticity; and the poet laureate, Alfred Tennyson, thought fit to eulogize the monarch as "Mother, Wife, and Queen."

A middle-class way of life was defined according to a firmly established pattern; a nonmanual job (usually in trade, manufacture, or the professions) with a steady income, a villa in a fashionable part of the town, a wife and family,

servants and a carriage, and a Public School education for
the children. Underpinning the whole structure were the
twin concepts of Respectability and Duty.

53. [THE GREAT EXHIBITION, 1851]

by THE PRINCE CONSORT

There had been industrial exhibitions before 1851 but the
Great Exhibition of the Industry of all Nations held in Hyde
Park, London, became the symbol of an age. Through the
combination of the organizing ability of the civil servant,
Henry Cole, the influential support of the Prince Consort,
and the brilliant design of Joseph Paxton for a "Crystal
Palace," the exhibition was an outstanding success. During
the five months it was open over six million people visited
it. The Queen was there frequently, and cheap railway ex-
cursions from all parts of Britain enabled the working
classes to participate in the national enthusiasm. Impressive as were the numbers and ingenuity of the exhibits, and
the technical achievement of the building, it was the great
themes of Progress, Work, Religion, and Peace that contemporary commentators most liked to dwell on. The following is from a speech by the Prince Consort (1819–
1861) at a preparatory banquet in 1850, in *Principal
Speeches and Addresses of H.R.H. the Prince Consort*
(1862), pp. 110–112.

NOBODY . . . who has paid any attention to the peculiar features
of our present era, will doubt for a moment that we are living at a
period of most wonderful transition, which tends rapidly to accomplish
that great end, to which, indeed, all history points—*the realization of
the unity of mankind.* Not a unity which breaks down the limits and
levels the peculiar characteristics of the different nations of the earth,
but rather a unity, the *result and product* of those very national
varieties and antagonistic qualities.

The distances which separated the different nations and parts of
the globe are rapidly vanishing before the achievements of modern
invention, and we can traverse them with incredible ease; the languages of all nations are known, and their acquirement placed within

the reach of everybody; thought is communicated with the rapidity, and even by the power, of lightning. On the other hand, the *great principle of division of labour,* which may be called the moving power of civilization, is being extended to all branches of science, industry, and art.

Whilst formerly the greatest mental energies strove at universal knowledge, and that knowledge was confined to the few, now they are directed on specialities, and in these, again, even to the minutest points; but the knowledge acquired becomes at once the property of the community at large; for, whilst formerly discovery was wrapped in secrecy, the publicity of the present day causes that no sooner is a discovery or invention made than it is already improved upon and surpassed by competing efforts. The products of all quarters of the globe are placed at our disposal, and we have only to choose which is the best and the cheapest for our purposes, and the powers of production are intrusted to the stimulus of *competition and capital.*

So man is approaching a more complete fulfilment of that great and sacred mission which he has to perform in this world. His reason being created after the image of God, he has to use it to discover the laws by which the Almighty governs His creation, and, by making these laws his standard of action, to conquer nature to his use; himself a divine instrument.

Science discovers these laws of power, motion, and transformation; industry applies them to the raw matter, which the earth yields us in abundance, but which becomes valuable only by knowledge. Art teaches us the immutable laws of beauty and symmetry, and gives to our productions forms in accordance to them.

Gentlemen—the Exhibition of 1851 is to give us a true test and a living picture of the point of development at which the whole of mankind has arrived in this great task, and a new starting-point from which all nations will be able to direct their further exertions.

54. SELF-HELP

by SAMUEL SMILES

Every age has its popular prototypes who epitomize the dominant social values of the time. Samuel Smiles (1812–1904) was the most popular of many authors of a success literature which elevated the self-made man into an almost mystical figure in Victorian England. *Self-Help* was published in 1859 and sold a quarter of a million copies during Smiles' lifetime. It originated in a series of talks which he gave to a little mutual improvement society in Leeds in 1845, and consisted of a series of potted biographies of men who had risen by their own efforts from obscurity to wealth and influence. Lessons of the benefits of steady work, thrift, perseverance and temperance were drawn from these examples, and the gospel of self-help was presented as a practical method of working-class improvement. These passages are from *Self-Help* (1859), pp. 1–2, 232–234.

"HEAVEN helps those who help themselves" is a well-tried maxim, embodying in a small compass the results of vast human experience. The spirit of self-help is the root of all genuine growth in the individual; and, exhibited in the lives of many, it constitutes the true source of national vigour and strength. Help from without is often enfeebling in its effects, but help from within invariably invigorates. Whatever is done *for* men or classes, to a certain extent takes away the stimulus and necessity of doing for themselves; and where men are subjected to over-guidance and over-government, the inevitable tendency is to render them comparatively helpless.

Even the best institutions can give a man no active aid. Perhaps the utmost they can do is, to leave him *free* to develop himself and improve his individual condition. But in all times men have been prone to believe that their happiness and well-being were to be secured by means of institutions rather than by their own conduct. Hence the value of legislation as an agent in human advancement has always been greatly over-estimated. To constitute the millionth part of a Legislature, by voting for one or two men once in three or five years, however conscientiously this duty may be performed, can exercise but little active influence upon any man's life and character. Moreover, it is every day becoming more clearly understood, that the function of Government is negative and restrictive, rather than positive and active; being resolvable principally into protection—protection of life, liberty, and property. Hence the chief "reforms" of the last fifty years have consisted mainly in abolitions and disenactments. But there is no power of law that can make the idle man industrious, the thriftless provident, or the drunken sober; though every individual can be each and all of these if he will, by the exercise of his own free powers of action and self-denial. Indeed all experience serves to prove that the worth and strength of a State depend far less upon the form of its institutions than upon the character of its men. For the nation is only the aggregate of individual conditions, and civilization itself is but a question of personal improvement.

National progress is the sum of individual industry, energy, and uprightness, as national decay is of individual idleness, selfishness, and vice. What we are accustomed to decry as great social evils, will, for the most part, be found to be only the outgrowth of our own perverted life; and though we may endeavour to cut them down and extirpate them by means of Law, they will only spring up again with fresh luxuriance in some other form, unless the conditions of human life and character are radically improved. If this view be correct, then it follows that the highest patriotism and philanthropy consist, not so much in altering laws and modifying institutions, as in helping and stimulating men to elevate and improve themselves by their own free and independent action.

. . . [Mr. Bright observed in 1847] "There is only one way that is safe for any man, or any number of men, by which they can maintain their present position if it be a good one, or raise themselves above it if it be a bad one,—that is, by the practice of the virtues of industry, frugality, temperance, and honesty. There is no royal road by which men can raise themselves from a position which they feel to be uncomfortable and unsatisfactory, as regards their mental or physical condition, except by the practice of those virtues by which they find numbers amongst them are continually advancing and bettering themselves. What is it that has made, that has in fact created, the middle class in this country, but the virtues to which I have alluded? There was a time when there was hardly any class in England, except the highest, that was equal in condition to the poorest class at this moment. How is it that the hundreds of thousands of men now existing in this our country of the middle class, are educated, comfortable, and enjoying an amount of happiness and independence, to which our forefathers were wholly unaccustomed? Why, by the practice of those very virtues; for I maintain that there has never been in any former age as much of these virtues as is now to be found amongst the great middle class of our community. When I speak of the middle class, I mean that class which is between the privileged class, the richest, and the very poorest in the community; and I would recommend every man to pay no attention whatever to public writers or speakers, whoever they may be, who tell them that this class or that class, that this law or that law, that this Government or that Government, can do all these things for them. I assure you, after long reflection and much observation, that there is no way for the working classes of this country to improve their condition but that which so many of them have already availed themselves of,—that is, by the practice of those virtues, and by reliance upon themselves."

There is no reason why the condition of the average workman in this country should not be a useful, honourable, respectable, and happy one. The whole body of the working classes might (with few exceptions) be as frugal, virtuous, well-informed, and well-conditioned as many individuals of the same class have already made themselves. What some men are, all without difficulty might be. Employ the same means, and the same results will follow. That there should be a class of men who live by their daily labour in every state is the ordinance of God, and doubtless is a wise and righteous one; but that this class should be otherwise than frugal, contented, intelligent, and happy, is not the design of Providence, but springs solely from the weakness, self-indulgence, and perverseness of man himself. The healthy spirit of self-help created amongst working people would more than any other measure serve to raise them as a class, and this, not by pulling down others, but by levelling them up to a higher and still advancing standard of religion, intelligence, and virtue.

55. [A SUCCESSFUL INDUSTRIALIST]: SIR TITUS SALT

by R. BALGARNIE

No better example of Smilesian precepts could be found than Titus Salt (1803–1876), a successful woolen manufacturer of Bradford. He made a fortune out of alpaca wool, built a model factory and village community for his workers (named Saltaire), was successively mayor and M. P. for Bradford, and was created a baronet in 1869. After his death he was commemorated by an elaborate white marble statue in front of Bradford town hall. This account of the reasons for his success is from a eulogistic biography by a Wesleyan minister, R. Balgarnie, *Sir Titus Salt, Baronet: His Life and its Lessons* (1877), pp. 80–85.

. . . HE [Titus Salt] was a very *early riser,* and his unvarying rule was to be at the works before the engine was started. Is it not written, "the hand of the diligent maketh rich"? and here is a signal illustration of it. It used to be said in Bradford, "Titus Salt makes a thousand pounds before other people are out of bed." Whether the sum thus specified was actually realised by him we cannot say, but it is the habit of early rising we wish to point out, and inculcate on those whose business career is about to begin. In these times of artificiality and self-indulgence, when the laws of nature are often wantonly violated, the chances of success are dead against those who follow such a course. Let young men especially avoid it; yea, let them take Mr. Titus Salt as an example of early rising. . . .

It is almost superfluous to mention that his early presence at "the works" exercised a high moral influence over his workpeople. Well they knew they had not merely to do with delegated authority, but with that which was supreme. If any of them were late, it was the master's rebuke they feared. If any were conspicuous above the rest for regularity and skill in their duties, it was the master's approval they expected, and this approval was shewn by the promotion of those who served him best. Some who entered his employment in the humblest capacity have been raised to the highest positions in it. There was thus a personal acquaintance formed, and a mutual sympathy established, that greatly helped to bridge the gulf which too often has separated master and workpeople, and sometimes placed them in an attitude of antagonism to each other. Throughout his manufacturing career he had great moral power in attaching the workpeople to himself; they all looked up to him as a friend rather than a master, and they obeyed and served him with all the devotion of a Highland clan to their noble chieftain. . . .

Another striking feature of his character, and one which enabled him to accomplish so much work, was his *punctuality.* Never was military despot more rigid than he in the observance of this rule: when he made an engagement he was punctual to the minute, and he expected the same in others who had dealings with him. . . . Such was his punctuality that he was hardly ever known to miss a train, or to be in a hurry for one. It was the same at home as in business; the hour of meals was observed with precision, and all other domestic arrangements were conducted on the same principle of order. With watch in hand he would await the time for evening prayers, and then the bell was instantly rung for the household to assemble. When the usual hour arrived for his family and household to retire to rest, the signal was at once given and observed. When guests were staying at his house, he was the timekeeper of their movements, and in regulating themselves accordingly they were seldom mistaken. When a journey was to be taken with his wife and family, say to the metropolis or the seaside, nothing was left to chance; but the day and hour of starting, together with other minor arrangements, were written down some time beforehand.

Another marked characteristic in the prosecution of his immense business was his *methodical exactness;* but for this habit, which was natural to him, he never could have personally controlled the various departments in connection with "the works." He was scrupulously exact in the arrangement of his papers, and knew where to lay his hand on any document when required. His letters were always promptly answered. He was exact in his accounts, exact in the words he spoke—which never had the colour of exaggeration about them— exact in his purchases and sales. When he had fixed his price he stood by it, so that no one ever thought of arguing with him to take a farthing less. . . .

But if we were to sum up all the qualities that conduced to his success at this period, all those mental characteristics that enabled him to prosecute his immense business single-handed, it would be expressed in the word *whole-heartedness.* . . . How many men drag out a miserable existence, owing to the very consciousness that they have been mistaken in their occupation? As a consequence of this, they have never followed it with their whole heart, they have always hankered after something else, and that to which they have originally put their hands, has, of course, turned out a failure. Better for a young man carefully to watch the bias of his mind, and the particular taste evinced; then in that direction his future course ought to be steered. This is just nature giving a broad hint, and what she thus indicates is likely to prosper; then let him determine to succeed, and succeed he must. It was thus with Mr. Salt; his early proclivities found their true sphere in the occupation he now pursued.

56. ENGLISH TRAITS

by RALPH WALDO EMERSON

Among the most perspicacious visitors to England was the
New England transcendentalist, Ralph Waldo Emerson
(1803–1882), who toured in the north in 1847–1848, lecturing at mechanics' institutes. His impressions were published
in *English Traits* (1856) and the following extracts (*Works*,
1884 ed., Vol. 5, pp. 145–158) describe the same dynamic
qualities in Victorian England as a later generation ascribed
to American society in the twentieth century.

THE creation of wealth in England in the last ninety years is a main
fact in modern history. The wealth of London determines prices all
over the globe. All things precious, or useful, or amusing, or intoxicating, are sucked into this commerce and floated to London. Some
English private fortunes reach, and some exceed a million of dollars
a year. A hundred thousand palaces adorn the island. All that can
feed the senses and passions, all that can succor the talent or arm
the hands of the intelligent middle class, who never spare in what
they buy for their own consumption; all that can aid science, gratify
taste, or soothe comfort, is in open market . . .

There is no country in which so absolute a homage is paid to wealth.
In America there is a touch of shame when a man exhibits the evidences of large property, as if after all it needed apology. But the
Englishman has pure pride in his wealth, and esteems it a final certif-
icate. A coarse logic rules throughout all English souls; if you have
merit, can you not show it by your good clothes and coach and horses?
How can a man be a gentleman without a pipe of wine? . . .

The ambition to create value evokes every kind of ability; government becomes a manufacturing corporation, and every house a mill.
The headlong bias to utility will let no talent lie in a napkin,—if possible will teach spiders to weave silk stockings. An Englishman, while
he eats and drinks no more or not much more than another man,
labors three times as many hours in the course of a year as another
European; or, his life as a workman is three lives. He works fast.
Every thing in England is at a quick pace. They have reinforced their

own productivity by the creation of that marvellous machinery which differences this age from any other age . . .

The habit of brag runs through all classes, from the "Times" newspaper through politicians and poets, through Wordsworth, Carlyle, Mill and Sydney Smith, down to the boys of Eton. In the gravest treatise on political economy, in a philosophical essay, in books of science, one is surprised by the most innocent exhibition of unflinching nationality . . .

57. [DOMESTIC SERVANTS]

by ISABELLA BEETON

In 1851 the most numerous group of employed persons after agriculture was domestic servants, who totalled 1,039,000, which was more than the combined total for the great basic textile industries of cotton and wool. Moreover, the percentage of the occupied population in domestic service rose from 13.3 in 1851 to 15.8 in 1871. The keeping of servants became a distinguishing mark of membership of the middle class, and the precise number of domestics in a household indicated the standard of living enjoyed. An indication of the elaborateness of middle-class domestic economy is given in these instructions on servants from Isabella Beeton's *Book of Household Management* (1861), 1888 ed., pp. 1453–1481. "Mrs Beeton" (1836–1865) became a household name as the standard English cookbook, though the early editions were not merely recipe books but complete guides to all aspects of housekeeping.

THE CUSTOM OF "SOCIETY" is to abuse its servants: a *façon de parler* such as leads their lords and masters to talk of the weather, and, when ruefully inclined, of the crops, leads matronly ladies, and ladies just entering on their probation in that honoured and honourable state, to talk of servants, and, as we are told, wax eloquent over the greatest plague in life while taking a quiet cup of tea. Young men at their clubs, also, we are told, like to abuse their "fellows," perhaps not without a certain pride and pleasure at the opportunity of intimating that they enjoy such appendages to their state. It is a conviction of

"Society" that the race of good servants has died out, at least in England, although they do order these things better in France; that there is neither honesty, conscientiousness, nor the careful and industrious habits which distinguished the servants of our grandmothers and great-grandmothers; that domestics no longer know their place; that the introduction of cheap silks and cottons, and, still more recently, those ambiguous "materials" and tweeds, have removed the landmarks between the mistress and her maid, between the master and his man.

CHOICE OF SERVANTS.—When the distinction really depends on things so insignificant as dress, when the lady of fashion chooses her footman without any other consideration than his height, shape, and *tournure* of calf, it is not surprising that she should find a domestic who has no attachment for the family, who considers the figure he cuts behind her carriage, and the late hours he is compelled to keep, a full compensation for the wages he exacts, for the food he wastes, and for the perquisites he can lay his hands on. Nor should the fast young man, who chooses his groom for his knowingness in the ways of the turf and in the tricks of low horse-dealers, be surprised if he is sometimes the victim of these learned ways. But these are the exceptional cases, which prove the existence of a better state of things. The great masses of society among us are not thus deserted: there are few families of respectability, from the shopkeeper in the next street to the nobleman whose mansion dignifies the next square, which do not contain among their dependents attached and useful servants; and where these are absent altogether, there are good reasons for it.

MASTERS AND MISTRESSES.—It has been said that good masters and mistresses make good servants, and this to a great extent is true. There are certainly some men and women in the wide field of servitude whom it would be impossible to train into good servants, but the conduct of both master and mistress is seldom without its effect upon these dependents. They are not mere machines, and no one has a right to consider them in that light. The sensible master and the kind mistress know, that if servants depend on them for their means of living, in their turn they are dependent on their servants for very many of the comforts of life; and that, using a proper amount of care in choosing servants, treating them like reasonable beings, and making slight excuses for the shortcomings of human nature, they will, save in some exceptional cases, be tolerably well served, and, in most instances, surround themselves with attached domestics.

This remark, which is applicable to all domestics, is especially so to men-servants. Families accustomed to such attendants have always about them humble dependents, whose children have no other prospect than domestic service to look forward to; to them it presents no degradation, but the reverse, to be so employed; they are initiated step by step into the mysteries of the household, with the prospect of rising in the service, if it is a house admitting of promotion, to the respectable position of butler or house-steward. In families of humbler pretensions, where they must look for promotion elsewhere, they know that can only be attained by acquiring the goodwill of their employers. Can there be any stronger security for their good conduct—any doubt that, in the mass of domestic servants, good conduct is the rule, the reverse the exception?

WOMEN SERVANTS are specially likely to be influenced by their mistress's treatment of them, and yet we venture to assert that good mistresses are rarer than good masters, so many of the former lacking consideration for their servants.

In many cases they do not give them the help which it is their duty to afford. A timely hint or even a few words of quiet reproof may be lacking when needed, and still more so the kind words and the deserved praise for work well and carefully done. It is a fact that we must take some *trouble* with our servants. The wheels of domestic machinery will not run well without constant care. There is no necessity for a mistress to be continually fussing round and superintending her servants' work, but she must first make sure that they do it thoroughly and well. Also she must take time and pains to show her domestics *how* she likes the work done. . . .

THE NUMBER OF MEN-SERVANTS IN A FAMILY varies according to the wealth and position of the master, from the owner of the ducal mansion, with a retinue of attendants, at the head of which is the chamberlain and house-steward, to the occupier of the humbler house, where a single footman, or even the odd man-of-all-work, is the only male retainer. The majority of gentlemen's establishments probably comprise a servant out of livery, or butler, a footman and coachman, or coachman and groom, where the horses exceed two or three.

To a certain extent the number of men-servants kept is regulated by the number of women servants, this statement, of course, not applying to such out-door servants as coachman, groom, or gardener.

Occasionally a parlour-maid is kept instead of a second footman, or a kitchen or scullery-maid does the work in the way of boot-cleaning, etc., that would fall to a third footman or page. A man cook is now more rarely to be found in private service than formerly, women having found it expedient to bring their knowledge of the culinary art more to the level of the *chef;* while in many cases those who have a talent for cooking have risen superior to him both in the way they flavour and serve the various dishes that call for skill and taste. . . .

THE FIRST DUTY OF THE HOUSEMAID in winter is to open the shutters of all the lower rooms in the house, and take up the hearthrugs in those rooms which she is going to "do" before breakfast. In some families, where there are only a cook and housemaid kept, and where the drawing-rooms are large, the cook has the care of the dining-room, and the housemaid that of the breakfast-room, library and drawing-rooms. After the shutters are all opened, she sweeps the breakfast-room, sweeping the dust towards the fireplace, of course previously removing the fender. She should then lay a cloth (generally made of coarse wrapping) over the carpet in front of the stove, and on this should place her housemaid's box, containing black-lead brushes, leathers, emery-paper, cloth, black-lead, and all utensils necessary for cleaning a grate, with the cinder-pail on the other side. She now sweeps up the ashes, and deposits them in her cinder-pail, which is a japanned tin pail, with a wire sifter inside, and a closely-fitting top. In this pail the cinders are sifted, and reserved for use in the kitchen or under the copper, the ashes only being thrown away. The cinders disposed of, she proceeds to black-lead the grate, producing the black lead, the soft brush for laying it on, her blacking and polishing brushes, from the box which contains her tools. The housemaid's box should be kept well stocked. Having blackened, brushed and polished every part, and made all clean and bright, she now proceeds to lay the fire. Sometimes it is very difficult to get a proper polish to black grates, particularly if they have been neglected and allowed to rust at all. But later on we give recipes for treating them that will be found useful.

Bright grates require unceasing attention to keep them in perfect order. A day should never pass without the housemaid rubbing with a dry leather the polished parts of a grate, as also the fender and fire-irons. A careful and attentive housemaid should have no occasion ever to use emery-paper for any part but the bars, which, of course, become blacked by the fire. (Some mistresses, to save labour, have a double set of bars, one set bright for the summer, and another black set to use when fires are in requisition.)

The several fires lighted, the housemaid proceeds with her dusting, and polishing the several pieces of furniture in the breakfast-parlour, leaving no corner unvisited. Before sweeping the carpet, it is a good practice to sprinkle it all over with tea-leaves, which not only lay all dust, but give a slightly fragrant smell to the room. It is now in order for the reception of the family, and where there is neither footman or parlour-maid, she now proceeds to the dressing-room, and lights her mistress's fire, if she is in the habit of having one to dress by. Her mistress is called, hot water placed in the dressing-room for her use, her clothes—as far as they are under the housemaid's charge—put before the fire, hanging a fire-guard on the bars where there is one, while she proceeds to prepare the breakfast. . . .

BEDROOM WORK.—Breakfast served, the housemaid proceeds to the bed-chambers, throws up the sashes, if not already done, pulls up the blinds, throwing back the curtains at the same time, and opens the beds, by removing the clothes, placing them over a horse, or failing that, over the backs of chairs. She now proceeds to empty the slops. In doing this, everything is emptied into the slop-pail, leaving a little scalding-hot water for a minute in vessels that require it; adding a drop of turpentine to the water, when that is not sufficient to cleanse them. The basin is emptied, well rinsed with clean water, and carefully wiped; the ewers emptied and washed; finally, the water-jugs themselves emptied out and rinsed, and wiped dry. As soon as this is done, she should remove and empty the pails, taking care that they also are well washed, scalded and wiped as soon as they are empty. Next follows bed-making, at which one of the other servants usually assists; but, before beginning, velvet chairs, or other things injured by dust, should be removed to another room. In bed-making, the fancy of its occupant should be consulted: some like beds sloping from the top towards the feet, swelling slightly in the middle; others, perfectly flat; a good housemaid will accommodate each bed to the taste of the sleeper, taking care to shake, beat and turn it well in the process. Some persons prefer sleeping on the mattress; in which case a feather bed is usually beneath, resting on a second mattress, and a straw palliasse at the bottom. In this case, the mattresses should change places daily; the feather bed placed on the mattress shaken, beaten, taken up and opened several times, so as thoroughly to separate the feathers; if too large to be thus handled, the maid should shake and beat one end first, and then the other, smoothing it afterwards equally all over into the required shape, and place the mattress gently over it. Any feathers which escape in this process a tidy servant will put back through the seam of the tick; she will also be careful to sew up any stitch that gives way the moment it is discovered. The bed-clothes are laid on, beginning with an under blanket and sheet, which are tucked under the mattress at the bottom. The bolster is then beaten and shaken, and put on, the top of the sheet rolled round it, and the sheet tucked in all round. The pillows and other bed-clothes follow, and the counterpane over all, which should fall in graceful folds, and at equal distance from the ground all round. The curtains are drawn to the head and folded neatly across the bed, and the whole finished in a smooth and graceful manner. Where spring mattresses are used, care should be taken that the over one is turned every day. The housemaid should now take up in a dustpan any pieces that may be on the carpet; she should dust the room, shut the door, and proceed to another room. When all the bedrooms are finished, she should dust the stairs and polish the hand-rail of the banisters, and see that all ledges, window-sills, &c., are quite free from dust.

Chapter 12.

The Athenian Age of English Democracy

The Chartists failed in their attempt to win the vote for working men, and after 1848 the movement for the extension of the suffrage did not gain any substantial support for several years. In 1859 however the franchise question was revived and Disraeli introduced an unsuccessful reform bill in the Commons. From then until 1867, when the second Reform Bill was passed, the movement to extend the franchise gathered strength. Support came from a variety of sources: from middle-class radicals such as John Bright, from the trade unions organized behind the Reform League, from Whigs and Liberals such as Lord John Russell and William Ewart Gladstone, and finally from moderate Conservatives led by Lord Derby and Benjamin Disraeli. The opposition to reform was equally diverse; it was not along straight party lines, and until the death of Lord Palmerston in 1865 was able to hold its own. But thereafter the reform tide began to flow more strongly. Gladstone's moderate reform bill of 1866 was defeated; and the new Conservative government of Derby and Disraeli introduced its own plan, which after considerable amendment became the Reform Act of 1867.

This second Reform Act enfranchised in the boroughs all householders paying rates and lodgers occupying rooms of £10 annual value, and in the counties occupiers of property valued at £12 per year. In effect, this gave the vote to settled working men in the towns but not to the miners and agricultural laborers in the rural areas. A further redistribution of seats from small towns to larger ones was also effected. In 1865 there were about one million voters out of a total adult male population of some five millions. The 1867 Act added another 938,000 voters to the electorate.

The transition from the political system of 1832 to a limited (but expandable) democracy was not effected without grave misgivings by most of the principal leaders of the nation. Lord Derby, the prime minister, referred to the 1867 bill as a "leap in the dark," and Thomas Carlyle wrote of "shooting Niagara." Discussion of all the issues involved was thorough and protracted. From 1859 to 1867 the nation conducted a prolonged debate in parliament, at public meetings, and in pamphlets and journals on all aspects of the coming democracy. The brilliant intellectual quality of much of this great debate comes through in the writings of John Stuart Mill, Walter Bagehot, and Robert Lowe, and in the speeches of Gladstone and Disraeli. From the select democracy of the England of the 1860s the implications of mass democracy were clearly seen, and deliberately but fearfully the next step along the democratic road was taken.

58. THE ENGLISH CONSTITUTION

by WALTER BAGEHOT

It is a remarkable tribute to *The English Constitution* (1867) that it can still be used as a profitable introduction to English politics. Written originally as a series of articles in *The Fortnightly,* it appeared in book form in the same year as the second Reform Act, and was reissued in 1872 with important revisions. Walter Bagehot (1826–1877) began his career as a banker in London but soon moved into literary journalism, becoming editor of *The Economist* from 1861 to 1877. The fascination of his work lies in his ability to probe beneath the surface of politics and uncover the social and psychological springs of action. These passages, which illustrate his concern with the difference between the outward appearance and inner reality of English politics, are from *The English Constitution* (1872 ed.), pp. 4–5, 12–13, 33, 57, 59, 265–268.

NO one can approach to an understanding of the English institutions, or of others, which, being the growth of many centuries, exercise a wide sway over mixed populations, unless he divide them into two classes. In such constitutions there are two parts (not indeed separable with microscopic accuracy, for the genius of great affairs abhors nicety of division): first, those which excite and preserve the reverence of the population—the *dignified* parts, if I may so call them; and next, the *efficient* parts—those by which it, in fact, works and rules. There are two great objects which every constitution must attain to be successful, which every old and celebrated one must have wonderfully achieved: every constitution must first *gain* authority, and then *use* authority; it must first win the loyalty and confidence of mankind, and then employ that homage in the work of government.

There are indeed practical men who reject the dignified parts of government. They say, we want only to attain results, to do business: a constitution is a collection of political means for political ends, and if you admit that any part of a constitution does no business, or that a simpler machine would do equally well what it does, you admit that this part of the constitution, however dignified or awful it may be, is nevertheless in truth useless. And other reasoners, who distrust this bare philosophy, have propounded subtle arguments to prove that these dignified parts of old governments are cardinal opponents of the essential apparatus, great pivots of substantial utility; and so they manufactured fallacies which the plainer school have well exposed. But both schools are in error. The dignified parts of government are those which bring it force—which attract its motive power. The efficient parts only employ that power. The comely parts of a government *have* need, for they are those upon which its vital strength depends. They may not do anything definite that a simpler polity would not do better; but they are the preliminaries, the needful pre-requisites of *all* work. They raise the army, though they do not win the battle.

. . . We have in England an elective first magistrate as truly as the Americans have an elective first magistrate. The Queen is only at the head of the dignified part of the constitution. The prime minister is at the head of the efficient part. The Crown is, according to the saying, the "fountain of honour;" but the Treasury is the spring of business. Nevertheless, our first magistrate differs from the American. He is not elected directly by the people; he is elected by the representatives of the people. He is an example of "double election." The legislature chosen, in name, to make laws, in fact finds its principal business in making and in keeping an executive.

The leading minister so selected has to choose his associates, but he only chooses among a charmed circle. The position of most men in parliament forbids their being invited to the cabinet; the position of a few men ensures their being invited. Between the compulsory list whom he must take, and the impossible list whom he cannot take, a prime minister's independent choice in the formation of a cabinet is not very large; it extends rather to the division of the cabinet offices than to the choice of cabinet ministers. Parliament and the nation have pretty well settled who shall have the first places; but they have not discriminated with the same accuracy which man shall have which place. The highest patronage of a prime minister is, of course, a considerable power, though it is exercised under close and imperative restrictions—though it is far less than it seems to be when stated in theory, or looked at from a distance.

The cabinet, in a word, is a board of control chosen by the legislature, out of persons whom it trusts and knows, to rule the nation. The particular mode in which the English ministers are selected; the fiction that they are, in any political sense, the Queen's servants; the rule which limits the choice of the cabinet to the members of the legislature—are accidents unessential to its definition—historical incidents separable from its nature. . . .

The use of the Queen, in a dignified capacity, is incalculable. Without her in England, the present English Government would fail and pass away. Most people when they read that the Queen walked on the slopes at Windsor—that the Prince of Wales went to the Derby—have imagined that too much thought and prominence were given to little things. But they have been in error; and it is nice to trace how the actions of a retired widow and an unemployed youth become of such importance.

The best reason why Monarchy is a strong government is, that it is an intelligible government. The mass of mankind understand it, and they hardly anywhere in the world understand any other. It is often said that men are ruled by their imaginations; but it would be truer to say they are governed by the weakness of their imaginations. . . .

The House of Commons has inquired into most things, but has never had a committee on "the Queen." There is no authentic blue-book to say what she does. Such an investigation cannot take place; but if it could, it would probably save her much vexatious routine, and many toilsome and unnecessary hours.

. . . Above all things our royalty is to be reverenced, and if you begin to poke about it you cannot reverence it. When there is a select committee on the Queen, the charm of royalty will be gone. Its mystery is its life. We must not let in daylight upon magic.

. . . It [cabinet government] is only possible in what I may venture to call *deferential* nations. It has been thought strange, but there *are* nations in which the numerous unwiser part wishes to be ruled by the less numerous wiser part. The numerical majority—whether by custom or by choice, is immaterial—is ready, is eager to delegate its power of choosing its ruler to a certain select minority. It abdicates in favour of its *élite,* and consents to obey whoever that *élite* may confide in. It acknowledges as its secondary electors—as the choosers of its government—an educated minority, at once competent and unresisted; it has a kind of loyalty to some superior persons who are fit to choose a good government, and whom no other class opposes. A nation in such a happy state as this has obvious advantages for constructing a cabinet government. It has the best people to elect a legislature, and therefore it may fairly be expected to choose a good legislature— a legislature competent to select a good administration.

England is the type of deferential countries, and the manner in which it is so, and has become so, is extremely curious. The middle classes—the ordinary majority of educated men—are in the present day the despotic power in England. "Public opinion," nowadays, "is the opinion of the bald-headed man at the back of the omnibus." It is *not* the opinion of the aristocratical classes as such; or of the most educated or refined classes as such; it is simply the opinion of the ordinary mass of educated, but still commonplace mankind. If you look at the mass of the constituencies, you will see that they are not very interesting people; and perhaps if you look behind the scenes and see the people who manipulate and work the constituencies, you will find that these are yet more uninteresting. The English constitution in its palpable form is this—the mass of the people yield obedience to a select few; and when you see this select few, you perceive that though not of the lowest class, nor of an unrespectable class, they are yet of a heavy sensible class—the last people in the world to whom, if they were drawn up in a row, an immense nation would ever give an exclusive preference.

In fact, the mass of the English people yield a deference rather to something else than to their rulers. They defer to what we may call the *theatrical show* of society. A certain state passes before them; a certain pomp of great men; a certain spectacle of beautiful women;

a wonderful scene of wealth and enjoyment is displayed, and they are coerced by it. Their imagination is bowed down; they feel they are not equal to the life which is revealed to them. Courts and aristocracies have the great quality which rules the multitude, though philosophers can see nothing in it—visibility. Courtiers can do what others cannot. A common man may as well try to rival the actors on the stage in their acting, as the aristocracy in *their* acting. The higher world, as it looks from without, is a stage on which the actors walk their parts much better than the spectators can. This play is played in every district. Every rustic feels that his house is not like my lord's house; his life like my lord's life; his wife like my lady. The climax of the play is the Queen: nobody supposes that their house is like the court; their life like her life; her orders like their orders. There is in England a certain charmed spectacle which imposes on the many, and guides their fancies as it will. As a rustic on coming to London finds himself in presence of a great show and vast exhibition of inconceivable mechanical things, so by the structure of our society, he finds himself face to face with a great exhibition of political things which he could not have imagined, which he could not make—to which he feels in himself scarcely anything analogous.

Philosophers may deride this superstition, but its results are inestimable. By the spectacle of this august society, countless ignorant men and women are induced to obey the few nominal electors—the £10 borough renters, and the £50 county renters—who have nothing imposing about them, nothing which would attract the eye or fascinate the fancy. What impresses men is not mind, but the result of mind. And the greatest of these results is this wonderful spectacle of society, which is ever new, and yet ever the same; in which accidents pass and essence remains; in which one generation dies and another succeeds, as if they were birds in a cage or animals in a menagerie; of which it seems almost more than a metaphor to treat the parts as limbs of a perpetual living thing, so silently do they seem to change, so wonderfully and so perfectly does the conspicuous life of the new year take the place of the conspicuous life of last year. The apparent rulers of the English nation are like the most imposing personages of a splendid procession: it is by them the mob are influenced; it is they whom the spectators cheer. The real rulers are secreted in second-rate carriages; no one cares for them or asks about them, but they are obeyed implicitly and unconsciously by reason of the splendour of those who eclipsed and preceded them.

59. [THE EXTENSION OF THE SUFFRAGE]

by JOHN STUART MILL

The greatest intellectual figure among the radicals of the nineteenth century was John Stuart Mill (1806–1873). A child of Utilitarianism (for his father, James Mill, was a close disciple of Jeremy Bentham), and filled with zeal to promote the good of the community, Mill ultimately escaped from the limitations of his environment. To Gladstone he was the "saint of rationalism"; to others he was the apostle of individualism and the champion of women's rights. These passages from his *Considerations on Representative Government* (1861), pp. 156–176, show his dilemma of how to reconcile democratic convictions with apprehension of working-class power.

. . . ALL trust in constitutions is grounded on the assurance they may afford, not that the depositaries of power will not, but that they cannot, misemploy it. Democracy is not the ideally best form of government unless this weak side of it can be strengthened; unless it can be so organized that no class, not even the most numerous, shall be able to reduce all but itself to political insignificance, and direct the course of legislation and administration by its exclusive class interest. The problem is, to find the means of preventing this abuse, without sacrificing the characteristic advantages of popular government.

These twofold requisites are not fulfilled by the expedient of a limitation of the suffrage, involving the compulsory exclusion of any portion of the citizens from a voice in the representation. Among the foremost benefits of free government is that education of the intelligence and of the sentiments, which is carried down to the very lowest ranks of the people when they are called to take a part in acts which directly affect the great interests of their country.

. . . It is by political discussion that the manual labourer, whose employment is a routine, and whose way of life brings him in contact with no variety of impressions, circumstances, or ideas, is taught that remote causes, and events which take place far off, have a most sensible effect even on his personal interests; and it is from political discussion, and collective political action, that one whose daily occupations concentrate his interests in a small circle round himself, learns to feel for and with his fellow-citizens, and becomes consciously a member of a great community. But political discussions fly over the heads of those who have no votes, and are not endeavouring to acquire them. Their position, in comparison with the electors, is that of the audience in a court of justice, compared with the twelve men in the jury-box. It is not *their* suffrages that are asked, it is not their opinion that is sought to be influenced; the appeals are made, the arguments addressed, to others than them; nothing depends on the decision they may arrive at, and there is no necessity and very little inducement to them to come to any. Whoever, in an otherwise popular government, has no vote, and no prospect of obtaining it, will either be a permanent malcontent, or will feel as one whom the general affairs of society do not concern; for whom they are to be managed by others; who 'has no business with the laws except to obey them,' nor with public interests and concerns except as a looker-on. What he will know or care about them from this position, may partly be measured by what an average woman of the middle class knows and cares about politics, compared with her husband or brothers.

Independently of all these considerations, it is a personal injustice to withhold from any one, unless for the prevention of greater evils, the ordinary privilege of having his voice reckoned in the disposal of affairs in which he has the same interest as other people. If he is compelled to pay, if he may be compelled to fight, if he is required implictly to obey, he should be legally entitled to be told what for; to have his consent asked, and his opinion counted at its worth, though not at more than its worth. There ought to be no pariahs in a full-grown and civilized nation; no persons disqualified, except through their own default. Every one is degraded, whether aware of it or not, when other people, without consulting him, take upon themselves unlimited power to regulate his destiny. And even in a much more improved state than the human mind has ever yet reached, it is not in nature that they who are thus disposed of should meet with as fair play as those who have a voice. Rulers and ruling classes are under a necessity of considering the interests and wishes of those who have the suffrage; but of those who are excluded, it is in their option whether they will do so or not; and however honestly disposed, they are in general too fully occupied with things which they *must* attend to, to have much room in their thoughts for anything which they can with impunity disregard. No arrangement of the suffrage, therefore, can be permanently satisfactory, in which any person or class is peremptorily excluded; in which the electoral privilege is not open to all persons of full age who desire to obtain it.

There are, however, certain exclusions, required by positive reasons, which do not conflict with this principle, and which, though an evil in themselves, are only to be got rid of by the cessation of the state of things which requires them. I regard it as wholly inadmissible that any person should participate in the suffrage, without being able to read, write, and, I will add, perform the common operations of arithmetic. Justice demands, even when the suffrage does not depend on it, that the means of attaining these elementary acquirements should be within the reach of every person, either gratuitously, or at an expense not exceeding what the poorest, who earn their own living, can afford. . . .

It is also important, that the assembly which votes the taxes, either general or local, should be elected exclusively by those who pay something towards the taxes imposed. Those who pay no taxes, disposing by their votes of other people's money, have every motive to be lavish, and none to economize. As far as money matters are concerned, any power of voting possessed by them is a violation of the fundamental principle of free government; a severance of the power of control, from the interest in its beneficial exercise. It amounts to allowing them to put their hands into other people's pockets, for any purpose which they think fit to call a public one. . . . That representation should be co-extensive with taxation, not stopping short of it, but also not going beyond it, is in accordance with the theory of British institutions. But to reconcile this, as a condition annexed to the representation, with universality, it is essential, as it is on many other accounts desirable, that taxation, in a visible shape, should descend to the poorest class.

. . . I regard it as required by first principles, that the receipt of parish relief should be a peremptory disqualification for the franchise. He who cannot by his labour suffice for his own support, has no claim to the privilege of helping himself to the money of others. By becoming dependent on the remaining members of the community for actual subsistence, he abdicates his claim to equal rights with them in other respects. . . .

In the long run, therefore (supposing no restrictions to exist but those of which we have now treated), we might expect that all, except that (it is to be hoped) progressively diminishing class, the recipients of parish relief, would be in possession of votes, so that the suffrage would be, with that slight abatement, universal. That it should be thus widely expanded, is, as we have seen, absolutely necessary to an enlarged and elevated conception of good government. Yet in this state of things, the great majority of voters, in most countries, and emphatically in this, would be manual labourers; and the twofold danger, that of too low a standard of political intelligence, and that of class legislation, would still exist, in a very perilous degree. It remains to be seen whether any means exist by which these evils can be obviated.

They are capable of being obviated, if men sincerely wish it; not by any artificial contrivance, but by carrying out the natural order of human life, which recommends itself to every one in things in which he has no interest or traditional opinion running counter to it. In all human affairs, every person directly interested, and not under positive tutelage, has an admitted claim to a voice, and when his exercise of it is not inconsistent with the safety of the whole, cannot justly be excluded from it. But though every one ought to have a voice—that every one should have an equal voice is a totally different proposition.

. . . An employer of labour is on the average more intelligent than a labourer; for he must labour with his head, and not solely with his hands. A foreman is generally more intelligent than an ordinary labourer, and a labourer in the skilled trades than in the unskilled. A banker, merchant, or manufacturer, is likely to be more intelligent than a tradesman, because he has larger and more complicated interests to manage. In all these cases it is not the having merely undertaken the superior function, but the successful performance of it, that tests the qualifications; for which reason, as well as to prevent persons from engaging nominally in an occupation for the sake of the vote, it would be proper to require that the occupation should have been persevered in for some length of time (say three years). Subject to some such condition, two or more votes might be allowed to every person who exercises any of these superior functions. The liberal professions, when really and not nominally practised, imply, of course, a still higher degree of instruction; and wherever a sufficient examination, or any serious conditions of education, are required before entering on a profession, its members could be admitted at once to a plurality of votes. The same rule might be applied to graduates of universities; and even to those who bring satisfactory certificates of having passed through the course of study required by any school at which the higher branches of knowledge are taught, under proper securities that the teaching is real, and not a mere pretence. . . .

In the preceding argument for universal, but graduated suffrage, I have taken no account of difference of sex. I consider it to be entirely irrelevant to political rights, as difference in height, or in the colour of the hair. All human beings have the same interest in good government; the welfare of all is alike affected by it, and they have equal need of a voice in it to secure their share of its benefits. If there be any difference, women require it more than men, since, being physically weaker, they are more dependent on law and society for protection. Mankind have long since abandoned the only premises which will support the conclusion that women ought not to have votes. No one now holds that women should be in personal servitude; that they should have no thought, wish, or occupation, but to be the domestic drudges of husbands, fathers, or brothers. It is allowed to unmarried, and wants but little of being conceded to married women, to hold property, and have pecuniary and business interests, in the same manner as men. It is considered suitable and proper that women should think, and write, and be teachers. As soon as these things are admitted, the political disqualification has no principle to rest on. The whole mode of thought of the modern world is, with increasing emphasis, pronouncing against the claim of society to decide for individuals what they are and are not fit for, and what they shall and shall not be allowed to attempt. . . .

60. [THE DANGERS OF DEMOCRACY]

by ROBERT LOWE

"He cannot help being brilliant," wrote Walter Bagehot of his contemporary, Robert Lowe (1811–1892); and it was this dazzling intellectualism of the Oxford first-class mind which was both Lowe's strength and undoing. As a Liberal M.P. he became the most formidable opponent of an extension of the franchise and the leader of a small group in the Commons labelled by John Bright the Adullamites (since they formed a cabal, sheltering in their cave). Lowe's fear of democracy was based essentially on his conviction that government should be in the hands of an elite—not an elite of birth but of intellect and ability. This passage is from the preface to his *Speeches and Letters on Reform* (1867), pp. 3–16.

NO assertion is more frequently met with in the speeches of the supporters of a democratic Reform than this,—that the arguments are all on one side, that the question is an easy one, depending merely on arithmetic, and such as any man possessed of ordinary common sense may decide on the first inspection. To me the question appears very difficult to treat in a popular, and, at the same time, in a fair and intelligible way, because it involves not merely the balancing of adverse arguments, but a decision as to what kind of argument should have weight on such a subject. A consideration of the speeches delivered on both sides will show that the arguments in favour of Democracy are mostly metaphysical, resting on considerations prior to, and therefore independent of, experience, appealing to abstract maxims and terms, and treating this peculiarly practical subject as if it were a problem of pure geometry. The arguments against a democratic change, on the other hand, are all drawn, or profess to be drawn, from considerations purely practical. The one side deals in such terms as right, equality, justice; the other, with the working of institutions, with their faults, with their remedies, with the probable influence which such changes will exert. Are both these methods right, and if not both, which of the two? There are, as a great thinker has taught, three ways of treating political subjects:—the Theological, the Metaphysical, and the Inductive, or experimental. The doctrine of the divine right of kings is an instance of the first kind of treatment of a political subject; the argument so much relied on at Reform meetings in favour of extended suffrage, and the writings of James and John Mill, are examples of the second; and discussions of the House of Commons on almost every other subject except Reform, and the arguments against Reform, of the third. It is considered, I believe, by most thinkers that the second of these methods is superior to the first, and the third superior to the first and second—so superior as entirely to supersede them, and to afford the only safe guide in political and in many other branches of speculation. I certainly entertain this opinion. When I find a book or a speech appealing to abstract *a priori* principles I put it aside in despair, being well aware that I can learn nothing useful from it. Such works only present to us the limited and qualified propositions which experience has established, without their limitations and qualifications, and elevate them into principles by a rash generalization which strips them of whatever truth they originally possessed. Thus the words *right* and *equality* have a perfectly clear and defined meaning when applied to the administration of justice under a settled law, but are really without meaning, except as vague and inappropriate metaphors, when applied to the distribution of political power. The proper answer to a statement, for instance, that all men free from crime or pauperism have a right to the franchise, is—that this is a question of experience, not of *a priori* assumption, and that the assertion, whether true or false, is inadmissible in political discussion. But how is this truth to be made evident to a large multitude when we find men from whom better things might have been expected, speaking of those who deny the existence of rights as if they sought to deprive men of something they really possess, instead of to explode a vague and meaningless assumption? The position may be further illustrated by observing, that if the propositions of this nature which we hear were true, they would not lead, as they do, to false conclusions, such as—that men, women, and children, should have the franchise; that this right applies to every race in the world; that this right being prior to and independent of experience cannot be limited by experience, and that it is therefore the duty of a State to do what may be foreseen to lead to immediate ruin in order to satisfy these abstract principles which it has imposed on itself as its guides. The first step, therefore, in the discussion of democratic changes is to clear the mind of these delusive notions, and to employ the teaching of experience, not to qualify or limit, but absolutely to supersede them.

What, then, is the professed object of Reform? It is to improve the structure of the House of Commons. The natural order of investigation is—What are the faults which require correction, and then how will the proposed measures cure those faults? Passion or party spirit may drive men to plunge into the details of a Reform Bill without clearly putting to themselves and answering these questions, but no really conscientious investigator can pass them by unconsidered.

. . . It is not for the evils that exist, but for the evils which it is in its power to prevent, that Parliament should be held responsible. Everybody admits this when he judges another in private life, but when we are dealing with public bodies, we cast candour aside, and censure them for things over which they have no control, or which they have done very wisely to let alone. The theory of uneducated or half-educated persons in general is, that Government is almost omnipotent, and that when an evil is not remedied the fault lies in the indolence, the selfishness, or the shortsightedness of Parliament. It is much pleasanter to an audience of non-electors to be told that the franchise would enable them to remedy the evils of their condition than to be told the real truth, that the evils they endure are remediable by themselves, in their individual rather than in their collective capacity—by their own thrift and self-denial, not by pressing on Government to do that for them which they are able, if they will, to do without it. It were ludicrous, if it were not so sad, to hear speeches which urge working-men to seek for the franchise, that they may compel Parliament to compel them to educate their children, or to practise an involuntary abstinence from intoxicating liquors. When one man is willing to sell his vote and another to buy it, what machinery does Parliament possess to prevent a secret bargain for its purchase? The Ballot nowhere secures secrecy, and the elections of America show that in large constituencies bribery is used as well as in small, especially when parties are evenly divided. Till Parliament can give health, strength, providence, and self-control, how can it deal with the evil of pauperism? If the poor were willing to pay a rent sufficient to provide them with decent and healthy dwellings, capital would flow into the business just as it does into the business of building public-houses and gin-shops. With what justice can Parliament be called upon to tax the community at large for that which it is in the power of all who receive fair wages to provide for themselves? These may suffice as specimens of the complaints of neglect of the interests of the poor which are brought against Parliament. Parliament does not command boundless resources. A course of the kind indicated would be felt very sensibly in heavier taxation, and a violation of sound principles would avenge itself on the very classes for whose supposed interest they were violated.

The attempts to enlarge the sphere of Government action, which the impatience of benevolent persons urges upon us, can only be made at a heavy sacrifice of individual liberty. It is said Parliament should remedy the unequal distribution of land. This can only be done by curtailing individual liberty of disposition. That it should give compensation for improvements to tenants, this can only be done by invading the freedom of contract. Is it not at least conceivable that a Legislature which declines to enter on this retrograde course may be in the right, and actuated by better motives than prejudice in favour of one class or antipathy to another?

For my own part, I disclaim such motives. The end of good government appears to me to be the good of all, and, if that be not attainable, the good of the majority; but I must pause when I am told that the majority, told by the head, should have the supreme power because they will be sure to do that which is for their own interest. If this be so, the solution of all questions is easy indeed. Let us burn our books, and send round the ballot-box on every question as it arises? No position can be more unsound. If the Queen's Council, as the men of Kent complained, be no good craftsmen, neither are good craftsmen necessarily wise councillors. I cannot blow a glass bottle because it would be my interest to do so, nor discern political truth merely because I shall suffer if I am wrong. *Cuique in suâ arte credendum.* The popular view of the obstacles which prevent the accomplishment of our wishes for the happiness of our fellow-creatures is, that there is a want of good-will in those who have the power to make laws, while the view which is forced on every thoughtful man who has practical experience of human affairs, is, that the real obstacle is most frequently the difficulty of knowing how the end is to be gained. The more complicated and artificial society becomes, and the better we know the principles which underlie all sound legislation, the more difficult do we find it to do things which to our ancestors, three hundred years ago, presented no difficulty at all. Protection, for instance, is the political economy of the poor, simply because they are not able to follow the chain of reasoning which demonstrates that they themselves are sure to be the victims of the waste of capital which protection implies. I dare say that a democratic House of Commons would deal with many of these questions, especially those relating to protection, to the distribution of wealth, and the giving direct assistance to the poor from the public purse; but that does not prove that they would, by doing so, benefit the poor, or that the interest of the poor would be promoted by placing in their hands a more extended power of injuring themselves. From these considerations, it follows that, of those things which Parliament is blamed for not doing, many are impossible, others inexpedient, while some, such as the regulation of sanitary matters, have actually been attained without our censors being aware of it; that what is wanted is not more power to urge on change, but more intelligence to decide on what that change ought to be, and therefore that the standard of intelligence, in constituencies or members, should on no account be lowered, nor the impulse to inconsiderate action increased.

. . . But I would point out that the working classes, under the modest claim to share in electoral power, are really asking for the whole of it. Their claim is to pass from the position of non-electors to the position of sovereign arbiters in the last resort of the destinies of the nation. They who set up such a claim must show that they are masters of themselves before they can hope to be masters of others. One of the first qualifications for power should be the willingness to hear both sides—those who say what is unpleasing, as well as those who say what is smooth. They must not seek to limit the field of discussion by their own susceptibilities. They must expect to be critically surveyed and canvassed before they can persuade the present depositaries of power to abdicate in their favour. If it is competent to me to argue that with a little self-denial the franchise is already within the reach of many of them; that they will swamp the less numerous classes; that the expenses of elections will be increased, and the character of the House of Commons impaired; it is also competent for me to urge that since corruption and the other electoral vices prevail most in the lower ranks of the present constituencies, it is unwise and unsafe to go lower in search of electoral virtue. It is no answer to such an argument to abuse its author. Either the statement is false, in which case it can be refuted, and will only recoil upon him who made it, or it is true, in which case it is worthy of the most serious consideration, not only by the upper classes, but by the very class which is instructed to resent it, because that class more than any other will suffer if Parliament should, through any ill-considered change, become less fit for the discharge of its duties.

61. [THE DEMAND FOR PARLIAMENTARY REFORM]

by JOHN BRIGHT

Not all participants in the great debate on democracy in the 1860s argued with the intellectual depth of a Mill or a

Lowe. John Bright (1811–1889) spoke as a nonconformist manufacturer and the leader of middle-class parliamentary radicalism. His was the voice of that liberal individualism which had earlier triumphed in the struggle of the Anti-Corn Law League, and which was sustained throughout all vicissitudes by a strong religious faith. This speech was made in Birmingham town hall on Jan. 18, 1865. (*Speeches by John Bright,* James E. Thorold Rogers, ed. [1869], Vol. II, pp. 111–127).

. . . THE Tories, and those Whigs who are like Tories, have an uncomfortable feeling which approaches almost to a shiver. What is this apparition which alarms them? . . . I will tell you what it is. They are afraid of the five or six millions of Englishmen, grown-up men who are allowed to marry, to keep house, to rear children, who are expected to earn their living, who pay taxes, who must obey the law, who must be citizens in all honourable conduct—they are afraid of the five or six millions who by the present system of representation are shut out, and insultingly shut out, from the commonest rights of citizenship.

. . . You know the boast we have of what takes place when negro-slaves land in England; you know what one of our best poets has said, that if their lungs but breathe our air, that moment they are free; they touch our country, and their shackles fall. But how is it with an Englishman? An Englishman, if he goes to the Cape, can vote; if he goes further, to Australia, to the nascent empires of the New World, he can vote; if he goes to the Canadian Confederation, he can vote; and if he goes to those grandest colonies of England not now dependent upon the English Crown, there, in twenty free, and, in the whole, in thirty-five different States, he can give his free and independent vote. It is only in his own country, on his own soil, where he was born, the very soil which he has enriched with his labour and with the sweat of his brow, that he is denied this right which in every other community of Englishmen in the world would be freely accorded to him.

. . . This state of things I hold to be dangerous, and one that cannot last. It may happen, as it happened thirty years ago, that the eyes of the five millions all through the United Kingdom may be fixed with an intense glare upon the doors of Parliament; it was so in the years 1831–32. There are men in this room who felt then, and know

now, that it required but an accident—but one spark to the train, and this country would have been in the throes of revolution; and these gentlemen who are so alarmed now lest a man who lives in a 10*l*. house in a county, and a 6*l*. house in a borough, should have a vote, would have repented in sackcloth and ashes that they had ever said one word or given one vote against Lord Grey's Reform Bill. I say that accidents always are happening, not to individuals only, but to nations. It was the accident of the French Revolution of 1830 that preceded that great movement in this country. You may have accidents again, but I do not hold that to be statesmanship which allows the security, the tranquillity, the loyalty of a people to be disturbed by any accident which they are able to control. If the five millions should once unitedly fix their eyes with an intense look upon the door of that House where my hon. Friend and I expect so soon to enter, I would ask who shall say them nay? Not the mace upon the table of the House; not the four hundred easy gentlemen of the House of Lords who lounge in and out of that decorated chamber; not the dozen gentlemen who call themselves statesmen, and who meet in Downing-street; perhaps not even those more appalling and more menacing personages who have their lodgment higher up Whitehall. I say there is no power in this country, as opinion now stands, and as combination is now possible, there is no power in this country that can say 'Nay' for one single week to the five millions, if they are intent upon making their way within the doors of Parliament. . . .

But perhaps our friends who oppose us will say, 'We do not fear about elections and order. What we fear is this—the legislative results of this wide extension of the franchise.' I am ready to test it in any country by the results of legislation. I say, whether you go to South Africa, or to Australia, or to the British North American provinces, or to the States of the American Union, you will find—excluding always those States where slavery injures the state of society—you will find that life and property are as secure, you will find that education is much more extended amongst the people, that there is quite as wide a provision for their religious interests, that the laws are as merciful and just, that taxes are imposed and levied with as great equality, and that the millions of your countrymen who are now established in those countries are at least as well off in all the circumstances of life as are the people of this country whom they have left behind them. I confess that I never yet heard of a man who returned to this country from any of those countries under the impression that he would be more secure here than he would be there. . . .

But this, I suspect, is what they fear. I have sought a good deal into this question, and it seems to me as if they had a notion that in this country we have some institutions which have come down to us from the middle ages—from what some people call the dark ages—and that these institutions may not permanently harmonize with the intelligence and the necessities of the nineteenth century in which we live. The 'institutions' are truly safe enough if the Government be in the hands of the institution; and if the Peerage and the Established Church are to rule in England, then I presume that the Peerage and the Established Church, in their present condition, will be permanently safe; and if the great patronage of our vast expenditure is to be dispensed perpetually amongst the ruling class, the ruling class as a matter of course will take extreme care of the patronage. There is something very sacred in that patronage. There are many families in this country with long lines of ancestry, who, if patronage were curtailed, would feel very much as some of us feel in Lancashire when the American war has stopped our supplies of cotton. They look upon patronage as a holy thing, not to be touched by profane hands.

. . . These gentlemen do not comprehend our Constitution at all. They do not know, apparently, that it is only because there is something which the people still believe to be in some degree a representative body, and which stands between them and monarchical and aristocratic despotism—that it is only the existence of that House which makes the institution they are so fond of safe and permanent at all—and they are afraid that the five millions somehow or other will get into it. Now, I beg to tell them that the five millions will get into it, though they may not get into it all at once; and perhaps few men desire that they should, for I am opposed myself to great and violent changes, which create needless shocks, and which are accepted, if they are accepted, with great alarm.

But I will undertake to say that some portion, a considerable and effective portion, of those five millions will before many years are passed be freely allowed to vote for Members of the House of Commons. It is not the democracy which these gentlemen are always afraid of that is the peril of this country. It was not democracy in 1832 that was the peril. It was the desperate antagonism of the class that then had power to the just claims and rights of the people. And at this moment, when they dine and when I speak, I tell them that Conservatism—they give it that name, but it is worthy of a very different name—that Conservatism, be it Tory or be it Whig, is the true national peril which we have to face. They may dam the stream, they may keep back the waters, but the volume is ever increasing, and it descends with accelerated force, and the time will come when, in all probability, and to a certainty, if wisdom does not take the place of folly, the waters will burst their banks, and these men, who fancy they are stemming this imaginary apparition of democracy, will be swept away by the resolute will of a united and determined people.

Chapter 13.
Religion and Science

At the meeting of the British Association in Oxford in June 1860 the most sensational episode was the discussion of Charles Darwin's recently published book, *The Origin of Species*. The climax of the attack on Darwin's theory of evolution came when Bishop Wilberforce turned with affected politeness to Professor Huxley and "begged to know, was it through his grandfather or his grandmother that he claimed descent from a monkey?" Huxley, who had been wondering how best to refute Wilberforce's ignorant but popular remarks, slapped his knee and murmured softly to his neighbor, "The Lord hath delivered him into mine hands." He then rose to his feet and quietly but effectively exposed the shallowness of the Bishop's argument, adding that although he would not be ashamed to have a monkey for his ancestor, he would be "ashamed to be connected with a man who used great gifts to obscure the truth."

This incident dramatized an intellectual conflict that had been growing steadily during the previous decades, and which after 1859 burst forth with heated publicity. *The Origin of Species* was an epoch-making book, in the sense that it altered irrevocably the direction of men's thought. After its publication it was no longer possible for intelligent men to go on thinking in the same way as they had done previously. This of course was profoundly disquieting and its implications were at first fiercely resisted. By the end of the century it was apparent that what had begun as an intellectual, scientific revolt against traditional authority had become a challenge to the moral, religious, and social bases of Victorian England.

The mood of doubt and questioning of religious faith had been present always in the nineteenth century. Religious orthodoxy had been challenged by the historical criticism of the Bible and by geological discoveries before 1859. There were also those, like George Eliot and Francis Newman, who were outraged by the apparent immorality of

some aspects of Christian teaching. The *Origin* presented
a mass of data which could only be explained by a theory
of evolution which seemed to destroy many traditional
Christian doctrines. By the 1860s the need to reconcile
science and Christian belief was considered the most important question of the day by many liberal churchmen.
But the Broad Churchmen who attempted this task earned
few thanks from either the Evangelicals or the Tractarians.

62. THE ORIGIN OF SPECIES

by THOMAS HENRY HUXLEY

It was fortunate for the cause of Darwinism that it found
such an able defender and propagandist as Thomas Henry
Huxley (1825–1895). Charles Darwin was by nature a
sickly, retiring Victorian gentleman, and no suitable leader
for a movement which started as a scientific theory but soon
became a national debate on fundamental questions of religion and ethics. Huxley's review of the *Origin* appeared in
the *Westminster Review*, April 1860, and was reprinted in
his *Lay Sermons, Addresses and Reviews* (1870). These extracts are from pp. 279–297.

THE hypotheses respecting the origin of species which profess to
stand upon a scientific basis, and, as such, alone demand serious attention, are of two kinds. The one, the "special creation" hypothesis,
presumes every species to have originated from one or more stocks,
these not being the result of the modification of any other form of
living matter—or arising by natural agencies—but being produced,
as such, by a supernatural creative act.

The other, the so-called "transmutation" hypothesis, considers that
all existing species are the result of the modification of pre-existing
species, and those of their predecessors, by agencies similar to those
which at the present day produce varieties and races, and therefore
in an altogether natural way; and it is a probable, though not a
necessary consequence of this hypothesis, that all living beings have
arisen from a single stock. With respect to the origin of this primitive
stock, or stocks, the doctrine of the origin of species is obviously
not necessarily concerned. The transmutation hypothesis, for example,

is perfectly consistent either with the conception of a special creation of the primitive germ, or with the supposition of its having arisen, as a modification of inorganic matter, by natural causes.

The doctrine of special creation owes its existence very largely to the supposed necessity of making science accord with the Hebrew cosmogony; but it is curious to observe that, as the doctrine is at present maintained by men of science, it is as hopelessly inconsistent with the Hebrew view as any other hypothesis.

. . . Deserving no aid from the powerful arm of bibliolatry, then, does the received form of the hypothesis of special creation derive any support from science or sound logic? Assuredly not much. The arguments brought forward in its favour all take one form: If species were not supernaturally created, we cannot understand the facts *x*, or *y*, or *z*; we cannot understand the structure of animals or plants, unless we suppose they were contrived for special ends; we cannot understand the structure of the eye, except by supposing it to have been made to see with; we cannot understand instincts, unless we suppose animals to have been miraculously endowed with them.

As a question of dialectics, it must be admitted that this sort of reasoning is not very formidable to those who are not to be frightened by consequences. It is an *argumentum ad ignorantiam*—take this explanation or be ignorant. But suppose we prefer to admit our ignorance rather than adopt a hypothesis at variance with all the teachings of Nature? Or, suppose for a moment we admit the explanation, and then seriously ask ourselves how much the wiser are we; what does the explanation explain? Is it any more than a grandiloquent way of announcing the fact, that we really know nothing about the matter? A phenomenon is explained when it is shown to be a case of some general law of Nature; but the supernatural interposition of the Creator can, by the nature of the case, exemplify no law, and if species have really arisen in this way, it is absurd to attempt to discuss their origin.

Or, lastly, let us ask ourselves whether any amount of evidence which the nature of our faculties permits us to attain, can justify us in asserting that any phenomenon is out of the reach of natural causation. To this end it is obviously necessary that we should know all the consequences to which all possible combinations, continued through unlimited time, can give rise. If we knew these, and found none competent to originate species, we should have good ground for denying their origin by natural causation. Till we know them, any hypothesis is better than one which involves us in such miserable presumption.

But the hypothesis of special creation is not only a mere specious mask for our ignorance; its existence in Biology marks the youth and imperfection of the science. For what is the history of every science but the history of the elimination of the notion of creative, or other interferences, with the natural order of the phenomena which are the subject-matter of that science? . . .

The Darwinian hypothesis has the merit of being eminently simple and comprehensible in principle, and its essential positions may be stated in a very few words: all species have been produced by the development of varieties from common stocks by the conversion of these first into permanent races and then into new species, by the process of *natural selection,* which process is essentially identical with that artificial selection by which man has originated the races of domestic animals—the *struggle for existence* taking the place of man, and exerting, in the case of natural selection, that selective action which he performs in artificial selection.

The evidence brought forward by Mr. Darwin in support of his hypothesis is of three kinds. First, he endeavours to prove that species may be originated by selection; secondly, he attempts to show that natural causes are competent to exert selection; and thirdly, he tries to prove that the most remarkable and apparently anomalous phenomena exhibited by the distribution, development, and mutual relations of species, can be shown to be deducible from the general doctrine of their origin, which he propounds, combined with the known facts of geological change; and that, even if all these phenomena are not at present explicable by it, none are necessarily inconsistent with it.

There cannot be a doubt that the method of inquiry which Mr. Darwin has adopted is not only rigorously in accordance with the canons of scientific logic, but that it is the only adequate method. Critics exclusively trained in classics or in mathematics, who have never determined a scientific fact in their lives by induction from experiment or observation, prate learnedly about Mr. Darwin's method, which is not inductive enough, not Baconian enough, forsooth, for them. . . .

Now, the conditions which have determined the existence of species are not only exceedingly complex, but, so far as the great majority of them are concerned, are necessarily beyond our cognizance. But . . . Mr. Darwin . . . has endeavoured to determine certain great facts inductively, by observation and experiment; he has then reasoned from the data thus furnished; and lastly, he has tested the validity of his ratiocination by comparing his deductions with the observed facts of Nature. Inductively, Mr. Darwin endeavours to prove that species arise in a given way. Deductively, he desires to show that, if they arise in that way, the facts of distribution, development, classification, &c., may be accounted for, *i.e.* may be deduced from their mode of origin, combined with admitted changes in physical geography and climate, during an indefinite period. And this explanation, or coincidence of observed with deduced facts, is, so far as it extends, a verification of the Darwinian view.

. . . The discussion of Mr. Darwin's arguments in detail would lead us far beyond the limits within which we proposed, at starting, to confine this article. Our object has been attained if we have given an intelligible, however brief, account of the established facts connected with species, and of the relation of the explanation of those facts offered by Mr. Darwin to the theoretical views held by his predecessors and his contemporaries, and, above all, to the requirements of scientific logic. We have ventured to point out that it does not, as yet, satisfy all those requirements; but we do not hesitate to assert that it is as superior to any preceding or contemporary hypothesis, in the extent of observational and experimental basis on which it rests, in its rigorously scientific method, and in its power of explaining biological phenomena, as was the hypothesis of Copernicus to the speculations of Ptolemy. . . .

63. [THE REJECTION OF DARWINISM]

by SAMUEL WILBERFORCE

The first reaction of many churchmen to *The Origin of Species* was one of confusion and indignation. Prominent among the confident rejectors of Darwinism was the Bishop of Oxford, Samuel Wilberforce (1805–1873), a son of the great Evangelical, William Wilberforce (see Reading No. 26). "Soapy Sam," as he was nicknamed, was an able ecclesiastical administrator, but intellectually was no match for the able defenders of Darwin's views. This review of the *Origin* appeared in the *Quarterly Review*, Vol. 108 (1860), pp. 247–259.

WE come then to these conclusions. All the facts presented to us in the natural world tend to show that none of the variations produced in the fixed forms of animal life, when seen in its most plastic condition under domestication, give any promise of a true transmutation of species; first, from the difficulty of accumulating and fixing variations within the same species; secondly, from the fact that these variations, though most serviceable for man, have no tendency to improve the individual beyond the standard of his own specific type, and so to afford matter, even if they were infinitely produced, for the supposed power of natural selection on which to work; whilst all variations from the mixture of species are barred by the inexorable law of hybrid sterility. Further, the embalmed records of 3000 years show that there has been no beginning of transmutation in the species of our most familiar domesticated animals; and beyond this, that in the countless tribes of animal life around us, down to its lowest and most variable species, no one has ever discovered a single instance of such transmutation being now in prospect; no new organ has ever been known to be developed—no new natural instinct to be formed—whilst, finally, in the vast museum of departed animal life which the strata of the earth imbed for our examination, whilst they contain far too complete a representation of the past to be set aside as a mere imperfect record, yet afford no one instance of any such change as having ever been in progress, or give us anywhere the missing links of the assumed chain, or the remains which would enable now existing variations, by gradual approximations, to shade off into unity.

On what then is the new theory based? We say it with unfeigned regret, in dealing with such a man as Mr. Darwin, on the merest hypothesis, supported by the most unbounded assumptions. . . .

Mr. Darwin writes as a Christian, and we doubt not that he is one. We do not for a moment believe him to be one of those who retain in some corner of their hearts a secret unbelief which they dare not vent; and we therefore pray him to consider well the grounds on which we brand his speculations with the charge of such a tendency. First, then, he not obscurely declares that he applies his scheme of the action of the principle of natural selection to MAN himself, as well as to the animals around him. Now, we must say at once, and openly, that such a notion is absolutely incompatible not only with single expressions in the word of God on that subject of natural science with which it is not immediately concerned, but, which in our judgment is of far more importance, with the whole representation of that moral and spiritual condition of man which is its proper subject-matter. Man's derived supremacy over the earth; man's power of articulate speech; man's gift of reason; man's free-will and responsibility; man's fall and man's redemption; the incarnation of the Eternal Son; the indwelling of the Eternal Spirit,—all are equally and utterly irreconcilable with the degrading notion of the brute origin of him who was created in the image of God, and redeemed by the Eternal Son assuming to himself his nature. Equally inconsistent, too, not with any passing expressions, but with the whole scheme of God's dealings with man as recorded in His word, is Mr. Darwin's daring notion of man's further development into some unknown extent of powers, and shape, and size, through natural selection acting through that long vista of ages which he casts mistily over the earth upon the most favoured individuals of his species. We care not in these pages to push the argument further. We have done enough for our purpose in thus succinctly intimating its course. . . .

Nor can we doubt, secondly, that this view, which thus contradicts the revealed relation of creation to its Creator, is equally inconsistent with the fulness of His glory. It is, in truth, an ingenious theory for diffusing throughout creation the working and so the personality of the Creator. And thus, however unconsciously to him who holds them, such views really tend inevitably to banish from the mind most of the peculiar attributes of the Almighty.

How, asks Mr. Darwin, can we possibly account for the manifest plan, order, and arrangement which pervade creation, except we allow to it this self-developing power through modified descent? . . .

How can we account for all this? By the simplest and yet the most comprehensive answer. By declaring the stupendous fact that all creation is the transcript in matter of ideas eternally existing in the mind of the Most High—that order in the utmost perfectness of its relation pervades His works, because it exists as in its centre and highest fountain-head in Him the Lord of all. Here is the true account of the fact which has so utterly misled shallow observers, that Man himself, the Prince and Head of this creation, passes in the earlier stages of his being through phases of existence closely analogous, so far as his earthly tabernacle is concerned, to those in which the lower animals ever remain. At that point of being the development of the protozoa is arrested. Through it the embryo of their chief passes to the perfection of his earthly frame. But the types of those lower forms of being must be found in the animals which never advance beyond them—

not in man for whom they are but the foundation for an afterdevelopment; whilst he too, Creation's crown and perfection, thus bears witness in his own frame to the law of order which pervades the universe.

64. [GEOLOGY AND GENESIS]

by EDMUND GOSSE

The acute nature of the challenge of new scientific theories of evolution to traditional Christian interpretations of the Bible is brought out in the following passage from Sir Edmund Gosse's autobiography, *Father and Son* (1907), pp. 111–117, 128–129. His father, Philip Gosse (1810–1888) was a rather undistinguished naturalist who was also a zealous member of a fundamentalist sect, the Plymouth Brethren.

. . . THROUGH my Father's brain, in that year of scientific crisis, 1857, there rushed two kinds of thought, each absorbing, each convincing, yet totally irreconcilable. There is a peculiar agony in the paradox that truth has two forms, each of them indisputable, yet each antagonistic to the other. It was this discovery, that there were two theories of physical life, each of which was true, but the truth of each incompatible with the truth of the other, which shook the spirit of my Father with perturbation. It was not, really, a paradox, it was a fallacy, if he could only have known it, but he allowed the turbid volume of superstition to drown the delicate stream of reason. He took one step in the service of truth, and then he drew back in an agony, and accepted the servitude of error.

This was the great moment in the history of thought when the theory of the mutability of species was preparing to throw a flood of light upon all departments of human speculation and action. It was becoming necessary to stand emphatically in one army or the other. Lyell was surrounding himself with disciples, who were making strides in

the direction of discovery. Darwin had long been collecting facts with
regard to the variation of animals and plants. Hooker and Wallace,
Asa Gray and even Agassiz, each in his own sphere, were coming
closer and closer to a perception of that secret which was first to reveal itself clearly to the patient and humble genius of Darwin. In the
year before, in 1856, Darwin, under pressure from Lyell, had begun
that modest statement of the new revelation, that 'abstract of an
essay,' which developed so mightily into 'The Origin of Species.' Wol-
laston's 'Variation of Species' had just appeared, and had been a nine
days' wonder in the wilderness.

On the other side, the reactionaries, although never dreaming of the
fate which hung over them, had not been idle. In 1857 the astounding
question had for the first time been propounded with contumely,
'What, then, did we come from orang-outang?' The famous 'Vestiges
of Creation' had been supplying a sugar-and-water panacea for those
who could not escape from the trend of evidence, and who yet clung
to revelation. Owen was encouraging reaction by resisting, with all
the strength of his prestige, the theory of the mutability of species.

In this period of intellectual ferment, as when a great political
revolution is being planned, many possible adherents were confi-
dentially tested with hints and encouraged to reveal their bias in
a whisper. It was the notion of Lyell, himself a great mover of men,
that, before the doctrine of natural selection was given to a world
which would be sure to lift up at it a howl of execration, a certain
body-guard of sound and experienced naturalists, expert in the description of species, should be privately made aware of its tenour.
Among those who were thus initiated, or approached with a view
towards possible illumination, was my Father. He was spoken to by
Hooker, and later on by Darwin, after meetings of the Royal Society
in the summer of 1857.

My Father's attitude towards the theory of natural selection was
critical in his career, and oddly enough, it exercised an immense influence on my own experience as a child. Let it be admitted at once,
mournful as the admission is, that every instinct in his intelligence
went out at first to greet the new light. It had hardly done so, when
a recollection of the opening chapter of 'Genesis' checked it at the
outset. He consulted with Carpenter, a great investigator, but one who
was fully as incapable as himself of remodelling his ideas with regard
to the old, accepted hypotheses. They both determined, on various
grounds, to have nothing to do with the terrible theory, but to hold

steadily to the law of the fixity of species. It was exactly at this juncture that we left London, and the slight and occasional, but always extremely salutary personal intercourse with men of scientific leading which my Father had enjoyed at the British Museum and at the Royal Society came to an end. His next act was to burn his ships, down to the last beam and log out of which a raft could have been made. By a strange act of wilfulness, he closed the doors upon himself for ever.

My Father had never admired Sir Charles Lyell. I think that the famous 'Lord Chancellor manner' of the geologist intimidated him, and we undervalue the intelligence of those whose conversation puts us at a disadvantage. For Darwin and Hooker, on the other hand, he had a profound esteem, and I know not whether this had anything to do with the fact that he chose, for his impetuous experiment in reaction, the field of geology, rather than that of zoology or botany. Lyell had been threatening to publish a book on the geological history of Man, which was to be a bomb-shell flung into the camp of the catastrophists. My Father, after long reflection, prepared a theory of his own, which, as he fondly hoped, would take the wind out of Lyell's sails, and justify geology to godly readers of 'Genesis.' It was, very briefly, that there had been no gradual modification of the surface of the earth, or slow development of organic forms, but that when the catastrophic act of creation took place, the world presented, instantly, the structural appearance of a planet on which life had long existed.

The theory, coarsely enough, and to my Father's great indignation, was defined by a hasty press as being this—that God hid the fossils in the rocks in order to tempt geologists into infidelity. In truth, it was the logical and inevitable conclusion of accepting, literally, the doctrine of a sudden act of creation; it emphasised the fact that any breach in the circular course of nature could be conceived only on the supposition that the object created bore false witness to past processes, which had never taken place. For instance, Adam would certainly possess hair and teeth and bones in a condition which it must have taken many years to accomplish, yet he was created full-grown yesterday. He would certainly—though Sir Thomas Browne denied it—display an 'omphalos,' yet no umbilical cord had ever attached him to a mother.

Never was a book cast upon the waters with greater anticipations of success than was this curious, this obstinate, this fanatical volume. My Father lived in a fever of suspense, waiting for the tremendous issue. This 'Omphalos' of his, he thought, was to bring all the turmoil of scientific speculation to a close, fling geology into the arms of Scripture, and make the lion eat grass with the lamb. It was not surprising, he admitted, that there had been experienced an ever-increasing discord between the facts which geology brings to light and the direct statements of the early chapters of 'Genesis.' Nobody was to blame for that. My Father, and my Father alone, possessed the secret of the enigma; he alone held the key which could smoothly open the lock of geological mystery. He offered it, with a glowing gesture, to atheists and Christians alike. This was to be the universal panacea; this the system of intellectual therapeutics which could not but heal all the maladies of the age. But, alas! atheists and Christians alike looked at it, and laughed, and threw it away.

In the course of that dismal winter, as the post began to bring in private letters, few and chilly, and public reviews, many and scornful, my Father looked in vain for the approval of the churches, and in vain for the acquiescence of the scientific societies, and in vain for the gratitude of those 'thousands of thinking persons,' which he had rashly assured himself of receiving. As his reconciliation of Scripture statements and geological deductions was welcomed nowhere; as Darwin continued silent, and the youthful Huxley was scornful, and even Charles Kingsley, from whom my Father had expected the most instant appreciation, wrote that he could not 'give up the painful and slow conclusion of five and twenty years' study of geology, and believe that God has written on the rocks one enormous and superfluous lie,'—as all this happened or failed to happen, a gloom, cold and dismal, descended upon our morning teacups.

Up to this point in his career, [my Father] had . . . nourished the delusion that science and revelation could be mutually justified, that some sort of compromise was possible. With great and ever greater distinctness, his investigations had shown him that in all departments of organic nature there are visible the evidences of slow modification of forms, of the type developed by the pressure and practice of aeons. This conviction had been borne in upon him until it was positively irresistible. Where was his place, then, as a sincere and accurate observer? Manifestly, it was with the pioneers of the new truth, it was with Darwin, Wallace and Hooker. But did not the second chapter of 'Genesis' say that in six days the heavens and earth were finished, and the host of them, and that on the seventh day God ended his work which he had made?

Here was a dilemma! Geology certainly *seemed* to be true, but the Bible, which was God's word, *was* true. If the Bible said that all things in Heaven and Earth were created in six days, created in six days they were,—in six literal days of twenty-four hours each. The evidences of spontaneous variation of form, acting, over an immense space of time, upon ever-modifying organic structures, *seemed* overwhelming, but they must either be brought into line with the six-day labour of creation, or they must be rejected. . . .

65. THE INTERPRETATION OF SCRIPTURE

by BENJAMIN JOWETT

It is difficult today, after reading *Essays and Reviews*, to appreciate the furor which this book aroused after its publication in 1860. Few of the opinions of the seven authors (six clergy and a pious layman) would not now be accepted without difficulty by most Christians; yet the writers were denounced as "septem contra Christum," two of them were brought to trial for heresy, and the volume was condemned by Convocation. The most significant essay was that by Benjamin Jowett (1817–1893) on "The Interpretation of Scripture." Jowett was Regius Professor of Greek in the University of Oxford and later Master of Balliol College. The following extracts are from *Essays and Reviews* (12th ed., 1865), pp. 453–512.

. . . AS the time has come when it is no longer possible to ignore the results of criticism, it is of importance that Christianity should be seen to be in harmony with them. That objections to some received views should be valid, and yet that they should be always held up as the objections of infidels, is a mischief to the Christian cause. It is a mischief that critical observations which any intelligent man can make for himself, should be ascribed to atheism or unbelief. It would be a strange and almost incredible thing that the Gospel, which at first made war only on the vices of mankind, should now be opposed to one of the highest and rarest of human virtues—the love of truth. And that in the present day the great object of Christianity should be, not to change the lives of men, but to prevent them from changing their opinions; that would be a singular inversion of the purposes for which Christ came into the world. The Christian religion is in a false position when all the tendencies of knowledge are opposed to it. Such position cannot be long maintained, or can only end in the withdrawal of the educated classes from the influences of religion. It is a grave consideration whether we ourselves may not be in an earlier stage of the same religious dissolution, which seems to have gone further in Italy and France. The reason for thinking so is not to be sought in the external circumstances of our own or any other religious communion, but in the progress of ideas with which Christian teachers seem to be ill at ease. Time was when the Gospel was before the age; when it breathed a new life into a decaying world— when the difficulties of Christianity were difficulties of the heart only, and the highest minds found in its truths not only the rule of their lives, but a well-spring of intellectual delight. Is it to be held a thing impossible that the Christian religion, instead of shrinking into itself, may again embrace the thoughts of men upon the earth? Or is it true that since the Reformation 'all intellect has gone the other way'? and that in Protestant countries reconciliation is as hopeless as Protestants commonly believe to be the case in Catholic?

Those who hold the possibility of such a reconcilement or restoration of belief, are anxious to disengage Christianity from all suspicion of disguise or unfairness. They wish to preserve the historical use of Scripture as the continuous witness in all ages of the higher things in the heart of man, as the inspired source of truth and the way to the better life. They are willing to take away some of the external supports, because they are not needed and do harm; also, because they interfere with the meaning. They have a faith, not that after a period of transition all things will remain just as they were before, but that they will all come round again to the use of man and to the glory of God. When interpreted like any other book, by the same rules of evidence and the same canons of criticism, the Bible will still remain unlike any other book; its beauty will be freshly seen, as of a picture which is restored after many ages to its original state; it will create a new interest and make for itself a new kind of authority by the life which is in it. It will be a spirit and not a letter; as it was in the beginning, having an influence like that of the spoken word, or the book newly found.

INTERPRET THE SCRIPTURE LIKE ANY OTHER BOOK

There are many respects in which Scripture is unlike any other book; these will appear in the results of such an interpretation. The first step is to know the meaning, and this can only be done in the same careful and impartial way that we ascertain the meaning of Sophocles or of Plato.

. . . It may be observed, that a change in some of the prevailing modes of interpretation is not so much a matter of expediency as of necessity. The original meaning of Scripture is beginning to be clearly understood. But the apprehension of the original meaning is inconsistent with the reception of a typical or conventional one. The time will come when educated men will be no more able to believe that the words, 'Out of Egypt have I called my son' (Matt. ii. 15; Hosea xi. i), were *intended* by the prophet to refer to the return of Joseph and Mary from Egypt, than they are now able to believe the Roman Catholic explanation of Gen. iii. 15, 'Ipsa conteret caput tuum.' They will no more think that the first chapters of Genesis relate the same tale which Geology and Ethnology unfold, than they now think the meaning of Joshua x. 12, 13, to be in accordance with Galileo's discovery.

. . . It has to be considered whether the intellectual forms under which Christianity has been described may not also be in a state of transition and resolution, in this respect contrasting with the never-changing truth of the Christian life. (I Cor. xiii. 8.) Looking backwards at past ages, we experience a kind of amazement at the minuteness of theological distinctions, and also at their permanence. They seem to have borne a part in the education of the Christian world, in an age when language itself had also a greater influence than now-a-days. It is admitted that these distinctions are not observed in the New Testament, and are for the most part of a later growth. But little is gained by setting up theology against Scripture, or Scripture against theology; the Bible against the Church, or the Church against the Bible. At different periods either has been a bulwark against some form of error; either has tended to correct the abuse of the other. . . .

And now, as the Interpretation of Scripture is receiving another character, it seems that distinctions of theology, which were in great measure based on old Interpretations, are beginning to fade away. A change is observable in the manner in which doctrines are stated and defended; it is no longer held sufficient to rest them on texts of Scripture, one, two, or more, which contain, or appear to contain, similar words or ideas. They are connected more closely with our moral nature; extreme consequences are shunned; large allowances are made for the ignorance of mankind. It is held that there is truth on both sides; about many questions there is a kind of union of opposites; others are admitted to have been verbal only; all are regarded in the light which is thrown upon them by church history and religious experience. . . .

Chapter 14.

Critics of Victorian Civilization

Despite the affluence, optimism, and complacency of much of mid-Victorian life, there were always those who doubted and questioned the assumptions and values of Victorian society. Most of these critics attacked the commercialization of life, to which they attributed the social evils of big cities, the bad taste in art and architecture, and the false values of the middle classes. Thomas Carlyle had written against "mammon worship" in the 1840s; and in the 1860s the revolt against Victorianism was expressed in other forms. In the novels of Charles Dickens the shams and pomposities of middle-class life were amusingly exposed; in the art and the crafts and the socialism of William Morris the escape from Podsnappery was proclaimed; while Matthew Arnold showed the cultured, humanist alternative to the aridities of puritanism.

That Victorian society could produce its own critics of the stature of John Stuart Mill, Karl Marx, and Matthew Arnold is a testimony to the greatness of the age. But inevitably many of the problems they posed were insoluble within the framework of Victorianism itself. Only when the certainties of Victorian society began to crumble in the 1880s was the logic of the working out of their ideas apparent.

66. THE TYRANNY OF THE MAJORITY

by JOHN STUART MILL

In his classic essay *On Liberty* (1859) John Stuart Mill (see Reading No. 59) analyzed "the nature and limits of the

259

power which can be legitimately exercised by society over the individual." Whereas in the past the danger to the liberty of the individual had come from despots and tyrannical governments, in mid-Victorian England, argued Mill, the danger came from the "tyranny of the majority," exercised in innumerable and subtle ways. These extracts are from *On Liberty* (1859), pp. 13–14, 33–34, 64, 67, 83, 110, 118–119, 120–121, 126.

. . . IN political speculations "the tyranny of the majority" is now generally included among the evils against which society requires to be on its guard.

Like other tyrannies, the tyranny of the majority was at first, and is still vulgarly, held in dread, chiefly as operating through the acts of the public authorities. But reflecting persons perceived that when society is itself the tyrant—society collectively over the separate individuals who compose it—its means of tyrannizing are not restricted to the acts which it may do by the hands of its political functionaries. Society can and does execute its own mandates; and if it issues wrong mandates instead of right, or any mandates at all in things with which it ought not to meddle, it practices a social tyranny more formidable than many kinds of political oppression, since, though not usually upheld by such extreme penalties, it leaves fewer means of escape, penetrating much more deeply into the details of life, and enslaving the soul itself. Protection, therefore, against the tyranny of the magistrate is not enough; there needs protection also against the tyranny of the prevailing opinion and feeling, against the tendency of society to impose, by other means than civil penalties, its own ideas and practices as rules of conduct on those who dissent from them; to fetter the development and, if possible, prevent the formation of any individuality not in harmony with its ways, and compel all characters to fashion themselves upon the model of its own.

. . . Let us suppose . . . that the government is entirely at one with the people, and never thinks of exerting any power of coercion unless in agreement with what it conceives to be their voice. But I deny the right of the people to exercise such coercion, either by themselves or by their government. The power itself is illegitimate. The best government has no more title to it than the worst. It is as noxious, or more noxious, when exerted in accordance with public opinion than when in opposition to it. If all mankind minus one were of one opinion, mankind would be no more justified in silencing that one person than he, if he had the power, would be justified in silencing mankind. Were an opinion a personal possession of no value except to the owner, if to be obstructed in the enjoyment of it were simply a private injury, it would make some difference whether the injury was inflicted only on a few persons or on many. But the peculiar evil of silencing the expression of an opinion is that it is robbing the human race, posterity as well as the existing generation—those who dissent from the opinion, still more than those who hold it. If the opinion is right, they are deprived of the opportunity of exchanging error for truth; if wrong, they lose, what is almost as great a benefit, the clearer perception and livelier impression of truth produced by its collision with error.

It is necessary to consider separately these two hypotheses, each of which has a distinct branch of the argument corresponding to it. We can never be sure that the opinion we are endeavoring to stifle is a false opinion; and if we were sure, stifling it would be an evil still.

First, the opinion which it is attempted to suppress by authority may possibly be true. Those who desire to suppress it, of course, deny its truth; but they are not infallible. They have no authority to decide the question for all mankind and exclude every other person from the means of judging. To refuse a hearing to an opinion because they are sure that it is false is to assume that *their* certainty is the same thing as *absolute* certainty. All silencing of discussion is an assumption of infallibility. Its condemnation may be allowed to rest on this common argument, not the worse for being common. . . .

Let us now pass to the second division of the argument, and dismissing the supposition that any of the received opinions may be false, let us assume them to be true and examine into the worth of the manner in which they are likely to be held when their truth is not freely and openly canvassed. However unwillingly a person who has a strong opinion may admit the possibility that his opinion may be false, he ought to be moved by the consideration that, however true it may be, if it is not fully, frequently, and fearlessly discussed, it will be held as a dead dogma, not a living truth.

. . . He who knows only his own side of the case knows little of that. His reasons may be good, and no one may have been able to refute them. But if he is equally unable to refute the reasons on the opposite side, if he does not so much as know what they are, he has no ground for preferring either opinion.

. . . But there is a commoner case than either of these: when the conflicting doctrines, instead of being one true and the other false, share the truth between them, and the nonconforming opinion is needed to supply the remainder of the truth of which the received doctrine embodies only a part. Popular opinions, on subjects not palpable to sense, are often true, but seldom or never the whole truth. They are a part of the truth, sometimes a greater, sometimes a smaller part, but exaggerated, distorted, and disjointed from the truths by which they ought to be accompanied and limited.

. . . In our times, from the highest class of society down to the lowest, everyone lives as under the eye of a hostile and dreaded censorship. Not only in what concerns others, but in what concerns only themselves, the individual or the family do not ask themselves, what do I prefer? or, what would suit my character and disposition? or, what would allow the best and highest in me to have fair play and enable it to grow and thrive? They ask themselves, what is suitable to my position? what is usually done by persons of my station and pecuniary circumstances? or (worse still) what is usually done by persons of a station and circumstances superior to mine? I do not mean that they choose what is customary in preference to what suits their own inclination. It does not occur to them to have any inclination except for what is customary. Thus the mind itself is bowed to the yoke: even in what people do for pleasure, conformity is the first thing thought of; they like in crowds; they exercise choice only among things commonly done; peculiarity of taste, eccentricity of conduct are shunned equally with crimes, until by dint of not following their own nature they have no nature to follow: their human capacities are withered and starved; they become incapable of any strong wishes or native pleasures, and are generally without either opinions or feelings of home growth, or properly their own. . . .

In sober truth, whatever homage may be professed, or even paid, to real or supposed mental superiority, the general tendency of things throughout the world is to render mediocrity the ascendant power among mankind.

. . . At present individuals are lost in the crowd. In politics it is almost a triviality to say that public opinion now rules the world. The only power deserving the name is that of masses, and of governments while they make themselves the organ of the tendencies and instincts of masses. This is as true in the moral and social relations of private life as in public transactions. Those whose opinions go by the name of public opinion are not always the same sort of public: in America, they are the whole white population; in England, chiefly the middle class. But they are always a mass, that is to say, <u>collective mediocrity</u>. And what is a still greater novelty, the mass do not now take their opinions from dignitaries in Church or State, from ostensible leaders, or from books. Their thinking is done for them by men much like themselves, addressing them or speaking in their name, on the spur of the moment, through the newspapers. . . . <u>In this age, the mere example of nonconformity, the mere refusal to bend the knee to custom, is itself a service.</u> Precisely because the tyranny of opinion is such as to make eccentricity a reproach, it is desirable, in order to break through that tyranny, that people should be eccentric. Eccentricity has always abounded when and where strength of character has abounded; and the amount of eccentricity in a society has generally been proportional to the amount of genius, mental vigor, and moral courage it contained. That so few now dare to be eccentric marks the chief danger of the time. . . .

The despotism of custom is everywhere the standing hindrance to human advancement, being in unceasing antagonism to that disposition to aim at something better than customary, which is called, according to circumstances, the spirit of liberty, or that of progress or improvement. The spirit of improvement is not always a spirit of liberty, for it may aim at forcing improvements on an unwilling people; and the spirit of liberty, in so far as it resists such attempts, may ally itself locally and temporarily with the opponents of improvement; but the only unfailing and permanent source of improvement is liberty, since by it there are as many possible independent centers of improvement as there are individuals. . . .

67. BARBARIANS, PHILISTINES, POPULACE

by MATTHEW ARNOLD

There was no more telling indictment of the insufficiency of middle-class Nonconformity and industrialism for the Good Life than Matthew Arnold's *Culture and Anarchy* (1869). Arnold (1822–1888) was the eldest son of the great Dr. Thomas Arnold, Headmaster of Rugby School, and made a reputation for himself as a poet, critic, and educationist.

From 1851 to 1886 he was an Inspector of Schools. *Culture
and Anarchy* is a plea for humanism (especially "sweetness
and light") as an alternative to the unloveliness, bigotry,
and crude individualism of English society. These passages
are from chap. 3, "Barbarians, Philistines, Populace," pp.
100–105.

. . . FOR the middle class, for that great body which, as we know,
"has done all the great things that have been done in all departments," . . . we have a designation which now has become pretty
well known, and which we may as well still keep for them, the designation of Philistines.

. . . For *Philistine* gives the notion of something particularly stiff-
necked and perverse in the resistance to light and its children; and
therein it specially suits our middle class, who not only do not pursue
sweetness and light, but who even prefer to them that sort of machinery
of business, chapels, tea-meetings, . . . which makes up the dismal
and illiberal life on which I have so often touched.

. . . I have in my own mind often indulged myself with the fancy
of employing, in order to designate our aristocratic class, the name of
The Barbarians. The Barbarians, to whom we all owe so much, and
who reinvigorated and renewed our worn-out Europe, had, as is well
known, eminent merits; and in this country, where we are for the most
part sprung from the Barbarians, we have never had the prejudice
against them which prevails among the races of Latin origin. The
Barbarians brought with them that staunch individualism, as the
modern phrase is, and that passion for doing as one likes, for the assertion of personal liberty, which appears to Mr. Bright the central
idea of English life, and of which we have, at any rate, a very rich
supply. The stronghold and natural seat of this passion was in the
nobles of whom our aristocratic class are the inheritors; and this class,
accordingly, have signally manifested it, and have done much by their
example to recommend it to the body of the nation, who already,
indeed, had it in their blood. The Barbarians, again, had the passion
for field-sports; and they have handed it on to our aristocratic class,
who of this passion too, as of the passion for asserting one's personal
liberty, are the great natural stronghold. The care of the Barbarians
for the body, and for all manly exercises; the vigour, good looks, and
fine complexion which they acquired and perpetuated in their families
by these means,—all this may be observed still in our aristocratic class.

The chivalry of the Barbarians, with its characteristics of high spirit, choice manners, and distinguished bearing,—what is this but the attractive commencement of the politeness of our aristocratic class?

. . . Only, all this culture (to call it by that name) of the Barbarians was an exterior culture mainly. It consisted principally in outward gifts and graces, in looks, manners, accomplishments, prowess. The chief inward gifts which had part in it were the most exterior, so to speak, of inward gifts, those which come nearest to outward ones; they were courage, a high spirit, self-confidence. <u>Far within, and unawakened, lay a whole range of powers of thought and feeling, to which these interesting productions of nature had, from the circumstances of their life, no access.</u> Making allowances for the difference of the times, surely we can observe precisely the same thing now in our aristocratic class. In general its culture is exterior chiefly; all the exterior graces and accomplishments, and the more external of the inward virtues, seem to be principally its portion. It now, of course, cannot but be often in contact with those studies by which, from the world of thought and feeling, true culture teaches us to fetch sweetness and light; but its hold upon these very studies appears remarkably external, and unable to exert any deep power upon its spirit. . . .

It is obvious that that part of the working class which . . . looks forward to the happy day when it will sit on thrones with . . . middle-class potentates, to survey, as Mr. Bright beautifullly says, "the cities it has built, the railroads it has made, the manufactures it has produced, the cargoes which freight the ships of the greatest mercantile navy the world has ever seen,"—it is obvious, I say, that this part of the working class is, or is in a fair way to be, one in spirit with the industrial middle class. It is notorious that our middle-class Liberals have long looked forward to this consummation, when the working class shall join forces with them, aid them heartily to carry forward their great works, go in a body to their tea-meetings, and, in short, enable them to bring about their millennium. That part of the working class, therefore, which does really seem to lend itself to these great aims, may, with propriety, be numbered by us among the Philistines. That part of it, again, which so much occupies the attention of philanthropists at present,—the part which gives all its energies to organising itself, through trades' unions and other means, so as to constitute, first, a great working-class power, independent of the middle and aristocratic classes, and then, by dint of numbers, give the law to them, and itself reign absolutely,—this lively and interesting part must also, according to our definition, go with the Philistines; because it is its class and its class-instinct which it seeks to affirm, its ordinary self, not its best self; and it is a machinery, an industrial machinery, and power and pre-eminence and other external goods, which fill its thoughts, and not an inward perfection. It is wholly occupied, according to Plato's subtle expression, with the things of itself and not its real self, with the things of the State and not the real State. But that vast portion, lastly, of the working class which, raw and half-developed, has long lain half-hidden amidst its poverty and squalor, and is now issuing from its hiding-place to assert an Englishman's heaven-born privilege of doing as he likes, and is beginning to perplex us by marching where it likes, meeting where it likes, bawling what it likes, breaking what it likes,—to this vast residuum we may with great propriety give the name of *Populace*.

Thus we have got three distinct terms, *Barbarians, Philistines, Populace,* to denote roughly the three great classes into which our society is divided . . .

68. UNTO THIS LAST

by J O H N R U S K I N

The attack on orthodox political economy could be mounted from several directions. John Ruskin (1819–1900), the art critic, criticized the complacent atmosphere in which the comfortable middle classes lived and questioned the whole basis of money making and the values and attitudes associated with it. His writings were widely read and influenced many working men who subsequently joined the socialist movement. *Unto this Last,* which first appeared in *The Cornhill Magazine* in August–November 1860, was published in book form in 1862, and the following passages from pp. 1–174 indicate the nature of Ruskin's critique.

AMONG the delusions which at different periods have possessed themselves of the minds of large masses of the human race, perhaps the most curious—certainly the least creditable—is the modern *soi-disant* science of political economy, based on the idea that an advantageous code of social action may be determined irrespectively of the influence of social affection.

Of course, as in the instances of alchemy, astrology, witchcraft, and other such popular creeds, political economy has a plausible idea at the root of it. "The social affections," says the economist, "are accidental and disturbing elements in human nature; but avarice and the desire of progress are constant elements. Let us eliminate the inconstants, and, considering the human being merely as a covetous machine, examine by what laws of labour, purchase, and sale, the greatest accumulative result in wealth is obtainable. Those laws once determined, it will be for each individual afterwards to introduce as much of the disturbing affectionate element as he chooses, and to determine for himself the result on the new conditions supposed."

. . . I neither impugn nor doubt the conclusions of the science, if its terms are accepted. I am simply uninterested in them, as I should be in those of a science of gymnastics which assumed that men had no skeletons. It might be shown, on that supposition, that it would be advantageous to roll the students up into pellets, flatten them into cakes, or stretch them into cables; and that when these results were effected, the re-insertion of the skeleton would be attended with various inconveniences to their constitution. The reasoning might be admirable, the conclusions true, and the science deficient only in applicability. Modern political economy stands on a precisely similar basis. Assuming, not that the human being has no skeleton, but that it is all skeleton, it founds an ossifiant theory of progress on this negation of a soul; and having shown the utmost that may be made of bones, and constructed a number of interesting geometrical figures with death's-heads and humeri, successfully proves the inconvenience of the reappearance of a soul among these corpuscular structures. I do not deny the truth of this theory: I simply deny its applicability to the present phase of the world. . . .

The whole question . . . respecting not only the advantage, but even the quantity, of national wealth, resolves itself finally into one of abstract justice. It is impossible to conclude, of any given mass of acquired wealth, merely by the fact of its existence, whether it signifies good or evil to the nation in the midst of which it exists. Its real value depends on the moral sign attached to it, just as sternly as that of a mathematical quantity depends on the algebraical sign attached to it Any given accumulation of commercial wealth may be indicative, on the one hand, of faithful industries, progressive energies, and productive ingenuities; or, on the other, it may be indicative of mortal luxury, merciless tyranny, ruinous chicane.

Some treasures are heavy with human tears, as an ill-stored harvest with untimely rain; and some gold is brighter in sunshine than it is in substance. And these are not, observe, merely moral or pathetic attributes of riches, which the seeker of riches may, if he chooses, despise; they are literally and sternly, material attributes of riches, depreciating or exalting, incalculably, the monetary signification of the sum in question. One mass of money is the outcome of action which has created,—another, of action which has annihilated,—ten times as much in the gathering of it; such and such strong hands have been paralyzed, as if they had been numbed by nightshade: so many strong men's courage broken, so many productive operations hindered; this and the other false direction given to labour, and lying image of prosperity set up, on Dura plains dug into seven-times-heated furnaces. That which seems to be wealth may in verity be only the gilded index of far-reaching ruin; a wrecker's handful of coin gleaned from the beach to which he has beguiled an argosy; a camp-follower's bundle of rags unwrapped from the breasts of goodly soldiers dead; the purchase-pieces of potter's fields, wherein shall be buried together the citizen and the stranger.

And, therefore, the idea that directions can be given for the gaining of wealth, irrespectively of the consideration of its moral sources, or that any general and technical law of purchase and gain can be set down for national practice, is perhaps the most insolently futile of all that ever beguiled men through their vices. So far as I know, there is not in history record of anything so disgraceful to the human intellect as the modern idea that the commercial text, "Buy in the cheapest market and sell in the dearest," represents, or under any circumstances could represent, an available principle of national economy. Buy in the cheapest market?—yes; but what made your market cheap? Charcoal may be cheap among your roof timbers after a fire, and bricks may be cheap in your streets after an earthquake; but fire and earthquake may not therefore be national benefits. Sell in the dearest?—yes, truly; but what made your market dear? You sold your bread well to-day; was it to a dying man who gave his last coin for it, and will never need bread more, or to a rich man who to-morrow will buy your farm over your head; or to a soldier on his way to pillage the bank in which you have put your fortune?

None of these things you can know. One thing only you can know, namely, whether this dealing of yours is a just and faithful one, which is all you need concern yourself about respecting it; sure thus to have done your own part in bringing about ultimately in the world a state of things which will not issue in pillage or in death. And thus every question concerning these things merges itself ultimately in the great question of justice . . .

I said . . . that nothing in history had ever been so disgraceful to human intellect as the acceptance among us of the common doctrines of political economy as a science. I have many grounds for saying this, but one of the chief may be given in few words. I know no previous instance in history of a nation's establishing a systematic disobedience to the first principles of its professed religion. The writings which we (verbally) esteem as divine, not only denounce the love of money as the source of all evil, and as an idolatry abhorred of the Deity, but declare mammon service to be the accurate and irreconcileable opposite of God's service; and, wherever they speak of riches absolute, and poverty absolute, declare woe to the rich, and blessing to the poor. Whereupon we forthwith investigate a science of becoming rich, as the shortest road to national prosperity.

. . . THERE IS NO WEALTH BUT LIFE. Life, including all its powers of love, of joy, and of admiration. That country is the richest which nourishes the greatest number of noble and happy human beings; that man is richest who, having perfected the functions of his own life to the utmost, has also the widest helpful influence, both personal, and by means of his possessions, over the lives of others.

A strange political economy; the only one, nevertheless, that ever was or can be: all political economy founded on self-interest being but the fulfilment of that which once brought schism into the policy of angels, and ruin into the economy of Heaven.

"The greatest number of human beings noble and happy." But is the nobleness consistent with the number? Yes, not only consistent with it, but essential to it. The maximum of life can only be reached by the maximum of virtue. In this respect the law of human population differs wholly from that of animal life. The multiplication of animals is checked only by want of food, and by the hostility of races; the population of the gnat is restrained by the hunger of the swallow, and that of the swallow by the scarcity of gnats. Man, considered as an animal, is indeed limited by the same laws: hunger, or plague, or war, are the necessary and only restraints upon his increase,—effectual restraints hitherto,—his principal study having been how most swiftly to destroy himself, or ravage his dwelling-places, and his highest skill directed to give range to the famine, seed to the plague, and sway to the sword. But, considered as other than an animal, his increase is not limited by these laws. It is limited only by the limits of his courage and his love. Both of these *have* their bounds; and ought to have: his race has its bounds also; but these have not yet been reached, nor will be reached for ages.

In all the ranges of human thought I know none so melancholy as the speculations of political economists on the population question. It is proposed to better the condition of the labourer by giving him higher wages. "Nay," says the economist, "if you raise his wages, he will either people down to the same point of misery at which you found him, or drink your wages away." He will. I know it. Who gave him this will? Suppose it were your own son of whom you spoke, declaring to me that you dared not take him into your firm, nor even give him his just labourer's wages, because if you did, he would die of drunkenness, and leave half a score of children to the parish. "Who gave your son these dispositions?"—I should inquire. Has he them by inheritance or by education? By one or other they *must* come; and as in him, so also in the poor. Either these poor are of a race essentially different from ours, and unredeemable (which, however often implied, I have heard none yet openly say), or else by such care as we have ourselves received, we may make them continent and sober as ourselves—wise and dispassionate as we are—models arduous of imitation. But, it is answered, they cannot receive education. Why not? That is precisely the point at issue. Charitable persons suppose the worst fault of the rich is to refuse the people meat; and the people cry for their meat, kept back by fraud, to the Lord of Multitudes. Alas! it is not meat of which the refusal is cruelest, or to which the claim is validest. The life is more than the meat. The rich not only refuse food to the poor; they refuse wisdom; they refuse virtue; they refuse salvation. Ye sheep without shepherd, it is not the pasture that has been shut from you, but the presence. Meat! perhaps your right to that may be pleadable; but other rights have to be pleaded first. Claim your crumbs from the table, if you will; but claim them as children, not as dogs; claim your right to be fed, but claim more loudly your right to be holy, perfect, and pure.

. . . We continually hear it recommended by sagacious people to complaining neighbours, (usually less well placed in the world than themselves), that they should "remain content in the station in which Providence has placed them." There are perhaps some circumstances of life in which Providence has no intention that people *should* be content. Nevertheless, the maximum is on the whole a good one; but it is peculiarly for home use. That your neighbour should, or should not, remain content with *his* position, is not your business; but it is very much your business to remain content with your own. What is chiefly needed in England at the present day is to show the quantity of pleasure that may be obtained by a consistent, well-administered competence, modest, confessed, and laborious. We need examples of people who, leaving Heaven to decide whether they are to rise in the world, decide for themselves that they will be happy in it, and have resolved to seek—not greater wealth, but simpler pleasure; not higher fortune, but deeper felicity; making the first of possessions, self-possession; and honouring themselves in the harmless pride and calm pursuits of peace. . . .

And if, on due and honest thought over these things, it seems that the kind of existence to which men are now summoned by every plea of pity and claim of right, may, for some time at least, not be a luxurious one;—consider whether, even supposing it guiltless, luxury would be desired by any of us, if we saw clearly at our sides the suffering which accompanies it in the world. Luxury is indeed possible in the future—innocent and exquisite; luxury for all, and by the help of all; but luxury at present can only be enjoyed by the ignorant; the cruelest man living could not sit at his feast, unless he sat blindfold. Raise the veil boldly; face the light; and if, as yet, the light of the eye can only be through tears, and the light of the body through sackcloth, go thou forth weeping, bearing precious seed, until the time come, and the kingdom, when Christ's gift of bread, and bequest of peace shall be Unto this last as unto thee; and when, for earth's severed multitudes of the wicked and the weary, there shall be holier reconciliation than that of the narrow home, and calm economy, where the Wicked cease—not from trouble, but from troubling—and the Weary are at rest.

69. IN A MANUFACTURING TOWN

by EDWARD CARPENTER

The revolt against Victorianism was one of the factors in
the revival of socialism in England in the 1880s. Edward
Carpenter (1844–1929) resigned his fellowship at Trinity
Hall, Cambridge, in 1873, and became a University Extension lecturer because he thought it would enable him to
"throw in his lot with the mass-people and the manual
workers." But he was disappointed in this expectation and
so in 1881, under the inspiration of Walt Whitman, he
turned from lecturing to writing *Towards Democracy*, and
established for himself a Thoreau-like existence on a small-
holding near Sheffield. There he joined a local branch of
William Morris' Socialist League; and for many years lived
as a writer, socialist sage, and advocate of the "simplifica-
tion of life." This poem is from *Towards Democracy*, pp.
148–150, which was first published in 1883 but which is essentially a critique of bourgeois society in its hey-day
during the preceding decades.

IN A MANUFACTURING TOWN

AS I walked restless and despondent through the gloomy city,
    And saw the eager unresting to and fro—as of ghosts in some sul-
phurous Hades—
    And saw the crowds of tall chimneys going up, and the pall of
smoke covering the sun, covering the earth, lying heavy against the
very ground—
    And saw the huge refuse-heaps writhing with children picking them
over,
    And the ghastly half-roofless smoke-blackened houses, and the
black river flowing below,—
    As I saw these, and as I saw again far away the Capitalist quarter,
    With its villa residences and its high-walled gardens and its well-
appointed carriages, and its face turned away from the wriggling
poverty which made it rich,—

As I saw and remembered its drawing-room airs and affectations and its wheezy pursy Church-going and its gas-reeking heavy-furnished rooms and its scent-bottles and its other abominations—

I shuddered:

For I felt stifled, like one who lies half-conscious—knowing not clearly the shape of the evil—in the grasp of some heavy nightmare.

Then out of the crowd descending towards me came a little ragged boy;

Came—from the background of dirt disengaging itself—an innocent wistful child-face, begrimed like the rest but strangely pale, and pensive before its time.

And in an instant (it was as if a trumpet had been blown in that place) I saw it all clearly, the lie I saw and the truth, the false dream and the awakening.

For the smoke-blackened walls and the tall chimneys, and the dreary habitations of the poor, and the drearier habitations of the rich, crumbled and conveyed themselves away as if by magic;

And instead, in the backward vista of that face, I saw the joy of free open life under the sun:

The green sun-delighting earth and rolling sea I saw—

The free sufficing life—sweet comradeship, few needs and common pleasures—the needless endless burdens all cast aside,

Not as a sentimental vision, but as a fact and a necessity existing, I saw

In the backward vista of that face.

Stronger than all combinations of Capital, wiser than all the Committees representative of Labour, the simple need and hunger of the human heart.

Nothing more is needed.

All the books of political economy ever written, all the proved impossibilities, are of no account.

The smoke-blackened walls and tall chimneys duly crumble and convey themselves away;

The falsehood of a gorged and satiated society curls and shrivels together like a withered leaf,

Before the forces which lie dormant in the pale and wistful face of a little child.

FURTHER READING: *Part Three*

Annan, Noel G., *Leslie Stephen* (1951).

Briggs, Asa, *Victorian People* (1954).

Brinton, Crane, *English Political Thought in the 19th Century* (1962 ed.).

British Broadcasting Corporation, *Ideas and Beliefs of the Victorians* (1949).

Buckley, Jerome Hamilton, *The Victorian Temper* (1951).

Edwards, Maldwyn, *Methodism and England* (1943).

Eiseley, Loren, *Darwin's Century* (1958).

Gillespie, Charles Coulston, *Genesis and Geology* (1951).

Hanham, H. J., *Elections and Party Management: Politics in the Time of Disraeli and Gladstone* (1959).

Hobhouse, Christopher, *1851 and the Crystal Palace* (1950 ed.).

Houghton, Walter E., *The Victorian Frame of Mind, 1830–1870* (1957).

Packe, M. St. John, *Life of John Stuart Mill* (1954).

St. John-Stevas, Norman, *Walter Bagehot* (1959).

Vidler, Alec R., *The Church in an Age of Revolution, 1789 to the Present Day* (1961).

Young, G. M., *Victorian England: Portrait of an Age* (1953 ed.).

PART FOUR.
TOWARDS A MASS
DEMOCRACY,
1870-1914

Chapter 15.

Agricultural and Industrial Society

By 1870 the Victorian social and political edifice was complete; thereafter the golden age of the middle classes began to wane. Politically the extension of the franchise in 1867 and 1884 signalled the spread of democracy far beyond its middle-class boundaries to the whole of the people. Economically the so-called Great Depression beginning in 1873 marked a change in Britain's world trading position. The rise of Germany and the flood of wheat from America marked the end of many of the assumptions and certainties of Victorian England. In the early 1870s these signs of change were barely perceptible; by 1914 their implications were everywhere apparent.

The Workshop of the World had been solidly built, and until 1914 Britain remained a prosperous and powerful nation. Her great basic industries continued to grow and maintained their relative importance in the national economy. The total industrial production and real national income both increased 2¼–2½ times between 1870 and 1913. But the great industrial lead over all other nations was cut down as Germany and the United States rapidly expanded their coal and steel production and surpassed the British output. Changes within industry tended to be along conventional lines—the continued superseding of handicraft techniques, completion of the railroad system, and the adoption of new forms of company organization. In the older industries there was a slowness in changing over to new methods and the initiative in new developments such as electric power and the internal combustion engine was lost to America and Germany.

In agriculture the changes between 1870 and 1914 were of a more fundamental nature. On top of a series of disastrous harvests in the 1870s came imports of abundant cheap wheat from the Middle West of America. Falling prices, with consequent reductions in profits and rents, put an end to the prosperity of English agriculture. After the grain imports came meat. Refrigeration and cold storage, together with the development of the canning industry, enabled American meat—and later Australian, New Zealand, and Argentine products—to compete with home output. English farmers attempted to meet this situation by switching more of their efforts to dairy farming and decreasing the amount of arable land. By 1914 Britain supplied all her own fresh milk and about three-fifths of her meat, but relied on imports for four-fifths of her wheat and a considerable part of her animal feeding stuffs.

The net result of these changes was to intensify the predominantly industrial nature of England, and to reduce still further the relative importance of the countryside. Not that the values and traditions of rural England were easily and suddenly set aside; but the economic position of the landed interest was undermined, and village society was eroded by piecemeal changes.

70. [THE BASES OF ENGLISH SOCIETY]

by THOMAS ESCOTT

It is significant that in his book, *England: Her People, Polity and Pursuits* (1879), T. H. S. Escott (1844–1924), a literary journalist and editor of the *Fortnightly Review*, should have ascribed so much importance to the landed interest and its influence in English life. The book was regarded by a contemporary reviewer in the *Economist* as giving a "wonderfully faithful picture of our daily life" and its tone and spirit as "eminently English . . . conservative without being reactionary, liberal, yet not subversive." These passages are from the 1891 ed., pp. 314–315, 331–340.

IN the constitution of English society at the present day, the three rival elements—the aristocratic, the plutocratic, and the democratic—are closely blended. The aristocratic principle is still paramount, forms the foundation of our social structure, and has been strengthened and extended in its operation by the plutocratic, while the democratic instinct of the race has all the opportunities of assertion and gratification which it can find in a career conditionally open to talent.

The antagonism between the aristocracy of wealth and birth has long been disappearing. The son of the newly-enriched father is identified in education, social training, habits, prejudices, feelings, with the scions of the houses of Norman descent. At all times there has been a tendency on the part of birth to ally itself with wealth, and it would be found upon examination that for the greater part of their princely rentals many a noble English stock is indebted to purely commercial sources. Judicious matrimonial alliances have largely assisted in identifying the two principles of wealth and birth. This has continued down to the present day, and the consequence is that though English society may be divided into the higher classes, the middle classes, the lower middle, and that vast multitude which for the sake of convenience may be described as the proletariat, the feud between the aristocracy of lineage and of revenue is almost at an end. There are typical country gentlemen in the House of Commons and in society, but the country interest is no longer the sworn enemy of the urban interest. Our territorial nobles, our squires, our rural landlords great and small, have become commercial potentates; our merchant princes have become country gentlemen. The possession of land is the guarantee of respectability, and the love of respectability and land is inveterate in our race.

The great merchant or banker of to-day is an English gentleman of a finished type. He is possibly a peer, and an active partner in a great City firm; if he is not a peer, the chances are that he is a member of the House of Commons. He is a man of wide culture, an authority upon paintings, or china, or black-letter books; upon some branch of natural science, upon the politics of Europe, upon the affairs of the world. Does he then neglect his business? By no means. He has, indeed, trustworthy servants and deputies; but he consults personally with his partners, gentlemen in culture and taste scarcely inferior, it may be, to himself; he goes into the City as punctually as his junior clerks; and when he returns from the City he drops for a few minutes into the most exclusive of West-end clubs. His grandfather would have lived with his family above the countinghouse, and regarded a trip to Hyde Park as a summer day's journey. As for the descendant, his town-house is in Belgravia or Mayfair. He occupies it for little more than six months out of the twelve, and during the rest of the year lives in his palace in the country, takes a keen interest in the breeding of stock, the cultivation of the soil, and the general improvement of his property. There is, in fact, but one standard of "social position" in England, and it is that which is formed by a blending of the plutocratic and aristocratic elements. If it is realized imperfectly in one generation, if will be approximated to more closely in the next, and thus it will go on till the ideal is reached.

. . . Whatever its levities and frivolities, the foundation on which English society rests is essentially serious, the result of the traditional and pre-eminently English habit of taking grave and earnest views of life. Religion is not now spoken of; what is meant is, that pure enjoyment is not the ideal of the typical Englishman in whatever class. He takes his pleasures heartily indeed, and with gusto, if he finds them in his path. Occasionally, . . . he may make the mistake of forsaking the true path of his career and following the phantom of pleasure till it lands him in disaster. These are our failures. The ordinary Englishman has ambitions, social and professional, and he subordinates all other things to them. He is bent upon improving his position, or immortalising his name. His dominant motive is the desire to rise, or the resolution to do to the utmost his duty in the sphere of life in which his lot has been cast. The plan of existence, thus regarded as the great and only opportunity for the accomplishment of a definite work, acquires an energising solemnity. The Englishman may stumble sometimes, but after the fall he picks himself up and pushes on to the goal. . . .

The gradations of esteem allotted to the different English professions are exactly what might be expected in a society organised upon such a basis and conscious of such aims. Roughly it may be said professions in England are valued according to their stability, their remunerativeness, their influence, and their recognition by the State. These conditions may partially explain the difference which English society draws between the callings of the merchant and the stockbroker. Stockbrokers make immense fortunes; but there attaches to them a suspicion of precariousness infinitely in excess of that which, in some measure, necessarily attaches to all fortunes accumulated by commerce or trade. The merchant represents an interest which is almost deserving of a place among the estates of the realm, and with the development of which the prosperity and prestige of England are bound up. His house of business is practically a public institution, and the speculative element—the fluctuation of prices and the uncertainty of markets—enters as little as possible into it. Merchants have from time immemorial been the friends and supporters of monarchs— have taken their place in the popular chamber of the legislature, have been elevated to distinguished stations among the titular aristocracy of the land. We have had not only our merchant-princes, but our merchant-peers and merchant-statesmen. The calling has been recognised in our social hierarchy for centuries, and if not exactly a liberal, is an eminently respectable and dignified one. Nor is the merchant, as a rule, so much absorbed in the affairs of his own business as to be unable to devote as much time as is requisite to the pursuits of society and the affairs of the country. His operations run in a comparatively equal and tranquil channel, and to hint that he lives in an atmosphere of feverish excitement is equivalent to insinuating a doubt of his solvency. It is different with the stockbroker, whose social position is so quickly acquired that it cannot yet be looked upon as assured— whose wealth, though great, has the garish hue of luck and glories which may dissolve themselves at any moment into thin air, like Aladdin's palace, and who himself is popularly supposed to be more or less on the tenterhooks of expectation and anxiety from morning to night. The merchant drives to his place of business in a family brougham or barouche; the stockbroker drives to the station, where he takes the morning express to the City, in a smart dog-cart, with a high-stepping horse between the shafts and a very knowing-looking groom at his side. . . .

It is the fashion to say that, since the English people have been taken into partnership in the work of National government by the Reform Acts of 1832 and 1867, and we have fairly entered upon the broad road which is thought to lead to pure democracy, the influence of rank and fashion, in other words of what is called "society," upon politics has ceased to exist.

. . . Nevertheless, it would be a great mistake to conclude that the great houses are without influence on the formation of cabinets, or that there are no points of contact between aristocratic drawing-rooms and a Parliament in which the popular chamber is elected by household suffrage. That the English masses can secure at the head of an Administration any statesman upon whom they have set their hearts, and that the Government which is to have the national confidence must be composed of men approved by the constituencies, is

certain. Still there is left a fair margin in which the machinery of society may be brought to bear upon the politics and politicians of the
day.

. . . Democratic as our tendencies may be, there never was a time
when rank and fashion, when everything which is comprised in the
single word position, had so signal an opportunity of influencing the
popular mind. The reason for this has been to some extent explained
in the preceding chapters. The process that has been going on for
years is that of levelling up. The increase of the wealth of the middle
classes, and their intermarriage with their social superiors, have caused
them to assimilate the tastes and prejudices of their new connections.
Property grows, and the holders of property naturally take the colour
of their views from those who are above them, and not from those
who are below. The consequences of this, whether socially or politically considered, are identical. It is the aristocratic principle which
dominates our political as it dominates our social system. . . .

71. THE LANDED INTEREST

by JAMES CAIRD

This description by the agriculturist, Sir James Caird
(1816–1892), is from his book, *The Landed Interest,* pp.
41–67, which was published in 1878. But the society he describes was little different several decades earlier, and
continued in outward form until 1914, despite the agricultural depression of the later part of the nineteenth century: such was the continuity and stability of squire-
archical England.

THE distribution of landed property in England, so far as ownership
is concerned, is, by the growing wealth of the country, constantly
tending to a reduction in the number of small estates. This tendency
is further promoted by the law, which permits entails and settlements,
thus hindering the natural sale of land so dealt with; and also by
rights of primogeniture, which prevent subdivision of landed property
among the family in case of intestacy. Cultivation thus passes out of
the hands of small owners into those of tenant-farmers, causing a

gradual decrease of the agricultural population, and a proportionate increase of the towns. This has been much accelerated by a policy of Free Trade, which has at once opened up the markets of the world for our commerce, and for the produce of our mines and manufactures. These are advantageously interchanged for the corn and other agricultural products of foreign lands. This will go on while the commerce is found mutually profitable. And it will be profitable so long as, by superior skill and enterprise, combined with exceptional mineral advantages, we can undersell other countries in the produce of our manufactories and mines, while they can supply us with corn at a cheaper rate than we can grow it at home. Our present relation with foreign countries is becoming like that of a crowded capital, which draws its fresh supplies of vegetables, milk, and meat, from the market-gardens, meadows, and rich grazings in its vicinity, but looks to more distant lands for the corn and other commodities which bear long transport from cheaper and more distant farms. More than one-half of our corn is now of foreign growth, and nearly one-fourth of our meat and dairy produce; whilst year by year our cornland is giving place to the more profitable produce afforded by the milk and grazing and market-garden farms, which are gradually extending their circle. Such produce renders the land more valuable, more tempting prices are offered for it to the small landowners, and their numbers decrease. Wealthy men from the mines and manufactories and shipping and colonial interests, and the learned professions, desire to become proprietors of land; and some competition exists between them and those landowners whose increasing wealth tempts them on suitable opportunities to enlarge the boundaries of their domains. Thus small proprietors are bought out, and agricultural landowners diminish in number; while, side by side with them, vast urban populations are growing up, having little other connection with the land than that of affording the best market for its produce.

The Domesday Book for the United Kingdom, lately published, divides the landowners into two classes—those who have less than one acre of land, and those who have one acre and upwards. The former comprise 70 per cent. of the whole; but as none of this class has so much as an acre, and they hold together less than a two-hundredth part of the land, they may be regarded as householders only. Excluding these as not properly agricultural landowners, it may then fairly be said that one person in every hundred of the entire population is a landowner. Subdividing that figure by the average numbers of each family, it may be concluded that every twentieth head of a family is an owner of land.

But the tenant-farmers are entitled also to be reckoned as part owners of agricultural property, for in the crops and live and dead stock they own equal to one-fifth of the whole capital value of the land. Part of this is incorporated with the soil, and it is all as indispensable for the production of crops as the land itself. As cultivators, they employ and possess individually a larger capital than the peasant proprietors of other countries in their double capacity as owners and cultivators. They are 1,160,000 in number, and when added to 320,000 owners of one acre and upwards, make 1,480,000 altogether, engaged in the ownership and cultivation of the soil. When reckoned as heads of families they comprise more than one-fifth of the total male adult population; and it is thence not unreasonable to infer that, in that proportion, the people of this country are more or less interested in the preservation of landed property.

When we come more closely to analyse the landowning class, the aggregation of land amongst small numbers becomes very conspicuous. One-fourth of the whole territory, excluding those under one acre, is held by 1,200 persons, at an average for each of 16,200 acres; another fourth by 6,200 persons, at an average for each of 3,150 acres; another fourth by 50,770 persons, at an average for each of 380 acres; whilst the remaining fourth is held by 261,830 persons, at an average for each of 70 acres. An interesting compilation from the Domesday Books by the *Scotsman* newspaper, shows that the Peerage of the United Kingdom, about 600 in number, possess among them rather more than a fifth of all the land, and between a tenth and an eleventh of its annual income. . . .

The landowners are the capitalists to whom the land belongs. Their property comprises the soil and all that is beneath it, and the buildings and other permanent works upon it, required for the accommodation of the people, and of the working stock employed in its cultivation. Thus, where the land itself may be worth £35 an acre, the buildings, roads, fences, and drainage may have cost the landowners £15 an acre more. The landowner has thus two capitals in the land, one of which is permanent and growing rapidly in value with the prosperity of the country, the other liable to decay and occasioning cost in repair. In nearly all permanent improvements arising from the progress of agriculture he is also expected to share the cost. And he is necessarily concerned in the general prosperity and good management of his estate, and in the welfare of those who live upon it, with which his own is so closely involved. He takes a lead in the business of his parish, and from his class the magistrates who administer the criminal affairs of the county, and superintend its roads, its public buildings, and charitable institutions, are selected. Nor do his duties end here, for the landowner, from his position, is expected to be at the head of all objects of public utility, to subscribe to, and, if so inclined, to ride with the hounds, showing at once an example to the farmers and tradesmen, and meeting them on terms of neighbourly friendship and acquaintance. The same example is carried out in his intercourse with the clergy and schoolmaster, and his influence, where wisely exercised, is felt in the church, the school, the farm, and the cottage.

This class in the United Kingdom comprises a body of about 180,-000, who possess among them the whole of the agricultural land from 10 acres upwards. The owners of less than 10 acres each hold not more than one-hundredth part of the land, and may here be regarded as householders only. The property of the landowners, independent of minerals, yields an annual rent of sixty-seven millions sterling, and is worth a capital value of two thousand millions. There is no other body of men in the country who administer so large a capital on their own account, or whose influence is so widely extended and universally present. From them the learned professions, the church, the army, and the public services are largely recruited.

The tenant-farmers are the second class, and a much more numerous one. Their business is the cultivation of the land, with a capital quite independent of that of the landowner. They occupy farms of very various extent, 70 per cent. of them under 50 acres each, 12 per cent. between 50 and 100 acres, and 18 per cent. farms of more than 100 acres each. 5,000 occupy farms of between 500 and 1,000 acres, and 600 occupy farms exceeding 1,000 acres. Many of them are men of liberal education, and some of these are found in most parishes and in every county. A spirit of emulation exists among them, elicited by county, provincial, and national exhibitions of agricultural stock, and by a natural desire, in a country where everything is open to comment, not to be behind their neighbours in the neatness, style, and success of their cultivation, or in the symmetry and condition of their live-stock. They are brought into the closest relations with their labourers, and although, occasionally, feelings of keen antagonism have arisen, there is generally a very friendly understanding between them. The farmer knows that it is for his interest that the labourers should find their position made so comfortable as to value it.

To the farmer is committed the management of the details of the parish, as those of the county to the landowner. His intimate knowledge of the condition of the labourer, and constant residence in the parish, fit him best for the duty of Overseer of the Poor, member of the Board of Guardians, Churchwarden, and Surveyor of the Roads. He is frank and hospitable to strangers, as a rule; in favour of the established political institutions of the country; loyal as a subject; generally available in case of need as a mounted yeoman; and constantly in requisition as a juryman in the Courts of Law.

The farmers are six times as numerous as the landowners, there being 560,000 in Great Britain, and 600,000 in Ireland, the holdings there being on a smaller scale. They employ a vast capital in the aggregate, upwards of four hundred millions sterling, and, unlike that of the landowners, much of it is in daily use, circulating among tradesmen and labourers. . . .

The third class comprises the agricultural labourers, who are necessarily much more numerous than both landowners and tenants. They cannot be said to have any other capital than the furniture of their dwellings, their well-acquired experience in all the details of husbandry, and the bodily strength to use it. The English labourer, of the southern counties especially, has hitherto had but little education, except in his business. . . .

To these three classes are committed the agricultural interest and industry of the kingdom. The two first have duties entrusted to them by the constitution, for the management of the public and local interests of their counties and parishes, in addition to their special business as landowners and agriculturists. Each of the three classes is constantly being altered and recruited by changes and additions. Landed property of the value of several millions sterling a year changes hands, and as there is necessarily a larger body of persons capable of competing for small properties, there is a natural tendency to subdivision on sale. . . .

In short, our system is that of large capitalists owning the land; of smaller capitalists, each cultivating five times more of it than they would have means to do if they owned their farms; and of labourers free to carry their labour to any market which they consider most remunerative. . . .

72. THE WHEELWRIGHT'S SHOP

by GEORGE STURT

The tough resilience of rural traditions and the economic prosperity of Victorian farming enabled many parts of England to withstand the impact of industrialism and commercialization until the last quarter of the nineteenth century. But from the 1880s village society began to crumble. The changes were not sudden and in themselves often appeared trivial—the substitution of a machine-made product for one locally produced, or the introduction of quicker, "improved" methods of doing things. But in the aggregate they undermined the traditional balance of rural life and ultimately destroyed the organic community of the village. These changes are described with discernment and subtlety by George Sturt (1863–1927) who in 1884 entered a firm of wheelwrights at Farnham (Surrey) in which his ancestors had worked since 1706. The passages are from his book, *The Wheelwright's Shop* (1923), pp. 17–24, 53–55, 197–201.

TO say that the business I started into in 1884 was old-fashioned is to understate the case: it was a "folk" industry, carried on in a "folk" method. And circumstances made it perhaps more intensely so to me than it need have been. My father might just possibly, though I don't think he would, have shown me more modern aspects of it; but within my first month he took ill of the illness he died of five months later. Consequently I was left to pick up the business as best I could from "the men." There were never any "hands" with us. Eight skilled workmen or apprentices, eight friends of the family, put me up to all they could: and since some of them had been born and trained in little old country shops, while this of my father's was not much better, the lore I got from them was of the country through and through.

The objects of the work too were provincial. There was no looking far afield for customers. Farmers rarely more than five miles away; millers, brewers, a local grocer or builder or timber-merchant or hop-grower—for such and no others did the ancient shop still cater, as it had done for nearly two centuries. And so we got curiously intimate with the peculiar needs of the neighbourhood. In farm-waggon or dung-cart, barley-roller, plough, water-barrel, or what not, the dimensions we chose, the curves we followed (and almost every piece of timber was curved) were imposed upon us by the nature of the soil in this or that farm, the gradient of this or that hill, the temper of this or that customer or his choice perhaps in horseflesh. The carters told us their needs. To satisfy the carter, we gave another half-inch of curve to the waggon-bottom, altered the hooks for harness on the shafts, hung the water-barrel an inch nearer to the horse or an inch farther away, according to requirements.

. . . Reasoned science for us did not exist. "Theirs not to reason why." What we had to do was to live up to the local wisdom of our kind; to follow the customs, and work to the measurements, which had been tested and corrected long before our time in every village shop all across the country. A wheelwright's brain had to fit itself to this by dint of growing into it, just as his back had to fit into the supplenesses needed on the saw-pit, or his hands into the movements that would plane a felloe "true out o' wind." Science? Our two-foot rules took us no nearer to exactness than the sixteenth of an inch: we used to make or adjust special gauges for the nicer work; but very soon a stage was reached when eye and hand were left to their own cleverness, with no guide to help them. So the work was more of an art—a very fascinating art—than a science; and in this art, as I say, the brain had its share. A good wheelwright knew by art but not by reasoning the proportion to keep between spokes and felloes; and so too a good smith knew how tight a two-and-a-half inch tyre should be made for a five-foot wheel and how tight for a four-foot, and so on. He felt it, in his bones. It was a perception with him. But there was no science in it; no reasoning. Every detail stood by itself, and had to be learnt either by trial and error or by tradition.

This was the case with all dimensions. I knew how to "line out" a pair of shafts on a plank, and had in fact lined and helped saw on the saw-pit hundreds of them, years before I understood, thinking it over, why this method came right. So too it was years before I understood why a cart wheel needed a certain convexity although I had seen wheels fall to pieces for want of it. It was a detail most carefully attended to by the men in my shop; but I think none of them, any more than myself, could have explained why it had to be so.

. . . Any piece of work had to last for years. Fashion, or invention, didn't affect it. So it was held a shame to have to do work twice over because the original material had been faulty; and I have known old-fashioned workmen refuse to use likely-looking timber because they held it to be unfit for the job.

And they knew. The skilled workman was the final judge. Under the plane (it is little used now) or under the axe (it is all but obsolete) timber disclosed qualities hardly to be found otherwise. My own eyes know because my own hands have felt, but I cannot teach an outsider, the difference between ash that is "tough as whip-cord," and ash that is "frow as a carrot," or "doaty," or "biscuity." In oak, in beech, these differences are equally plain, yet only to those who have been initiated by practical work. These know how "green timber" (that is, timber with some sap left in it, imperfectly "sea-soned") does not look like properly dried timber, after planing. With axe or chisel or draw-shave they learn to distinguish between the heart of a plank and the "sap." And again, after years of attention, but nohow else, timber-users can tell what "shakes" are good and what bad. For not all shakes, all natural splits, in seasoned timber are injurious. On the contrary it was an axiom in my shop that good timber in drying was bound to "open" (care had to be taken to prevent it from opening too far) and that timber must be bad, must have lost all its youthful toughness, if the process of drying developed no shakes in it. . . .

I should soon have been bankrupt in business in 1884 if the public temper then had been like it is now—grasping, hustling, competitive. But then no competitor seems to have tried to hurt me. To the best of my remembrance people took a sort of benevolent interest in my doings, put no difficulties in my way, were slow to take advantage of my ignorance. Nobody asked for an estimate—indeed there was a fixed price for all the new work that was done. The only chance for me to make more profit would have been by lowering the quality of the output; and this the temper of the men made out of the question. But of profits I understood nothing. My great difficulty was to find out the customary price. The men didn't know. I worked out long lists of prices from the old ledgers, as far as I could understand their technical terms. . . .

The steadiness of the men was doubtless what saved me from ruin. Through them I felt the weight of the traditional public attitude towards industry. They possibly (and properly) exaggerated the respect for good workmanship and material; and I cannot blame them if they slowed down in pace. Workmen even to-day do not understand what a difference this may make to an employer. The main thing after all (and the men in my shop were faithful to it) was to keep the business up to a high level, preserving the reputation my father and grandfather had won for it. To make it pay—that was not their affair. Certainly they taught me how to be economical, in "lining-out" the timber and so on; but the time came when I found it needful to curb their own extravagance, scheming all sorts of ways, for instance, to get three shafts out of a plank, where a too fastidious workman would have cut only two. It rarely happened the other way about, rarely happened that the condemnation of a piece of timber came from me; but it did happen, not infrequently, that a disgusted workman would refuse to use what I had supplied to him.

. . . Two things [were] notable about these men. Of the first, indeed, I have already given some hint: it is, that in them was stored all the local lore of what good wheelwright's work should be like. The century-old tradition was still vigorous in them. They knew each customer and his needs; understood his carters and his horses and the nature of his land; and finally took a pride in providing exactly what was wanted in every case. So, unawares, they lived as integral parts in the rural community of the English. Overworked and underpaid, they none the less enjoyed life, I am sure. They were friends, as only a craftsman can be, with timber and iron. The grain of the wood told secrets to them.

The other point is, that these men had a special bond of comfort in the regard they felt for my own family. This was of old standing. Consideration had been shown to them—a sort of human thoughtfulness—for very long.

. . . Having no other guidance, I priced the work to my customers by my father's and my grandfather's charges, making schedules of figures from an old ledger. This plan was only not quite disastrous because . . . there was in fact a local traditional price for new work and new parts, which nobody dared to exceed. This much was painfully proved to me long afterwards. A certain standard cart, I ascertained, was being sold throughout the neighbourhood at less than cost price. Accordingly I tried to get sundry rivals to join me in raising the price. One of these however made the project known to a good customer of mine and succeeded in getting that customer's work away from me. This was one of the many occasions when I should have welcomed pressure from a strong Trade Union, to compel other employers to make the changes I could not introduce alone.

My father had probably known for years how unprofitable some of the trade was. New work, he used to say, did not pay. Even in his time, and under his able management, it was only worth doing at all for the sake of keeping the staff together and getting the "jobbing"— the repairs; for, as there could be no standard in them, it was still possible to make a profit at jobbing. On the subject of profits other tradesmen in the district were as ignorant and simple as myself. Although Farnham fancied itself a little town, its business was being conducted in the spirit of the village—almost indeed of the mediaeval manor. Men worked to oblige one another. Aldershot was almost as bad; Alton was if possible worse; and the most conservative village in the whole neighbourhood set the rate to which my own trade lived down. I doubt if there was a tradesman in the district—I am sure there was no wheelwright—who really knew what his output cost, or what his profits were, or if he was making money or losing it on any particular job. In later years, after the habit of giving estimates had become common (as it was unknown in 1884), I several times lost work to rivals who, I found out, were working for less than the mere iron and timber were to cost them. They never knew. Nor did they know if on to-morrow's estimate they were to make a fabulous profit. Well on into the present century these matters, in my trade, were settled by guess-work, not by calculation. We knew nothing, thought nothing, of how much we ought to have. But it was very needful to know how much our customer would pay. . . .

But by the time I dropped into the business many changes had begun. Some of the old work was growing obsolete, unexampled work was coming into vogue all round. Not only was it that "The Iron Age" . . . was on the move again, after years of quiescence. Better roads, and imported foodstuffs too, broke up the old farm-life on which my shop had waited. Instead of waggons, vans to run twice as fast were wanted, and their springs and brakes and lighter wheels revolutionised the industry my men had taught me. At the same time the break-down of village industries was introducing changes which were reflected in my shop in the shape of butchers' carts and bread-carts—unknown of old—and in brewers' drays and in millers' vans, not to mention vehicles for bricks and other building materials.

While novelties were pouring in upon the trade from one side, on the other side an unexampled competition began to be felt, keeping the prices still low. Things were not as in the pre-railway days. Now, discontented customers would buy "steam wheels" from London. Lighter wheels than any that could be made in my shop—wheels imported ready-made from America—had to be kept in stock along with the ancient sort of naves and felloes. But the prices were effectually kept down also by competition of another sort, or rather of a very ancient sort. Dorset villages, Wiltshire villages, entered into the rivalry. Thanks to their lower wages and rents, and their far less costly timber, places one had never heard of were able to supply local farmers at so cheap a rate that it was worth the farmers' while to ignore, or to sacrifice, the advantage of vehicles made locally with a view to local conditions. The circle of my competitors widened out by hundreds of miles.

In all these circumstances it is not wonderful that the price of wheelwright's work by no means kept pace with the cost of it. To tell the truth, the figures in my shop in 1884 (as extracted by myself from the old books) were not much in excess of those which Arthur Young found current in the southern counties in 1767. For a waggon the price had risen from about £21 then, to £29 or £30 in my father's time; but carts, which at the later date were but £12 or less, had averaged as much as £10 even a century earlier. . . .

In these circumstances it is not surprising that I began at last to feel a need of some change or other. It is true, I knew nothing about "Costing." Methods for that were not devised until years later; but, in the simpler things, I did after four or five years—say in 1889—know well enough that some of the work was not paying its way—was even being done at a loss. Yet too often I saw work going elsewhere which I felt ought to have come to me. And one thing, if not certain, was probable: under my ignorant management the men had grown not so much lazy as leisurely. I knew this but too well; but I did not know how to mend the matter. . . .

What was to be done? How long I thought it over is more than I can at all tell now; but eventually—probably in 1889—I set up machinery: a gas-engine, with saws, lathe, drill and grindstone. And this device, if it saved the situation, was (as was long afterwards plain) the beginning of the end of the old style of business, though it did just bridge over the transition to the motor-trade of the present time.

I suppose it did save the situation. At any rate there was no need for dismissals, and after a year or two there was trade enough—of the more modern kind—to justify my engaging a foreman, whom I ultimately took into partnership. It proved a wise move from every point of view save the point of sentiment. The new head had experience and enterprise enough, without offending the men too, to develop the new commercial side—the manufacture of trade-vans and carts—when the old agricultural side of the business was dying out. Wood-work and iron-work were still on equal terms. Neither my partner nor myself realised at all that a new world (newer than ever America was to the Pilgrim Fathers) had begun even then to form all around us; we neither of us dreamt that the very iron age itself was passing away or that a time was actually near at hand when (as now) it would not be worth any young man's while to learn the ancient craft of the wheelwright or the mysteries of timber-drying. It might be that improved roads and plentiful building were changing the type of vehicles wheelwrights would have to build; but while horses remained horses and hill and valley were hill and valley, would not the old English provincial lore retain its value? We had no provocation to think otherwise, and yet:—

And yet, there in my old-fashioned shop the new machinery had almost forced its way in—the thin end of the wedge of scientific engineering. And from the first day the machines began running, the use of axes and adzes disappeared from the well-known place, the saws and saw-pit became obsolete. We forgot what chips were like. There, in that one little spot, the ancient provincial life of England was put into a back seat. It made a difference to me personally, little as I dreamt of such a thing. "The Men," though still my friends, as I fancied, became machine "hands." Unintentionally, I had made them servants waiting upon gas combustion. No longer was the power of horses the only force they had to consider. Rather, they were under the power of molecular forces. But to this day the few survivors of them do not know it. They think "Unrest" most wicked.

73. [THE GROWTH OF MIDDLESBROUGH]

by LADY BELL

The geography of the Industrial Revolution was clearly established by the 1830s, and the attraction of industry to the northern coalfields continued until the 1880s. One of the last developments within this pattern was the iron and steel industry of the northeast, located on Teesside. The rapid exploitation of local iron ore deposits in Cleveland and the proximity to the Durham coalfield made Middlesbrough a boom town in the second half of the nineteenth century. This account of the town is from *At the Works* (1907), 1911 ed., pp. 22–35, written by Lady (Florence) Bell (1851–1930), the wife of Sir Hugh Bell, a local ironmaster.

. . . WHEN iron is found in a district, it means that there will be employment not only for the man skilful and deft with his hands, who has a turn, perhaps, for mechanics, for science, for what may be called the higher branches of ironmaking, but there will be employment for countless numbers besides; any man with a pair of strong arms can join in the rush for the new great opportunity. For the majority of the ironworkers, the main equipment needed is health and strength. They must be hale enough and strong enough to lift bars of iron and carry them from one place in the works to another, or to wheel a barrow full of ironstone from the kiln to the furnace.

It is obvious, then, what a field for labour is suddenly opened by the discovery of iron in any part of the country. The genesis of an iron-making town which follows such a discovery is breathless and tumultuous, and the onslaught of industry which attends the discovery of mineral wealth, whether ironstone or coal mines, has certain characteristics unlike any other form of commercial enterprise. The unexpectedness of it, the change in the condition of the district, which suddenly becomes swamped under a great rush from all parts of the country of people often of the roughest kind, who are going to swell the ranks of unskilled labour; the need for housing these people; all this means that there springs, and too rapidly, into existence a community of a pre-ordained inevitable kind, the members of which must live near their work. They must therefore have houses built as quickly as possible; the houses must be cheap, must be as big as the workman wants, and no bigger; and as they are built, there arise, hastily erected, instantly occupied, the rows and rows of little brown streets, of the aspect that in some place or another is familiar to all of us. A town arising in this way cannot wait to consider anything else than time and space: and none of either must be wasted on what is merely agreeable to the eye, or even on what is merely sanitary. There can be no question under these conditions of building model cottages, or of laying out a district into ideal settlements. As one owner after another starts ironworks in the growing place, there is a fresh inrush of workmen, and day by day the little houses spring hurriedly into existence, until at last we find ourselves in the middle of a town. It is, unhappily, for the most part a side issue for the workman whether he and his family are going to live under healthy conditions. The main object of his life is to be at work: that is the one absolute necessity.

Most of the houses run up in this way consist of four rooms: two rooms on the ground floor, one of them a kitchen and living-room, which in many of them opens straight from the street, and in some has a tiny lobby with another door inside it, and another room behind, sometimes used as a bedroom, sometimes shut up as a parlour. A little steep dark staircase goes up from the kitchen to the next floor, where there are two more rooms. Sometimes there is a little scullery besides, sometimes a place hardly big enough to be called a room, just big enough to contain a bed, off the kitchen. Such abodes can house comfortably a couple and two or three children, but not the families of ten, twelve, and more, that are sometimes found in them.

Nearly every town of any considerable size that has not remained stagnant has of course in the newer portions of it quarters such as we have described, which, to keep pace with the development of the town, add themselves on to the older part of it. And whether it is a manufacturing quarter added to a town which had none before, or whether it is a whole new manufacturing town where before there was nothing, the conditions of life in such a quarter must be the same until we have found some more desirable way of dealing with them. Such a place must always necessarily present the same general characteristics. The workmen all struggle to be as near as possible to their work, to waste no time or money in transit; they are bound, therefore, to be crowded together, to have no open spaces round them in the places where the majority of them live. There will always be the rows of small cheap houses, the successive streets built as the district prospers, with no point of view but that of affording further dwellings as soon as possible for the throng of workers.

As we look down the unending vista of street after street, all alike, we are somehow apt to consider the aspect as being more discouraging than any one of the houses would look if it stood by itself. But perhaps in this we are mistaken. There is no reason in any sort of street why the life of each individual should be the more monotonous because his next-door neighbour has a front door resembling his own. Life, happily, is not governed only, if at all, by the outward aspect of the home. The dwellers in South Kensington squares and streets, who have houses all alike with columned porticoes, may have lives entirely and interestingly differentiated one from another, and so may the dwellers in the small streets of the ironmaking town, where you may open two doors side by side into houses of identically the same accommodation, and find one of them a bright and seemly home and the other an abode hardly fit to be entered by human beings. . . .

In towns of an older tradition and history, in which the newer portion has been added to a more ancient nucleus, such little monotonous streets as we have described are often erected within measurable distance of something entirely different, of more dignified dwellings in which a succession of people with a secure foothold in life have handed on one to the other a worthy tradition, adding to existence not only the useful and essential, but that which is able to beautify. In such a case the older town insensibly leavens the newer, while it is leavened by it; the older order can help to organize the growth and development of the rough, teeming life which lives side by side with it. But where there is no older nucleus of habitation, when the whole community springs into existence at once from the top to the bottom, then, indeed, it is bound to be rough-hewn. The more educated in such a community,—those who should be able to bring a leaven of art, of literature, of thought, to the toilers round them,—are toiling also themselves; they are part of the immense machine, and it is impossible for them to stand aside from it and to judge of it with a free mind. This is the condition of Middlesbrough, the town we are describing, in which leisure, that all-important factor in the development of the mind and soul, is almost unknown: a typical town in which to study the lives of those engaged in the making of iron, for it has come into existence for that purpose and for nothing else. It is obviously not a place that people would be likely to settle in unless there were very practical reasons for their doing so. There are no immediate surroundings, either of buildings or of country, to appeal to the æsthetic side of imagination, although five or six miles south of the town the beautiful Yorkshire moors begin. There is nothing to appeal to a sense of art or of beauty. There is no building in the town more than seventy years old; most of them, indeed, are barely half that age. There is no picture-gallery: indeed, there is not a picture anywhere that the ordinary public can go to see. But yet imagination can be stirred,—must be stirred,—by the story of the sudden rise of the place, by the Titanic industry with which it deals, by the hardy, strenuous life of the North, the seething vitality of enterprise with which the town began. And to-day all this has consolidated into something more potent still, for the energy of those first fashioners has been transmitted to their successors, and in every layer of the social scale the second generation is now continuing the work of the first. The employers, the professional men, the tradesmen, are handing on their work to the sons who come after them. In many cases the sons of the workmen are going on working for the same employers as their fathers did before them. All this is gradually creating a precedent, a tradition, a spirit of cohesion and of solidarity. Many of the inhabitants of to-day have been born in the town or the district, and to a large proportion of them the associations of home and childhood, of leisure and enjoyment, as well as of work, are already centred in a place which to the first restless generation of new-comers who started it was nothing but a centre of industrial activity.

The whole town, as a place of residence, is designed for the working hours of the people who live in it, and not for their leisure; so far, that is, as the more prosperous inhabitants are concerned. It is a matter of ordinary experience that as a man succeeds in his business he moves his home farther away from it, and that the distance he lives from his daily work is in direct proportion to his success in it. In compliance with this instinctive custom, the more successful and prosperous citizens of the town we are describing have gradually moved their abodes towards the outskirts, and there have grown up round the town detached villas with gardens, forming agreeable semi-country abodes which will one day no doubt be engulfed and surrounded by houses. There are fine public buildings of the kind that grow up with the development of a municipality: a Town Hall, a Free Library, the various offices of the Corporation, churches, schools, a fine park on the outskirts of the town, a big public square in the middle of it, several wide streets with good shops, and towards the south of the town broad roads planted with trees. But towards the centre and the north, serried together in and out of the better quarters, there are hundreds of the little streets we have described, in which lives a struggling, striving crowded population of workmen and their families: some of them, as will be shown, prospering, anchored, tolerably secure, some in poverty and want, the great majority on the borderland between the two. It is a population recruited by the incessant influx of fresh workers into the town, of which a great part is for ever changing and shifting, restlessly moving from one house to another, or going away altogether, in the constant hope that the mere fact of change must be an improvement.

. . . The working people greatly outnumber the rest of the inhabitants, since they amount to five-sixths of the whole population; and of these one-third are children. But of whatever age or class, all are directly or indirectly concerned in the iron trade. The majority of the population, consisting of the workmen employed at the various works and their employers, are, of course, actively taking part in it: and the rest—the clergymen of various denominations, the doctors, the teachers, the tradesmen—represent all the callings that so large and flourishing a community demands for its spiritual, intellectual, and material needs. . . .

It is somewhat surprising, when one sees the thronged, overflowing Middlesbrough of to-day, to realize that so late as 1801 it only had twenty-five inhabitants. It was no larger, in fact, than the little hamlet of the same name which six or seven centuries before had stood on the banks of the Tees at a place where the monks going between Whitby and Durham were ferried across.

The population of Middlesbrough
In 1811 was . . . . 35.
In 1821 was . . . . 40.
In 1831 was . . . . 154.
In 1841 (after railways had begun) was . . . 5,463.

In 1850 the ironstone was discovered in the Cleveland Hills, ten miles from Middlesbrough, and then the great town we have described rose on the banks of the Tees, within reach, on the one hand, of the Durham coal-fields, and on the other of the Cleveland ironstone. There could not have been a more favourable place for an ironmaking centre.

The population in 1861, after the discovery of the iron, had
risen to . . . . 18,892.
The population in 1871 was . . . . 39,284.

The population in 1881 was . . . . 55,288.
The population in 1891 was . . . . 75,532.
The population in 1901 was . . . . 91,302.

And at the moment of writing returns of the census of 1911 come to hand, giving the population of the Municipal Borough as 104,787.

Chapter 16.
The Rise of Labor

England, arise! The long, long night is over,
Faint in the East behold the dawn appear.

This song by Edward Carpenter, which soon rivalled the
Red Flag in popularity, appeared in 1886. It celebrated the
revival of socialism in England. The old tradition of popular radicalism which had been so vigorous in the 1840s
had by the 1880s become submerged beneath the overwhelming tide of Liberal complacency. The organizations
of the working class—their trade unions, friendly societies,
and cooperative societies—remained intact, but had for the
most part become so saturated with social liberalism as to
make them agencies of self-help rather than radical challenge. Yet within the ten years 1883–1893 the whole climate
of the English working-class movement changed—old unions were revivified, unorganized workers were recruited
into new unions, and a political labor party was established. The dynamic behind this change was the gospel of
socialism.

Until 1888 the number of committed socialists in England
was small. The Social Democratic Federation (founded
in 1881 as the Democratic Federation) was the pioneer
Marxist organization; and from it in 1884 there broke off
the Socialist League. In the same year the Fabian Society
was formed from an earlier body, the Fellowship of the
New Life. But the total membership of these organizations
was probably no more than 2000 in the 1880s.

From 1888 the situation was transformed by the growth
of a mass movement in the trade union world. New unions
for unskilled and semi-skilled workers—dockers, gas workers, and general laborers—were founded between 1889 and
1891, and their leaders were often closely associated with
socialist organizations. The older unions for the skilled
men ("the aristocracy of labor") also expanded. Hitherto
most working men had supported the Liberals and a pat-

tern of limited "Lib-Lab" cooperation was worked out. But the great upsurge of labor strengthened the demand for independent labor representation in parliament; and out of this agitation came the Independent Labour Party in 1893. The I.L.P. was a socialist party and its failure to attract large working class support in the 1890s showed the need to win over the trade unions if a mass workers' party was to be established. The steps by which such an alliance between the socialist parties and the labor unions was built were carefully planned by James Keir Hardie, and in 1900 his goal of "the labour alliance" was achieved through the foundation of the Labour Representation Committee. In 1906 this body secured the return of 29 labor M.P.s and the name was changed to the Labour Party.

74. [PIONEERING DAYS IN YORKSHIRE]

by BEN TURNER

The revival of the labor movement was strongest in the industrial areas, notably in the West Riding of Yorkshire. Here the role of the small band of socialists in helping the formation of new unions and providing leadership in various aspects of labor struggle was clearly demonstrated. Ben Turner (1863–1942) was a Yorkshire weaver who successfully organized the textile workers in the woolen trade, and played a leading part in local labor politics. He became president of the National Union of Textile Workers, Member of Parliament for Batley, and was knighted in 1931. These passages are from his autobiography, *About Myself* (1930), pp. 77–115.

I JOINED my Trade Union towards the end of 1882. It was the old Weavers' Union, established in 1881. The contributions were nil. We paid for our cards and rules, and the funds were raised by a very slight monthly, quarterly or special levy. It was really playing at Trades Unionism, but was as far advanced as the old Radical section felt able to go. I was a delegate to the union from our weavers in January, 1883. . . .

The biggest lock-out in our own trade was that in Huddersfield in 1883. It was here that I got my trades union baptism. . . . Each firm of weavers paying their levies was entitled to send one or more delegates. I happened to work at a small commission weaving place, and my co-weavers made me their delegate. Early in the new year of 1883 there were rumblings and rumours about a new scale or rate of wages being prepared by the employers' association, and in February it came to a head. . . . It was a revision of wages downwards. There was a new loom coming along, speeded up by 33 per cent., and the employers' new price list was so built up that it took all the 33 per cent. benefit of extra speeds. In those days the bulk of the weavers were men, and the finest of fine cloths were manufactured in that area. I think it is the premier town for cloths for men's wear to this day. These men weavers felt angry at the new move, and the new scale, and rejected it. There were various attempts by well-meaning folks to get a settlement, but it was in vain, and in March the lock-out began and 90 per cent. of the looms and, therefore, the mills, closed down. It raged for eleven weeks. It was, generally speaking, a peaceful dispute. There were few blacklegs, for the employers, in place of running that costly risk, sent a quantity of their easier woven cloths to Bradford and Halifax. Generally, the sympathy of the workers in the town was with the locked out weavers, but the tradesmen and business men, as usual, backed the employers, and wanted the workpeople to settle—however they settled. . There were demonstrations and processions, mass meetings and intrigues with intermediaries, but it dragged on its way and became a fight with hunger and despair, ranged against a wealthy plutocracy, and after eleven weeks it ended in a compromise, mostly in favour of the employers. . . .

The next big strike I had anything to do with was the strike at Leeds. It was of tailoresses at a big clothing factory, and it was in this trouble that I became closely acquainted with three sisters of one old Leeds family—the Misses Bessie, Emily and Isabella Ford. Emily is still living, and is a famous church artist. Her sister Bessie helped on unpopular causes, and was a social and musical helper for the poorer people of Leeds; and Miss Isabella, the youngest of the three, became a noted Labour woman, a foundation member of the Independent Labour Party and a fighter for women's franchise. She called me in to help her, and we used to address the strikers in various halls and meeting places. It ended in a compromise, but it stirred Leeds up a bit, and from it came the Leeds Tailoresses' Union which is now merged in the Tailors and Garment Workers' Union. From it also came the old Clothiers' Operatives' Union, which is also merged in the national body. We were able to get a little help for the women, and on two occasions we distributed strike pay to the tune of 4s. and 5s. respectively, which in those days was looked upon as moderate.

Another strike I remember very vividly was that of the Leeds Gasworkers. The men had just become members of the newly-formed Gasworkers' Union, and they had caught the new spirit and were determined they would try for the eight hours' day. London gasworkers had won it, the Dockers' Union had won their "tanner per hour," and New Unionism, as it was termed, as distinct from Craft Unionism, was the order of the day. They made their demands to the Leeds Gas Committee, who turned them down. This challenge the men met by going on strike, and for about a week Leeds was a most lively and darkened place. The Gas Committee were unwise enough to try and fill the men's places with blacklegs, and train-loads of them coming to Leeds set the town afire. The Gas Committee got beds and food and beer into Meadow Lane, and New Wortley Gasworks, and believed they had won, but the gas stokers had their blood up, and lamps were broken in the streets and attacks were made upon the gasworks and the blacklegs. I well remember being with the men at the battle of the bridge at New Wortley when the soldiers charged the crowd. . . .

Another big dispute with which I was closely connected was the lock-out or strike at Manningham Mills, Bradford. In December, 1890, Mr. S. Cunliffe-Lister, who later on became Lord Masham, decided that a big reduction should be made in the wages of his operatives. It ranged upwards of 25 per cent. These very fine mills employed towards 5,000 workpeople. All of them were not affected by the dispute, but the weavers, to the number of many hundreds, were faced with the proposal just on the eve of Christmas. . . . A courteous note was sent to the firm, but it received no response. The reduction was placarded, and the workpeople, after a ballot vote, declined to accept it, and the strike, lock-out or dispute began. What a hectic time it was! It lasted nearly six months, and twice and sometimes three times a week we had processions of the workpeople marching from near the millgates by several routes to the centre of Bradford. Sometimes we held meetings in the Skating Rink, sometimes in St. George's Hall, other times in Peckover Square, and other times at the end of the Town Hall. There were no funds to start with, only odd ones were financial members of their union, and we had to do many things to raise the wind to help the hardest hit in that long struggle. The total funds raised came to over £11,000—a tidy sum in those days. It was my duty, along with a working member of the committee, or on my own, to visit trades union centres in Dundee, Forfar, Edinburgh, Newcastle, London and other places. For many week-ends I went with the collectors into mining centres and spoke at Barnsley, Wakefield, and Rotherham, and in some Lancashire towns I visited a number of the Trades Councils. It was a hard time for my wife and three very little children, for they seldom saw their father, who was, as they say, up to the neck in it.

The women strikers established a well-conducted soup kitchen, and the sympathy of the shopkeepers was very broad and the butchers gave their bones and greengrocers and grocers and bakers gave peas, lentils and loaves, and thus children were fed. Every Thursday 200 to 300 cigar boxes would be fastened up, handbills placed over them, holes cut in for coins to be placed in, and these brave women and a number of the men would set out on the Friday and Saturday to mills and workshops, mines and factories, for miles around. Each who went got a shilling and their fares, and when the boxes were brought in on the Saturday afternoon the totals were made up and a distribution followed to the most needy and extra supplies were provided for the soup kitchen. We instituted a prize draw of a big sort, and scores of thousands of penny tickets were sold. The first prize was a £28 piano. . . .

The dispute went on until well into May, when a number of public men got Sam Lister to bend a little, and a settlement was arrived at. It was really a defeat, and many of the best men and women went overseas to make a new home in a new land. . . .

In 1890, we started the *Workman's Times*. In promoting it, it was my business to go out to address many Trades Councils, and I visited Birmingham, Wolverhampton, Dudley, Kidderminster, Sheffield, Leicester, Derby, Newcastle and other places on that mission.

I did it by night-travelling and day-time writing, for I did work both for the *Factory Times* and the *Workman's Times*. I used to do all sorts of writing, notes, leaders, special articles, news from villages, reports of meetings. . . .

I kept up my Union work, and really the two fitted in as the paper gave us ample room for our mill news and textile views, and for several years the paper was a success and our union rose to bigger membership at the same time. As Leeds and District Secretary for the Union with a wage of five shillings a week, we took a little office at three shillings per week, and I went into the "hurly-burly" of Leeds Labour life.

I joined at once the Leeds Socialist Party. The membership was mixed, but not large. A few were Jews, employed in Leeds clothing houses, a few were men with anarchist views. There were a few Englishmen and Irishmen—left-wing Socialists of that period—composed the membership. The club was about a mile and a quarter from our house, and whilst enjoying myself there with intellectual debates and disquisitions, I did not always go home as early as I should have done. Put it down that I was young and active and in my element taking part in the advanced Labour and Socialist movement. I also joined the Leeds Trades Council in 1889, and during the two years I lived in Leeds took part in its work and in its discussions. The Socialist Club folks were anti-Trades Council, and because I would stand up for the Council the anarchist element in the Socialist Club were at political enmity with me. It was at this club that I met Cunninghame Graham, Michael Davitt, Edward Carpenter, William Thorne and many another old Labour Socialist and land reformer.

. . . It was about this time that we younger folks wanted to lead the Trades Union movement out of the Liberal Party fold, and as the unions grew stronger the Socialist or Labour force grew stronger, and a large number of Labour Unions and Labour Clubs were formed, especially in the Industrial areas of the West Riding. I helped in the formation of Labour Clubs in many parts of Leeds, Huddersfield, Colne Valley, Holme Valley, Bradford and other places. We enjoyed doing it for nothing, paying our own expenses to this place and that place, being repaid, as it were, by the success we obtained. Street meetings were numerous, and although we were young men with no Oxford accent, but a Yorkshire twang, we didn't hesitate to thunder forth our views on Trades Unionism, Labour politics, on independent lines, nearly always concluding, of course, with the old slogan "The Socialisation of the means of production, distribution and exchange." . . .

75. [THE RELIGION OF SOCIALISM]

by J A M E S   K E I R   H A R D I E

The leader of the movement for a national Labour Party based upon an alliance of the socialists and the labor unions was James Keir Hardie (1856–1915). He came from a poor Scottish family and first made his mark as an organizer of the Scottish coal miners. Starting as a Liberal, he soon became convinced of the need for independent labor representation and devoted his life to the attainment of this goal. His socialism was of a simple, ethical type and derived from Nonconformist traditions. The following report of a speech at Merthyr Tydfil (South Wales) in August 1910 protesting the Liberal government's use of troops in a railway men's strike is a fair example of Hardie's style and simple, biblical oratory (from *Keir Hardie's Speeches and Writings*, Emrys Hughes, ed. [1927], pp. 146–147).

"MY friends, let us have law and order by all means, but in the name of the God we worship do not call it law and order to shoot down strikers who are simply asking for their unions to be recognised.

"The moral of this thing is two-fold. First of all, the old idea of separate unions has passed away. The colliers, the ironworkers, the steelworkers, the artisans, the railwaymen, the shop assistants, the school teachers, the gasworkers, and the street cleaners have all got to stand together, not as members of different trades, but as members of one class—(hear, hear)—fighting for the improvement of conditions all round.

"That is the first point. And the second is like unto it. We have exposed the hypocrisy of Liberal professions once more. (Loud cheers.) The last time that men were shot down by the military was at Featherstone, when Asquith was Home Secretary and a Liberal Government was in power. Once more when the Liberals are in office, and Asquith is Prime Minister, the troops are let loose upon the people to shoot them down if need be whilst they are fighting for their legitimate rights. My friends and comrades, you cannot mix oil and water. There are some men in the meeting who are half Liberal, half Labour—who want to be friends with both parties. The thing cannot be done, men. ('Quite right,' and loud cheers.) They will give you Insurance Bills, they will give you all kinds of soothing syrups to keep you quiet, but in the end your Liberal Party, just like your Tory Party, is the party of the rich, and exists to protect the rich when Labour and Capital come into conflict.

"And, therefore, my friends, make up your minds this day whom you will serve: Labour and Socialism, or Liberalism and Capitalism. (Loud applause.) That is the choice that lies before you. The day for fooling has gone past. The day for temporising is over and done with. This is real war we are in, and if the people stand together the time will come, and come speedily, when every City Council like Liverpool will be manned by Labour men, when the House of Commons will have its majority of Labour men—(loud cheers)—and when the forces of the Crown will not be used to help the rich to oppress the poor, but to uplift the masses of the people to a higher plane." (Cheers.)

The hon. member concluded:—

"On this Sunday afternoon, speaking on this tip, with all that glorious scenery round about, with God's sun overhead, with the birds full of song, with the harvest ripe for reaping, with the fruit in the orchard, the flower in the field, and the lamb in the meadow, there is joy, beauty, peace, and prosperity everywhere, except in the homes and lives of the Common People. (Applause.) Oh, men and women, in the name of that God whom you profess to believe in, in the name of Jesus of Nazareth who died to save your souls, how long do you intend to submit to a system which is defacing God's image upon you, which is blurring and marring God's handiwork, which is destroying the lives of men, women, and children? Do not you think that God, who made everything else beautiful, intended men to be beautiful also; that God, who made the birds as free as the wind, intended you to be free also? And here you are, in bondage. Come out from the House of Bondage—(hear, hear)—fight for freedom—(cheers)—fight for manhood, fight for the coming day when in body, soul, and spirit you will be free to live your own lives—(applause)—and give glory to your Creator." (Loud and prolonged cheering.)

76. HOW I BECAME A SOCIALIST

by WILLIAM MORRIS

One of the most attractive figures in the early socialist movement was William Morris (1834–1896). He had already won fame as an artist, craftsman, and poet when he joined the Social Democratic Federation in 1883. However, his dislike of H. M. Hyndman, the leader of the S.D.F., led to Morris's break-away and the foundation of the Socialist League in 1884. He edited and financed *The Commonweal* until 1890, when the anarchists secured control of the League. The following passages are from Morris's pamphlet, *How I became a Socialist* (1896), pp. 9–13, reprinted from articles in *Justice*, June 1894.

. . . WHAT I mean by Socialism is a condition of society in which there should be neither rich nor poor, neither master nor master's man, neither idle nor overworked, neither brain-sick brain workers nor heart-sick hand workers, in a word, in which all men would be living in equality of condition, and would manage their affairs unwastefully, and with the full consciousness that harm to one would mean harm to all—the realisation at last of the meaning of the word COMMONWEALTH.

Now this view of Socialism which I hold to-day, and hope to die holding, is what I began with; I had no transitional period, unless you may call such a brief period of political radicalism during which I saw my ideal clear enough, but had no hope of any realisation of it. That came to an end some months before I joined the (then) Democratic Federation, and the meaning of my joining that body was that I had conceived a hope of the realisation of my ideal. If you ask me how much of a hope, or what I thought we Socialists then living and working would accomplish towards it, or when there would be affected any change in the face of society, I must say, I do not know. I can only say that I did not measure my hope, nor the joy that it brought me at the time. For the rest when I took that step I was blankly ignorant of economics; I had never so much as opened Adam Smith, or heard of Ricardo, or of Karl Marx. Oddly enough I *had* read some of Mill, to wit, those posthumous papers of his (published was it in the *Westminster Review* or the *Fortnightly?*) in which he attacks Socialism in its Fourierist guise. In those papers he put the arguments, as far as they go, clearly and honestly, and the result so far as I was concerned was to convince me that Socialism was a necessary change, and that it was possible to bring it about in our own days. Those papers put the finishing touch to my conversion to Socialism. Well, having joined a Socialist body (for the Federation soon became definitely Socialist), I put some conscience into trying to learn the economical side of Socialism, and even tackled Marx, though I must confess that, whereas I thoroughly enjoyed the historical part of "Capital," I suffered agonies of confusion of the brain over reading the pure economics of that great work. Anyhow, I read what I could, and will hope that some information stuck to me from my reading; but more, I must think, from continuous conversation with such friends as Bax and Hyndman and Scheu, and the brisk course of propaganda meetings which were going on at the time, and in which I took my share. Such finish to what of education in practical Socialism as I am capable of I received afterwards from some of my Anarchist friends, from whom I learned, quite against their intention, that Anarchism was impossible, much as I learned from Mill against *his* intention that Socialism was necessary.

But in thus telling how I fell into *practical* Socialism I have begun, as I perceive, in the middle, for in my position of a well-to-do man, not suffering from the disabilities which oppress a working man at every step, I feel that I might never have been drawn into the practical side of the question if an ideal had not forced me to seek towards it. For politics as politics, *i.e.*, not regarded as a necessary if cumbersome and disgustful means to an end, would never have attracted me, nor when I had become conscious of the wrongs of society as it now is, and the oppression of poor people, could I have ever believed in the possibility of a *partial* setting right of those wrongs. In other words, I could never have been such a fool as to believe in the happy and "respectable" poor.

If, therefore, my ideal forced me to look for practical Socialism, what was it that forced me to conceive of an ideal? Now, here comes in what I said of my being (in this paper) a type of a certain group of mind.

Before the uprising of *modern* Socialism almost all intelligent people either were, or professed themselves to be, quite contented with the civilisation of this century. Again, almost all of these really were thus contented, and saw nothing to do but to perfect the said civilisation by getting rid of a few ridiculous survivals of the barbarous ages. To be short, this was the *Whig* frame of mind, natural to the modern prosperous middle-class men, who, in fact, as far as mechanical progress is concerned, have nothing to ask for, if only Socialism would leave them alone to enjoy their plentiful style.

But besides these contented ones there were others who were not really contented, but had a vague sentiment of repulsion to the triumph of civilisation, but were coerced into silence by the measureless power of Whiggery. Lastly there were a few who were in open rebellion against the said Whiggery—a few, say two, Carlyle and Ruskin. The latter, before my days of practical Socialism, was my master towards the ideal aforesaid, and, looking backward, I cannot help saying, by the way, how deadly dull the world would have been twenty years ago but for Ruskin! It was through him that I learned to give form to my discontent, which I must say was not by any means vague. Apart from the desire to produce beautiful things, the leading passion of my life has been and is hatred of modern civilisation. What shall I say of it now, when the words are put into my mouth, my hope of its destruction—what shall I say of its supplanting by Socialism?

What shall I say concerning its mastery of, and its waste of mechanical power, its commonwealth so poor, its enemies of the commonwealth so rich, its stupendous organisation—for the misery of life! Its contempt of simple pleasures which everyone could enjoy but for its folly? Its eyeless vulgarity which has destroyed art, the one certain solace of labour? All this I felt then as now, but I did not know why it was so. The hope of the past times was gone, the struggles of mankind for many ages had produced nothing but this sordid, aimless, ugly confusion; the immediate future seemed to me likely to intensify all the present evils by sweeping away the last survivals of the days before the dull squalor of civilisation had settled down on the world. This was a bad look out indeed, and, if I may mention myself as a personality and not as a mere type, especially so to a man of my disposition, careless of metaphysics and religion, as well as of scientific analysis, but with a deep love of the earth and the life on it, and a passion for the history of the past of mankind. Think of it! Was it all to end in a counting-house on the top of a cinder-heap, with Podsnap's drawing-room in the offing, and a Whig committee dealing out champagne to the rich and margarine to the poor in such convenient proportions as would make all men contented together, though the pleasure of the eyes was gone from the world, and the place of Homer was to be taken by Huxley. Yet believe me, in my heart when I really forced myself to look towards the future, that is, what I saw in it, and, as far as I could tell, scarce anyone seemed to think it worth while to struggle against such a consummation of civilisation. So there I was in for a fine pessimistic end of life, if it had not somehow dawned on me, that amidst all this filth of civilisation the seeds of a great chance, what we others call Social Revolution, were beginning to germinate. The whole face of things was changed to me by that discovery, and all I had to do then in order to become a Socialist was to hook myself on to the practical movement, which, as before said, I have tried to do as well as I could.

To sum up, then, the study of history and the love and practice of art forced me into a hatred of the civilisation, which, if things were to stop as they are, would turn history into inconsequent nonsense, and make art a collection of the curiosities of the past, which would have no serious relation to the life of the present.

But the consciousness of revolution stirring amidst our hateful modern society prevented me, luckier than many others of artistic perceptions, from crystallising into a mere railer against "progress" on the one hand, and on the other from wasting time and energy in any of the numerous schemes by which the quasi-artistic of the middle-classes hope to make art grow when it has no longer any root, and thus I became a practical Socialist.

77. MERRIE ENGLAND

by ROBERT BLATCHFORD

Not since the days of William Cobbett's *Political Register* had there been a radical journal which enjoyed the popularity of the *Clarion*. Founded in 1891 by Robert Blatchford (1851–1943), the *Clarion* spread socialist ideas in readable, entertaining form. A penny edition of *Merrie England,* which was a reprint of articles by Blatchford in the *Clarion,* sold a million copies in 1894–1895. This passage is from pp. 43–45 of the 1st ed. (1893).

JOHN SMITH, do you know what Socialism is? You have heard it denounced many a time, and it is said that you do not believe in it; but do you know what it is?

Good or bad, wise or foolish, it is all I have to offer as a remedy of the many evils of which I have been complaining.

Good or bad, wise or foolish, Socialism is the only remedy in sight. None of its opponents, none of your friends, the members of Parliament, old trade union leaders, Tory and Liberal editors, parsons, priests, lawyers, and men of substance have any remedy to offer at all.

Some of them are sorry, or profess to be sorry, that there is so much misery in the land; some of them offer a little mild charity, some a little feeble legislation, but there is no great radical cure to be heard of except Socialism.

What is Socialism? I am going to tell you, and I ask you to listen patiently, and to judge fairly. You have heard Socialism reviled by speakers and writers. You know that the Pope has denounced it, and that the Bishop of Manchester has denounced it. You know that men like Herbert Spencer, Charles Bradlaugh, and John Morley have written and spoken against it, and doubtless you have got an idea that it is as unworthy, as unwise, and as unworkable as such men say it is. Now I will describe it for you and you shall draw your own conclusions.

But before I tell you what Socialism is, I must tell you what Socialism is not. For half our time as champions of Socialism is wasted in denials of false descriptions of Socialism; and to a large extent the anger, the ridicule, and the argument of the opponents of Socialism are hurled against a Socialism which has no existence except in their own heated minds.

Socialism does not consist in violently seizing upon the property of the rich and sharing it out amongst the poor.

Socialists do not propose by a single Act of Parliament or by a sudden revolution, to put all men on an equality, and compel them to remain so. Socialism is not a wild dream of a happy land where the apples will drop off the trees into our open mouths, the fish come out of the rivers and fry themselves for dinner, and the looms turn out ready-made suits of velvet with gold buttons without the trouble of coaling the engine. Neither is it a dream of a nation of stained-glass angels, who never say damn, who always love their neighbours better than themselves, and who never need to work unless they wish to.

No. Socialism is none of these things. It is a scientific scheme of national Government, entirely wise, just and practical. And now let us see.

For convenience sake, Socialism is usually divided into two kinds. These are called—

1. Practical Socialism.
2. Ideal Socialism.

Really they are only part of one whole; Practical Socialism being a kind of preliminary step towards Ideal Socialism, so that we might with more reason call them Elementary and Advanced Socialism.

I am an Ideal Socialist, and desire to have the whole Socialist programme carried out.

Practical Socialism is so simple that a child may understand it. It is a kind of national scheme of co-operation, managed by the State. Its programme consists, essentially, of one demand, that the land and other instruments of production shall be the common property of the people, and shall be used and governed by the people for the people.

Make the land and all the instruments of production State property; put all farms, mines, mills, ships, railways, and shops under State control, as you have already put the postal and telegraphic services under State control, and Practical Socialism is accomplished.

The postal and telegraphic service is the standing proof of the capacity of the State to manage the public business with economy and success.

That which has been done with the post-offices may be done with mines, trams, railways, and factories.

The difference between Socialism and the state of things now in existence will now be plain to you.

At present the land—that is, England—does not belong to the people—to the English—but to a few rich men. The mines, mills, ships, shops, canals, railways, houses, docks, harbours and machinery do not belong to the people, but to a few rich men.

Therefore, the land, the factories, the railways, ships, and machinery are not used for the general good of the people, but are used to make wealth for the few rich men who own them.

Socialists say that this arrangement is unjust and unwise, that it entails waste as well as misery, and that it would be better for all, even for the rich, that the land and other instruments of production should become the property of the State, just as the post-office and the telegraphs have become the property of the State.

Socialists demand that the State shall manage the railways and the mines and the mills just as it now manages the post-offices and the telegraphs.

Socialists declare that if it is wicked and foolish and impossible for the State to manage the factories, mines and railways, then it is wicked and foolish and impossible for the State to manage the telegraphs.

Socialists declare that as the State carries the people's letters and telegrams more cheaply and more efficiently than they were carried by private enterprise, so it could grow corn and weave cloth and work the railway systems more cheaply and more efficiently than they are now worked by private enterprise.

Socialists declare that as our Government now makes food and clothing and arms and accoutrements for the army and navy and police, so it could make them for the people.

Socialists declare that as many corporations make gas, provide and manage the water-supply, look after the paving and lighting and cleansing of the streets, and often do a good deal of building and farming, so there is no reason why they should not get coal and spin yarn, and make boots, and bread, and beer for the people.

Socialists point out that if all the industries of the nation were put under State control, all the profit which now goes into the hands of a few idle men, would go into the coffers of the State—which means that the people would enjoy the benefits of all the wealth they create.

This, then, is the basis of Socialism, that England should be owned by the English, and managed for the benefit of the English, instead of being owned by a few rich idlers, and mismanaged by them for the benefit of themselves.

But Socialism means more than the mere transference of the wealth of the nation to the nation.

Socialism would not endure competition. Where it found two factories engaged in under-cutting each other at the price of long hours and low wages to the workers, it would step in and fuse the two concerns into one, save an immense sum in cost of working, and finally produce more goods and better goods at a lower figure than were produced before.

But Practical Socialism would do more than that. It would educate

the people. It would provide cheap and pure food. It would extend
and elevate the means of study and amusement. It would foster literature and science and art. It would encourage and reward genius and
industry. It would abolish sweating and jerry work. It would demolish
the slums and erect good and handsome dwellings. It would compel
all men to do some kind of useful work. It would recreate and nourish
the craftsman's pride in his craft. It would protect women and children. It would raise the standard of health and morality; and it would
take the sting out of pauperism by paying pensions to honest workers
no longer able to work.

Why nationalise the land and instruments of production? To save
waste; to save panics; to avert trade depressions, famines, strikes, and
congestion of industrial centres; and to prevent greedy and unscrupu-
lous sharpers from enriching themselves at the cost of the national
health and prosperity. In short, to replace anarchy and war by law
and order. To keep the wolves out of the fold, to tend and fertilise the
field of labour instead of allowing the wheat to be strangled by the
tares, and to regulate wisely the distribution of the seed-corn of industry so that it might no longer be scattered broadcast—some falling
on rocks and some being eaten up by the birds of the air.

78. [THE FABIAN SOCIETY]

by GEORGE BERNARD SHAW

Very different from the Social Democratic Federation, the
Socialist League, and the labor unions was the Fabian Society, founded in 1884 by a small group of intellectuals.
Their socialism was derived not from Marx, nor from concepts of ethical or religious justice, but from Benthamite
utilitarianism. Later, when the Society grew in influence,
it provided important elements in the distinctive social
philosophy of the Labour Party. In its early days the two
most notable members of the Fabian Society were Sidney
Webb (1859–1947) and George Bernard Shaw (1856–
1950). *Tract No. 70: Report on Fabian Policy* (1896) was
written by Shaw for the meeting of the International Socialist Workers and Trade Union Congress in London in
1896, and is reprinted in full.

I. THE MISSION OF THE FABIANS

THE object of the Fabian Society is to persuade the English people to make their political constitution thoroughly democratic and so to socialize their industries as to make the livelihood of the people entirely independent of private Capitalism.

The Fabian Society endeavours to pursue its Socialist and Democratic objects with complete singleness of aim. For example:

It has no distinctive opinions on the Marriage Question, Religion, Art, abstract Economics, historic Evolution, Currency, or any other subject than its own special business of practical Democracy and Socialism.

It brings all the pressure and persuasion in its power to bear on existing forces, caring nothing by what name any party calls itself, or what principles, Socialist or other, it professes, but having regard solely to the tendency of its actions, supporting those which make for Socialism and Democracy, and opposing those which are reactionary.

It does not propose that the practical steps towards Social-Democracy should be carried out by itself, or by any other specially organised society or party.

It does not ask the English people to join the Fabian Society.

II. FABIAN ELECTORAL TACTICS

The Fabian Society does not claim to be the people of England, or even the Socialist party, and therefore does not seek direct political representation by putting forward Fabian candidates at elections. But it loses no opportunity of influencing elections and inducing constituencies to select Socialists as their candidates. No person, however, can obtain the support of the Fabian Society, or escape its opposition, by merely repeating a few shibboleths and calling himself a Socialist or Social-Democrat. As there is no Second Ballot in England, frivolous candidatures give great offence, and discredit the party in whose name they are undertaken, because any third candidate who is not well supported will not only be beaten himself, but may also involve in his defeat the better of the two candidates competing with him. Under such circumstances the Fabian Society throws its weight against the third candidate whether he calls himself a Socialist or not, in order to secure the victory to the better of the two candidates between whom the contest really lies. But when the third candidate is not only a serious representative of Socialism, but can organise his party well, and is likely to poll sufficient votes to make even his defeat a respectable demonstration of the strength and growth of Socialism in the constituency, the Fabian Society supports him resolutely under all circumstances and against all other parties.

III. FABIAN TOLERATION

The Fabian Society, far from holding aloof from other bodies, urges its members to lose no opportunity of joining them and permeating them with Fabian ideas as far as possible. Almost all organizations and movements contain elements making for Socialism, no matter how remote the sympathies and intentions of their founders may be from those of the Socialists. On the other hand, unintentionally reactionary proposals are constantly being brought forward in Socialist bodies. Fabians are therefore encouraged to join all other organizations, Socialist or non-Socialist, in which Fabian work can be done.

IV. FABIAN CONSTITUTIONALISM

The Fabian Society is perfectly constitutional in its attitude; and its methods are those usual in political life in England.

The Fabian Society accepts the conditions imposed on it by human nature and by the national character and political circumstances of the English people. It sympathises with the ordinary citizen's desire for gradual, peaceful changes, as against revolutionary, conflict with the army and police, and martyrdom. It recognises the fact that Social-Democracy is not the whole of the working-class program, and that every separate measure towards the socialization of industry will have to compete for precedence with numbers of other reforms. It therefore does not believe that the moment will ever come when the whole of Socialism will be staked on the issue of a single General Election or a single Bill in the House of Commons as between the proletariat on one side and the proprietariat on the other. Each instalment of Social-Democracy will only be a measure among other measures, and will have to be kept to the front by an energetic socialist section. The Fabian Society therefore begs those Socialists who are looking forward to a sensational historical crisis, to join some other Society.

V. FABIAN DEMOCRACY

Democracy, as understood by the Fabian Society, means simply the control of the administration by freely elected representatives of the people. The Fabian Society energetically repudiates all conceptions of Democracy as a system by which the technical work of government administration and the appointment of public officials, shall be carried on by referendum or any other form of direct popular decision. Such arrangements may be practical in a village community, but not in the complicated industrial civilizations which are ripening for Social Democracy. When the House of Commons is freed from the veto of the House of Lords and thrown open to candidates from all classes by an effective system of Payment of Representatives and a more rational method of election, the British parliamentary system will be, in the opinion of the Fabian Society, a first-rate practical instrument of democratic government.

Democracy, as understood by the Fabian Society, makes no political distinction between men and women.

VI. FABIAN COMPROMISE

The Fabian Society, having learnt from experience that Socialists cannot have their own way in everything any more than other people, recognises that in a Democratic community Compromise is a necessary condition of political progress.

VII. FABIAN SOCIALISM

Socialism, as understood by the Fabian Society, means the organization and conduct of the necessary industries of the country and the appropriation of all forms of economic rent of land and capital by the nation as a whole, through the most suitable public authorities, parochial, municipal, provincial, or central.

The Socialism advocated by the Fabian Society is State Socialism exclusively. The foreign friends of the Fabian Society must interpret this declaration in view of the fact that since England now possesses an elaborate democratic State machinery, graduated from the Parish Council or Vestry up to the central Parliament, and elected under a franchise which enables the working class vote to overwhelm all others, the opposition which exists in the continental monarchies between the State and the people does not hamper English Socialists. For example, the distinction made between State Socialism and Social-Democracy in Germany, where the municipalities and other local bodies are closed against the working classes, has no meaning in England. The difficulty in England is not to secure more political power for the people, but to persuade them to make any sensible use of the power they already have.

VIII. FABIAN INDIVIDUALISM

The Fabian Society does not suggest that the State should monopolise industry as against private enterprise or individual initiative further than may be necessary to make the livelihood of the people and their access to the sources of production completely independent of both. The freedom of individuals to test the social value of new inventions; to initiate improved methods of production; to anticipate and lead public enterprise in catering for new social wants; to practise all arts, crafts and professions independently; in short, to complete the social organization by adding the resources of private activity and judgment to those of public routine, is, subject to the above conditions, as highly valued by the Fabian Society as Freedom of Speech, Freedom of the Press or any other article in the charter of popular liberties.

IX. FABIAN FREEDOM OF THOUGHT

The Fabian Society strenuously maintains its freedom of thought and speech with regard to the errors of Socialist authors, economists, leaders and parties, no less than to those of its opponents. For instance, it insists on the necessity of maintaining as critical an attitude towards Marx and Lassalle, some of whose views must by this time be discarded as erroneous or obsolete, as these eminent Socialists themselves maintained towards their predecessors, St. Simon and Robert Owen.

X. FABIAN JOURNALISM

The Fabian Society, in its relations with the Press, makes no such distinction as that indicated by the phrase "the Capitalist Press." In England all political papers without exception are conducted with private capital under the control of the owners of the capital. Some of them profess Socialist opinions, others Conservative opinions, others Liberal and Radical opinions, and so forth. The Socialists papers are in no way more independent of social pressure than the others; and the superiority of a Socialist paper from the Socialist point of view is of exactly the same nature as the superiority of a Conservative paper from the Conservative point of view. The Fabian Society, in securing journalistic expression for its ideas, has no preference, except for the largest circulation.

XI. FABIANS AND THE MIDDLE CLASS

In view of the fact that the Socialist movement has been hitherto inspired, instructed, and led by members of the middle class or "bourgeoisie," the Fabian Society though not at all surprised to find these middle class leaders attacking with much bitterness the narrow social ideals current in their own class, protests against the absurdity of Socialists denouncing the very class from which Socialism has sprung as specially hostile to it. The Fabian Society has no romantic illusions as to the freedom of the proletariat from these same narrow ideals. Like every other Socialist society, it can only educate the people in Socialism by making them conversant with the conclusions of the most enlightened members of all classes. The Fabian Society, therefore, cannot reasonably use the words "bourgeois" or "middle class" as terms of reproach, more especially as it would thereby condemn a large proportion of its own members.

XII. FABIAN NATURAL PHILOSOPHY

The Fabian Society endeavours to rouse Social compunction by making the public conscious of the evil condition of society under the present system. This it does by the collection and publication of authentic and impartial statistical tracts, compiled, not from the works of Socialists, but from official sources. The first volume of Karl Marx's *Das Capital*, which contains an immense mass of carefully verified facts concerning modern capitalistic civilization, and practically nothing about Socialism, is probably the most successful propagandist work ever published. The Fabian Society, in its endeavours to continue the work of Marx in this direction, has found that the guesses made by Socialists at the condition of the people almost invariably flatter the existing system instead of, as might be suspected, exaggerating its evils. The Fabian Society therefore concludes that in the natural philosophy of Socialism, light is a more important factor than heat.

XIII. FABIAN REPUDIATIONS

The Fabian Society discards such phrases as "the abolition of the wage system," which can only mislead the public as to the aims of Socialism. Socialism does not involve the abolition of wages, but the establishment of standard allowances for the maintenance of all workers by the community in its own service, as an alternative to wages fixed by the competition of destitute men and women for private employment, as well as to commercial profits, commissions, and all other speculative and competitive forms of remuneration. In short, the Fabian Society, far from desiring to abolish wages, wishes to secure them for everybody.

The Fabian Society resolutely opposes all pretentions to hamper the socialization of industry with equal wages, equal hours of labour, equal official status, or equal authority for everyone. Such conditions are not only impracticable, but incompatible with the equality of subordination to the common interest which is fundamental in modern Socialism.

The Fabian Society steadfastly discountenances all schemes for securing to any person, or any group of persons "the entire product of their labor." It recognises that wealth is social in its origin and must be social in its distribution, since the evolution of industry has made it impossible to distinguish the particular contribution that each person makes to the common product, or to ascertain its value.

The Fabian Society desires to offer to all projectors and founders of Utopian communities in South America, Africa, and other remote localities, its apologies for its impatience of such adventures. To such protectors, and all patrons of schemes for starting similar settlements and workshops at home, the Society announces emphatically that it does not believe in the establishment of Socialism by private enterprise.

XIV. FINALLY

The Fabian Society does not put Socialism forward as a panacea for the ills of human society, but only for those produced by defective organization of industry and by a radically bad distribution of wealth.

79. PROGRAM OF THE INDEPENDENT LABOUR PARTY

Dissatisfaction with the consequences of relying on the Liberals, together with the spread of socialism and the upsurge of labor unionism, led to the formation of local independent labor parties in the north, especially in Yorkshire and in the Manchester area. In January 1893 in Bradford a national conference of these and other socialist organizations was held, at which was born the Independent Labour Party. Despite its name, which had been selected to disarm the fears which "socialism" might arouse, the new party adopted a socialist program. Its great objective at first was to win over the trade unions to an independent policy. Although it did not grow into a mass party in the 1890s, it became in 1900 the kernel of a Labour Party based on the trade unions. This was effected through the Labour Representation Committee which in 1906 took the name of Labour Party (see Reading No. 80). After the foundation of the Labour Party the I.L.P. continued to have a separate existence, as well as being a constituent part of the Labour Party which was federal in structure. This program of the I.L.P. is dated 1906–1907.

NAME

"THE Independent Labour Party."

MEMBERSHIP

Open to all Socialists who endorse the principles and policy of the Party, are not members of either the Liberal or Conservative Party, and whose application for membership is accepted by a Branch.

Any member expelled from membership of a Branch of the I.L.P. shall not be eligible for membership of any other Branch without having first submitted his or her case for adjudication of the N.A.C.

OBJECT

The object of the Party is to establish the Socialist State, when land and capital will be held by the community and used for the well-being of the community, and when the exchange of commodities will be organized also by the community, so as to secure the highest possible standard of life for the individual. In giving effect to this object it shall work as part of the International Socialist movement.

METHOD

The Party, to secure its objects, adopts—
1. EDUCATIONAL METHODS, including the publication of Socialist literature, the holding of meetings, etc.
2. POLITICAL METHODS, including the election of its members to local and national administrative and legislative bodies.

PROGRAMME

The true object of industry being the production of the requirements of life, the responsibility should rest with the community collectively, therefore—

The land, being the storehouse of all the necessaries of life, should be declared and treated as public property.

The capital necessary for industrial operations should be owned and used collectively.

Work, and wealth resulting therefrom, should be equitably distributed over the population.

As a means to this end, we demand the enactment of the following measures:—

1. A maximum forty-eight hours' working-week, with the retention of all existing holidays, and Labour Day, May 1, secured by law.

2. The provision of work to all capable adult applicants at recognized trade-union rates, with a statutory minimum of sixpence per hour.

In order to remuneratively employ the applicants, parish, district, borough, and county councils to be invested with power to—

(*a*) Organize and undertake such industries as they may consider desirable.

(*b*) Compulsorily acquire land; purchase, erect, or manufacture, buildings, stock, or other articles for carrying on such industries.

(*c*) Levy rates on the rental values of the district, and borrow money on the security of such rates for any of the above purposes.

3. State pensions for every person over fifty years of age, and adequate provision for all widows, orphans, sick and disabled workers.

4. Free, secular, moral, primary, secondary and university education, with free maintenance while at school or university.

5. The raising of the age of child labour, with a view of its ultimate extinction.

6. Municipalization and public control of the drink traffic.

7. Municipalization and public control of all hospitals and infirmaries.

8. Abolition of indirect taxation, and the gradual transference of all public burdens on to unearned incomes, with a view to their ultimate extinction.

The Independent Labour Party is in favour of adult suffrage, with full political rights and privileges for women, and the immediate extension of the franchise to women on the same terms as granted to men; also triennial parliaments and second ballot.

80. CONSTITUTION OF THE LABOUR PARTY

Throughout the 1890s Keir Hardie fought strenuously to convert the labor unions to a policy of independent labor representation in parliament. Within the Trades Union Congress he encountered stiff resistance from the "Lib-Labs," but eventually he was able, by means of an innocuously worded resolution, to secure the establishment of a Labour Representation Committee in 1900. This consisted of representatives of the trade unions and socialist bodies, and its purpose was to secure the return of labor members to parliament. In 1906 it changed its name to the Labour Party and adopted the following constitution.

ORGANIZATION

I.—AFFILIATION

1. THE Labour Party is a Federation consisting of Trade-Unions, Trades-Councils, Socialist Societies, and Local Labour Parties.

2. A Local Labour Party in any constituency is eligible for affiliation, provided it accepts the constitution and policy of the Party, and that there is no affiliated Trades Council covering the constituency, or that, if there be such council, it has been consulted in the first instance.

3. Co-operative Societies are also eligible.

4. A National Organization of Women, accepting the basis of this Constitution and the policy of the Party, and formed for the purpose of assisting the Party, shall be eligible for affiliation as though it were a Trades Council without having the right to vote in the election of the Executive.

II.—OBJECT

To secure the election of Candidates to Parliament and organize and maintain a Parliamentary Labour Party, with its own whips and policy.

III.—CANDIDATES AND MEMBERS

1. Candidates and members must accept this constitution; agree to abide by the decisons of the Parliamentary Party in carrying out the aims of this constitution; appear before their constituencies under the title of Labour candidates only; abstain strictly from identifying themselves with or promoting the interests of any Parliamentary Party not affiliated, or its candidates; and they must not oppose any candidate recognized by the Executive Committee of the party.

2. Candidates must undertake to join the Parliamentary Labour Party, if elected.

IV.—THE NATIONAL EXECUTIVE

The National executive shall consist of fifteen members, eleven representing the Trade-Unions, one the Trades-Councils and Local Labour Parties, and three the Socialist Societies, and shall be elected by ballot at the annual conference by their respective sections.

V.—DUTIES OF THE NATIONAL EXECUTIVE

The National Executive Committee shall—

1. Appoint a chairman, vice-chairman, and treasurer, and shall transact the general business of the party;

2. Issue a list of its candidates from time to time, and recommend them for the support of the electors;

3. Report to the affiliated organization concerned any Labour member, candidate, or chief official who opposes a candidate of the party, or who acts contrary to the spirit of this constitution;

4. And its members shall strictly abstain from identifying themselves with or promoting the interests of any Parliamentary party not affiliated, or its candidates.

VI.—THE SECRETARY

The secretary shall be elected by the annual conference, and shall be under the direction of the National Executive.

VII.—AFFILIATION FEES AND DELEGATES

1. Trade-Unions and Socialist Societies shall pay 15s. per annum for every 1000 members or fraction thereof, and may send to the annual conference one delegate for each thousand members.

2. Trades-Councils and Local Labour Parties with 5000 members

or under shall be affiliated on annual payment of 15s.; similar organizations with a membership of over 5000 shall pay £1 10s., the former Councils to be entitled to send one delegate with one vote to the annual conference, the latter to be entitled to send two delegates and have two votes.

3. In addition to these payments a delegate's fee to the annual conference may be charged.

VIII.—ANNUAL CONFERENCE

The National Executive shall convene a conference of its affiliated societies in the month of January each year.

Notice of resolutions for the conference and all amendments to the constitution shall be sent to the secretary by November 1st, and shall be forthwith forwarded to all affiliated organizations.

Notice of amendments and nominations for secretary and National Executive shall be sent to the secretary by December 15th, and shall be printed on the agenda.

IX.—VOTING AT ANNUAL CONFERENCE

There shall be issued to affiliated societies represented at the annual conference voting cards as follows:—

1. Trade-Unions and Socialist Societies shall receive one voting card for each thousand members, or fraction thereof paid for.

2. Trades-Councils and Local Labour Parties shall receive one card for each delegate they are entitled to send.

Any delegate may claim to have a vote taken by card.

PARLIAMENTARY FUND

I.—OBJECT

To assist in paying the election expenses of candidates adopted in accordance with this constitution, and in maintaining them when elected, and to provide the salary and expenses of a national party agent.

II.—AMOUNT OF CONTRIBUTION

Affiliated societies, except Trades-Councils and Local Labour Parties, shall pay a contribution to this fund at the rate of 2d. per member per annum, not later than the last day of each financial year.

On all matters affecting the financial side of the Parliamentary Fund only contributing societies shall be allowed to vote at the annual conference.

III.—TRUSTEES

The National Executive of the Party shall, from its number, select three to act as trustees, any two of whom, with the secretary, shall sign cheques.

IV.—EXPENDITURE

1. *Maintenance.*—All members elected under the auspices of the Labour Party shall be paid from the fund equal sums not to exceed £200 per annum, provided that this payment shall only be made to members whose candidatures have been promoted by societies which have contributed to this fund: provided further that no payment from this fund shall be made to a member or candidate of any society which has not contributed to this fund for one year, and that any society over three months in arrears shall forfeit all claim to the fund on behalf of its members or candidates, for twelve months from the date of payment.

2. *Returning Officers' Expenses.*—Twenty-five per cent. of the returning officers' net expenses shall be paid to the candidates, subject to the provisions of the preceding clause, so long as the total sum so expended does not exceed twenty-five per cent. of the fund.

3. *Administration.*—Five per cent. of the annual income of the fund shall be transferred to the general funds of the party to pay for administrative expenses of the fund.

Chapter 17.
Some Representative
Social Patterns

The long reign of Queen Victoria (1837–1901) can be misleading in suggesting a false unity of the mid- and late-nineteenth-century periods. Although the investigations of Charles Booth in London and Seebohm Rowntree in York revealed poverty and squalor comparable to that of the 1840s, the reaction to these conditions was different. The Education Act of 1870 appeared to do little more than fill in the gaps of the existing provision of schools by the religious bodies; but by the end of the century the effects of a free, compulsory, national system of education were apparent in the national life. Again, the new journalism of the 1880s and 1890s drew heavily upon many of the traditional staples of the popular press; but the combination of advertising and greatly increased circulation transformed the press into a new kind of social phenomenon. Against a background of working-class suffrage, socialism, new unionism, and the demand for women's rights, the sureties and respectability of the Victorian age faded away. The social patterns of Edwardian England foreshadowed the 1940s and the old skin of Victorianism was sloughed off.

81. POVERTY

by B. SEEBOHM ROWNTREE

The great social investigations of the 1830s and 1840s had aroused the conscience of the middle classes and strengthened the social reformers in their attempts to deal with the "condition-of-England-question." Great therefore was the shock when Charles Booth and Seebohm Rowntree showed by their investigations of living conditions in London and York that half a century later these problems were still unsolved. That one quarter of the population should be existing in poverty in the midst of the wealthiest society hitherto known was a damning indictment of nineteenth-century civilization.

Seebohm Rowntree (1871–1954) was a member of the Quaker dynasty of cocoa manufacturers in York, and a pioneer of "scientific management" in England. His reputation as a sociologist was first established by his book, *Poverty: a Study of Town Life* (1901), the material for which was collected by a survey in the fall of 1899. The following summary of his study is from the 1903 ed., pp. 295–305.

METHOD AND SCOPE OF INQUIRY

THE information regarding the numbers, occupation, and housing of the working classes was gained by direct inquiry, which practically covered every working-class family in York. In some cases direct information was also obtained regarding earnings, but in the majority of cases these were estimated, the information at the disposal of the writer enabling him to do this with considerable accuracy.

THE POVERTY LINE

Having thus made an estimate, based upon carefully ascertained facts, of the earnings of practically every working-class family in York, the next step was to show the proportion of the total population living in poverty. Families regarded as living in poverty were grouped under two heads:—

(*a*) Families whose total earnings were insufficient to obtain the minimum necessaries for the maintenance of merely physical efficiency. Poverty falling under this head was described as "primary" poverty.

(*b*) Families whose total earnings would have been sufficient for the maintenance of merely physical efficiency were it not that some portion of it was absorbed by other expenditure, either useful or wasteful. Poverty falling under this head was described as "secondary" poverty.

To ascertain the total number living in "primary" poverty it was necessary to ascertain the minimum cost upon which families of various sizes could be maintained in a state of physical efficiency.

. . . For a family of father, mother, and three children, the minimum weekly expenditure upon which physical efficiency can be maintained in York is 21s. 8d., made up as follows:

	s.	d.
Food	12	9
Rent (say)	4	0
Clothing, light, fuel, etc.	4	11
	21	8

The necessary expenditure for families larger or smaller than the above will be correspondingly greater or less. This estimate was based upon the assumptions that the diet is selected with a careful regard to the nutritive values of various food stuffs, and that these are all purchased at the lowest current prices. It only allows for a diet less generous as regards variety than that supplied to able-bodied paupers in workhouses. It further assumes that no clothing is purchased which is not absolutely necessary for health, and assumes too that it is of the plainest and most economical description.

No expenditure of any kind is allowed for beyond that which is absolutely necessary for the maintenance of *merely physical efficiency*.

The number of persons whose earnings are so low that they cannot meet the expenditure necessary for the above standard of living, stringent to severity though it is, and bare of all creature comforts, was shown to be no less than 7230, or almost exactly 10 per cent of the total population of the city. These persons, then, represent those who are in "primary" poverty.

The number of those in "secondary" poverty was arrived at by ascertaining the *total* number living in poverty, and subtracting those living in "primary" poverty. The investigators, in the course of their house-to-house visitation, noted those families who were obviously living in a state of poverty, *i.e.* in obvious want and squalor. Sometimes they obtained definite information that the bulk of the earnings was spent in drink or otherwise squandered, sometimes the external evidence of poverty in the home was so clear as to make verbal evidence superfluous.

In this way 20,302 persons, or 27.84 per cent of the total population, were returned as living in poverty. Subtracting those whose poverty is "primary," we arrive at the number living in "secondary" poverty, viz. 13,072, or 17.93 per cent of the total population. . . .

As the investigation into the conditions of life in this typical provincial town has proceeded, the writer has been increasingly impressed with the gravity of the facts which have unfolded themselves.

That in this land of abounding wealth, during a time of perhaps unexampled prosperity, probably more than one-fourth of the population are living in poverty, is a fact which may well cause great searchings of heart. There is surely need for a greater concentration of thought by the nation upon the well-being of its own people, for no civilisation can be sound or stable which has at its base this mass of stunted human life. The suffering may be all but voiceless, and we may long remain ignorant of its extent and severity, but when once we realise it we see that social questions of profound importance await solution. What, for instance, are the primary causes of this poverty? How far is it the result of false social and economic conditions? If it be due in part to faults in the national character, what influences can be exerted to impart to that character greater strength and thoughtfulness?

The object of the writer, however, has been to state facts rather than to suggest remedies. He desires, nevertheless, to express his belief that however difficult the path of social progress may be, a way of advance will open out before patient and penetrating thought if inspired by a true human sympathy.

The dark shadow of the Malthusian philosophy has passed away, and no view of the ultimate scheme of things would now be accepted under which multitudes of men and women are doomed by inevitable law to a struggle for existence so severe as necessarily to cripple or destroy the higher parts of their nature.

82. [AN EARLY BOARD SCHOOL]

by JAMES RUNCIMAN

Until 1870 all attempts to establish a national system of public education had been wrecked on the rock of religious divisions. But in that year an Education Act was passed which provided that elementary schooling should be made available to every English child. In 1880 attendance was made compulsory. The 1870 Education Act filled in the gaps left by the voluntary school provision of the religious bodies. Locally elected School Boards were established to build and manage new schools where required, and provided new accommodation for 2,200,000 scholars between 1870 and 1895.

Firsthand accounts of conditions in these early Board schools are not very numerous. One of the few surviving records by a teacher is James Runciman's *Schools and Scholars* (1887), in which he gave vivid descriptions of life in schools in the East End of London. In the following account (from pp. 4–10), Palliser, the young teacher, is drawn from the author's own experiences.

YOUNG Palliser had no gloomy forebodings when he took his place among the murmuring mob that filled the shed in which he was to begin work. The Board were eager to start, so they did not wait until a new school could be built, and they fitted up a long, hideous drill-room with rough desks that served to seat 250 youngsters. . . .

They were a wild lot that gathered in the Willow Alley shed. Not one boy had experienced any but parental discipline before and Palliser soon saw that most of the little fellows had been used to blows. His face was always sternly set, and he noticed that when he spoke to a lad the youngster's hands were instinctively made ready to protect the head; the cold calmness of the young man's face was misunderstood. . . .

Palliser was bewildered by the intense restlessness of his pupils. Their minds were in a turmoil, their curiosity was at fever pitch, and the master soon saw that he must let the excitement simmer down before he tried to establish order. Some of the boys were hardy enough, some were very intelligent in appearance, some were cowed and sly but vicious, and some were dulled into semi-imbecility by hunger, disease, ill-usage. For three days Palliser made no attempt to go on with book-work. The lads had no conception of the meaning of an order, and the master was obliged to drill them again and again in the simplest movements. Sometimes, after a class had been told to stand, a dreamy boy would sit still, calmly gazing at a map on the wall. The power of paying attention was almost wanting in them, and Palliser had unpleasant apprehensions as to his probable fate when he should begin with the alphabet. So far as attainments were concerned, the boys were tolerably level; not one knew the entire alphabet, and those who had picked up a slight idea of the letters from the street hoardings were decidedly vague. Palliser found it best to teach each group by brief snatches, for he invariably found it impossible to interest them in any subject for more than five minutes. They had the fluid mind of the true barbarian, and it was quite useless to attempt any species of coercion. Some impatient men are apt to punish a boy for an indifference which is quite remote from insolence, but the very boy who has suffered forgets all about his pain in five minutes, and his wits go woolgathering once more. Patience, patience, indomitable and tender patience, must be brought to bear when the wastrels are to be taught. Palliser learned that fine health, perfect nerve, and, above all, perfect temper, are essential to a teacher. Those who only know the charming children who come from good homes cannot form any conception of the kind of work which must be done among children who do not come from homes, but from lairs. The savage who excused himself for flinging a stick at a missionary by saying, "I could not help it; your arms moved so quick that they made me do it," was rather an easy subject for instruction compared with the raw street arab.

With keen delight the young master found that his steady kindness produced good effects by degrees. Had he scolded and shouted, the boys would never have minded him, because they were all seasoned to violence; but the calm, polite voice first of all amazed them, and then subdued them. Some little rascals grinned when they were courteously addressed, but they learned to like the gentleness, and made elaborate attempts to imitate their master.

Palliser began to teach singing as soon as he managed to impress on his flock the necessity for sitting still. In the early days a boy thought nothing of rising from the desk, and wriggling along the floor to pick up a marble, or a pin, or any stray object that took his fancy, and as the truant could hardly resist the chance of pinching his comrades' legs, the occasional interruptions were embarrassing. Palliser conquered this troublesome volatility without using hard measures, and he speedily contrived to delight the lads with their music lesson. Nearly all arabs have a true ear for music, and they certainly like it, though they are given to imitating the dolorous cadences of the ballad-singers. Palliser never cared a whit for the apparent waste of time, and he had five minutes of singing out of every half-hour, so that many of the scholars came to think they were having quite a rollicking time. The drudgery of teaching the alphabet was cruel, but the master always treated the lessons as great fun, and eased the work directly he saw signs of boredom. Yet, although the young man kept a cheerful face in presence of his trouble, he was heavy at heart; he seemed to be pressing against a cruel obstacle, which yielded for a moment, only to sway back with crushing force. Often in the evening he flung himself on the sofa and wished he had the power to sob like a woman; his throat was parched, he loathed the sight of food, and only a long, resolute walk in the open enabled him to shake off his weariness of nerve and dull heartache. All this did not prevent him from making the school a very happy place, and he casually heard from parents that some boys would cry at the very notion of being kept away.

83. [THE WORKERS' EDUCATIONAL ASSOCIATION]

by ALBERT MANSBRIDGE

Only in English society is it possible to imagine a successful workers' education movement with such an unlikely basis as the Workers' Educational Association. On the one hand it was regarded as the educational expression of the rising labor movement and was supported by enthusiastic socialists, and on the other it won the support of Anglican bishops, Oxford dons, and the Board of Education. The W.E.A. was essentially the creation of Albert Mansbridge (1876–1952), a clerk in the Cooperative Wholesale Society's warehouse in Whitechapel, London. He was not a socialist, nor a trade unionist; and his favorite phrase was "the glory of education." The W.E.A., working closely with the universities, became an extremely effective agency of adult education; it enabled intelligent working men to remedy the deficiencies of their early education and equip themselves for leadership roles in their trade unions, in the Labour Party, and in the community. This account of the foundation and early days of the W.E.A. is from Albert Mansbridge, *An Adventure in Working Class Education* (1920), pp. 10–43.

THE two streams of labour and scholarship unite to make a great and powerful river of education, which must by an unerring law draw to itself most, if not all, the runnels and rivulets of thought making their way to the open sea of a free people.

That is, at once, the condition and meaning of the Workers' Educational Association. . . .

In 1897 I entered the service of the Co-operative Wholesale Society, after a varied career in which commerce and education were strangely mixed. My experience in both these directions proved to be of use. After a short time I was appointed to teach the History and Principles of Co-operation to such of my fellow employees as would listen after an arduous and long day's work. In the meantime, both by occasional contributions to the *Co-operative News* and by speeches in numerous conferences, I sought to bring about an actual working alliance between the Universities and the people. . . .

It was not until Christmas 1902 that I again began to plan an educational alliance. In the meantime I had been teaching in the Higher Commercial Schools of the London Board, on five evenings a week during the winter. This in addition to a full working day at the Co-operative Wholesale Society left me little or no leisure. But I had never forgotten the invitation given to me to write an article for the *University Extension Journal* on the lines of my Conference paper. At the first opportunity 'Democracy and Education' was prepared and published in the January 1903 number of the Journal. At the time of writing I had little or no idea of organising a movement, but it soon became clear that I should either have to do it myself, or induce someone else to do so. The Editor of the Journal, Dr. Holland Rose, was instant in his encouragement and printed two further articles, also one in commendation by Robert Halstead. In the course of these articles the plan of action revealed itself as a working alliance between Co-operation, Trade Unionism, and University Extension. A triple cord is not easily broken.

A small group of working men gathered round me, including some who had formed a 'Christian Economic Society,' which met at my house. With this help at hand, together with the encouragement of Dr. Holland Rose, my wife and I decided to take action by becoming the first two members of 'An Association to Promote the Higher Education of Working Men,' and at that symbolical meeting by democratic vote I was appointed Hon. Secretary (*pro tem.*). . . .

On July 14, 1903, the Provisional Committee, consisting entirely of Co-operators and Trade Unionists, met in Toynbee Hall for the first time. There were present, Mr. A. H. Thomas (Brushmaker) in the chair, Mr. George Alcock (Trustee National Union of Railwaymen),

Mr. W. R. Salter (Engineer), Mr. L. Idle (Co-operative Employee), Mr. J. W. Cole (Co-operative Employee), and myself as Hon. Secretary. The first organisation to enter into affiliation with the provisional body was the Co-operative Society at Annfield Plain, Co. Durham. On Saturday, 25th August, in the Examination Schools at Oxford, the Association received public recognition from the representatives of nearly all the Universities and a large number of labour organisations. Dr. Percival, then Bishop of Hereford, was in the chair, and his place was taken afterwards by Dean Kitchin, of Durham, both of whom possessed the confidence of the working people in a remarkable degree. . . .

The work which followed the Conference was exciting and interesting as it has seldom been since, in spite of the expansion of the Association and the multitude of its adherents. It was a great privilege to see the rapid working of the magnetic power of the new idea. Representative workers, such as D. J. Shackleton, then President of the Trades Union Congress, and representative University lecturers such as Hudson Shaw, declared their unqualified adherence to its principles. Financial support was accorded by working-class societies of all kinds and degrees. The Co-operative Union, the Working Men's Club and Institute Union, and the Parliamentary Committee of the Trades Union Congress entered into an association, which has never been broken, but, on the contrary, has increased in power every year. They did not merely express a sentiment, nor did they content themselves with an annual grant; they sent their best men to co-operate in the work of the Association, and these have been—and still are— amongst the most ardent advocates of the movement.

By the beginning of 1906, branches had been formed in eight towns, four in the South of England, one in the Midlands, and three in the North. District Committees were at work covering the North-Western and South-Western areas. Great meetings had been held, including that which formed the first branch at Reading and that which formed the first district at Manchester. . . .

It will be obvious from what has been said that goodwill and desire for the success of the new movement animated most of those persons who came into contact with its influence. Indeed, it is almost safe to say that it had become a replica in miniature of English life. The Second Annual Report analyses the individual members as—authors, churchmen, co-operators, educationalists, headmasters, journalists, lawyers, nonconformists, scholars, statesmen, trade unionists, and adds,

'The last two members to join were a shop assistant and a labourer.' All the public utterances of the time make it clear that the first condition of the power and life of the Association was that at least three-quarters of its members should be actual labouring men and women. Had it been otherwise, the scholars of the time would have regarded it as an unnecessary body; but they realised that the W.E.A. did itself naturally represent the fundamental life of working people, who made it abundantly clear in conferences and elsewhere that, in the words of a leading article in the *Manchester Guardian*, they desired 'a liberal as against a merely bread-and-butter education.' . . .

Many people regard the W.E.A. and the University Tutorial Class Movement as one and the same thing. They treat the terms as interchangeable, probably because the system of University Tutorial Classes has been the most prominent constructive work of the Association; and that is the feature which has earned the commendation of educational experts wherever they are found. . . .

There were not wanting those who, in the early years of the W.E.A., said that its success would depend upon its ability to create serious students. Among those especially experienced in the problems of adult education, the names of Canon Barnett and Dr. Roberts stand out prominently. The former, ever since the foundation of Toynbee Hall, had striven with all his might to bring the University to the workers. The latter, as secretary to the Syndicate for Local Lectures at Cambridge, and latterly as Registrar of the University of London Extension Board, had perhaps given more attention than anyone else to the question of the recognition by Universities of extra-mural studies. It was the united stimulus of these two men that caused the formation of a class in Battersea, of which Professor Patrick Geddes was appointed tutor; but, serious though the intention of this class was, it was not a University Tutorial Class, and did not become one for some two or three years.

The formation of the first class in 1906 was due to a very wise use of University Extension at Rochdale, where the W.E.A. branch, under the name of the Rochdale Education Guild, had become powerful owing to the truly wonderful work of L. V. Gill, F. Greenwood, and A. Carter, the three secretaries of the branch. Working men and women began to attend lectures in large numbers, and because they reached out for something more, a new problem arose. After long reflection I came to the conclusion that the best thing to do would be to ask Rochdale to get thirty students to pledge themselves to make every attendance for two years and to write regular essays. If they would do this we could get the best tutor in England. Our part of the bargain was certainly a large one, but we meant it, and it represented our enthusiasm at the time. As the result of a letter I addressed to them the Rochdale students pledged themselves for two years, and R. H. Tawney, a Balliol scholar, agreed to teach the class for the time being under the auspices of the Oxford University Extension Delegacy. Mr. Tawney was at that time Lecturer in Economics at Glasgow; he was quite prepared to undertake arduous work for the W.E.A. at any cost. In this way a pioneer experiment was initiated of far-reaching consequence for the education of the workers. . . .

The remarkable progress of the classes up to the time of the war, and throughout its course, can best be realised by a consideration of the statistics . . . Let it be said at once that students as a rule keep their pledges, that the first Rochdale Class continued for four, and the Longton class for eight years: indeed, the latter is in effect still at work, although the personnel has changed. The quality of the work done revealed itself rapidly as good. The judgment of Mr. A. L. Smith, the Master of Balliol, was much quoted at the time. He declared that 25 per cent. of the essays written were as good as the work done by men who obtain First-Class Honours in the Final Schools of Modern History at Oxford. He was astonished, not so much at the 'quality of the work as at the quantity of the quality.' This high standard was the direct result of keenness in unifying the practical experience of the students' lives with the knowledge gained in the class.

Obviously, the men and women who would undertake such a course were thoughtful people to begin with. Many of them had read a good deal, if discursively. Their technical equipment was not great at the outset, but that rapidly righted itself; such minor matters as spelling and punctuation soon ceased to trouble them unduly. The principles upon which the classes were founded, in themselves secured good results. No one was encouraged to join a class who did not really wish to study the proposed subject; the class was also allowed to select its tutor and to formulate its syllabus. The adoption of these two methods caused some to be scornful who had underestimated the psychological importance of this concession to the initiative of students of mature years.

The tutor must of course in the first place have been approved by the University Joint Committee established in connection with each

University, but a really good tutor would never stand in danger of not being accepted by a class. Moreover, the syllabus would also have to be approved. There is a vital impulse in a class which starts the study of a subject at the point which it desires, although, naturally, this must be a suitable point. It is always best in dealing with the education of people of any type to start from the known in the investigation of the unknown. There is much artificiality in teaching which deals with remote matters. Perhaps, however, the principle which gave most life and vigour to the classes was that each student was held to be a teacher and each teacher held to be a student. A tutorial class, it was said, consisted of thirty-one teachers and thirty-one students. 'The lecture is one but the discussion is one thousand' runs the old Persian proverb. The power of the operation of this principle and the rapid development of the subject as a result must be seen to be appreciated. The joy in work which it produces makes tired men fresh. Otherwise, how could men working seventy hours a week come to the classes and write their essays regularly, as so many have done?

This freshness and joy in work was one of the main notes in the Report on the Classes published by the Board of Education, and drawn up by Mr. J. W. Headlam and Professor L. T. Hobhouse. They record there the case of a student who, hampered by conditions at home, rose in the night, wrote his essay for two hours, and then turned to sleep again. The recognised period of a class meeting is two hours, on twenty-four occasions during each of three consecutive years. No really good class ever keeps to the two hours. They break up, as a rule, only when compelled by necessity. There are limits to the time during which buildings with caretakers may be left open, but there always remains the street. A class in Philosophy at Birmingham habitually continued its sessions on the sidewalk, until an energetic policeman threatened to charge the tutor with causing an obstruction. On one occasion an Economics class, after a pavement session, accompanied the tutor to the railway station; and the argument not being finished, some of the students entered the train with him and went as far as they dared. The early tutors became the friends of the students, visited them in their houses, joined them on all possible occasions, and, in fact, acted towards them in much the same way as a tutor at Oxford towards his pupils, subject, of course, to the limitations imposed by working hours, and allowing for the more intimate friendship which is possible between tutor and W.E.A. students of the same age.

As a rule the subjects studied are economic; and a large number of classes take industrial history. After a little while students become keenly interested in literature and philosophy. The preponderance of Economics studied has been deplored by those who only know the Economics of the Universities. In any case the actual subject of study is not of so much concern as the spirit in which it is studied. In a tutorial class there is little or no danger of narrow treatment. . . .

It is difficult and perhaps unprofitable to try to trace an effect such as the good and thoughtful work of the classes would undoubtedly produce. It is a matter for speculation whether or not the public mind would have been very different during the great war if there had been no tutorial classes. Certain it is that some 5,000 active working men and women had received systematic and careful education in History and Economics over a period of no less than three years. Many trade union officials have as a result found that their work was more powerful, and that they themselves were better informed and equipped to deal with the problems which have arisen in their meetings with the representatives of the employers. There is abundant detailed evidence to this effect.

84. [*THE DAILY MAIL*]

by HENRY HAMILTON FYFE

In 1855 the Stamp Duty on newspapers (the last of the "taxes on knowledge") was finally abolished, and in the second half of the century a daily and Sunday press developed steadily. *The Times* continued to cater to the "educated classes," but in addition new papers such as the *Daily Telegraph* appeared for lower-middle and upper working-class readers. The biggest circulations were in the Sunday newspapers, which throve on the traditional mixture of sex, violent crime, and sentiment.

However, in 1880 George Newnes started a weekly of a new type, accurately named *Tit-Bits*. Working for Newnes was a young journalist, Alfred Harmsworth (later Lord Northcliffe), 1865–1922, who in 1888 started his own weekly, *Answers to Correspondents*, which incorporated many of the features of *Tit-Bits* and became its rival. *Answers* attained a circulation of 250,000, and this success encouraged Harmsworth to extend his "new journalism." In 1894 he bought the *Evening News;* and two years later launched *The Daily Mail.* The significance of this venture is brought out in the following account by one of his journalists who knew him closely. It is from Henry Hamilton Fyfe, *Northcliffe: An Intimate Biography* (1930), pp. 66–70, 84–87.

THE idea behind *The Daily Mail* was that it should appear to be a penny paper sold for a halfpenny. Other halfpenny papers had been on the market for some little time before it; they had devoted their front pages to news instead of advertisements, thus making a difference plain at sight between themselves and the "heavies." Northcliffe would not do this. He made his front page resemble as closely as possible those of the old-established papers. Nor was there much novelty at first in the appearance of the other pages. He did not want to startle people, to suggest to them that they had got hold of something to which they were altogether unaccustomed. *The Daily Mail* had a lighter, brighter look than the older journals, for the reason that the matter was broken up and shorter; it seemed to have more in it than they contained. But it was only when the pages were looked into that the far-reaching nature of the experiment could be grasped.

Now at last Fleet Street does get a shock. The 4th of May, 1896, becomes a leading date in newspaper history. The new venture does not have to fight its way. Of its first number, 367,215 copies are bought; the demand is not satisfied even then. . . .

The Daily Mail settles down with a circulation of 170,000 a day during its first months. During the first year its daily sale averages 202,000. Then it increases steadily week by week. There is prejudice to be overcome. It is usually spoken of by educated persons as "that rag." It is sneered at by the Marquis of Salisbury, Prime Minister of the day, as "a journal produced by office-boys for office-boys." The Conservatives, his followers, applaud—without a suspicion that the day is coming when they will be truckling to these "office-boys," begging for their support. In the variety theatres jokes are made about it. A song, "By kind permission of *The Daily Mail,*" is sung. All the better; good advertisement. "Of course, I don't believe a word I read in it," say solemn and ponderous pillars of society, but they continue to read it—furtively, perhaps, poking it into their pockets until they are at home.

Here is something that the chief proprietor has not understood until now . . . Those who have been the supporters of the older journalism do not really like it. They find it dull. They are glad to get a paper that is more lively than any they are accustomed to—though they dare not as yet confess this. They can read the whole of *The Daily Mail* in a short time and be entertained by all of it. Flitting from one topic to another, running their eyes over informative head-lines, finding subjects for conversation, knowing more about events because they are explained, they soon get the habit of looking through it. If they do not see it, they feel they may have missed something of interest. That is exactly what the proprietors aim at making every-body feel. The result is in three years a daily sale of 543,000. It is ad-vertised as The Busy Man's Paper. Eight pages only, not so un-wieldy in size as the old-established sheets. It claims as a merit, in its first issue, that it has not so many advertisements as the other dailies. Strange, when we recollect how it came to have more than any! But this is before the Advertising Age. The Store announcements covering whole pages will not begin for many years yet. Publicity is still an in-fant. Far distant the time, not even to be imagined, when there will be twelve, sixteen, twenty, even twenty-four pages, when the Busy Man will have to hunt for his reading-matter through acres of ad-vertisement.

Just at the right moment to catch the new reading public comes the New Journalism, as it is slightingly, sarcastically spoken of among the high-priests of the Old. Not one of these has made any move to provide what that public has been waiting for. Not one of them has given any sign of being aware even that such a public exists.

Just at the right moment, too, for another reason. The number of men who now travel to and fro, between suburban homes and offices, out in the morning, back at night, has been growing with the growth of cities. Farther and farther out the small householder must go. And to the troops of men who are daily travellers by train or omnibus or street-car are beginning to be added women—not in troops as yet, though before long they will be equalling and then outnumbering the men. These travellers want something to read in the morning, some-thing of a lighter, more diverting character than the news which the old-established pages contain. The new daily gives them exactly what they require. It amuses them, they can get through it during their journey, they are satisfied they have got all the news of the day. And men take it home in the evening so that their wives can glance over it and read the serial story.

Always convinced of the value of women's support, Northcliffe has insisted on following the example of French newspapers and printing every day an instalment of a tale calculated to carry all who have begun to read it along with it until the end. He argues that this will do more than add an interest and increase the numbers of "readers per copy." It will also lengthen the life of each day's issue. Most morning newspapers, he has noticed, are dead before the morning is through. This one will not be dead until night. It will live for twelve hours instead of two. That must be brought to the notice of advertisers. They will appreciate his reason for including a serial story. . . .

The props of Old Journalism feel bewildered. Their task, they believe, is to enlighten such of the public as can profit by enlightenment on political questions, on foreign policy. Their duty, they maintain, is to guide opinion concerning matters which may affect national well-being, cause changes of Government, raise the issue of peace or war. They have nothing to do with increase of circulation. They call this "pandering to mob interest in trivialities" commercial, undignified. Their standard of importance is set by the chiefs of Political parties, Foreign Office and the Treasury; by the famous clubs (Reform, Carlton, Athenaeum); by the great country houses, the country rectories; by the Universities, by Bench and Bar. Now the standard is to be set by the mass of people; the New Journalism will put in the foreground whatever is of interest to them, whatever will make them "hand the paper about."

"Our policy of twenty years ago," Northcliffe said in 1920, "was to do big things big, and little things little." So long as we keep up to that, he added, we shall do well. He did not say then that the cause of his revolution in journalism was a difference of opinion between him and the directors of the old-established newspapers. He did at other times discuss this with a just appreciation of what had happened. "Values," he said, "had been changed by the social reform which taught everyone to read. The newspapers had up to this time been published for a small number, and out of that small number a tiny class set the standard at which the newspapers should aim.

"The tiny class was the class which ruled the British Empire, and it was, in the jargon of the day, 'highly educated,' which means, in the literal sense, that it once had a smattering of Latin and Greek; it had also learned to shoot and ride and play cricket.

"In another sense, however, this tiny class could rightly be called educated, for it had studied in the school of life. Its members had few ideas, no ideals; but they did possess an understanding of the nature of things, rough and ready perhaps, but based on accumulated experience and what they would have called 'common knowledge.'

"For them the big things were politics and money. They did not expect to find in newspapers anything much besides. They certainly did not look for light reading, entertaining scraps. If they had a taste for gossip, they got it at their clubs, at their dinner-tables. Their 'talking-points' were made for them in social intercourse. They did not read, though they always glanced at their newspapers (it seems unlikely that anyone really read them!); they were satisfied, they did not want anything different.

"If you had said that a class was growing up which had no use for that kind of newspaper, which would welcome one that told what was going on in the world, not merely what politicians were saying and how the money market had been, they would have looked blankly at you, without knowing what you meant.

"For this tiny class the big thing of one day would be a speech foreshadowing a change of Government or some new combination in politics; of another day a rise or fall in stocks and shares. The new sort of newspaper reader cares little about Government nor is he excited about investments; he has none. Most of the things that interest him are things which the pre-*Mail* newspapers never used to mention. The reason why the *Mail* caused such a sensation was that it dealt with these things, played them up, increased the interest in them a hundred-fold.

"You could search the Victorian newspapers in vain for any reference to changing fashions, for instance. You could not find in them anything that would help you to understand the personalities of public men. We cannot get from them a clear and complete picture of the times in which they were published, as one could from *The Daily Mail*. Before that was published, journalism dealt with only a few aspects of life. What we did was to extend its purview to life as a whole.

"This was difficult. It involved the training of a new type of journalist. The old type was convinced that anything which would be a subject of conversation ought to be kept out of the papers.

"Did you know there was a sub-editor on *The Times* who once spiked an elephant? Yes, an elephant escaped from a circus in South

London and went careering about the streets. When this sub-editor received an account of the incident, he stuck it on the waste-file with other rejected copy. It was too interesting!

"Most journalists of that time had that kind of mentality, though perhaps not quite so pronounced. Or else they thought that the way to sell a newspaper was to have first-class criticisms of books and pictures and music and plays. The only thing that will sell a newspaper in large numbers is news, and news is anything out of the ordinary. You know, of course, the great American editor's definition? Dana said, 'If a dog bites a man, that's nothing, but if a man bites a dog, that's news.' In *The Daily Mail* we paid little or no attention to the dogs which bit men—and the dogs didn't like it—I mean the politicians, the bigwigs, the people who laid foundation-stones and presided at banquets and opened Church bazaars. On the other hand we gave the men who bit dogs such prominence as they never had before, and we were accused of lowering the dignity of journalism!"

Chapter 18.

Conservatives
and Liberals

Now nature always does contrive
That every boy and every gal
That's born into this world alive
Is either a little Liberal
Or else a little Conservative.

GILBERT AND SULLIVAN OPERA, *Iolanthe* (1882)

From the death of Palmerston in 1865 until the death of
Disraeli in 1881 English politics was dominated by the personalities of the two great party leaders, Benjamin Disraeli and William Ewart Gladstone. The duel between
these two in the 1870s was echoed in every part of the
country, and the proceedings in parliament were very
widely followed. Behind each leader was a political party
formed out of a coalition of disparate elements from the
preceding two decades; and despite some outward appearance of parliamentary unity, held together only by his
strength and skill.

The Liberal party, as formed by Gladstone in 1868, was
created by an amalgamation of the Whigs, Peelites, and
Radicals; thus representing an alliance between a section
of the old landed interest, the industrial middle classes,
and the newly enfranchised artisans. It was characterized
by strong Nonconformist and urban support, and a highly
moralistic attitude to public affairs.

Similarly Disraeli provided the basis for a new Conservative party, which while it included the traditional
Tory interests went beyond them in extending the ideal of
an organic society to the whole of the people. Against the
sectional interests of middle-class Liberal industrialists the
Conservative party presented itself as the truly national,
inclusive party.

After 1886, however, the party alignments began to change. The effects of the shift in political power brought about by the Reform Acts of 1867 and 1884 became increasingly insistent; and the great issues of Home Rule for Ireland, imperialism, and the rise of labor necessitated a reorientation of the parties. For the Conservatives a solution was sought in Tory Democracy, and for their opponents in the New Liberalism.

85. ENGLAND'S MISSION

by WILLIAM EWART GLADSTONE

In his youth, William Ewart Gladstone (1809–1898) had been (in the historian Macaulay's words) "the rising hope of those stern and unbending Tories." He had held office under Peel; and thereafter progressed from Peelite Conservatism to become the leader of a new Liberal party. A devout High Churchman, Gladstone was basically conservative in outlook; and yet as he grew older he became more and more radical. He was four times prime minister, and his first administration (1868–1874) left behind a solid achievement of overdue reform legislation. In opposition in the 1870s he conducted a sustained attack on Disraeli's foreign policy, which reached a climax in that "pilgrimage of passion," the Midlothian campaign of 1879–1880. The following article, "England's Mission," appeared in the *Nineteenth Century* (September 1878), pp. 560–584, and was written as a comment on Disraeli's return from the Congress of Berlin in July 1878, bringing "peace with honour."

THE honour to which the recent British policy is entitled is this: that, from the beginning of the Congress to the end, the representatives of England, instead of taking the side of freedom, emancipation, and national progress, took, in every single point where a practical issue was raised, the side of servitude, of reaction, and of barbarism. With a zeal worthy of a better cause, they laboured to reduce the limits within which the populations of European Turkey are to be masters of their own destinies; to keep as much as they could of direct Turkish rule; and to enfeeble as much as they could the limitations upon that rule. Nor was this only to restrain or counterwork the influence of Russia. For, upon the record, they have done more than any other power to assist Russia in despoiling Roumania of her Bessarabian territory; they have worked energetically against Greece, which represented the only living anti-Russian force in the Levant . . . The honour, which the Government have earned for us at Berlin, is that of having used the name and influence, and even, by their preparations, the military power of England, to set up the principles of Metternich, and to put down the principles of Canning. We, who have helped Belgium, Spain, and Portugal to be free, we who led the way in the establishment of free Greece, and gave no mean support to the liberation and union of Italy, have at Berlin wrought actively to limit everywhere the area of self-government, and to save from the wreck as much as possible of a domination which has contributed more than any other that ever existed to the misery, the debasement, and the extermination of mankind. . . . For a vigorous, that is to say, a narrow, restless, blustering, and self-asserting foreign policy, no Ministry has ever been punished in this country. . . . The vigorous foreign policy exhibits all the advantages of a good and available political speculation. First, by forcing upon the public mind a stronger excitement, it produces a comparative indifference to the humdrum detail of legislation, and effectually covers all domestic shortcomings. Secondly, instead of asserting what are, or may be called, the views of a party, a vigorous foreign policy asserts what are presumptively claims and interests of the nation, and thus sheds a halo round its acts. Thirdly, in thus appealing to the self-love and pride of the community, it is pretty certain to carry its influence and drawing power for a time beyond the circle of its sworn followers, and to enlist the support of all those good citizens who, from the shilling gallery and elsewhere, enthusiastically applaud the lines—

> Methought upon one pair of English legs
> Did march three Frenchmen.

But last, and best of all, as they are contending, forsooth, on behalf of the greatness of England, it follows that they are enabled at once to place all opponents in the category of contenders for its littleness. . . .

. . . Territorial aggrandisement, backed by military display, is the *cheval de bataille* of the administration. Empire is greatness; leagues of land are empire; your safety is measured by the fear you strike into other nations; trade follows the flag: he that doubts is an enemy to his country. This creed of aggrandisement, made real to the public imagination by the acquisition of a Mediterranean and virtually European island, has operated a relative success: it has covered the miscarriages of the Government, and it enables them to say that they have not been condemned to capital punishment by the country.

It is very disagreeable for an Englishman to hint to Englishmen that the self-love and pride, which all condemn in individuals, have often lured nations to their ruin or their loss; that they are apt to entail a great deal of meanness, as well as a great deal of violence; that they begin with a forfeiture of respect abroad, and end even in the loss of self-respect; that their effect is to destroy all sobriety in the estimation of human affairs, and to generate a temperament of excitability which errs alternately on the side of arrogance, and of womanish and unworthy fears. For the performance of this disagreeable duty, we are entitled to look in the first place to the Queen's Government; which ought in foreign affairs invariably to play, and which in other times usually has played, the part of moderator. . . .

. . . The doctrines of national self-restraint, of the equal obligations of States to public law, and of their equal rights to fair construction as to words and deeds, have been left to unofficial persons. The Government, not uniformly nor consistently, but in the main and on the whole, have opened up and relied on an illegitimate source of power, which never wholly fails: they have appealed, under the prostituted name of patriotism, to exaggerated fears, to imaginary interests, and to the acquisitiveness of a race which has surpassed every other known to history in the faculty of appropriating to itself vast spaces of the earth, and establishing its supremacy over men of every race and language. Now I hold that to stimulate these tendencies, to overlook the proportion between our resources and our obligations, and above all to claim anything more than equality of rights in the moral and political intercourse of the world, is not the way to make England great, but to make it both morally and materially little. . . .

The sentiment of empire may be called innate in every Briton. If there are exceptions, they are like those of men born blind or lame among us. It is part of our patrimony: born with our birth, dying only with our death; incorporating itself in the first elements of our knowledge, and interwoven with all our habits of mental action upon public affairs. It is a portion of our national stock, which has never been deficient, but which has more than once run to rank excess, and brought us to mischief accordingly, mischief that for a time we have weakly thought was ruin. In its normal action, it made for us the American colonies, the grandest monument ever erected by a people of modern times, and second only to the Greek colonisation in the whole history of the world. In its domineering excess, always under the name of British interests and British honour, it lost them by obstinacy and pride. Lord Chatham who forbade us to tax, Mr. Burke who forbade us to legislate for them, would have saved them. But they had to argue for a limitation of English power; and to meet the reproach of the political wiseacres, who first blustered on our greatness, and then, when they reaped as they had sown, whined over our calamities. Undoubtedly the peace of 1782–3, with its adjuncts in exasperated feeling, was a terrible dismemberment. But England was England still: and one of the damning signs of the politics of the school is their total blindness to the fact, that the central strength of England lies in England. Their eye travels with satisfaction over the wide space upon the map covered by the huge ice-bound deserts of North America or the unpenetrated wastes of Australasia, but rests with mortification on the narrow bounds of latitude and longitude marked by nature for the United Kingdom. They are the materialists of politics: their faith is in acres and in leagues, in sounding titles and long lists of territories. They forget that the entire fabric of the British Empire was reared and consolidated by the energies of a people, which was (though it is not now) insignificant in numbers, when compared with the leading States of the Continent; and that if by some vast convulsion our transmarine possessions could be all submerged, the very same energies of that very same people would either discover other inhabited or inhabitable spaces of the globe on which to repeat its work, or would without them in other modes assert its undiminished greatness. Of all the opinions disparaging to England, there is not one which can lower her like that which teaches that the source of strength for this almost measureless body lies in its extremities, and not in the heart which has so long propelled the blood through all its regions, and in the brain which has bound and binds them into one.

In the sphere of personal life, most men are misled through the medium of the dominant faculty of their nature. It is round that dominant faculty that folly and flattery are wont to buzz. They play upon vainglory by exaggerating and commending what it does, and by piquing it on what it sees cause to forbear from doing. It is so with nations. For all of them the supreme want really is, to be warned against the indulgence of the dominant passion. The dominant passion of France was military glory. Twice, in this century, it has towered beyond what is allowed to man; and twice has paid the tremendous forfeit of opening to the foe the proudest capital in the world. The dominant passion of England is extended empire. It has heretofore been kept in check by the integrity and sagacity of her statesmen, who have not shrunk from teaching her the lessons of self-denial and self-restraint. But a new race has arisen; and the most essential or the noblest among all the duties of government, the exercise of moral control over ambition and cupidity, have been left to the intermittent and feeble handling of those who do not govern. . . .

The truth is that, turn where we will, we are met on every side with proofs that the cares and calls of the British Empire are already beyond the strength of those who govern and have governed it. A protracted experience of public affairs, not unattended with a high estimate of the general diligence, devotion, and ability of the Parliamentary as well as the civil servants of the Crown, has long convinced me that of the more difficult descriptions of the public business, apart from simple routine, it is only a small part that is transacted with the requisite knowledge, care, and thoroughness. We have undertaken, in the matter of government, far more than ever in the history of the world has been previously attempted by the children of men. . . .

86. [HOME RULE FOR IRELAND]

by WILLIAM EWART GLADSTONE

"Too little and too late" is a just verdict on the failure of successive British governments to deal with the special problems of Ireland in the nineteenth century. By the 1880s a barrier of bitterness, compounded of religious, economic and political grievances, frustrated all well-meaning but piecemeal attempts at a solution. The insufficiency of such measures as his disestablishment of the Irish Church and the Irish Land Acts convinced Gladstone of the need to grant Home Rule for Ireland; and in 1886 he introduced his first Home Rule bill in parliament. The following extract is from his speech on that occasion (*Hansard,* 3rd series [1886], pp. 1037–1045, 1080–1084). The Home Rule issue split the Liberals, and Joseph Chamberlain, the leader of the Radical wing, left the party.

IT is felt on both sides of the House, unless I am much mistaken, that we have arrived at a stage in our political transactions with Ireland, where two roads part one from the other, not soon probably to meet again. The late Government—I am not now referring to this as a matter of praise or blame, but simply as a matter of fact—the late Government felt that they had reached the moment for decisive resolution when they made the announcement, on the last day of their Ministerial existence, that their duty compelled them to submit to Parliament proposals for further repressive criminal legislation. We concur entirely in that conclusion, and we think that the time is come when it is the duty of Parliament, when the honour of Parliament and its duty alike require, that it should endeavour to come to some decisive resolution in this matter; and our intention is, Sir, to propose to the House of Commons that which, as we think, if happily accepted, will liberate Parliament from the restraints under which of late years it has ineffectually struggled to perform the Business of the country; will restore legislation to its natural, ancient, unimpeded course; and will, above all, obtain an answer—a clear, we hope, and definite answer—to the question whether it is or is not possible to establish good and harmonious relations between Great Britain and Ireland on the footing of those free institutions to which Englishmen, Scotchmen, and Irishmen are alike unalterably attached. . . .

. . . And, Sir, the first point to which I would call your attention is this, that whereas exceptional legislation—legislation which introduces exceptional provisions into the law—ought itself to be in its own nature essentially and absolutely exceptional, it has become for us not exceptional, but habitual. We are like a man who, knowing that medicine may be the means of his restoration to health, endeavours to live upon medicine. Nations, no more than individuals, can find a subsistence in what was meant to be a cure. But has it been a cure? Have we attained the object which we desired, and honestly desired, to attain? No, Sir, agrarian crime has become, sometimes upon a larger and sometimes upon a smaller scale, as habitual in Ireland as the legislation which has been intended to repress it. . . .

But the agrarian crime in Ireland is not so much a cause as it is a symptom. It is a symptom of a yet deeper mischief of which it is only the external manifestation. That manifestation is mainly threefold. In the first place, with certain exceptions for the case of winter juries, it is impossible to depend in Ireland upon the finding of a jury in a case of agrarian crime according to the facts as they are viewed by the Government, by the Judges, and by the public, I think, at large. That is a most serious mischief, passing down deep into the very groundwork of civil society. It is also, Sir, undoubtedly a mischief that, in cases where the extreme remedy of eviction is resorted to by the landlord—possibly, in some instances, unnecessarily resorted to, but, in other instances, resorted to after long patience has been exhausted —these cases of eviction, good, bad, and indifferent as to their justification, stand pretty much in one and the same discredit with the rural population of Ireland, and become, as we know, the occasion of transactions that we all deeply lament. Finally, Sir, it is not to be denied that there is great interference in Ireland with individual liberty in the shape of intimidation. . . . I will simply record the fact that intimidation does prevail, not to the extent that is supposed, yet to a material and painful extent in Ireland. The consequence of that is to weaken generally the respect for law, and the respect for contract, and that among a people who, I believe, are as capable of attaining to the very highest moral and social standard as any people on the face of the earth. So much for coercion—if I use the phrase it is for brevity for repressive legislation generally—but there is one circumstance to which I cannot help calling the special attention of the House.

Nothing has been more painful to me than to observe that, in this matter, we are not improving, but, on the contrary, we are losing ground. Since the last half-century dawned, we have been steadily engaged in extending, as well as in consolidating, free institutions. I divide the period since the Act of Union with Ireland into two—the first from 1800 to 1832, the epoch of what is still justly called the great Reform Act; and, secondly, from 1833 to 1885. I do not know whether it has been as widely observed as I think it deserves to be that, in the first of those periods—32 years—there were no less than 11 years—it may seem not much to say, but wait for what is coming—there were no less than 11 of those 32 years in which our Statute Book was free throughout the whole year from repressive legislation of an exceptional kind against Ireland. But in the 53 years since we advanced far in the career of Liberal principles and actions—in those 53 years, from 1833 to 1885—there were but two years which were entirely free from the action of this special legislation for Ireland. Is not that of itself almost enough to prove that we have arrived at the point where it is necessary that we should take a careful and searching survey of our position? For, Sir, I would almost venture, trusting to the indulgent interpretation of the House, to say that the coercion we have heretofore employed has been spurious and ineffectual coercion, and that if there is to be coercion—which God forbid—it ought to be adequate to attain its end. If it is to attain its end it must be different, differently maintained, and maintained with a different spirit; courage, and consistency compared with the coercion with which we have been heretofore familiar. . . .

. . . If it be true that our system, such as I have exhibited it, has been—we may hide it from ourselves, we cannot hide it from the world—a failure in regard to repressive legislation, will that other coercion, which it is possible to conceive, be more successful? I can, indeed, conceive, and in history we may point to circumstances in which coercion of that kind, stern, resolute, consistent, might be, and has been, successful. But it requires, in my judgment, two essential conditions, and these are—the autocracy of Government, and the secrecy of public transactions. With those conditions, that kind of coercion to which I am referring might possibly succeed. But will it succeed in the light of day, and can it be administered by the people of England and Scotland against the people of Ireland by the two nations which, perhaps, above all others upon earth—I need hardly except America—best understand and are most fondly attached to the essential principles of liberty?

Now, I enter upon another proposition to which I hardly expect broad exception can be taken. I will not assume, I will not beg, the question, whether the people of England and Scotland will ever administer that sort of effectual coercion which I have placed in contrast with our timid and hesitating repressive measures; but this I will say, that the people of England and Scotland will never resort to that alternative until they have tried every other. Have they tried every other? Well, some we have tried, to which I will refer. I have been concerned with some of them myself. But we have not yet tried every alternative, because there is one—not unknown to human experience—on the contrary, widely known to various countries in the world, where this dark and difficult problem has been solved by the comparatively natural and simple, though not always easy, expedient of stripping law of its foreign garb, and investing it with a domestic character, I am not saying that this will succeed; I by no means beg the question at this moment; but this I will say, that Ireland, as far as I know, and speaking of the great majority of the people of Ireland, believes it will succeed, and that experience elsewhere supports that conclusion. The case of Ireland, though she is represented here not less fully than England or Scotland, is not the same as that of England or Scotland. England, by her own strength, and by her vast majority in this House, makes her own laws just as independently as if she were not combined with two other countries. Scotland—a small country, smaller than Ireland, but a country endowed with a spirit so masculine that never in the long course of history, excepting for two brief periods, each of a few years, was the superior strength of England such as to enable her to put down the national freedom beyond the border —Scotland, wisely recognized by England, has been allowed and encouraged in this House to make her own laws as freely and as effectually as if she had a representation six times as strong. The consequence is that the mainspring of law in England is felt by the people to be English; the mainspring of law in Scotland is felt by the people to be Scotch; but the mainspring of law in Ireland is not felt by the people to be Irish, and I am bound to say—truth extorts from me the avowal—that it cannot be felt to be Irish in the same sense as it is English and Scotch. The net results of this statement which I have laid before the House, because it was necessary as the groundwork of my argument, are these—in the first place, I admit it to be little less than a mockery to hold that the state of law and of facts conjointly, which I have endeavoured to describe, conduces to the real unity of this great, noble, and world-wide Empire. In the second place, something must be done, something is imperatively demanded from us to restore to Ireland the first conditions of civil life—the free course of law, the liberty of every individual in the exercise of every legal right, the confidence of the people in the law, and their sympathy with the law, apart from which no country can be called, in the full sense of the word, a civilized country, nor can there be given to that country the blessings which it is the object of civilized society to attain. . . .

But, Sir, I do not deny the general good intentions of Parliament on a variety of great and conspicuous occasions, and its desire to pass good laws for Ireland. But let me say that, in order to work out the purposes of government, there is something more in this world occasionally required than even the passing of good laws. It is sometimes requisite not only that good laws should be passed, but also that they should be passed by the proper persons. The passing of many good laws is not enough in cases where the strong permanent instincts of the people, their distinctive marks of character, the situation and history of the country require not only that these laws should be good, but that they should proceed from a congenial and native source, and besides being good laws should be their own laws. . . .

The principle that I am laying down I am not laying down exceptionally for Ireland. It is the very principle upon which, within my recollection, to the immense advantage of the country, we have not only altered, but revolutionized our method of governing the Colonies. . . . The Colonies said—"We do not want your good laws; we want our own." We admitted the reasonableness of that principle, and it is now coming home to us from across the seas. We have to consider whether it is applicable to the case of Ireland. Do not let us disguise this from ourselves. We stand face to face with what is termed Irish nationality. Irish nationality vents itself in the demand for local autonomy, or separate and complete self-government in Irish, not in Imperial, affairs. Is this an evil in itself? Is it a thing that we should view with horror or apprehension? . . . Sir, I hold that it is not. . . . I ask that in our own case we should practise, with firm and fearless hand, what we have so often preached—the doctrine which we have so often inculcated upon others—namely, that the concession of local self-government is not the way to sap or impair, but the way to strengthen and consolidate unity. I ask that we should learn to rely less upon merely written stipulations, and more upon those better stipulations which are written on the heart and mind of man. I ask that we should apply to Ireland that happy experience which we have gained in England and in Scotland, where the course of generations has now taught us, not as a dream or a theory, but as practice and as life, that the best and surest foundation we can find to build upon is the foundation afforded by the affections, the convictions, and the will of the nation; and it is thus, by the decree of the Almighty, that we may be enabled to secure at once the social peace, the fame, the power, and the permanence of the Empire.

87. [THE CONCEPT OF EMPIRE]

by BENJAMIN DISRAELI

Just as Gladstone, with his early Tory views and devotion to the Church of England, seems an unlikely leader for the Liberal party, so Benjamin Disraeli (1804–1881) appears at first glance to be an odd choice for a Conservative prime minister. An Anglicized Jew, with a youthful background of literary radicalism, his colorful and dramatic personality was far removed from the imaginations of the Tory rank and file. He successfully transformed the old Tory image of a party representing the squires and parsons into a Conservatism which was the natural defender of the ancient institutions and rights of the people. His cult of the Queen went hand in hand with his championing of a revived imperialism. In 1876, during his second premiership, he was created Earl of Beaconsfield. His speech at the Crystal Palace on June 24, 1872, from which these passages are taken (*Selected Speeches of the Earl of Beaconsfield,* T. E. Kebbel, ed. [1882], pp. 530–534), is usually regarded as marking the beginning of the new conception of the British Empire.

IF you look to the history of this country since the advent of Liberalism—forty years ago—you will find that there has been no effort so continuous, so subtle, supported by so much energy, and carried on with so much ability and acumen, as the attempts of Liberalism to effect the disintegration of the Empire of England.

And, gentlemen, of all its efforts, this is the one which has been the nearest to success. Statesmen of the highest character, writers of the most distinguished ability, the most organised and efficient means, have been employed in this endeavour. It has been proved to all of us that we have lost money by our colonies. It has been shown with precise, with mathematical demonstration, that there never was a jewel in the Crown of England that was so truly costly as the possession of India. How often has it been suggested that we should at once emancipate ourselves from this incubus. Well, that result was nearly accomplished. When those subtle views were adopted by the country under the plausible plea of granting self-government to the Colonies, I confess that I myself thought that the tie was broken. Not that I for one object to self-government. I cannot conceive how our distant colonies can have their affairs administered except by self-government. But self-government, in my opinion, when it was conceded, ought to have been conceded as part of a great policy of Imperial consolidation. It ought to have been accompanied by an Imperial tariff, by securities for the people of England for the enjoyment of the unappropriated lands which belonged to the Sovereign as their trustee, and by a military code which should have precisely defined the means and the responsibilities by which the colonies should be defended, and by which, if necessary, this country should call for aid from the colonies themselves. It ought, further, to have been accompanied by the institution of some representative council in the metropolis, which would have brought the Colonies into constant and continuous relations with the Home Government. All this, however, was omitted because those who advised that policy—and I believe their convictions were sincere —looked upon the Colonies of England, looked even upon our connection with India, as a burden upon this country, viewing everything in a financial aspect, and totally passing by those moral and political considerations which make nations great, and by the influence of which alone men are distinguished from animals.

Well, what has been the result of this attempt during the reign of Liberalism for the disintegration of the Empire? It has entirely failed. But how has it failed? Through the sympathy of the Colonies with the Mother Country. They have decided that the Empire shall not be destroyed, and in my opinion no minister in this country will do his duty who neglects any opportunity of reconstructing as much as possible our Colonial Empire, and of responding to those distant sympathies which may become the source of incalculable strength and happiness to this land. Therefore, gentlemen, with respect to the second great object of the Tory party also—the maintenance of the Empire—public opinion appears to be in favour of our principles— that public opinion which, I am bound to say, thirty years ago, was not favourable to our principles, and which, during a long interval of controversy, in the interval had been doubtful. . . .

When you return to your homes, when you return to your counties and to your cities, you must tell to all those whom you can influence that the time is at hand, that, at least, it cannot be far distant, when England will have to decide between national and cosmopolitan principles. The issue is not a mean one. It is whether you will be content to be a comfortable England, modelled and moulded upon Continental principles and meeting in due course an inevitable fate, or whether you will be a great country,—an Imperial country—a country where your sons, when they rise, rise to paramount positions, and obtain not merely the esteem of their countrymen, but command the respect of the world. . . .

88. RECESSIONAL

by RUDYARD KIPLING

The popular poet of empire was Rudyard Kipling (1865–1936), the son of an artist who lived in India. To the practical policies of Joseph Chamberlain's active imperialism Kipling added an ideology compounded of simplified Darwinism, evangelicalism, and romanticism. His hero was the British "tommy," exiled on garrison duty in the remote parts of Asia; and his poems and stories popularized the idea of imperialism as the White Man's Burden. The following poem was written for the Queen's Diamond Jubilee in 1897 and was later incorporated in collections of hymns for use in church (from *The Five Nations* [1903], pp. 214–215).

JUNE 22, 1897

God of our fathers, known of old—
    Lord of our far-flung battle-line—
Beneath whose awful Hand we hold
    Dominion over palm and pine—
Lord God of Hosts, be with us yet,
Lest we forget, lest we forget!

The tumult and the shouting dies—
    The captains and the kings depart—
Still stands Thine ancient sacrifice,
    An humble and a contrite heart.

Lord God of Hosts, be with us yet,
Lest we forget, lest we forget!

Far-call'd our navies melt away—
    On dune and headland sinks the fire—
Lo, all our pomp of yesterday
    Is one with Nineveh and Tyre!
Judge of the Nations, spare us yet,
Lest we forget, lest we forget!

If, drunk with sight of power, we loose
    Wild tongues that have not Thee in awe—
Such boasting as the Gentiles use
    Or lesser breeds without the Law—
Lord God of Hosts, be with us yet,
Lest we forget, lest we forget!

For heathen heart that puts her trust
    In reeking tube and iron shard—
All valiant dust that builds on dust,
    And guarding calls not Thee to guard—
For frantic boast and foolish word,
Thy mercy on Thy People, Lord!

89. [TORY DEMOCRACY]

by RANDOLPH CHURCHILL

Disraeli was prime minister long enough only to elaborate rather than implement his theory of Tory democracy. It was left to his successors to try to win working men to the Conservative cause. Of the Conservative leaders after Disraeli, Lord Randolph Churchill (1849–1895) for a time seemed the most likely to be able to carry on the policy of the master. But his political career was cut short in 1886, when he resigned from the government over the issue of a radical budget. The following passages are from his famous speech, "Trust the People," at Birmingham on April 16, 1884, in *Speeches of Lord Randolph Churchill*, Louis J. Jennings, ed. (1889), Vol. I, pp. 134–140.

WHAT is the great and wide difference which distinguishes the two great political parties who endeavour to attract the support of the English people? It has been well and wisely said—but I do not think it can be too often repeated—that the Tory party clings with veneration and affection to the institutions of our country. The Radicals regard them with aversion and distrust and will always give multitudinous and specious reasons for their destruction. But can we, the Tory party, give no good convincing reasons to the people for the faith which is in us? We do not defend the Constitution from mere sentiment for the past, or from any infatuated superstition about Divine right or hereditary excellence. We defend the Constitution solely on the ground of its utility to the people. It is on the ground of utility alone that we go forth to meet our foes, and if we fail to make good our ground with utilitarian arguments and for utilitarian ends, then let the present combination of Throne, Lords, and Commons be for ever swept away. An hereditary throne is the surest device which has ever been imagined or invented for the perpetuation of civil order and for that first necessity of civilised society—continuity of government. . . . It would be impossible to devise a form of governmental summit as effectual, and yet cheaper and more simple . . . I maintain that the House of Lords should be preserved solely on the ground of its utility to the people. I do not put forward as an argument for its preservation its long history, in order to show you that it possesses great merit as an institution. I do not argue, as some do, that it has acquired stability from the circumstance that by its composition it is rooted in the soil. I content myself with the fact of its existence at the present moment, and I find in it not only a powerful check on popular impulses arising from imperfect information, not only an aggregation of political wisdom and experience such as no other country can produce, but, above all, because I find in it literally the only effectual barrier against that most fatal foe to freedom, the one-man power—that power which has more than once prostrated and enslaved the liberties of France, and which constantly gives anxiety to the citizens of the United States. From a national and imperial point of view, you need never be alarmed at the dangers cf one-man power so long as the House of Lords endures. Be he minister, be he capitalist, be he demagogue—be he Mr. Gladstone, or Mr. Chamberlain, or even Mr. Schnadhorst—against that bulwark of popular liberty and civil order he will dash himself in vain. The House of Lords may, perhaps, move slowly; they may, perhaps, be overcautious about accepting the merits of the legislation of the House of Commons; they may, perhaps, at times regard with some exaggeration of sentiment the extreme rights of property. That is the price you have to pay—and a small price it is for so valuable a possession—which guards you against so great a danger. They are essentially of the people. Year by year they are re-cruited from the people. Every privilege, every franchise, every liberty which is gained by the people, is treasured up and guarded by those who, animated by tradition and custom, by long descent and lofty name, fear neither monarchs, nor ministers, nor men, but only the people, whose trustees they are. . . .

I cannot pass from this subject of the House of Lords without al-luding to the other bugbear of the Radical party, the Church of Eng-land, and its connection with the State. . . . Again I adhere to my utilitarian line of defence, and I would urge upon you not to lend yourselves too hastily to any project for the demolition of the Es-tablished Church. But I would also, in dealing with this question, mingle a little of the wine of sentiment with the cold clear spring water of utilitarianism. I see in the Church of England an immense and omnipresent ramification of machinery working without cost to the people—and daily and hourly lifting the masses of the people, rich and poor alike, from the dead and dreary level of the lowest and most material cares of life, up to the comfortable contemplation of higher and serener forms of existence and of destiny. I see in the Church of England a centre, and a source, and a guide of charitable effort, miti-gating by its mendicant importunity the violence of human misery, whether mental or physical, and contributing to the work of alleviation from its own not superfluous resources. And I urge upon you not to throw that source of charity upon the haphazard almsgiving of a busy and a selfish world. I view the Church of England eagerly co-oper-ating in the work of national education, not only benefiting your chil-dren, but saving your pockets; and I remember that it has been the work of the Church to pour forth floods of knowledge, purely secular and scientific, even from the days when knowledge was not; and I warn you against hindering the diffusion of knowledge, inspired by religion, amongst those who will have devolved upon them the re-sponsibility for the government of this wide empire. But I own that my chief reason for supporting the Church of England I find in the fact that, when compared with other creeds and other sects, it is es-sentially the Church of religious liberty. Whether in one direction or another, it is continually possessed by the ambition, not of excluding, but of including, all shades of religious thought, all sorts and conditions of men; and, standing out like a lighthouse over a stormy ocean, it marks the entrance to a port where the millions and the masses of those who are wearied at times with the woes of the world, and troubled often by the trials of existence, may search for and may find that peace which passeth all understanding. I cannot, and will not, allow myself to believe that the English people, who are not only naturally religious, but also eminently practical, will ever consent, for the petty purpose of gratifying sectarian animosity, or for the wretched object of pandering to infidel proclivities—will ever consent to deprive themselves of so abundant a fountain of aid and consolation, or acquiesce in the demolition of an institution which elevates the life of the nation, and consecrates the acts of the State.

Last, but not least—no; rather first—in the scheme of Tory politics come the Commons of England, with their marvellous history; their ancient descent, combining the blood of many nations; their unequalled liberties, and, I believe, their splendid future. The social progress of the Commons by means of legislative reform under the lines and carried on under the protection of the institutions whose utility I have endeavoured to describe to you—that must be the policy of the Tory party. Their industries must be stimulated and protected by lightening the taxation, and by a large redistribution of the incidence of taxation. Their efforts to emancipate their brethren from the vices of an undeveloped civilisation, such as intemperance, crime, and a weak standard of morality, must be provoked, encouraged, and facilitated. No class interests should be allowed to stand in the way of this mighty movement, and with this movement the Tory party not only sympathise, but identify themselves. Social reform, producing direct and immediate benefit to the Commons—that must be our cry, as opposed to the Radicals, who foolishly scream for organic change, and waste their energies and their time in attacking institutions whose destruction would not only endanger popular freedom, but would leave the social condition of the people precisely where it was before. . . . I was much struck the other day in the House of Commons by a sentence which fell from the Prime Minister, when, leaning over the table and addressing directly the Tory party, he said to them, 'Trust the people.' I have long tried to make that my motto; but I know, and will not conceal, that there are still a few in our party who have that lesson yet to learn, and who have yet to understand that the Tory party of to-day is no longer identified with that small and narrow class which is connected with the ownership of land, but that its great strength can be found, and must be developed, in our large towns as well as in our country districts. Yes, trust the people. You, who are ambitious, and rightly ambitious, of being the guardians of the British Constitution, trust the people, and they will trust you —and they will follow you and join you in the defence of that Constitution against any and every foe.

I have no fear of democracy. I do not fear for minorities. . . . Modern checks and securities are not worth a brass farthing. Give me a fair arrangement of the constituencies, and one part of England will correct and balance the other. I do not think that electoral reform is a matter of national emergency. I should have been glad to see Parliament devote its attention and time to other matters, such as finance, local taxation, commerce, Ireland, and Egypt. But I think that electoral reform is a matter of ministerial urgency, of party urgency, and that it is being treated as a question of party tactics for the purpose of uniting and stimulating the shattered Liberal majority: and it was for these reasons that I voted against the Reform Bill. . . .

90. [THE NEW LIBERALISM]

by DAVID LLOYD GEORGE

Long before the death of Gladstone himself in 1898 it was clear that Gladstonian Liberalism was a spent force. Its intense concern for individualism, whether interpreted as "freedom of contract" in industry or "voluntaryism" in religion and philanthropy, no longer roused the enthusiasm of a generation which was finding collectivist ideas increasingly attractive. The old Liberal antithesis between the individual and society, with its corollary doctrines of self-help and laissez-faire, was due for replacement by a broader concept of freedom. This was provided by the radical wing of the Liberal party, which from 1906 to 1911 carried through a program of social reform and laid the foundations of the later Welfare State. The most dynamic of the leaders of this New Liberalism was David Lloyd George (1863–1945), a Welsh lawyer of humble origins, who in 1916 became prime minister. This speech was made

at Swansea, October 1, 1908, and is from David Lloyd
George, *Better Times* (1910), pp. 49–54.

WHAT is the work still waiting the Liberal Party in this country? It
is to establish complete religious equality in our institutions. There is
no religious equality so long as men of capacity and character are debarred from competing for teacherships in 14,000 State schools because they cannot conscientiously conform to the doctrines of some
dominant sect. There is no religious equality as long as one sect whose
dogmas, in Wales at any rate, are repudiated by the vast majority of
the people, is able to pose as the official exponent of the faith of the
Welsh people, and to enjoy all the privileges, emoluments, and endowments attached to that position. I place the establishment of complete
religious equality in the forefront, because it lies in the domain of
conscience . . . and nothing can save a people afflicted by such institutions from the spirit of bondage but an incessant protest against
them. . . .

The same observations apply to the question of civil equality. We
have not yet attained it in this country—far from it. You will not have
established it in this land until the child of the poorest parent shall
have the same opportunity for receiving the best education as the
child of the richest. . . . It will never be established so long as you
have five hundred men nominated by the lottery of birth to exercise
the right of thwarting the wishes of the majority of forty millions of
their countrymen in the determination of the best way of governing
the country. I hope no prospect of a temporary material advantage
will blind the people of this country to the permanent good for them
of vindicating in the laws and institutions of the land these great
principles, which lie at the root of freedom and good government for
the people.

On the other hand, I think there is a danger that Liberals may
imagine that their task begins and ends there. If they do so, then
they will not accomplish even that task.

British Liberalism is not going to repeat the fate of Continental
Liberalism. The fate of Continental Liberalism should warn them of
that danger. It has been swept on one side before it had well begun
its work, because it refused to adapt itself to new conditions. The
Liberalism of the Continent concerned itself exclusively with mending
and perfecting the machinery which was to grind corn for the people.
It forgot that the people had to live whilst the process was going on,

and people saw their lives pass away without anything being accomplished. British Liberalism has been better advised. It has not abandoned the traditional ambition of the Liberal Party to establish freedom and equality; but side by side with this effort it promotes measures for ameliorating the conditions of life for the multitude.

The old Liberals in this country used the natural discontent of the people with the poverty and precariousness of the means of subsistence as a motive power to win for them a better, more influential, and more honourable status in the citizenship of their native land. The new Liberalism, while pursuing this great political ideal with unflinching energy, devotes a part of its endeavour also to the removing of the immediate causes of discontent. It is true that men cannot live by bread alone. It is equally true that a man cannot live without bread. . . . It is a recognition of that elemental fact that has promoted legislation like the Old Age Pensions Act. It is but the beginning of things. . . . Poverty is the result of a man's own misconduct or misfortune. In so far as he brings it on himself, the State cannot accomplish much. It can do something to protect him. In so far as poverty is due to circumstances over which the man has no control, then the State should step in to the very utmost limit of its resources, and save the man from the physical and mental torture involved in extreme penury. . . . The aged we have dealt with during the present Session. We are still confronted with the more gigantic task of dealing with the rest—the sick, the infirm, the unemployed, the widows, and the orphans. No country can lay any real claim to civilisation that allows them to starve. Starvation is a punishment that society has ceased to inflict for centuries on its worst criminals, and at its most barbarous stage humanity never starved the children of the criminal. . . . Is it just, is it fair, is it humane, to let them suffer privation? I do not think the better-off classes, whose comfort is assured, realise the sufferings of the unemployed workmen. What is poverty? Have you felt it yourselves? If not, you ought to thank God for having been spared its sufferings and temptations. Have you ever seen others enduring it? Then pray God to forgive you if you have not done your best to alleviate it. By poverty I mean real poverty, not the cutting down of your establishment, not the limitation of your luxuries. I mean the poverty of the man who does not know how long he can keep a roof over his head, and where he will turn to find a meal for the pinched and hungry little children who look to him for sustenance and protection. That is what unemployment means.

FURTHER READING: Part Four

Brown, E. H. Phelps, *The Growth of British Industrial Relations: a Study from the Standpoint of 1906–14* (1959).

Cole, Margaret, *The Story of Fabian Socialism* (1961).

Dangerfield, George, *The Strange Death of Liberal England* (1936).

Fulford, Roger, *Votes for Women* (1957).

Jones, Thomas, *Lloyd George* (1951).

Lowndes, G. A. N., *The Silent Social Revolution: an Account of the Expansion of Public Education in England and Wales, 1895–1935* (1937).

Lynd, Helen Merrell, *England in the Eighteen Eighties* (1946).

Magnus, Sir Phillip, *Gladstone* (1954).

Monypenny, W. F., and G. Buckle, *Life of Disraeli*, 2 vols. (1929).

Morley, John, *Life of William Ewart Gladstone*, 3 vols. (1911 ed.).

Pelling, Henry, *The Origins of the Labour Party, 1880–1900* (1954).

Pelling, Henry, and Frank Bealey, *Labour and Politics, 1900–1906* (1958).

Poirier, Philip, *The Advent of the Labour Party* (1958).

Southgate, Donald, *The Passing of the Whigs, 1832–1886* (1962).

Thornton, A. P., *The Imperial Idea and its Enemies* (1959).

PART FIVE.
BETWEEN THE WARS, 1914-1939

Chapter 19.

The Revolutionary Years

The years immediately before World War I saw the growth of profound unrest and a trend towards extremism in English society. The labor movement was engaged in a series of widespread strikes, and syndicalism appealed strongly to some of the more militant trade union leaders. The agitation for women's suffrage moved into a new stage of violent tactics, using arson, assaults on police, and hunger strikes. In Ireland the northern counties of Ulster prepared to resist Home Rule by force of arms, and their action in raising a volunteer army for this purpose was matched by similar measures in southern Ireland. The constitution itself was by no means inviolate, as was demonstrated by the die-hard stand of the House of Lords against a popularly elected Liberal House of Commons in 1911.

This period of domestic anarchy was brought to a sudden end by the outbreak of war in August 1914; for the time being the appeal to close the ranks successfully shelved the issues which divided the nation. When the War ended in November 1918 it was clear that there could be no going back to the positions of 1914, though many conservatives instinctively thought of a return to "normalcy" as a re-establishment of prewar conditions. The War had decisively altered many social attitudes and assumptions; it had effected important changes in Britain's economic position; and the balance of political forces had been upset to the detriment of the Liberals and the advantage of Labour. Yet of the great movements which had been cut off by the outbreak of war, only the issue of women's suffrage was settled by 1918. The others remained as thorny problems, to be tackled now in a new context. In Ireland, after the Easter Rising of 1916, relations between the British government and the Irish nationalists became increasingly embittered; in 1919 open war was declared by the Irish Republican Army, and the "time of troubles" was not ended

371

until 1924. The demands of labor, which had not been met
before the war, were now presented with renewed mili-
tancy; and the alternation of economic booms and slumps
aggravated the conditions of the industrial struggle. In Europe the collapse of the Central Powers had been the signal
for revolutionary outbreaks; and the success of the Bol-
shevik Revolution in Russia remained to inspire or frighten
a whole generation of politicians and labor leaders. There
was an awareness in England that the great Victorian age
was now well and truly over. In its place there seemed only
social turmoil and cynical political bargaining. With par-
donable exaggeration Lloyd George declared that "only the
dole [i.e., unemployment relief] saved England from revolution."

91. LABOUR AND THE NEW SOCIAL ORDER

by THE LABOUR PARTY

Labor emerged from World War I greatly strengthened.
The trade unions benefited from the government's need of
their support on the home front, particularly in the munitions industries. The Labour Party itself, which had been
divided over support for the war, polled 2,400,000 votes
and gained 59 seats in the Commons at the "coupon" election of 1918; thus profiting from the split in the Liberal
Party and becoming the official Opposition. Its main problem was how to present itself as a truly national party,
claiming the allegiance of all radical and progressive elements as well as the labor union and socialist votes upon
which it had hitherto depended. A new constitution, providing for individual membership and local branches, was
adopted; and a new program entitled *Labour and the New
Social Order* cautiously committed the Party for the first
time to socialist objectives, though the word socialism was
avoided. This document was mainly drafted by Sidney
Webb of the Fabian Society. The following passages are
from the final version approved at the Labour Party Conference in June 1918, pp. 3–22.

IT behoves the Labour Party, in formulating its own programme for Reconstruction after the war, and in criticising the various preparations and plans that are being made by the present Government, to look at the problem as a whole. We have to make clear what it is that we wish to construct. It is important to emphasize the fact that, whatever may be the case with regard to other political parties, our detailed practical proposals proceed from definitely held principles.

THE END OF A CIVILISATION

We need to beware of patchwork. The view of the Labour Party is that what has to be reconstructed after the war is not this or that Government Department, or this or that piece of social machinery; but, so far as Britain is concerned, society itself. The individual worker, or for that matter the individual statesman, immersed in daily routine—like the individual soldier in a battle—easily fails to understand the magnitude and far-reaching importance of what is taking place around him. How does it fit together as a whole? How does it look from a distance? Count Okuma, one of the oldest, most experienced and ablest of the statesmen of Japan, watching the present conflict from the other side of the globe, declares it to be nothing less than the death of European civilisation. Just as in the past the civilisations of Babylon, Egypt, Greece, Carthage and the great Roman Empire have been successively destroyed, so, in the judgment of this detached observer, the civilisation of all Europe is even now receiving its death-blow. We of the Labour Party can so far agree in this estimate as to recognise, in the present world catastrophe, if not the death, in Europe, of civilisation itself, at any rate the culmination and collapse of a distinctive industrial civilisation, which the workers will not seek to reconstruct. At such times of crisis it is easier to slip into ruin than to progress into higher forms of organisation. That is the problem as it presents itself to the Labour Party to-day.

What this war is consuming is not merely the security, the homes, the livelihood and the lives of millions of innocent families, and an enormous proportion of all the accumulated wealth of the world, but also the very basis of the peculiar social order in which it has arisen. The individualist system of capitalist production, based on the private ownership and competitive administration of land and capital, which has in the past couple of centuries become the dominant form, with its reckless "profiteering" and wage-slavery; with its glorification of the unhampered struggle for the means of life and its hypocritical pretence of the "survival of the fittest"; with the monstrous inequality of circumstances which it produces and the degradation and brutalisation, both moral and spiritual, resulting therefrom, may, we hope, indeed have received a death-blow. With it must go the political system and ideas in which it naturally found expression. We of the Labour Party, whether in opposition or in due time called upon to form an Administration, will certainly lend no hand to its revival. On the contrary, we shall do our utmost to see that it is buried with the millions whom it has done to death. . . .

THE PILLARS OF THE HOUSE

We need not here recapitulate, one by one, the different items in the Labour Party's programme, which successive Party Conferences have adopted. These proposals, some of them in various publications worked out in practical detail, are often carelessly derided as impracticable, even by the politicians who steal them piecemeal from us! The members of the Labour Party, themselves actually working by hand or by brain, in close contact with the facts, have perhaps at all times a more accurate appreciation of what is practicable, in industry as in politics, than those who depend solely on academic instruction or are biased by great possessions. But to-day no man dares to say that anything is impracticable. The war, which has scared the old Political Parties right out of their dogmas, has taught every statesman and every Government official, to his enduring surprise, how very much more can be done along the lines that we have laid down than he had ever before thought possible. What we now promulgate as our policy, whether for opposition or for office, is not merely this or that specific reform, but a deliberately thought out, systematic, and comprehensive plan for that immediate social rebuilding which any Ministry, whether or not it desires to grapple with the problem, will be driven to undertake. The Four Pillars of the House that we propose to erect, resting upon the common foundation of the Democratic control of society in all its activities, may be termed, respectively:

(*a*) The Universal Enforcement of the National Minimum;
(*b*) The Democratic Control of Industry;
(*c*) The Revolution in National Finance; and
(*d*) The Surplus Wealth for the Common Good.

The various detailed proposals of the Labour Party, herein briefly summarised, rest on these four pillars, and can best be appreciated in connection with them.

THE UNIVERSAL ENFORCEMENT OF A NATIONAL MINIMUM

The first principle of the Labour Party—in significant contrast with those of the Capitalist System, whether expressed by the Liberal or by the Conservative Party—is the securing to every member of the community, in good times and bad alike (and not only to the strong and able, the well-born or the fortunate), of all the requisites of healthy life and worthy citizenship. . . .

THE LEGISLATIVE REGULATION OF EMPLOYMENT

Thus it is that the Labour Party to-day stands for the universal application of the Policy of the National Minimum, to which (as embodied in the successive elaborations of the Factory, Mines, Railways, Shops, Merchant Shipping, Trade Boards, and Truck Acts, the Public Health, Housing, and Education Acts, and the Minimum Wage Acts) the spokesmen of Labour have already gained the support of the enlightened statesmen and economists of the world. All these laws purporting to prevent any Degradation of the Standard of Life need considerable improvement and extension before they can fulfil their purpose of securing to every worker, by hand or by brain, at least the prescribed Minimum of Health, Education, Leisure, and Subsistence, whilst their administration leaves much to be desired. . . .

SECURING EMPLOYMENT FOR ALL

The Labour Party insists—as no other political party has thought fit to do—that what the soldiers and sailors will most seriously look to, is not the sum of money doled out to them, but the provision made for ensuring such of them as are not wholly disabled situations appropriate to their capacities and desires, and that the obligation to find suitable employment in productive work for all these men and women rests upon the Government for the time being. . . .

Nothing is more dangerous to the Standard of Life, or so destructive of those minimum conditions of healthy existence, which must in the interests of the community be assured to every worker, than any widespread or continued unemployment. It has always been a fundamental principle of the Labour Party (a point on which, singularly enough, it has not been followed by either of the other political parties) that, in a modern industrial community, it is one of the foremost obligations of the Government to find, for every willing worker, whether by hand or by brain, productive work at Standard Rates.

It is accordingly the duty of the Government to adopt a policy of deliberately and systematically preventing the occurrence of unemployment, instead of (as heretofore) letting unemployment occur, and then seeking, vainly and expensively, to relieve the unemployed. It is now known that the Government can, if it chooses, arrange the public works and the orders of National Departments and Local Authorities in such a way as to maintain the aggregate demand for labour in the whole kingdom (including that of capitalist employers) approximately at a uniform level from year to year; and it is therefore a primary obligation of the Government to prevent any considerable or widespread fluctuations in the total numbers employed in times of good or bad trade. . . .

SOCIAL INSURANCE AGAINST UNEMPLOYMENT

In so far as the Government fails to prevent Unemployment—whenever it finds it impossible to discover for any willing worker, man or woman, a suitable situation at the Standard Rate—the Labour Party holds that the Government must, in the interest of the community as a whole, provide him or her with adequate maintenance, either with such arrangements for honourable employment or with such useful training as may be found practicable, according to age, health and previous occupation. . . .

THE DEMOCRATIC CONTROL OF INDUSTRY

The universal application of the Policy of the National Minimum is, of course, only the first of the Pillars of the House that the Labour Party intends to see built. What marks off this Party most distinctively from any of the other political parties is its demand for the full and genuine adoption of the principle of Democracy. . . . But unlike the Conservative and Liberal Parties, the Labour Party insists on Democracy in industry as well as in government. It demands the progressive elimination from the control of industry of the private capitalist, individual or joint-stock; and the setting free of all who work, whether by hand or by brain, for the service of the community, and of the community only. And the Labour Party refuses absolutely to believe that the British people will permanently tolerate any reconstruction or perpetuation of the disorganisation, waste and inefficiency involved in the abandonment of British industry to a jostling crowd of separate private employers, with their minds bent, not on the service of the community, but—by the very law of their being—only on the utmost possible profiteering. . . . What the Labour Party looks to is a genuinely scientific reorganisation of the nation's industry, no longer deflected by individual profiteering, on the basis of the Common Ownership of the Means of Production; the equitable sharing of the proceeds among all who participate in any capacity and only among these, and the adoption, in particular services and occupations, of those systems and methods of administration and control that may be found, in practice, best to promote, not profiteering, but the public interest.

IMMEDIATE NATIONALISATION

The Labour Party stands not merely for the principle of the Common Ownership of the nation's land, to be applied as suitable opportunities occur, but also, specifically, for the immediate Nationalisation of Railways, Mines and the production of Electrical Power. . . .

But the sphere of immediate Nationalisation is not restricted to these great industries. We shall never succeed in putting the gigantic system of Health Insurance on a proper footing, or secure a clear field for the beneficent work of the Friendly Societies, or gain a free hand for the necessary development of the urgently called for Ministry of Health and the Local Public Health Service, until the nation expropriates the profit-making Industrial Insurance Companies, which now so tyrannously exploit the people with their wasteful house-to-house Industrial Life Assurance. . . .

In quite another sphere the Labour Party sees the key to Temperance Reform in taking the entire manufacture and retailing of alcoholic drink out of the hands of those who find profit in promoting the utmost possible consumption. This is essentially a case in which the people, as a whole, must assert its right to full and unfettered power for dealing with the licensing question in accordance with local opinion. For this purpose, in conjunction with any expropriation of private interests, localities should have conferred upon them facilities, at their own option:

(*a*) To prohibit the sale of alcoholic drink within their own boundaries;

(*b*) To reduce the number of places of sale and regulate the conditions of sale; and

(*c*) To determine, within the fundamental conditions prescribed by statute, the manner in which the public places of refreshment and social intercourse in their own districts shall be organised and controlled.

LOCAL GOVERNMENT

The Labour Party is alive to the evils of centralisation and the drawbacks of bureaucracy. To counteract these disadvantages it intends that the fullest possible scope shall be given, in all branches of social reconstruction, to the democratically elected local governing bodies. It holds that whilst the central Government Departments should assist with information and grants in aid, the local authorities should be given a free hand to develop their own services, over and above the prescribed national minimum, in whatever way they choose; that they should be empowered to obtain capital from the Government at cost price, and to acquire land cheaply and expeditiously, for any of the functions with which they are entrusted. The Labour Party holds, moreover, that the municipalities and County Councils should not confine themselves to the necessarily costly services of education, sanitation, and police, and the functions to be taken over from the Boards of Guardians, nor yet rest content with acquiring control of the local water, gas, electricity, and tramways, but that they should greatly extend their enterprises in housing and town planning, parks, and public libraries, the provision of music and the organisation of popular recreation, and also that they should be empowered to undertake, not only the retailing of coal, but also other services of common utility, particularly the local supply of milk, where this is not already fully and satisfactorily organized by a co-operative society. . . .

By far the most important function of the Local Authorities is the administration of Education. The first step to social reconstruction must be a genuine nationalisation of education, which shall get rid of all class distinctions and privileges, and bring effectively within the reach, not only of every boy and girl, but also of every adult citizen, all the training, physical, mental and moral, literary, technical, and artistic of which he is capable.

The Labour Party cannot be satisfied with a system which condemns the great bulk of the children to merely the elements of schooling with accommodation and equipment inferior to that of the secondary schools, in classes too large for efficient instruction, under teachers of whom at least one-third are insufficiently trained; which denies to the great majority of the teachers in the kingdom, whether in elementary or in secondary schools (and notably to most of the women), alike any opportunity for all-round culture as well as for training in their art, an adequate wage, reasonable prospects of advancement, and suitable superannuation allowances; and which, notwithstanding what is yet done by way of scholarships for exceptional talent, still reserves the endowed secondary schools, and even more the Universities, for the most part, to the sons and daughters of a small privileged class, whilst contemplating nothing better than eight or ten weeks a year continuation schooling up to 18 for 90 per cent. of the youth of the nation.

The Labour Party accordingly asks for a systematic reorganisation of the whole educational system, from the nursery school to the University, on the basis of (a) social equality; (b) the provision for each age, for child, youth, and adult, of the best and most varied education of which it is capable, with whatever provision by way of maintenance is needed to enable the students to obtain full advantage of the instruction provided; (c) the educational institutions, irrespective of social class or wealth, to be planned, equipped, and staffed according to their several functions, up to the same high level for elementary, secondary, or University teaching, with regard solely to the greatest possible educational efficiency, but without any military training; and (d) the recognition of the teaching profession, without distinction of grade, as one of the most valuable to the community. . . .

CONTROL OF CAPITALIST INDUSTRY

Meanwhile, however, we ought not to throw away the valuable experience now gained by the Government in its assumption of the importation of wheat, wool, metals, and other commodities, and in its control of the shipping, woollen, leather, clothing, boot and shoe, milling, baking, butchering, and other industries. The Labour Party holds that, whatever may have been the shortcomings of this Government importation and control, it has demonstrably prevented a lot of "profiteering." Nor can it end immediately on the Declaration of Peace. The people will be extremely foolish if they ever allow their indispensable industries to slip back into the unfettered control of private capitalists, who are, actually at the instance of the Government itself, now rapidly combining, trade by trade, into monopolist Trusts, which may presently become as ruthless in their extortion as the worst American examples.

A REVOLUTION IN NATIONAL FINANCE

In taxation, also, the interests of the professional and housekeeping classes are at one with those of the manual workers. Too long has our National Finance been regulated, contrary to the teaching of Political Economy, according to the wishes of the possessing classes and the profits of the financiers. The colossal expenditure involved in the present war (of which, against the protest of the Labour Party, only a quarter has been raised by taxation, whilst three-quarters have been borrowed at onerous rates of interest, to be a burden on the nation's future) brings things to a crisis. When peace comes, capital will be needed for all sorts of social enterprises, and the resources of Government will necessarily have to be vastly greater than they were before the war. Meanwhile innumerable new private fortunes are being heaped up by those who have taken advantage of the nation's needs; and the one-tenth of the population which owns nine-tenths of the riches of the United Kingdom, far from being made poorer, will find itself, in the aggregate, as a result of the war, drawing in rent and interest and dividends a larger nominal income than ever before. Such a position demands a revolution in national finance. How are we to discharge a public debt that may well reach the almost incredible figure of 7,000 million pounds sterling, and at the same time raise an annual revenue which, for local as well as central government, must probably reach 1,000 millions a year? It is over this problem of taxation that the various political parties will be found to be most sharply divided.

The Labour Party stands for such a system of taxation as will yield all the necessary revenue to the Government without encroaching on the prescribed National Minimum Standard of Life of any family whatsoever; without hampering production or discouraging any useful personal effort, and with the nearest possible approximation to equality of sacrifice. We definitely repudiate all proposals for a Protective Tariff, in whatever specious guise they may be cloaked, as a device for burdening the consumer with unnecessarily enhanced prices, to the profit of the capitalist employer or landed proprietor, who avowedly expects his profit or rent to be increased thereby. We shall strenuously oppose any taxation, of whatever kind, which would increase the price of food or of any other necessary of life. We hold that indirect taxation on commodities, whether by Customs or Excise, should be strictly limited to luxuries; and concentrated principally on those of which it is socially desirable that the consumption should be actually discouraged. We are at one with the manufacturer, the farmer, and the trader in objecting to taxes interfering with production or commerce, or hampering transport and communications. In all these matters—once more in contrast with the other political parties, and by no means in the interests of the wage-earners alone—the Labour Party demands that the very definite teachings of economic science should no longer be disregarded.

For the raising of the greater part of the revenue now required the Labour Party looks to the direct taxation of the incomes above the necessary cost of family maintenance; and for the requisite effort to pay off the National Debt, to the direct taxation of private fortunes both during life and at death. The Income Tax and Super-tax ought at once to be thoroughly reformed in assessment and collection, in abatements and allowances and in graduation and differentiation, so as to levy the required total sum in such a way as to make the real sacrifice of all the taxpayers as nearly as possible equal. This would involve assessment by families instead of by individual persons, so that the burden is alleviated in proportion to the number of persons to be maintained. It would involve the raising of the present unduly low minimum income assessable to the tax, and the lightening of the present unfair burden on the great mass of professional and small trading classes by a new scale of graduation, rising from a penny in the pound on the smallest assessable income up to sixteen or even nineteen shillings in the pound on the highest income of the millionaires. It would involve bringing into assessment the numerous windfalls of profit that now escape, and a further differentiation between essentially different kinds of income. The Excess Profits Tax might well be retained in an appropriate form; whilst so long as Mining Royalties exist the Mineral Rights Duty ought to be increased. The steadily rising Unearned Increment of urban and mineral land ought, by an appropriate direct Taxation of Land Values, to be wholly brought into the Public Exchequer. At the same time, for the service and redemption of the National Debt, the Death Duties ought to be regraduated, much more strictly collected, and greatly increased. In this matter we need, in fact, completely to reverse our point of view, and to rearrange the whole taxation of Inheritance from the standpoint of asking what is the maximum amount that any rich man should be permitted at death to divert, by his will, from the National Exchequer, which should normally be the heir to all private riches in excess of a quite moderate amount by way of family provision. But all this will not suffice. It will be imperative at the earliest possible moment to free the nation from at any rate the greater part of its new load of interest-bearing debt for loans which ought to have been levied as taxation; and the Labour Party stands for what is called the "Conscription of Wealth"—that is to say, for a special Capital Levy to pay off, if not the whole, a very substantial part of the entire National Debt—a Capital Levy chargeable like the Death Duties on all property, but (in order to secure approximate equality of sacrifice) with exemption of the smallest savings (say, up to £1,000), and for the rest at rates very steeply graduated, so as to take only a small contribution from the little people and a very much larger percentage from the millionaires. . . .

THE SURPLUS FOR THE COMMON GOOD

In the disposal of the surplus above the Standard of Life society has hitherto gone as far wrong as in its neglect to secure the necessary basis of any genuine industrial efficiency or decent social order. We have allowed the riches of our mines, the rental value of the lands superior to the margin of cultivation, the extra profits of the fortunate capitalists, even the material outcome of scientific discoveries—which ought by now to have made this Britain of ours immune from class poverty or from any widespread destitution—to be absorbed by individual proprietors; and then devoted very largely to the senseless luxury of an idle rich class. Against this misappropriation of the wealth of the community, the Labour Party—speaking in the interests not of the wage-earners alone, but of every grade and section of producers by hand or by brain, not to mention also those of the generations that are to succeed us, and of the permanent welfare of the community—emphatically protests. One main Pillar of the House that the Labour Party intends to build is the future appropriation of the Surplus, not to the enlargement of any individual fortune, but to the Common Good. It is from this constantly arising Surplus (to be secured, on the one hand, by Nationalisation and Municipalisation and, on the other, by the steeply graduated Taxation of Private Income and Riches) that will have to be found the new capital which the community day by day needs for the perpetual improvement and increase of its various enterprises, for which we shall decline to be dependent on the usury-exacting financiers. . . .

THE STREET OF TO-MORROW

The House which the Labour Party intends to build, the four Pillars of which have now been described, does not stand alone in the world. Where will it be in the Street of To-morrow? If we repudiate, on the one hand, the Imperialism that seeks to dominate other races, or to impose our own will on other parts of the British Empire, so we disclaim equally any conception of a selfish and insular "non-interventionism," unregarding of our special obligations to our fellow-citizens overseas; of the corporate duties of one nation to another; of the moral claims upon us of the non-adult races, and of our own indebtedness to the world of which we are part. We look for an ever-increasing intercourse, a constantly developing exchange of commodities, a steadily growing mutual understanding, and a continually expanding friendly co-operation among all the peoples of the world. With regard to that great Commonwealth of all races, all colours, all religions and all degrees of civilisation, that we call the British Empire, the Labour Party stands for its maintenance and its progressive development on the lines of Local Autonomy and "Home Rule All Round"; the fullest respect for the rights of each people, whatever its colour, to all the Democratic Self-Government of which it is capable, and to the proceeds of its own toil upon the resources of its own territorial home; and the closest possible co-operation among all the various members of what has become essentially not an Empire in the old sense, but a Britannic Alliance. . . .

92. THE ACQUISITIVE SOCIETY

by RICHARD HENRY TAWNEY

Hugh Gaitskell, the leader of the Labour Party from 1955 to 1963, declared that the influence of R. H. Tawney on the politically-minded members of his generation was profound. In particular, Tawney's *Acquisitive Society* (1921) and *Equality* (1931) were widely-read arguments for socialism, and showed clearly the strong ethical strand in British socialist thought. Tawney (1880–1962) came from a middle-class background, and after being educated at Rugby and Balliol College, Oxford, became a pioneer tutor for the Workers' Educational Association (see Reading No. 83). He was subsequently Professor of Economic History at the London School of Economics, and combined scholarly integrity with uncompromising moral protest. The following extracts are from *The Acquisitive Society* by R. H. Tawney (pp. 9–32, 222–227), copyright, 1920, by Harcourt, Brace & World, Inc., renewed, 1948, by R. H. Tawney and reprinted by permission of the publishers.

A FUNCTION may be defined as an activity which embodies and expresses the idea of social purpose. The essence of it is that the agent does not perform it merely for personal gain or to gratify himself, but recognizes that he is responsible for its discharge to some higher authority. The purpose of industry is obvious. It is to supply man with things which are necessary, useful, or beautiful, and thus to bring life to body or spirit. In so far as it is governed by this end, it is among the most important of human activities. In so far as it is diverted from it, it may be harmless, amusing, or even exhilarating to those who carry it on; but it possesses no more social significance than the orderly business of ants and bees, the strutting of peacocks, or the struggles of carnivorous animals over carrion.

Men have normally appreciated this fact, however unwilling or unable they may have been to act upon it; and therefore from time to time, in so far as they have been able to control the forces of violence and greed, they have adopted various expedients for emphasizing the social quality of economic activity. It is not easy, however, to emphasize it effectively, because to do so requires a constant effort of will, against which egotistical instincts are in rebellion, and because, if that will is to prevail, it must be embodied in some social and political organization, which may itself become so arbitrary, tyrannical and corrupt as to thwart the performance of function instead of promoting it. When this process of degeneration has gone far, as in most European countries it had by the middle of the eighteenth century, the indispensable thing is to break the dead organization up and to clear the ground. In the course of doing so, the individual is emancipated and his rights are enlarged; but the idea of social purpose is discredited by the discredit justly attaching to the obsolete order in which it is embodied.

It is not surprising, therefore, that in the new industrial societies which arose on the ruins of the old régime the dominant note should have been the insistence upon individual rights, irrespective of any social purpose to which their exercise contributed. . . .

The natural consequence of the abdication of authorities which had stood, however imperfectly, for a common purpose in social organization, was the gradual disappearance from social thought of the idea of purpose itself. Its place in the eighteenth century was taken by the idea of mechanism. The conception of men as united to each other, and of all mankind as united to God, by mutual obligations arising from their relation to a common end, ceased to be impressed upon men's minds, when Church and State withdrew from the centre of social life to its circumference. Vaguely conceived and imperfectly realized, it had been the keystone holding together the social fabric. What remained when the keystone of the arch was removed, was private rights and private interests, the materials of a society rather than a society itself. These rights and interests were the natural order which had been distorted by the ambitions of kings and priests, and which emerged when the artificial super-structure disappeared, because they were the creation, not of man, but of Nature herself. They had been regarded in the past as relative to some public purpose, whether religion or national welfare. Henceforward they were thought to be absolute and indefeasible, and to stand by their own virtue. They were the ultimate political and social reality; and since they were the ultimate reality, they were not subordinate to other aspects of society, but other aspects of society were subordinate to them. . . .

This doctrine has been qualified in practice by particular limitations to avert particular evils and to meet exceptional emergencies. But it is limited in special cases precisely because its general validity is regarded as beyond controversy, and, up to the eve of the recent war, it was the working faith of modern economic civilization. What it implies is, that the foundation of society is found, not in functions, but in rights; that rights are not deducible from the discharge of functions, so that the acquisition of wealth and the enjoyment of property are contingent upon the performances of services, but that the individual enters the world equipped with rights to the free disposal of his property and the pursuit of his economic self-interest, and that these rights are anterior to, and independent of, any service which he may render. . . .

A society which aimed at making the acquisition of wealth contingent upon the discharge of social obligations, which sought to proportion remuneration to service and denied it to those by whom no service was performed, which inquired first, not what men possess, but what they can make or create or achieve, might be called a Functional Society, because in such a society the main subject of social emphasis would be the performance of functions. But such a society does not exist, even as a remote ideal, in the modern world, though something like it has hung, an unrealized theory, before men's minds in the past. Modern societies aim at protecting economic rights, while leaving economic functions, except in moments of abnormal emergency, to fulfil themselves.

The motive which gives colour and quality to their public institutions, to their policy and political thought, is not the attempt to secure the fulfilment of tasks undertaken for the public service, but to increase the opportunities open to individuals of attaining the objects which they conceive to be advantageous to themselves. If asked the end or criterion of social organization, they would give an answer reminiscent of the formula the greatest happiness of the greatest number. But to say that the end of social institutions is happiness, is to say that they have no common end at all. For happiness is individual, and to make happiness the object of society is to resolve society itself into the ambitions of numberless individuals, each directed towards the attainment of some personal purpose.

Such societies may be called Acquisitive Societies, because their whole tendency and interest and pre-occupation is to promote the acquisition of wealth. The appeal of this conception must be powerful, for it has laid the whole modern world under its spell. . . .

The organization of society on the basis of functions, instead of on that of rights, implies three things. It means, first, that proprietary rights shall be maintained when they are accompanied by the performance of service and abolished when they are not. It means, second, that the producers shall stand in a direct relation to the community for whom production is carried on, so that their responsibility to it may be obvious and unmistakable, not lost, as at present, through their immediate subordination to shareholders whose interest is not service but gain. It means, in the third place, that the obligation for

the maintenance of the service shall rest upon the professional organizations of those who perform it, and that, subject to the supervision and criticism of the consumer, those organizations shall exercise
so much voice in the government of industry as may be needed to
secure that the obligation is discharged.

It is obvious, indeed, that no change of system or machinery can
avert those causes of social *malaise* which consist in the egotism,
greed, or quarrelsomeness of human nature. What it can do is to
create an environment in which those are not the qualities which are
encouraged. It cannot secure that men live up to their principles.
What it can do is to establish their social order upon principles to
which, if they please, they can live up and not live down. It cannot
control their actions. It can offer them an end on which to fix their
minds. And, as their minds are, so, in the long run and with exceptions, their practical activity will be.

The first condition of the right organization of industry is, then, the
intellectual conversion which, in their distrust of principles, Englishmen are disposed to place last or to omit altogether. It is that emphasis
should be transferred from the opportunities which it offers individuals
to the social functions which it performs; that they should be clear
as to its end and should judge it by reference to that end, not by
incidental consequences which are foreign to it, however brilliant or
alluring those consequences may be. What gives its meaning to any
activity which is not purely automatic is its purpose. It is because the
purpose of industry, which is the conquest of nature for the service of
man, is neither adequately expressed in its organization nor present to
the minds of those engaged in it, because it is not regarded as a function but as an opportunity for personal gain or advancement or display, that the economic life of modern societies is in a perpetual state
of morbid irritation. If the conditions which produce that unnatural
tension are to be removed, it can only be effected by the growth of a
habit of mind which will approach questions of economic organization
from the standpoint of the purpose which it exists to serve, and which
will apply to it something of the spirit expressed by Bacon when he
said that the work of men ought to be carried on "for the glory of
God and the relief of men's estate." . . .

The principle upon which our society professed to be based for
nearly a hundred years after 1789—the principle of free competition—
has clearly spent its force. In the last few years Great Britain—not to
mention America and Germany—has plunged, as far as certain great

industries are concerned, into an era of something like monopoly with the same light-hearted recklessness as a century ago it flung itself into an era of individualism. No one who reads the Reports of the Committee on Trusts appointed by the Ministry of Reconstruction and of the Committees set up under the Profiteering Act upon soap, or sewing cotton, or oil, or half-a-dozen other products, can retain the illusion that the consumer is protected by the rivalry of competing producers. The choice before him, to an increasing extent, is not between competition and monopoly, but between a monopoly which is irresponsible and private and a monopoly which is responsible and public. No one who observes how industrial agreements between workers and employers are actually reached can fail to see that they are settled by a trial of strength between two compactly organized armies, who are restrained from collision only by fear of its possible consequences. Fear is a powerful, but a capricious, motive, and it will not always restrain them. When prudence is overborne by rashness, or when the hope of gain outweighs the apprehension of loss, there will be a collision. No man can say where it will end. No man can even say with confidence that it will produce a more tolerable social order. It is idle to urge that any alternative is preferable to government by the greedy materialists who rule mankind at present, for greed and materialism are not the monopoly of a class. If those who have the will to make a better society have not at present the power, it is conceivable that, when they have the power, they too, like their predecessors, may not have the will.

So, in the long run, it is the principles which men accept as the basis of their social organization which matter. And the principle which we have tried to put forward is that industry and property and economic activity should be treated as functions, and should be tested, at every point, by their relation to a social purpose. Viewed from that angle, issues which are insoluble when treated on the basis of rights may be found more susceptible of reasonable treatment. For a purpose is, in the first place a principle of limitation. It determines the end for which, and therefore the limits within which, an activity is to be carried on. It divides what is worth doing from what is not, and settles the scale upon which what is worth doing ought to be done. It is, in the second place, a principle of unity, because it supplies a common end to which efforts can be directed, and submits interests, which would otherwise conflict, to the judgment of an over-ruling object. It is, in the third place, a principle of apportionment or distribution. It assigns to the different parties of groups engaged in a common undertaking the place which they are to occupy in carrying it out. Thus it establishes order, not upon chance or power, but upon a principle, and bases remuneration not upon what men can with good fortune snatch for themselves, nor upon what, if unlucky, they can be induced to accept, but upon what is appropriate to their function, no more and no less, so that those who perform no function receive no payment, and those who contribute to the common end receive honourable payment for honourable service. . . .

93. [THE GENERAL STRIKE]

by HENRY HAMILTON FYFE

The struggle between capital and labor in the postwar years came to a head in the coal industry. The miners were reluctant to give up their wartime gains and demanded the nationalization of the mines. Successive governments delayed making any decision about the future of the industry by appointing commissions of inquiry. But by 1926 these stalling tactics had been exhausted and government, employers, and miners' union prepared for a trial of strength. Outwardly the struggle was a miners' strike supported by the transport workers and other trade unions. Essentially it was a violent readjustment of industrial conditions after the war. The strike was conducted by the General Council of the Trades Union Congress, to whom the miners had entrusted their case. After nine days, during which the solidity of labor was completely maintained and the normal life of the nation came to a standstill, the T.U.C. leaders called off the strike. These extracts are from a diary of the events by Henry Hamilton Fyfe, *Behind The Scenes of the Great Strike* (1926), pp. 7–83. Fyfe (1869-1951) was at this time editor of the labor paper, *The Daily Herald.*

FIRST DAY

MAY 4th.–Well, it has come at last! I never thought–until a few weeks ago–that it would. Few people believed in the likelihood of it–until a few days ago.

My wife went into the milkman's shop just across the road yester-day. She said we had let our flat, and were wondering whether our tenants, who were coming from France, would be able to get to London and whether they would take the risk.

"What risk?" he inquired.

"Well, the strike, you know," my wife said.

"But that's nowhere near London," he replied scornfully. "It's the miners. Nothing to do with us."

"I'm afraid you don't quite realise. . . ."

"Nothing to do with us," he repeated dogmatically. He knows better now.

None but a few crazy idealists have ever wanted a General Strike. Now the very people who have always been most strongly opposed to it are forced to admit that there is no other way for the Trade Unions to carry out their pledge of support to the miners.

Either they had to break their promise or they had to withdraw their labour, to bring industry and transport to a standstill, in order to convince the mineowners, the Cabinet, and the nation generally that they are determined the miners shall have fair play.

This is the result of Baldwin's belief that he might muddle through the crisis without either making any sustained effort to understand the whole nature of the problem presented to him as Prime Minister, or facing with energy and determination the issues as they came up one by one.

The dispute between the miners and the mineowners has been mishandled all through. It ought to have been a dispute about the state of the coal industry. It has been allowed to become a dispute about wages. . . .

SECOND DAY

Noon.—All the reports coming in both to the T.U.C. and to the *British Worker* office (in response to telegrams we sent yesterday to Press correspondents in every part) show that the strike is general in fact as well as in name. I doubt if any one believed the stoppage of work would be so immediate, so complete. I am sure the Cabinet did not. Baldwin looks gloomy to-day, we hear. Churchill is said to have something up his sleeve. He is cheerful and energetic and seems to believe he can "smash the strike" single-handed with some new weapon he is now forging.

On the railways scarcely a wheel turns. The transport of food is by road. With this there will be no interference. The T.U.C. offered to provide men to run it. To that offer the Cabinet did not even reply.

Docks everywhere are empty and silent.

The roads, outside of the cities, have little traffic on them. Building has almost entirely stopped, except on housing schemes and hospital extensions. Iron and steel works are closed; so are the heavy chemical factories. There are none of the ordinary newspapers. Nothing like a strike on this scale has been seen before—anywhere. . . .

Midnight.—We have had a busy and exciting day of it, preparing the first number of the *British Worker*. It is now out, but it was touch and go until the moment when the machines began to work.

Firstly, there were more Trade Union complications to be smoothed out. Lastly, there was a police raid! . . .

FOURTH DAY

May 7th.—The Cabinet didn't foresee the *British Worker*. They thought their newspaper would have the field to itself and, with the aid of the wireless, influence public opinion unchecked. Churchill especially is for securing that influence, if they possibly can, even though it means suppressing the General Council's organ.

He rather admires us for getting it out. He reads it with keen interest. He speaks well of its appearance. But he wants to get rid of it all the same.

They dare not make a direct attack upon it. That, they realise, would provoke all moderate people against them. They go about their purpose in a round-about way.

This morning we received a letter commandeering our paper. That makes things difficult. We cut down at once to four pages—it is still a neat, compact little paper—and have explained the situation to our readers . . .

That the General Council's appeal to strikers to avoid any kind of disturbance has been successful is proved by the attempts which supporters of the Cabinet are now making to spread false news of outrages and riots. Yesterday and to-day fantastic stories have been in circulation of murdered policemen, Cabinet Ministers attacked, lorries looted, shops ransacked. Some of these fabrications are denied by the newspapers (gradually they are creeping out in miniature form), which, however, carefully print the rumours and so widen the area of mental disturbance and alarm. These are stimulated by the marching of troops about and the driving of lorries filled with them through the streets of cities.

Strong resentment is felt by ex-soldiers at the difference between the attitude of the comfortable classes towards them during the War and now. Many are wearing their medals as a reproach to those who expect them to work for low wages and live under conditions which, if wartime promises had been kept, would long ago have been swept away. There is special irritation against the ex-officers who are acting as strike-breakers under the direction of the O.M.S.

So far the organisation of this society has not made a very brilliant showing. At Newcastle it has broken down altogether. The Minister sent as Civil Commissioner to take charge of the city was compelled to appeal to the Trades Council for help and to admit that he had lost control of the situation. On one railway workers supplied by the O.M.S. blew out the cylinder heads of a locomotive as a consequence of failing to prepare properly for starting up.

Even railway officials are having trouble with trains. A line has been blocked near London by derailment and the Euston terminus points were overrun, traffic being held up for hours.

The end of the fourth day of the strike sees the stoppage of productive work more widely spread, with no sign whatever of weakening among the strikers, who regard themselves as pioneers in a glorious movement, aimed at freeing humanity from the tyranny under which millions of wage-earners are expected to accept a disgracefully low and degrading standard of life. . . .

FIFTH DAY

The demand for the *British Worker* is insatiable. We could sell to purchasers at the doors three times as many as we print, and we are printing half a million. The bundles are fought for as they come out of the office. One night there was a fierce scuffle. A bundle of papers was broken and scattered about. The street sellers snatched them up even then and sold them, soiled as they were. . . .

The story got about yesterday that the Russian Trade Unions had offered the General Council a very large sum of money as a contribution to the Strike Fund. It is quite true that they did so. Here is the sequel. The Council has informed the Russian Trade Unions, in a courteous communication, that it is unable to accept the offer, and the cheque has been returned.

A very prudent proceeding! Had the money been accepted, the other side would have yelled that it was a "subsidy from Moscow." Of course, it would have been nothing of the kind. The Russian Trade Unions are often at loggerheads with Moscow. But the truth wouldn't have had a look in when once the lie started.

What the General Council is asking all British Trade Unionists who are at work to do is to levy themselves for the benefit of those who are "out," and to hand 5 per cent. of their wages to their union officials, who will transmit it to Eccleston Square. . . .

SIXTH DAY

The Archbishop of Canterbury's sermon on the wireless this evening was a really moving appeal. He was down on those who talk about carrying on the struggle "to the bitter end." He was emphatic in his declaration that there should be no thought of making workers endure worse conditions of life. For the first time in its history, I think, the Church of England has put itself on the side of the People against the Privileged Class. The old Archbishop has been splendid.

Very different the pronouncement of Cardinal Bourne that "the General Strike is a sin against Almighty God." Five Labour M.P.'s— John Scurr, H. Murnin, J. Tinker, M. Conolly and J. Sullivan—who are members of the Catholic Church, have sent a letter to the Cardinal saying that they are "seriously disturbed" by this. . . .

SEVENTH DAY

May 10th.—It is possible now to say definitely that the "Revolution stunt" which Winston Churchill foisted upon the Cabinet has failed.

In spite of feverish efforts to alarm the public by its display of steel-helmeted troops, by sending out motor cars filled with special constables to rush through the streets at full speed, by gloomy speeches and articles in the Cabinet organ about the danger of civil war, the public has remained "more than usual calm."

The truth is that the character of the Trade Union leaders is too well known to admit any doubt about their detestation of violence or their determination to make changes only by constitutional means.

Meetings in many districts, attended by adherents of all parties, are discussing the strike as purely industrial in its origin and aims, and urging the renewal of discussion on the coal position, the strike being called off, and the miners' lock-out notices withdrawn.

The lead given by the Archbishops and other leaders of the

Churches is being widely followed. The Presbyterian Church of England has called on the Cabinet to open the door to further negotiations. . . .

May 11*th* (*Noon*).—The Cabinet and its supporters have now dropped Churchill's "Revolution" stunt.

The Times says to-day in a leading article: "No one suggests for a moment that any considerable number of men on strike are animated by revolutionary motives."

That marks the end of Churchill's foolish and dangerous gamble. Now the Cabinet's tactics are changed. Now the official gramophones are grinding out the statement that strikers are going back to work.

This is as much a fabrication as the other. The number of strikers has not diminished; it is increasing. There are more workers out to-day than there have been at any moment since the strike began.

They will stay out until they are instructed by Headquarters to return to work.

This may happen to-morrow. During the last twenty-four hours the Seven Negotiators appointed by the General Council to discuss with Herbert Samuel terms of peace have satisfied themselves that they can accept the general assurances which have been given to them. . . .

To-morrow, if the strike goes on, another section of trade unionists will be called into action. The order has gone out that the engineering shops and shipyards are to stop to-night. This applies to all unions in the engineering and shipbuilding trades affiliated to the T.U.C. It does not apply to men engaged at the Government dockyards, Admiralty establishments, or Government engineering works.

The men, so the General Council reports, have awaited the instructions impatiently, and all over the country they are receiving their "marching orders" with enthusiasm and a sense of relief. . . .

May 12*th.*—9 *a.m.*—To-day's the day!

A decision was reached in the night. The miners were still doubtful. At 1.15 this morning a secretary rang up Eccleston Square from Downing Street. "Are you coming to see the Prime Minister to-day?" he asked anxiously. But he could get neither "yes" nor "no," so the Cabinet went to bed. Later the vote was taken; it was unanimous.

Herbert Smith complains that he has been "left on the doormat," that the General Council has not kept the agreement that the miners should be consulted at every stage. The truth is, they neither gave the General Council power to act for them nor withheld it. They said: "We put our case into your hands, only you mustn't do anything unless we know all about it and agree that it is to be done."

This was an impossible position. It looks as if the strike might be called off without the miners' consent. They are meeting again now, all very weary, with tempers inclined to be edgy. Is it any wonder? Think of the responsibility that rests upon them!

There was a first-class row last night, I hear. Herbert Smith is suffering from gastritis, and ought to be in bed. Thomas declared he had never been so insulted in his life. Ben Tillett made the peace with one of his soft soapy orations.

The strikers are solid still. Even the *British Gazette* is obliged to admit that there is as yet little sign of a general collapse of the strike. It says also that "order and quiet reign throughout the whole island" and there have been "practically no attempts at sabotage."

But there is always a danger, if the situation remains as it is, of something happening to irritate either strikers or the other side, and then there would be fighting all over the place. And there is a great deal to be said for leaving off while the workers' forces are unbroken— so long as there is a clear understanding that they are to go back on honourable terms and that the conditions of the settlement will be observed by the other side.

Well, in an hour or two the strike will be called off. . . .

Noon.—Peace is declared. Pugh, Bevin and Thomas have gone to Downing Street. The General Council is issuing an announcement that the strike is ended because it has reached the conclusion that a satisfactory basis of settlement in the mining industry can now be formulated. ("The Movement," it says, "came out in order to ensure a fair deal for the miners. The G.C. is satisfied that this can now be achieved.")

Evening.—There is a feeling of intense relief everywhere. I saw just now a placard in a shop window, "Peace with Honour." I hope it is. . . .

THE AFTERMATH

May 13.— . . . Now it is clear that a plot was formed to hit back at the workers in every industry as soon as the strike ceased.

Their counter-attack began at once. They are paying no heed whatever to Baldwin's plea that "all vindictiveness" should be put aside. They are determined, it seems, to act upon an earlier *dictum* of his—his statement last July that:

All the workers of this country have got to take reductions of wages.

The nation went to bed on Wednesday night immensely relieved and happy in the belief that work would everywhere be restarted this morning. It has suffered a bitter disappointment. What was a General Strike has become almost a General Lockout. Now it is the employers who are holding up industry and transport.

When railway men reported for work this morning they were told they must re-engage on the understanding that the companies "reserved the rights they possessed in consequence of their breaking their contracts." The railway unions thereupon ordered the men not to resume work.

A large number of other transport workers were also told they could only be re-employed on fresh terms. The same threat was made to workers engaged in the production of newspapers. Some employers declare that henceforward they will only employ non-union labour. Many say they are resolved to have "open shops," where they can employ either union or non-union men.

Protesting against these attempts at victimisation, the General Council says it called off the strike believing that Baldwin meant what he said when he proclaimed his readiness to resume negotiations towards an honourable peace. Such peace, says the General Council, is not possible if employers seize the opportunity to humiliate and injure Trade Unionists. To this they cannot and will not submit.

At the same time they point out that Baldwin's personal honour is involved. He promised goodwill and co-operation. He said "no recriminations." Yet he allows employers in a spirit of mean revenge to endeavour to force important bodies of workers to surrender gains hardly won during many years.

The situation is now fraught with greater peril than before. During the strike every one was in a good temper; there was no malice or bitterness. Now vast numbers are indignant at what they call the dirty trick played on them. . . .

94. [THE DECLINE OF THE LIBERAL PARTY]

by HERBERT HENRY ASQUITH

In 1906 the Liberal Party was returned in overwhelming strength to the House of Commons, with 377 members and a large absolute majority over all other parties combined. Only twelve years later the independent Liberal Party was reduced to a handful of 33 M.P.s, and was never again able to form a government. The reasons for this strange eclipse of the Liberals were partly within the party itself and partly of a more objective nature. The immediate cause of the defeat in the 1918 election was the quarrel between the two rival leaders, Asquith and Lloyd George, which split the party into those who supported the Coalition (with the Conservatives) under Lloyd George, and the remainder who followed an independent line under Asquith. But the ultimate fate of the Liberal Party was signalled in Edwardian England by the successful launching of the Labour Party. The failure to keep the "Lib-Labs" within the Liberal fold showed that the working-class electorate had been lost; and the 1906–1911 Lloyd George brand of radicalism did not commend itself to the influential conservative wing of Liberalism. The disintegration of the Liberal Party after 1918 is recounted by Herbert Henry Asquith (1852–1928), who had been prime minister from 1908 to 1916, in the following document from his *Memories and Reflections, 1852–1927* (1928), Vol. 2, pp. 238–242.

CONFIDENTIAL AND SECRET

MEMORANDUM

THE disintegration of the Liberal Party began with the Coupon election of December, 1918. It then received a blow from which it has never since recovered. I myself was turned out of a seat which I had held against the Tories for thirty-two years. All my leading colleagues in the House of Commons suffered the same fate. The Liberal members in the new House were reduced to a handful of little more than thirty. The bulk of the old Liberal parliamentary party deserted to the Coalition.

I was much tempted to give up the formal Leadership (for it had become nothing more), but I did not think it right to leave old friends, who had remained loyal, in the lurch; and at the first available opportunity (January, 1920) I stood at a by-election for Paisley and was returned.

The Coalition House of Commons (1919–22) was the worst in which I have ever sat. The small band of Liberals whom Sir Donald Maclean had rallied were made to feel their impotence, and I myself, after I came back, was treated by the Coalition rank and file with studied contempt. I did my best with my colleagues to expose the stupidity and wickedness of Reprisals in Ireland. Outside, I urged (amidst the derision of the Coalition leaders) that Dominion Home Rule had become the only possible constructive policy. We opposed at its very outset and at every stage the legislation for the Safeguarding of Industries, supported as it was by so-called Free Traders like Sir Alfred Mond, who had become a member of the Coalition Cabinet.

Those were the darkest days for Liberalism which I have ever known. The manifest failure of the Black and Tan regime in Ireland, administered by a Liberal Coalitionist, Sir Hamar Greenwood, and strenuously defended by Mr. Lloyd George, and its growing unpopularity here, in time began to disquiet the Unionist members of the Coalition; and it was they (if we may believe Sir Austen Chamberlain) who were the first to urge its abandonment, with the substitution of the only possible alternative—Dominion Home Rule. After we had been brought to the verge of war by the adventure of Chanak, a section of the Conservatives already embittered by the "betrayal" of Unionism, became mutinous, and, under the leadership of Mr. Bonar Law and Mr. Baldwin, brought about the downfall of the Coalition, and the formation of a Bonar Law Government.

The folly of Mr. Baldwin, after Mr. Bonar Law's death, in hoisting the Protectionist flag brought about a strong movement for "Liberal Reunion." The fortunes of Free Trade were at stake, and for the purpose of the election of 1923 we joined forces with Mr. Lloyd George and the bulk of his Coalition or National Liberals. In the Parliament then elected, the "reunited" Liberals were a respectable, if not a formidable, minority.

We have now for nearly three years been trying the experiment of "Liberal Reunion." There is not one of us that does not know that in practice it has turned out to be a fiction, if not a farce. The control of the Party has throughout been divided between two separate authorities: the Liberal Central Office and Mr. Lloyd George's rival machine—the former very scantily, and the latter very richly, endowed. Things came very nearly to a crisis a year ago when the "Land Policy" as embodied in the Green Book was let loose, and followed up by an intensive and expansive propaganda. I insisted upon its being submitted to a representative Conference before it was incorporated in the Party programme. Prolonged negotiations between Sir Donald Maclean and Mr. Phillipps on the one side, and Mr. Lloyd George on the other, showed that he regarded his accumulated fund as at his own disposal, to be given to, or withheld from, the Central Office of the Party, as a dole, upon such conditions as he thought fit to impose. I was driven myself last December to the humiliating task of making a personal appeal to the better-to-do among our followers to come to the rescue and provide us with a wholly independent fund of adequate amount. Many generous contributions were made, but the fact remains that at this moment our Central Office is faced in the near future with the certainty of serious and perhaps fatal financial stress, in relief of which it is idle, in the present condition of the Party, to expect that a repetition of last year's appeal or any other expedient would meet with a substantial response.

Meanwhile, the rival organization, well supplied with material resources, is being enlarged in every direction, and has been recruited at its Head-quarters quite recently by an influx of skilled wire-pullers and propagandists.

Under such conditions, to talk of Liberal unity as a thing which either has been, or has any fair prospect of being, achieved, seems to me to be an abuse of language. If there are those who take a more sanguine view, I can only express a sincere hope that they may prove to be right.

I come now to my own personal position, which I have had to reconsider from every point of view, public and private, since the differences which arose in the early summer over the General Strike. After the fullest consideration, I find nothing to withdraw or qualify in my letter of June last to Sir Godfrey Collins. There are, it appears, not a few people in the Party who think that I acted on inadequate and even on unworthy grounds. No one has ever accused me before of being actuated in public matters by personal motives, and my career, which is sufficiently well known to my Party and the public, might, I think, have spared me any such imputation. In my judgment, then and now, grave matters of principle, vital to the Liberal Party and to its harmonious and effective working, were in peril.

I am equally resolved not to take any part, direct or indirect, in a sectional controversy in the Party, either about Leadership or funds.

I am now in my seventy-fifth year. I have been for the best part of half a century in public life. I have been Prime Minister for a longer consecutive time than anyone during the last 100 years, and for a still longer time I have been Leader of the Liberal Party. During the whole of that time I have given my time and strength without stint or reserve to the service of the Party and the State. From the principles of Liberalism, as I have always understood them, and understand them still, I have never swerved either to the right or the left, and I never shall.

I should therefore, in any case, consider that I had earned my title to release. But during the last few months I have had a serious warning, which I did not expect, but cannot ignore. My health, which has never troubled me before, gave way, and though it is now restored, I can no longer count upon it as I always have done in the past. The anxieties and responsibilities of Leadership, which do not diminish in these days, are enough to tax the strongest, and ought not to be undertaken or continued by anyone who cannot be reasonably sure that he can stand the strain.

I therefore feel it my duty to lay down the Leadership, and this decision, come to after much reflection and with many regrets, must be regarded as irrevocable.

OXFORD AND ASQUITH.

Chapter 20.
Crisis, 1929-1931

In the middle of the interwar period came the prolonged "crisis" of 1929–1931. Beginning with a financial collapse on the New York stock exchange in October 1929, following a great speculative boom in stocks and bonds, the distress spread rapidly to Europe, where large parts of the economy were dependent upon American loans. Britain could not escape from the general financial deterioration, and her dependence upon a precarious export-import balance made her vulnerable to any dislocation of world markets. As the international economy crumbled, unemployment in England mounted steadily, to a figure beyond anything hitherto reached (2½ millions by December 1930). In Austria and Germany the collapse was even more disastrous, and in 1931 the center of financial crisis shifted to London. The Labour government in office failed to agree on measures to deal with the situation; and the prime minister, Ramsay MacDonald, replaced his former colleagues by a National (i.e., coalition) government in August, 1931.

95. [THE SECOND LABOUR GOVERNMENT]

by BEATRICE WEBB

At the general election of 1929 the Labour Party won 287 seats, and was for the first time the largest party in the House. Although they did not have an absolute majority over the Conservatives (261) and the Liberals (59) combined, Labour accepted the challenge to form a government and James Ramsay MacDonald (as in the short-lived first Labour government of 1924) became prime minister. The government was made up of the right wing of the Party, and had neither the opportunity nor the taste for

much socialist legislation. An acute commentator on the
events of the time was Beatrice Webb (1858–1943), whose
husband, Sidney Webb, was a leading Fabian socialist
and member of the Labour governments of 1924 and 1929.
The remarkable intellectual partnership of the Webbs produced numerous historical and socialist works, and their
influence on the labor movement was profound. These extracts from *Beatrice Webb's Diaries, 1924–1932,* Margaret
Cole, ed. (1956), pp. 194–201, show the attitudes of middle-class socialists towards some of the problems of a Labour government.

JUNE 1st.—Sidney and I sat up with the Laskis till 2.30, listening to
the flowing tide of Labour victories—almost hysterical at the prospect
of Labour being in a majority in the House. Today the relative number of Labour and Tories has settled down near Sidney's forecast—
its difference being that the Tories excel in votes, and Labour in representatives, instead of *vice versa,* as he had predicted. What has been
accomplished is the final collapse of the Liberal Party. Considering
their money, their press, their brilliant demagogic leader with his
pledge "to cure unemployment in one year," the failure to add even
a score to their numbers is decisive. They will never again reach their
present number in the H. of C. How interesting it would be to look
into Mr. Trimblerigg's soul yesterday and to-day. Baldwin will be
smoking his pipe, philosophically enjoying the prospect of a rest from
responsibility, certain in his own mind he will come back to office
in a few years' time. J.R.M. will be enjoying the sensation of inflated
prestige and weighing the advantages of taking or not taking office.
But for Ll. George the future is blank. And yet he is too restlessly
ambitious and energetic to put up with a blank wall; he will try to
dodge round, under or over it. Futile scheming or stunt speaking are
not attractive in a rapidly ageing man and I doubt whether the Liberal M.P.'s, now that he has led them to disaster, will follow him; each
one will go his own way—some of them, before the end of this Parliament, will have gone definitely to the Right or to the Left out of the
Liberal Party. On the whole we are satisfied with the result of the
General Election.

June 4th.—Baldwin resigns. Informed public opinon—*The Times,*
the *Evening Standard,* insisted that the wisest course was dignified
resignation and acquiescence in the advent of a Labour Government.

Also B. must have felt that this step gives the "go by" to Ll. George and the Liberal party; it deprives them of their casting vote—or of any bargaining power. The idea that Ll.G. would intrigue with Austen & Winston to keep the Conservatives in office "on terms" must have been supremely distasteful to Baldwin, who loathes Ll.G. So Baldwin makes way for MacDonald and virtually agrees to support him so long as he does not introduce Socialism by instalments. But when the Labour measures are proposed Ll.G. and his followers will not dare to defeat them since they are all in the Yellow Book! From J.R.M.'s statement yesterday, I gather that he, Henderson, Snowden, Clynes and Thomas settled to take office and hold on for 2 years, bringing in just as much reform as the present House will accept. . . .

June 6th.—The interview ended in Sidney accepting a peerage in order to take over the Colonial Office. The immediate reason for this very handsome offer was that J.R.M., anxious to complete his Cabinet at once, had not complied with the constitutional requirements that there must be two Secretaries of State in the Lords. He immediately thought of Sidney for the job. Sidney was delighted with the C.O.: it is his old office as a civil servant, one about which he knows a good deal more than about some others. Meanwhile I was at Passfield awaiting the news by telephone amply disguised by code. . . .

June 20th. 41, *Grosvenor Road.*—When first it was mooted that Sidney should go to the Lords the question of becoming "Lord" & "Lady" was discussed between us. My instinct was against the use of a title and Sidney, tho' feeling less strongly, acquiesced. But breaking a convention which all accept, needs something more than mere dislike, which may arise from distorted pride, subconscious superiority, self-advertisement or other forms of egotism. The test is always: would it be desirable for all other people to do it? In breaking the convention are you making it easier to sweep away an evil thing or create a good one? Moreover if the use of a title is not desirable why should you put yourself in the position of having to refuse to use it? Why accept a peerage?

This last question is easily answered. The British Constitution being what it is, short of a physical force revolution, there have to be Labour peers in order to form and maintain a Government. Whatever objection there may be to accepting a peerage, it is immeasurably less objectionable than the refusal to take over the responsibilities of governing the country. In short, the acceptance, by a sufficient number of persons, of peerages helps to sweep away what you believe to be bad, and to create what you believe to be good. So far as Sidney is concerned, assuming that he thought himself fit to be in the Cabinet, he was in duty bound to go to the House of Lords.

The second question—and one which is not so easy to answer is: Having accepted the position why make a fuss about the title? And here it seems to me, and also to him, a question of manners and not of morals; and a question which was different for the peer and for the wife of the peer. We object to a *caste* of peers, and to all that honour and glamour that surrounds this social caste—we want to destroy the prestige enjoyed by the "ennobled"—in order to ease the way for destroying the constitution of an hereditary House of Lords, as part and parcel of the British Government. In particular, we do not want this liking for the institution of nobility to spread in the Labour Party—we do not want members of the Labour Party to seek the social esteem at present belonging to this venerable institution. Now one way of undermining the respect for the House of Lords is to give up the use of titles attached to peerages *as far as this is practicable*. It is clear that Sidney himself having accepted a peerage is bound to use the title in his official acts—he has accepted office on this condition—he might just as well refuse to call himself Secretary of State for the Colonies. But this obligation does not extend to his wife; nor, I think, to himself when out of office or in an unofficial capacity. By refusing to [be] come one of a social caste—honoured because it is a caste—I make it slightly more difficult for other Labour men to succumb to the temptation. By merely passing over my right to use a title I help to undermine the foundations of British snobbishness. There is far too much snobbishness—far too much regard for rank and social status in the British Labour Movement. It is a good thing to set the example of not considering a title as honourable to the person legally entitled to use it. And it is exactly this fact that by refusing to use a title you discredit it, that may cause a good deal of resentment on the part of the "powers that be" and may lead to a certain amount of disagreeableness. Owing to our peculiar position of acknowledged veterans in the Movement, our example will carry weight. Hence it seems worth while to break the convention. The more gently I break it—the less annoyance I rouse in breaking it—the more effective will be this little attack on the social prestige of the House of Lords. An honour ignored is an honour deflated. What amuses me is that the only possible retort, as far as I am concerned, on the part of the Court and London Society generally, is social ostracism, and that, of course, is the one that will best suit me. I *want* to be dropped out of the Buckingham Palace list, because it saves me from having to consider whether I am justified in refusing to attend Court functions. I respect our King and Queen and I acquiesce in a Constitutional Monarchy—the British Monarchy is an anachronism but it is a useful anachronism, an institution for which it would be precious difficult to find an equally good substitute. But its social environment of artistocracy and plutocracy is wholly bad; and the less the Labour Party accepts this environment the more wholesome will be its internal life. The ideal I set before me is to refuse to accept what seems to me a false scale of values, without bad manners or discourtesy. Anyway it is an interesting experiment, and if anything happens, I will record it. My present impression is that nothing will happen—I shan't be fussy or pedantic about it; if I find myself called "Lady Passfield" on official occasions, I shall not protest; obviously any one has a right to call me by that name. But I shall persistently call myself Mrs. Sidney Webb—and when once Sidney is out of office my intention will prevail. There is only one rock ahead. My action might mar Sidney's popularity in the House of Lords. I allay my fears by remembering the indifference of the Englishman as to how other people—especially those belonging to other sets—behave. . . .

96. [THE FORMATION OF THE NATIONAL GOVERNMENT]

by PHILIP SNOWDEN

The political outcome of the 1929–1931 crisis was the fall of the Labour government and its replacement by a National government, which (after the election in the fall of 1931) was in fact a Conservative government. The way in which Ramsay MacDonald acted towards his Labour colleagues in August 1931 led to bitter charges that he had betrayed his party; and the traumatic effect of the events of 1931 on the Labour Party remained throughout the 1930s. Philip Snowden (1864–1937) was one of the few Labour leaders who followed MacDonald into the National government. At that time he was Chancellor of the Exchequer. He had been a fervent member of the I.L.P.

in his youth and opposed participation in World War I. His account of the events of August 1931 is from Philip Viscount Snowden, *An Autobiography* (1934), Vol. 2, pp. 944–957.

. . . DURING the succeeding three days, that is, from Thursday 20th August to Sunday 23rd August, Mr. MacDonald and I, with the consent of the Cabinet, had frequent interviews with the leaders of the Opposition. They maintained their attitude that if the Government could not go beyond the figure of £56,250,000 as the total of their economies, they would feel compelled to call for an early meeting of the House of Commons, when they would unite and defeat the Government. Faced with this probability, the Cabinet turned its attention to seeking whether something more could be done. I ought to add that the Opposition leaders were wholly dissatisfied with the proposals of the Cabinet for reducing the cost of the Unemployment payments. The Cabinet, therefore, turned its attention to seeing what could be done to meet the demands of the Opposition leaders on this matter. There was, as I have said, an almost equal division of opinion in the Cabinet on the question of a reduction in the Unemployment benefits.

It was, therefore, decided that Mr. MacDonald and myself should be empowered to submit tentatively to the Opposition leaders a suggestion that if we could increase the economies by £20,000,000, namely, £12,500,000 from the Unemployment Grants and £7,500,000 from other sources, they would regard that as satisfactory. We were placed in a difficult position in making this suggestion, because we had no assurance that if it were accepted by the Opposition leaders the Cabinet would agree to do it. However, we put the proposal before them, and we received the impression that if this could be done they would regard the total of our economies as satisfactory. But they urged that this was a matter upon which the bankers should be consulted, and if they were satisfied the Opposition leaders would raise no further objection. . . .

. . . Mr. MacDonald and I put before the bankers the suggestion we had made to the Opposition leaders with the consent of the Cabinet that the total economies might be increased by £20,000,000 from the figure of £56,000,000 previously accepted. They thought that if this could be done it might satisfy New York, and the credits sought would be granted. I elaborate this matter because it was upon this that the Labour Government was finally broken up. . . .

. . . The split in the Labour Cabinet took place because unanimity could not be reached on the proposal to reduce Unemployment pay by 10 per cent. The May Committee had recommended a cut of 20 per cent. It may be mentioned that after a 10 per cent. cut in Unemployment pay the recipients of these payments would be in a better position than they were under the Labour Government of 1924 when there were abounding Budget surpluses. There had been in the meantime a fall in the cost of living which was equivalent to a 30 per cent. increase in the purchasing power of these benefits.

When this final test came the Cabinet would not agree to implement the authority they had given to Mr. MacDonald and myself to submit to the Opposition leaders and the bankers the suggestion for £20,-000,000 further economies which would include a reduction of 10 per cent. in Unemployment payments. A small majority of the Cabinet (and this became public property later) were in favour of these further economies, but as we could not have carried a united Cabinet in adopting them, and half the Cabinet would have resigned, the break-up of the Labour Government was inevitable. A cut in the Unemployment pay was repugnant to us all, but we had no choice in the matter. . . .

. . . When this final disagreement occurred it was evident that the Prime Minister had anticipated such a development, and had made his plans to deal with it. He asked the members of the Cabinet to place their resignations in his hands. This was done, and the Prime Minister immediately left the meeting to seek an audience with the King to acquaint him with the position, and to advise His Majesty to hold a conference with Mr. Baldwin, Sir Herbert Samuel and himself next morning. The Cabinet agreed to this course. Mr. MacDonald left at 10.10 p.m., and the members of the Cabinet remained in the room to await his return. He came back at 10.40, and told us that His Majesty had accepted his advice to meet Mr. Baldwin, Sir Herbert Samuel and himself next morning at 10 o'clock.

The Prime Minister, quite properly, had kept the King fully informed of the conversations with the Opposition leaders and of the difficulties within the Labour Cabinet. During the week before the resignation of the Labour Government the King had left Sandringham for Balmoral, but on the Saturday before the resignation of the Government the Prime Minister informed His Majesty of the critical situation, and that probably a change of Government might become necessary. His Majesty at once returned to London, and arrived there at eight o'clock on Sunday morning. Mr. Baldwin, who was at Aix, had been informed by his colleagues that his presence in London was urgently needed, so he came back at once and arrived in London on the Saturday evening.

Two hours after the arrival of the King from Balmoral, Mr. Mac-Donald had an audience with him at the Palace, and after this interview a statement was issued from 10 Downing Street, which read: "On the Prime Minister's advice the King has asked Mr. Baldwin and Sir Herbert Samuel to see him, because His Majesty wishes to hear from them themselves what the position of their respective Parties is."

In accordance with this statement, Sir Herbert Samuel and Mr. Baldwin had, separately, audiences with the King that Sunday afternoon.

That evening the fateful Cabinet Meeting was held when the resignation of the Labour Cabinet was agreed upon.

What took place at the meeting with the King and the three Party leaders at the Palace at ten o'clock on Monday morning I do not know beyond what was reported to us by Mr. MacDonald on his return. A meeting of the Labour Cabinet was called for twelve o'clock noon (24th August), and to this meeting Mr. MacDonald reported that it had been decided to form a Government of individuals whose task would be confined to dealing with the financial emergency. Mr. Baldwin and Sir Herbert Samuel were prepared to join such a Government, with Mr. MacDonald as Prime Minister.

The resignations of the Labour Ministers had already been given to Mr. MacDonald, and it was agreed that he should place them in the hands of the King that afternoon.

The developments from that Monday morning's audience with the King came to me quite unexpectedly. I left the Cabinet Meeting at 10.40 p.m. on the Sunday under the belief that the outcome of the resignation of the Labour Cabinet would be that Mr. Baldwin would be asked to form a Government, and with the help of the Liberals would carry through measures of economy and additional taxation which would balance the Budget and restore national stability. Whatever, at that time, may have been in Mr. MacDonald's mind as to a National Government with himself as Prime Minister he kept to himself, for at a meeting he had with the Opposition leaders at 11 p.m. on Sunday after his return from the Palace he gave them no hint of such a possible development. Mr. Neville Chamberlain, who was present at that meeting, stated publicly a few days later that he went to bed that night expecting that next day Mr. Baldwin would be called upon to form a Government.

Mr. MacDonald at the Palace meeting on the Monday morning agreed to the formation of a National Government, with himself as Prime Minister, without a word of previous consultation with any of his Labour colleagues. He knew he would have the great majority of the Labour Cabinet against him, and practically the whole of the Parliamentary Labour Party. He had, in fact, at that time, no assurance that he could take any of his late colleagues with him. Mr. Baldwin and Sir Herbert Samuel were in a different position. They could count confidently on carrying their Parties with them. Mr. MacDonald at the best could not hope to have the support of more than a mere handful of Labour members.

It was a very strange thing that Mr. MacDonlad should have taken this grave step without informing some at least of his Labour colleagues of his intention. He did tell his Cabinet, as I have mentioned, that he intended to advise the King to call the Opposition leaders into consultation, but this was not understood either by them or the Labour Cabinet as the prelude to a National Government.

When the Labour Cabinet as a whole declined to agree to a reduction of Unemployment pay, Mr. MacDonald assumed too hurriedly that this involved the resignation of his Government. He neither shewed nor expressed any grief at this regrettable development. On the contrary, he set about the formation of the National Government with an enthusiasm which shewed that the adventure was highly agreeable to him. . . .

. . . I do not think that Mr. MacDonald felt any regret that the break with his Labour colleagues had come to pass, and later developments have amply confirmed this belief. The day after the National Government was formed he came into my room at Downing Street in very high spirits. I remarked to him that he would now find himself very popular in strange quarters. He replied, gleefully rubbing his hands: "Yes, to-morrow every Duchess in London will be wanting to kiss me!"

Chapter 21.
The 1930s

Three dominant themes combined to give a distinctive tone to the years between 1931 and 1939. First, there was the slow economic recovery from the great slump. Bad as were conditions in England, they were not as severe as in Germany and the United States. Britain's trading position was such as to enable her to enjoy favorable terms of world trade, since on the world markets the prices of raw materials had fallen more than the prices of manufactured goods. To some extent therefore England was cushioned against the worst effects of the world slump, and her recovery was thereby facilitated. Nevertheless, on the outbreak of World War II there were still an army of unemployed and depressed areas of stagnant industry.

This was the second theme of the 1930s—the return of the old "condition-of-England question." At the bottom of the social pyramid was a hard core of long-unemployed men, and beyond them were social and economic inequalities throughout the whole class structure which seemed increasingly indefensible to large numbers of Englishmen. When they came to vote in 1945 it was these memories and experiences that caused the decisive defeat of the Conservative party which was associated with the men and measures of the 1930s.

Especially did the Conservatives incur the odium of a discredited foreign policy; and it was the growing predominance of foreign affairs in party politics after 1935 that was the third characteristic theme of the period. With the aggressions of the Nazi and Fascist dictators, and the civil war in Spain, domestic divisions became less urgent than issues of foreign policy. Against the government's stubborn support of nonintervention and appeasement, the Left sought to mobilize all opposition forces in a wide "popular front." So deep became their distaste for the prime minister, Neville Chamberlain, and his Conservative government, that even after the outbreak of war in September

1939, the Labour and Liberal leaders refused to join a coalition under his leadership; and it was not until May 1940 that England was again a united nation under the premiership of Winston Churchill.

97. MEN WITHOUT WORK

PILGRIM TRUST REPORT

In January 1933 there were 3 million unemployed workers, or 20 percent of all insured persons. Thereafter the numbers dropped steadily, but did not fall below 2 millions until July 1935. In 1938 there were still 1,800,000 unemployed. The incidence of unemployment was not uniform over the whole country, but was concentrated in the older industrial areas such as South Wales, Scotland, and northeast England. Three categories of unemployed were distinguishable: those temporarily out of work for a few weeks, young people who had never had a job since leaving school, and men who had not worked for many months or years. The last group presented the most serious problem. The "England of the dole" was perhaps the most bitter and unanswerable reproach to society in the 1930s. Something of the psychological effects of unemployment is conveyed in the following passage from *Men without Work: A Report made to the Pilgrim Trust* (1938), pp. 144–149. The report was the work of a committee of investigation under the chairmanship of Archbishop William Temple.

ONE of the main differences between the "working" classes and the "middle" classes is the difference of security. This is probably a more important distinction than income level. If working men and women seem to be unduly anxious to make their sons and daughters into clerks, the anxiety behind it is not for more money but for greater security. Rightly or wrongly, they feel that the black-coated worker has a more assured position. The semi-skilled man is at the mercy of rationalisation.

A week's notice may end half a lifetime's service, with no prospects, if he is elderly, but the dole, followed by a still further reduction in his means of livelihood when the old age pension comes. We take as an example a shoe laster from Leicester, who had worked thirty-seven years with one firm. "When I heard the new manager going through and saying: 'The whole of this side of this room, this room, and this room is to be stopped,' I knew it would be uphill work to get something." He went on to describe to us how he had not been able to bring himself to tell his wife the bad news when he got home, how she had noticed that something was wrong, how confident she had been that he would get work elsewhere, but how he had known that the chances were heavily against him. For months and indeed often for years such men go on looking for work, and the same is true of many casual labourers. There were in the sample old men who have not a remote chance of working again but yet make it a practice to stand every morning at six o'clock at the works gates in the hope that perhaps they may catch the foreman's eye. There were young men who said that they could never settle to anything, but must be out all day, every day, looking for work. We had instances of men who had bicycled all over Lancashire and Yorkshire from Liverpool in the hopes of finding something. A young married man (aged 29) in Leicester, who was for some reason strongly criticized by the authorities for not looking for work, had tramped about for nearly a year in the hopes of getting some permanent, or at least temporary employment (his wife had gone back into service to make it possible for him to do so), but the only substantial work he had done during the whole period was pea picking. Another man, a shoehand, 38 years old, had come down on his own initiative from Lancashire, where the factory in which he worked had closed down, to Leicester. He was a neat, rather reserved type of man and had not perhaps the necessary push to squeeze himself into work, but he wanted it desperately. He tried to join the army and was refused for it, apparently on account of his age, and it was clear that as time went on he was getting a more and more defeatist attitude to work. He might go on trying, but his efforts were vitiated more and more by the knowledge that he was not going to succeed. The sample brought out scores of similar instances, but these two of comparatively young men in a city which by ordinary standards is exceedingly prosperous must stand for all of them. When a man is thrown out of employment the first thing that he wants is work, and very few of those who have a good employment history can settle down to accept the fact of unemployment till they have been out of work for months.

But when a man who has had perhaps ten years' steady employment is thrown on the streets, to look for work effectively is not always easy. A large number of the sample cases had lost good jobs at
the time of the slump, when there was nothing else to be had. They
had gone round from one works to another with hundreds of others
all desperately anxious to secure employment, and failure after failure
had gradually "got them down." The restlessness of which many wives
spoke to us tells its own tale: "Now he's out of work he don't seem
to be able to settle down to anything." When a man is out of work,
anxiety is part of a vicious circle, and the more he worries, the more
he unfits himself for work.

There were other symptoms of this nerviness. The high proportions
of instances in which married men were living apart from their wives
is certainly in some degree to be explained by it. Among many of the
families visited, tension between man and wife was apparent. Thus
we saw a man of 25 in Liverpool, who had had previously to 1935 a
certain amount of work as a builder's labourer. At the time of the
visit his wife was 19; they had been married when she was 16. The
first child had died the day after it was born and the mother had
suffered from anaemia and kidney trouble at the time. There was
another baby a few months old, which was taken to hospital with
pneumonia the night before the visit occurred. The man gave the impression of one who had been not unhappy for a time lounging, but
was now getting to the end of his tether. Speaking of his wife, he
said: "She's always crying. But crying don't make things no better":
and the early marriage, poverty, illness, and finally the quarrel seemed
to summarise in a single instance several of the worst features of the
situation of the long unemployed. Friction may come out in other
ways, also. The children may get on a man's nerves if he is at home all
day. "When he was out of work we were always having rows over
the children. He will never let them do anything. It's much better now
he is at work." In several cases where the wife was earning but the
husband unemployed, there was evidently unhappiness as a result. A
striking example occurred among the Liverpool visits, the case of a
printer, 42 years old, who had lost his chance of re-employment at his
old trade, through a dispute with the union. A few weeks before our
visit occurred, he had left Liverpool in the hopes of finding work in
the Midlands, and the wife showed one of us a touching letter in
which he told her that he had got work at 25s. a week and enclosed
10s. for her. While he was out of work she had been working regularly,

with the result that he only drew 5s. Unemployment Assistance. She described how she used to lie awake at nights and hear him "tramping up and down the garden path, or up and down in the parlour, and it made her nearly mad; and it made her nearly mad to feel that she was keeping him by her earnings and they gaining nothing by her work." There was a somewhat similar case in Leicester, where the woman had left her work because she could not bear to be the breadwinner while her husband, young and fit, did nothing; another in Blackburn where a young married woman, working, with an unemployed husband, said that "it made him wild" to be about with no money in his pocket. It is in the light of such cases that we should read the figures showing the numbers of men in the sample who were living apart from their wives.

Similar questions are raised by the case of the man whose allowance takes into account the fact that his children are earning sums which permit of their contributing to his support and the general upkeep of the household. There were in the sample instances of men over 55 years of age who were either not in receipt of any income from the Unemployment Assistance Board, or in receipt of small amounts, 5s. or 7s. 6d., from the Board, because it was held that the household resources were otherwise sufficient. This view would be justified if the household were taken as a unit. The fact remains, however, that some men in this position feel the loss of an independent income, such as they enjoyed while on Unemployment Benefit, very acutely, and in many such cases the home appears to represent two standards, the earning children being often smartly dressed and happy, while the fathers were shabby and suffering from a sense of their dependence. Such men gave the impression that they purposely avoided making any effort to keep up appearances in case the children might think that they were drawing an undue share of the family income. While among the sample as a whole, bitterness against the Unemployment Assistance Board is the exception rather than the rule, in cases of this kind it was the rule rather than the exception. The question has two sides, and we came across several instances in which children were behaving most unreasonably in refusing to contribute towards the household expenses the sum, not large, which the regulations expect of them. Nevertheless, there may be a case, even here, for making some larger payment from State funds.

The depression and apathy which finally settles down in many of the homes of these long-unemployed men lies at the root of most of the problems which are connected with unemployment. It is one of the reasons why they fail to get back to work. It is one of the reasons why the majority of them "have not the heart" for clubs or activities of other kinds, and it is one of the reasons why their homes seem so poverty-stricken. "I don't know how it is," said a young married woman in Blackburn, "but these last few years since I've been out of the mills I don't seem able to take trouble, somehow; I've got no spirit for anything. But I didn't use to be like that." One of us who saw her had little doubt "how it was." The woman looked thin and ill, and it was clear that what food there was was going to the children. Such a simultaneous onset of physical and psychological hardship can hardly help having serious results.

98. THE ROAD TO WIGAN PIER

by GEORGE ORWELL

The depressing conditions of working-class life were vividly documented by writers with socialist sympathies; and agencies such as the Left Book Club helped to arouse middle-class social consciences. George Orwell (1903–1950) was a socialist of an independent cast of mind, and contributed some of the most powerful writing on social and literary subjects in the period. This account of working-class life is based on his experiences in Wigan, a depressed industrial town in Lancashire. From *The Road to Wigan Pier* (1937), pp. 48–67, by George Orwell. Reprinted by permission of Harcourt, Brace & World, Inc.

IN Wigan I stayed for a while with a miner who was suffering from nystagmus. He could see across the room but not much further. He had been drawing compensation of twenty-nine shillings a week for the past nine months, but the colliery company were now talking of putting him on "partial compensation" of fourteen shillings a week. It all depended on whether the doctor passed him as fit for light work "on top." Even if the doctor did pass him there would, needless to say, be no light work available, but he could draw the dole and the company would have saved itself fifteen shillings a week. Watching this man go to the colliery to draw his compensation, I was struck by the profound differences that are still made by *status*. Here was a man who had been half blinded in one of the most useful of all jobs and was drawing a pension to which he had a perfect right, if anybody has a right to anything. Yet he could not, so to speak, *demand* this pension—he could not, for instance, draw it when and how he wanted it. He had to go to the colliery once a week at a time named by the company, and when he got there he was kept waiting about for hours in the cold wind. For all I know he was also expected to touch his cap and show gratitude to whomever paid him; at any rate he had to waste an afternoon and spend sixpence in bus fares. It is very different for a member of the bourgeoisie, even such a down-at-heel member as I am. Even when I am on the verge of starvation I have certain rights attaching to my bourgeois status. I do not earn much more than a miner earns, but I do at least get it paid into my bank in a gentlemanly manner and can draw it out when I choose. And even when my account is exhausted the bank people are still passably polite.

This business of petty inconvenience and indignity, of being kept waiting about, of having to do everything at other people's convenience, is inherent in working-class life. A thousand influences constantly press a working man down into a *passive* rôle. He does not act, he is acted upon. He feels himself the slave of mysterious authority and has a firm conviction that "they" will never allow him to do this, that and the other. Once when I was hop-picking I asked the sweated pickers (they earn something under sixpence an hour) why they did not form a union. I was told immediately that "they" would never allow it. Who were "they"? I asked. Nobody seemed to know; but evidently "they" were omnipotent. . . .

As you walk through the industrial towns you lose yourself in labyrinths of little brick houses blackened by smoke, festering in planless chaos round miry alleys and little cindered yards where there are stinking dust-bins and lines of grimy washing and half-ruinous w.c's. The interiors of these houses are always very much the same, though the number of rooms varies between two and five. All have an almost exactly similar living-room, ten or fifteen feet square, with an open kitchen range; in the larger ones there is a scullery as well, in the smaller ones the sink and copper are in the living-room. At the back there is the yard, or part of a yard shared by a number of houses, just big enough for the dustbin and the w.c. Not a single one has hot water laid on. You might walk, I suppose, through literally hundreds of miles of streets inhabited by miners, every one of whom, when he is in work, gets black from head to foot every day, without ever passing a house in which one could have a bath. It would have been very simple to install a hot-water system working from the kitchen range, but the builder saved perhaps ten pounds on each house by not doing so, and at the time when these houses were built no one imagined that miners wanted baths.

For it is to be noted that the majority of these houses are old, fifty or sixty years old at least, and great numbers of them are by any ordinary standard not fit for human habitation. They go on being tenanted simply because there are no others to be had. And that is the central fact about housing in the industrial areas: not that the houses are poky and ugly, and insanitary and comfortless, or that they are distributed in incredibly filthy slums round belching foundries and stinking canals and slag-heaps that deluge them with sulphurous smoke—though all this is perfectly true—but simply that there are not enough houses to go round.

"Housing shortage" is a phrase that has been bandied about pretty freely since the war, but it means very little to anyone with an income of more than £10 a week, or even £5 a week for that matter. Where rents are high the difficulty is not to find houses but to find tenants. Walk down any street in Mayfair and you will see "To Let" boards in half the windows. But in the industrial areas the mere difficulty of getting hold of a house is one of the worst aggravations of poverty. It means that people will put up with anything—any hole and corner slum, any misery of bugs and rotting floors and cracking walls, any extortion of skinflint landlords and black-mailing agents—simply to get a roof over their heads. I have been into appalling houses, houses in which I would not live a week if you paid me, and found that the tenants had been there twenty and thirty years and only hoped they might have the luck to die there. In general these conditions are taken as a matter of course, though not always. Some people hardly seem to realise that such things as decent houses exist and look on bugs and leaking roofs as acts of God; others rail bitterly against their landlords; but all cling desperately to their houses lest worse should befall. So long as the housing shortage continues the local authorities cannot do much to make existing houses more livable. They can "condemn" a house, but they cannot order it to be pulled down till the tenant has another house to go to; and so the condemned houses remain standing and are all the worse for being condemned, because naturally the landlord will not spend more than he can help on a house which is going to be demolished sooner or later. In a town like Wigan, for instance, there are over two thousand houses standing which have been condemned for years, and whole sections of the town would be condemned *en bloc* if there were any hope of other houses being built to replace them. Towns like Leeds and Sheffield have scores of thousands of "back to back" houses which are all of a condemned type but will remain standing for decades.

I have inspected great numbers of houses in various mining towns and villages and made notes on their essential points. I think I can best give an idea of what conditions are like by transcribing a few extracts from my notebook, taken more or less at random. They are only brief notes and they will need certain explanations which I will give afterwards. Here are a few from Wigan:

House in Wallgate quarter. Blind back type. One up, one down. Living-room measures 12 ft. by 10 ft., room upstairs the same. Alcove under stairs measuring 5 ft. by 5 ft. and serving as larder, scullery and coal hole. Windows will open. Distance to lavatory 50 yards. Rent 4s. 9d., rates 2s. 6d., total 7s. 3d. . . .

House in Scholes quarter. Condemned house. One up, one down. Rooms 15 ft. by 15 ft. Sink and copper in living-room, coal hole under stairs. Floor subsiding. No windows will open. House decently dry. Landlord good. Rent 3s. 8d., rates 2s. 6d., total 6s. 2d.

Another near by. Two up, two down and coal hole. Walls falling absolutely to pieces. Water comes into upstairs rooms in quantities. Floor lopsided. Downstairs windows will not open. Landlord bad. Rent 6s., rates 3s. 6d., total 9s. 6d.

House in Greenough's Row. One up, two down. Living-room 13 ft. by 8 ft. Walls coming apart and water comes in. Back windows will not open, front ones will. Ten in family with eight children very near together in age. Corporation are trying to evict them for overcrowding but cannot find another house to send them to. Landlord bad. Rent 4s., rates 2s. 3d., total 6s. 3d. . . .

And so on and so on and so on. I could multiply examples by the score—they could be multiplied by the hundred thousand if anyone chose to make a house to house inspection throughout the industrial districts. Meanwhile some of the expressions I have used need explaining. "One up, one down" means one room on each storey—i.e. a two-roomed house. "Back to back" houses are two houses built in one, each side of the house being somebody's front door, so that if you walk down a row of what is apparently twelve houses you are in reality seeing not twelve houses but twenty-four. The front houses give on the street and the back ones on the yard, and there is only one way out of each house. The effect of this is obvious. The lavatories are in the yard at the back, so that if you live on the side facing the street, to get to the lavatory or the dust-bin you have to go out of the front door and walk round the end of the block—a distance that may be as much as two hundred yards; if you live at the back, on the other hand, your outlook is on to a row of lavatories. There are also houses of what is called the "blind back" type, which are single houses, but in which the builder has omitted to put in a back door—from pure spite, apparently. The windows which refuse to open are a peculiarity of old mining towns. Some of these towns are so undermined by ancient workings that the ground is constantly subsiding and the houses above slip sideways. In Wigan you pass whole rows of houses which have slid to startling angles, their windows being ten or twenty degrees out of the horizontal. Sometimes the front wall bellies outward till it looks as though the house were seven months gone in pregnancy. . . .

. . . The reasons given for the slow rate of building are lack of money and the difficulty of getting hold of sites—for Corporation houses are not erected piecemeal but in "estates," sometimes of hundreds of houses at a time. One thing that always strikes me as mysterious is that so many of the northern towns see fit to build themselves immense and luxurious public buildings at the same time as they are in crying need of dwelling houses. The town of Barnsley, for instance, recently spent close on £150,000 on a new town hall, although admittedly needing at least 2,000 new working-class houses, not to mention public baths. (The public baths in Barnsley contain *nineteen* men's slipper baths—this in a town of 70,000 inhabitants, largely miners, not one of whom has a bath in his house!) For £150,000 it could have built 350 Corporation houses and still had £10,000 to spend on a town hall. However, as I say, I do not pretend to understand the mysteries of local government. I merely record the fact that houses are desperately needed and are being built, on the whole, with paralytic slowness.

Still, houses *are* being built, and the Corporation building estates, with their row upon row of little red houses, all much liker than two peas (where did that expression come from? Peas have great individuality) are a regular feature of the outskirts of the industrial towns. . . .

99. FORWARD FROM LIBERALISM

by STEPHEN SPENDER

The economic breakdown and social misery of the 1930s convinced many of the most intelligent young minds in England that the capitalist system was finished. A system which could apparently offer nothing better than poverty for millions of people in the midst of potential plenty stood discredited. Its bourgeois values and attitudes seemed no longer relevant to the needs of the time. Marxism, in contrast, offered both a comprehensive explanation of the failure of capitalism and an alternative to it. For the first time in England Marxism began to attract a steadily growing number of adherents. Not all of these joined the Communist Party, and many more people were familiarized with Marxist thought than ever joined Marxist organizations. Among the intellectuals who were attracted to communism were several outstanding poets and writers, among whom was Stephen Spender (b. 1909) from whose book, *Forward from Liberalism* (1937), pp. 202–207 this reading is taken.

I AM a communist because I am a liberal. Liberalism seems to me to be the creed of those who, as far as it is possible in human affairs, are disinterested, if by disinterestedness one understands not mere passivity but a regard for objective truth, an active will towards political justice. During an era of peace and progress, the liberal spirit is identical not only with political discussion, but also with scientific inquiry, speculative thought and the disinterested creation of works of art.

In contrast to the liberal spirit, every form of scientific inquiry or creation which serves the ends of nationalism, reaction, prerogative, betrays standards of objectivity which have been attained by the greatest scientists and artists, and makes knowledge or imagination the servant of war, nationalist hatreds or aristocracy. The writings of Rudyard Kipling, some of the poems of Stefan George and almost the entire output of literature by writers in belligerent countries during the war, constitute such a betrayal.

The love of humanity rather than separate nationalities, of justice for all men rather than class privilege, of universal peace rather than imperialist competition and war—these are the features of disinterest. Faced with the collapse of liberalism all over the world as a principle of government, the spread of fascism with its lying nationalist propaganda, its repudiation of objective truth, and the threat of a world war more terrible even than the last, the intellectual must choose either to surrender every standard of objectivity and disinterest to the wave of hatred and nationalism followed by the overwhelming wave of war, or fight with political weapons for the political freedom which is the only environment in which he is free to create. He must oppose economic justice and internationalism to the power politics of nationalism and exploitation.

I do not doubt but that in the modern world communism—the classless, internationalist society—is the final goal of liberalism. But whereas formerly it seemed plausible to wait for the world gradually to progress towards this goal, whilst the intellectual could carry on his disinterested work without concerning himself at all with politics, today politics threaten us with the destruction of civilization, so that communism or international socialism becomes an immediate necessity: it is not too much to say that without it our civilization cannot survive. . . .

. . . There is truth in Julien Benda's main thesis that the intellectual, the artist, the "clerk," should take political action only in defence of justice and objectivity when they are threatened. The fact that Benda himself is a supporter of the French Popular Front may perhaps be taken as evidence that he believes such an occasion to exist now.

I have emphasized here that communism means to me a system of political justice, without which the disinterested view that humanity is more important than nationalities will not be able to survive. It follows therefore that communist tactics are only the means to achieve these ends, and that the ends are more important than strategy or dogma. From the point of view of the professional politician it may seem that party discipline is important even in the world of what men think: so that there are occasions when the whole party accepts a miscarriage of justice or a propagandist lie, in order that it may move forward in unison.

To me it seems that in the world of practical politics, wrongs may be necessary, just as mistakes or violence are inevitable: but that it would be a betrayal of his function for the clerk to become a politician in the sense of being a strategic liar or a false witness. Certainly the ends of communism cannot be achieved immediately: therefore it is all the more necessary that certain people should exist only for the ends, that they should judge and criticize the "party line" always by the final ends of political justice. No one pretends that practical necessity always coincides with truth; but on that account, it is fatal to sacrifice truth to the functions of discipline and dogma. Unless there is criticism the political movement is liable to fixation: for at some moment the dogma, the strategy, which is put outside the pale of criticism by party discipline, may cease to be measured against the final standard of communism, and become an end in itself.

I do not claim that anyone is completely disinterested, or even that it is possible to arrive at objective truths about contemporary history. Benda assumes too readily that a man's function as "clerk" is completely abstracted from his interests as a social animal. Nevertheless, there are degrees of objectivity; and it is only possible to measure these where criticism and discussion are allowed. Often the "party line" insults the intelligence. For example, in the recent Moscow trial of Zinoviev, Kameneff and the other "Trotskyists," the case, justly as it may have been tried, was pre-judged by the entire governmental press before sentence had been passed, whilst the whole judicial procedure was advertised so as to strike terror into the minds of everyone who at all deviated from the party line. It is difficult for an impartial reader of these proceedings to tell whether or not these men were guilty, and of what. Yet not only Russians but members of the communist party all over the world are expected to accept implicitly the fact that these men were found guilty of a crime, which may only have been criticism of the government.

This is precisely the point where the "clerk" must refuse to accept "necessity" and insist on an abstract justice, and a truth which is not invented by state policy. This does not mean that he opposes the revolution. On the contrary, he measures the means which the communists adopt by the ends of communism. He claims the right to criticize. He supports the revolution in his function as a "clerk," but he does not surrender such objectivity as he can attain. In this sense, he remains and has the right to remain unpractical; because the practical is policy and intrigue and injustice and armaments; and, whilst he may recognize the necessity of these things, he must not lie about them. He must certainly support the struggle to translate into terms of government and existence the principles of liberalism, which are impartial: and at the same time, he must remain impartial. He must abjure hatred, because in the last analysis, hatred, whether of class, nations, or creeds, is not a truth; it is an instrument of policy, a plaything of the will to power.

100. THE GENERAL THEORY OF EMPLOYMENT

by JOHN MAYNARD KEYNES

The grim experiences of slumps and mass unemployment provided the starting point for a new approach to economic theory. John Maynard Keynes (1883–1946), a Cambridge economist, analyzed unemployment and investment and questioned the soundness of the basic postulates of classical economics. Keynes was a Liberal; but the practical results of his teachings were to strengthen the argument for planning and government control of the economic process. At the same time he provided grounds for belief that a modified or welfare capitalism could be made to work and thus avoid the necessity for complete socialism. The social implications of his economic theories are set out in the following passages. From *The General Theory of Employment, Interest and Money* (1936), pp. 372–381, by J. M. Keynes. Reprinted by permission of Harcourt, Brace & World, Inc.

I

THE outstanding faults of the economic society in which we live are its failure to provide for full employment and its arbitrary and inequitable distribution of wealth and incomes. The bearing of the foregoing theory on the first of these is obvious. But there are also two important respects in which it is relevant to the second.

Since the end of the nineteenth century significant progress towards the removal of very great disparities of wealth and income has been achieved through the instrument of direct taxation—income tax and surtax and death duties—especially in Great Britain. Many people would wish to see this process carried much further, but they are deterred by two considerations; partly by the fear of making skilful evasions too much worth while and also of diminishing unduly the motive towards risk-taking, but mainly, I think, by the belief that the growth of capital depends upon the strength of the motive towards individual saving and that for a large proportion of this growth we are dependent on the savings of the rich out of their superfluity. Our argument does not affect the first of these considerations. But it may considerably modify our attitude towards the second. For we have seen that, up to the point where full employment prevails, the growth of capital depends not at all on a low propensity to consume but is, on the contrary, held back by it; and only in conditions of full employment is a low propensity to consume conducive to the growth of capital. Moreover, experience suggests that in existing conditions saving by institutions and through sinking funds is more than adequate, and that measures for the redistribution of incomes in a way likely to raise the propensity to consume may prove positively favourable to the growth of capital. . . .

Thus our argument leads towards the conclusion that in contemporary conditions the growth of wealth, so far from being dependent on the abstinence of the rich, as is commonly supposed, is more likely to be impeded by it. One of the chief social justifications of great inequality of wealth is, therefore, removed. I am not saying that there are no other reasons, unaffected by our theory, capable of justifying some measure of inequality in some circumstances. But it does dispose of the most important of the reasons why hitherto we have thought it prudent to move carefully. This particularly affects our attitude towards death duties; for there are certain justifications for inequality of incomes which do not apply equally to inequality of inheritances.

For my own part, I believe that there is social and psychological justification for significant inequalities of incomes and wealth, but not for such large disparities as exist to-day. There are valuable human activities which require the motive of money-making and the environment of private wealth-ownership for their full fruition. Moreover, dangerous human proclivities can be canalised into comparatively harmless channels by the existence of opportunities for money-making and private wealth, which, if they cannot be satisfied in this way, may find their outlet in cruelty, the reckless pursuit of personal power and authority, and other forms of self-aggrandisement. It is better that a man should tyrannise over his bank balance than over his fellow-citizens; and whilst the former is sometimes denounced as being but a means to the latter, sometimes at least it is an alternative. But it is not necessary for the stimulation of these activities and the satisfaction of these proclivities that the game should be played for such high stakes as at present. Much lower stakes will serve the purpose equally well, as soon as the players are accustomed to them. The task of transmuting human nature must not be confused with the task of managing it. Though in the ideal commonwealth men may have been taught or inspired or bred to take no interest in the stakes, it may still be wise and prudent statesmanship to allow the game to be played, subject to rules and limitations, so long as the average man, or even a significant section of the community, is in fact strongly addicted to the money-making passion.

II

There is, however, a second, much more fundamental inference from our argument which has a bearing on the future of inequalities of wealth; namely, our theory of the rate of interest. The justification for a moderately high rate of interest has been found hitherto in the necessity of providing a sufficient inducement to save. But we have shown that the extent of effective saving is necessarily determined by the scale of investment and that the scale of investment is promoted by a *low* rate of interest, provided that we do not attempt to stimulate it in this way beyond the point which corresponds to full employment. Thus it is to our best advantage to reduce the rate of interest to that point relatively to the schedule of the marginal efficiency of capital at which there is full employment.

There can be no doubt that this criterion will lead to a much lower rate of interest than has ruled hitherto; and, so far as one can guess at the schedules of the marginal efficiency of capital corresponding to increasing amounts of capital, the rate of interest is likely to fall steadily, if it should be practicable to maintain conditions of more or less continuous full employment—unless, indeed, there is an excessive change in the aggregate propensity to consume (including the State).

I feel sure that the demand for capital is strictly limited in the sense that it would not be difficult to increase the stock of capital up to a point where its marginal efficiency had fallen to a very low figure. This would not mean that the use of capital instruments would cost almost nothing, but only that the return from them would have to cover little more than their exhaustion by wastage and obsolescence together with some margin to cover risk and the exercise of skill and judgment. In short, the aggregate return from durable goods in the course of their life would, as in the case of short-lived goods, just cover their labour-costs of production *plus* an allowance for risk and the costs of skill and supervision.

Now, though this state of affairs would be quite compatible with some measure of individualism, yet it would mean the euthanasia of the rentier, and, consequently, the euthanasia of the cumulative oppressive power of the capitalist to exploit the scarcity-value of capital. Interest to-day rewards no genuine sacrifice, any more than does the rent of land. The owner of capital can obtain interest because capital is scarce, just as the owner of land can obtain rent because land is scarce. But whilst there may be intrinsic reasons for the scarcity of land, there are no intrinsic reasons for the scarcity of capital. An intrinsic reason for such scarcity, in the sense of a genuine sacrifice which could only be called forth by the offer of a reward in the shape of interest, would not exist, in the long run, except in the event of the individual propensity to consume proving to be of such a character that net saving in conditions of full employment comes to an end before capital has become sufficiently abundant. But even so, it will still be possible for communal saving through the agency of the State to be maintained at a level which will allow the growth of capital up to the point where it ceases to be scarce.

I see, therefore, the rentier aspect of capitalism as a transitional phase which will disappear when it has done its work. And with the disappearance of its rentier aspect much else in it besides will suffer a sea-change. It will be, moreover, a great advantage of the order of events which I am advocating, that the euthanasia of the rentier, of the functionless investor, will be nothing sudden, merely a gradual but prolonged continuance of what we have seen recently in Great Britain, and will need no revolution.

Thus we might aim in practice (there being nothing in this which is unattainable) at an increase in the volume of capital until it ceases to be scarce, so that the functionless investor will no longer receive a bonus; and at a scheme of direct taxation which allows the intelligence and determination and executive skill of the financier, the entrepreneur *et hoc genus omne* (who are certainly so fond of their craft that their labour could be obtained much cheaper than at present), to be harnessed to the service of the community on reasonable terms of reward.

At the same time we must recognise that only experience can show how far the common will, embodied in the policy of the State, ought to be directed to increasing and supplementing the inducement to invest; and how far it is safe to stimulate the average propensity to consume, without forgoing our aim of depriving capital of its scarcity-value within one or two generations. It may turn out that the propensity to consume will be so easily strengthened by the effects of a falling rate of interest, that full employment can be reached with a rate of accumulation little greater than at present. In this event a scheme for the higher taxation of large incomes and inheritances might be open to the objection that it would lead to full employment with a rate of accumulation which was reduced considerably below the current level. I must not be supposed to deny the possibility, or even the probability, of this outcome. For in such matters it is rash to predict how the average man will react to a changed environment. If, however, it should prove easy to secure an approximation to full employment with a rate of accumulation not much greater than at present, an outstanding problem will at least have been solved. And it would remain for separate decision on what scale and by what means it is right and reasonable to call on the living generation to restrict their consumption, so as to establish, in course of time, a state of full investment for their successors.

III

In some other respects the foregoing theory is moderately conservative in its implications. For whilst it indicates the vital importance of establishing certain central controls in matters which are now left in the main to individual initiative, there are wide fields of activity which are unaffected. The State will have to exercise a guiding influence on the propensity to consume partly through its scheme of taxation, partly by fixing the rate of interest, and partly, perhaps, in other ways. Furthermore, it seems unlikely that the influence of banking policy on the rate of interest will be sufficient by itself to determine an optimum rate of investment. I conceive, therefore, that a somewhat comprehensive socialisation of investment will prove the only means of securing an approximation to full employment; though this need not exclude all manner of compromises and of devices by which public authority will co-operate with private initiative. But beyond this no obvious case is made out for a system of State Socialism which would embrace most of the economic life of the community. It is not the ownership of the instruments of production which it is important for the State to assume. If the State is able to determine the aggregate amount of resources devoted to augmenting the instruments and the basic rate of reward to those who own them, it will have accomplished all that is necessary. Moreover, the necessary measures of socialisation can be introduced gradually and without a break in the general traditions of society.

Our criticism of the accepted classical theory of economics has consisted not so much in finding logical flaws in its analysis as in pointing out that its tacit assumptions are seldom or never satisfied, with the result that it cannot solve the economic problems of the actual world. But if our central controls succeed in establishing an aggregate volume of output corresponding to full employment as nearly as is practicable, the classical theory comes into its own again from this point onwards. If we suppose the volume of output to be given, *i.e.* to be determined by forces outside the classical scheme of thought, then there is no objection to be raised against the classical analysis of the manner in which private self-interest will determine what in particular is produced, in what proportions the factors of production will be combined to produce it, and how the value of the final product will be distributed between them. Again, if we have dealt otherwise with the problem of thrift, there is no objection to be raised against the modern classical theory as to the degree of consilience between private and public advantage in conditions of perfect and imperfect competition respectively. Thus, apart from the necessity of central controls to bring about an adjustment between the propensity to consume and the inducement to invest, there is no more reason to socialise economic life than there was before.

To put the point concretely, I see no reason to suppose that the existing system seriously misemploys the factors of production which are in use. There are, of course, errors of foresight; but these would not be avoided by centralising decisions. When 9,000,000 men are employed out of 10,000,000 willing and able to work, there is no evidence that the labour of these 9,000,000 men is misdirected. The complaint against the present system is not that these 9,000,000 men ought to be employed on different tasks, but that tasks should be available for the remaining 1,000,000 men. It is in determining the volume, not the direction, of actual employment that the existing system has broken down.

Thus . . . the result of filling in the gaps in the classical theory is not to dispose of the "Manchester System," but to indicate the nature of the environment which the free play of economic forces requires if it is to realise the full potentialities of production. The central controls necessary to ensure full employment will, of course, involve a large extension of the traditional functions of government. Furthermore, the modern classical theory has itself called attention to various conditions in which the free play of economic forces may need to be curbed or guided. But there will still remain a wide field for the exercise of private initiative and responsibility. Within this field the traditional advantages of individualism will still hold good.

Let us stop for a moment to remind ourselves what these advantages are. They are partly advantages of efficiency—the advantages of decentralisation and of the play of self-interest. The advantage to efficiency of the decentralisation of decisions and of individual responsibility is even greater, perhaps, than the nineteenth century supposed; and the reaction against the appeal to self-interest may have gone too far. But, above all, individualism, if it can be purged of its defects and its abuses, is the best safeguard of personal liberty in the sense that, compared with any other system, it greatly widens the field for the exercise of personal choice. It is also the best safeguard of the variety of life, which emerges precisely from this extended field of personal choice, and the loss of which is the greatest of all the losses of the homogeneous or totalitarian state. For this variety preserves the traditions which embody the most secure and successful choices of former generations; it colours the present with the diversification of its fancy; and, being the handmaid of experiment as well as of tradition and of fancy, it is the most powerful instrument to better the future.

Whilst, therefore, the enlargement of the functions of government, involved in the task of adjusting to one another the propensity to consume and the inducement to invest, would seem to a nineteenth-century publicist or to a contemporary American financier to be a terrific encroachment on individualism, I defend it, on the contrary, both as the only practicable means of avoiding the destruction of existing economic forms in their entirety and as the condition of the successful functioning of individual initiative.

For if effective demand is deficient, not only is the public scandal of wasted resources intolerable, but the individual enterpriser who seeks to bring these resources into action is operating with the odds loaded against him. The game of hazard which he plays is furnished with many zeros, so that the players *as a whole* will lose if they have the energy and hope to deal all the cards. Hitherto the increment of the world's wealth has fallen short of the aggregate of positive individual savings; and the difference has been made up by the losses of those whose courage and initiative have not been supplemented by exceptional skill or unusual good fortune. But if effective demand is adequate, average skill and average good fortune will be enough.

The authoritarian state systems of to-day seem to solve the problem of unemployment at the expense of efficiency and of freedom. It is certain that the world will not much longer tolerate the unemployment which, apart from brief intervals of excitement, is associated—and, in my opinion, inevitably associated—with present-day capitalistic individualism. But it may be possible by a right analysis of the problem to cure the disease whilst preserving efficiency and freedom. . . .

FURTHER READING: Part Five

Bassett, R. S., *Nineteen Thirty-One: Political Crisis* (1958).

Bullock, Alan, *The Life and Times of Ernest Bevin,* vol. I (1960).

Butler, D. E., *The Electoral System in Britain, 1918–1951* (1953).

Cole, G. D. H., *History of the Labour Party from 1914* (1948).

Graves, Robert, and Alan Hodge, *The Long Week-End: a Social History of Great Britain, 1918–1939* (1950 ed.).

Lewis, W. A., *Economic Survey, 1919–1939* (1949).

Lyman, R. W., *The First Labour Government, 1924* (1958).

McKenzie, R. T., *British Political Parties: the Distribution of Power within the Conservative and Labour Parties* (1955).

Nicolson, Harold, *King George the Fifth: his Life and Reign* (1953).

Pollard, Sidney, *The Development of the British Economy, 1914–1950* (1963).

Symons, Julian, *The General Strike* (1957).

Winkler, Henry R., *Great Britain in the Twentieth Century* (1960). [Bibliographical essay published by the Service Center for Teachers of History, American Historical Association]

PART SIX.
THE WELFARE STATE,
1940-1960

Chapter 22.
Wartime Origins

It is a significant comment on English society of the 1930s that the outbreak of World War II brought almost a feeling of relief; and—after the first few months of "phony war"—a new sense of national unity. For the first time for many years there was a job for everybody; and though food and consumers' goods were soon in short supply, the system of priorities and rationing satisfied demands for social justice more completely than the hollow pretences and unfulfilled promises of the preceding decade.

Under the compelling purposes of war English society underwent radical changes which had been unacceptable in peace time. At first the attempt was made to solve new problems in terms of prewar attitudes and assumptions. But when these proved inadequate they had to be replaced by new conceptions of social responsibility. The last relics of the Poor Law were swept away; ideas of a comprehensive system of public education replaced the legacy of instruction according to means and status; and the concept of full employment was made the foundation of all future social policy.

As early as the summer of 1940 plans for reconstruction after the war began to be aired; and in January, 1941 Arthur Greenwood, a Labour member of the coalition government, was put in charge of postwar planning. By the time the war ended Conservative and Labour leaders alike had committed themselves deeply to programs of social legislation far in advance of what had been practicable in 1939.

101. THEIR FINEST HOUR

by WINSTON SPENCER CHURCHILL

England entered World War II under the leadership of
Neville Chamberlain and a Conservative government whose
policy of appeasement of the dictators had so signally
failed. It was not until after the failures of the campaign
in Norway that pressure was sufficiently strong to force
Chamberlain to resign and make way for a genuinely national (i.e. coalition) government. The man who now came
forward as the prime minister, and one of the greatest war
leaders in the history of the nation, was Winston Churchill
(b. 1874), son of Lord Randolph Churchill (see Reading
No. 89) and a scion of the ducal house of Marlborough. Up
to this time (1940) Winston Churchill's political career had
been somewhat checkered, and he had remained aloof from
the Conservative leadership throughout the 1930s. In his
first speech to the House of Commons after becoming
prime minister he said that he had "nothing to offer but
blood, toil, tears and sweat," and that his policy was simply
to wage war until victory was won, at all costs. Throughout
the war his speeches rallied the nation and stirred depths
of patriotism probably unsurpassed in English history.
After the fall of France in June 1940 Britain and the Commonwealth stood alone; it was a solemn time, as England
prepared to withstand the full force of the German attack.
On June 18, 1940, Churchill made his great speech to the
House and the nation; these extracts are from Hansard,
Parliamentary Debates, House of Commons, 5th series,
Vol. 362 (1940), pp. 51–61.

THE military events which have happened during the past fortnight
have not come to me with any sense of surprise. Indeed, I indicated
a fortnight ago as clearly as I could to the House that the worst possibilities were open, and I made it perfectly clear then that whatever
happened in France would make no difference to the resolve of Britain
and the British Empire to fight on, "if necessary for years, if necessary
alone." During the last few days we have successfully brought off the

great majority of the troops we had on the lines of communication in France—a very large number, scores of thousands—and seven-eighths of the troops we have sent to France since the beginning of the war, that is to say, about 350,000 out of 400,000 men, are safely back in this country. Others are still fighting with the French, and fighting with considerable success in their local encounters with the enemy. We have also brought back a great mass of stores, rifles and munitions of all kinds which had been accumulated in France during the last nine months.

We have, therefore, in this island to-day a very large and powerful military force. This force includes all our best trained and finest troops and includes scores of thousands of those who have already measured their quality against the Germans and found themselves at no disadvantage. We have under arms at the present time in this island over a million and a quarter men. Behind these we have the Local Defence Volunteers, numbering half a million, only a portion of whom, however, are yet armed with rifles or other firearms. We have incorporated into our Defence Forces every man for whom we have a weapon. We expect a very large addition to our weapons in the near future, and in preparation for this we intend to call up, drill and train further large numbers at once. Those who are not called up or employed upon the vast business of munitions production in all its branches—and it runs through every kind of grade—serve their country best by remaining at their ordinary work until they are required.

We also have Dominions Armies here. The Canadians had actually landed in France but have now been safely withdrawn, much disappointed, but in perfect order, with all their artillery and equipment. These very high-class forces from the Dominions will now take part in the defence of the Mother Country. . . .

. . . It seems to me that as far as seaborne invasion on a great scale is concerned, we are far more capable of meeting it to-day than we were at many periods in the last war and during the early months of this war, before our other troops were trained, and while the B.E.F. was already abroad and still abroad. The Navy have never pretended to be able to prevent raids by bodies of 5,000 or 10,000 men flung suddenly across and thrown ashore at several points on the coast some dark night or foggy morning. The efficacy of sea-power, especially under modern conditions, depends upon the invading force being of large size. It has to be of large size, in view of our military strength, to be of any use. If it is of large size, then the Navy have something they can find and meet and as it were, bite on. Now we must remember that even five divisions, however lightly equipped, would require 200 to 250 ships, and with modern air reconnaissance and photography, it would not be easy to collect such an armada, marshal it and conduct it across the sea without any powerful naval forces to escort it, and with the very great possibility that it would be intercepted long before it reached the coast, and the men all drowned in the sea or, at the worst, blown to pieces with their equipment while they were trying to land. We also have a great system of minefields, recently strongly reinforced, through which we alone know the channel. If the enemy tries to sweep passages through these minefields, it will be the task of the Navy to destroy the minesweepers and any other forces employed to protect them. There should be no difficulty in this, owing to our great superiority at sea. . . .

This brings me, naturally, to the great question of invasion from the air and of the impending struggle between the British and German air forces. It seems quite clear that no invasion on a scale beyond the capacity of our land forces to crush speedily is likely to take place from the air until our Air Force has been definitely overpowered. In the meantime, there may be raids by parachute troops and attempted descents of airborne soldiers. We should be able to give those gentry a warm reception both in the air and if they reach the ground in any condition to continue the dispute. But the great question is, can we break Hitler's air weapon? Now, of course, it is a very great pity that we have not got an Air Force at least equal to that of the most powerful enemy within striking distance of these shores. But we have a very powerful Air Force which has proved itself far superior in quality, both in men and in many types of machine, to what we have met so far in the numerous fierce air battles which have been fought. In France, where we were at a considerable disadvantage and lost many machines on the ground, we were accustomed to inflict losses of as much as two to two and a half to one. In the fighting over Dunkirk, which was a sort of no man's land, we undoubtedly beat the German air force, and this gave us the mastery locally in the air, and we inflicted losses of three or four to one. Anyone who looks at the photographs which were published a week or so ago of the re-embarkation, showing the masses of troops assembled on the beach and forming an ideal target for hours at a time, must realise that this re-embarkation would not have been possible unless the enemy had resigned all hope of recovering air superiority at that point.

In the defence of this island the advantages to the defenders will be very great. We hope to improve on the rate of three or four to one which was realised at Dunkirk, and in addition all our injured machines and their crews which get down safely—and, surprisingly, a very great many injured machines and men do get down safely in modern air fighting—all of these will fall, in an attack upon these islands, on friendly soil and live to fight another day, whereas all injured enemy machines and their complements will be total losses as far as the war is concerned. . . .

There remains the danger of bombing attacks, which will certainly be made very soon upon us by the bomber forces of the enemy. It is true that the German bomber force is superior in numbers to ours, but we have a very large bomber force also which we shall use to strike at military targets in Germany without intermission. I do not at all underrate the severity of the ordeal which lies before us, but I believe our countrymen will show themselves capable of standing up to it, like the brave men of Barcelona, and will be able to stand up to it, and carry on in spite of it, at least as well as any other people in the world. Much will depend upon this, and every man and every woman will have the chance to show the finest qualities of their race and render the highest service to their cause. For all of us at this time, whatever our sphere, our station, our occupation, our duties, it will be a help to remember the famous lines:

> He nothing common did, or mean,
> Upon that memorable scene.

I have thought it right upon this occasion to give the House and the country some indication of the solid, practical grounds upon which we base our inflexible resolve to continue the war, and I can assure them that our professional advisers of the three Services unitedly advise that we should do so, and that there are good and reasonable hopes of final victory. We have also fully informed and consulted all the self-governing Dominions, and I have received from their Prime Ministers, Mr. Mackenzie King, Mr. Menzies, Mr. Fraser and General Smuts, messages couched in the most moving terms in which they endorse our decison and declare themselves ready to share our fortunes and to persevere to the end. . . .

. . . During the first four years of the last war the Allies experienced, as my right hon. Friend opposite the Member for Carnarvon Boroughs (Mr. Lloyd George) will remember, nothing but disaster and disappointment, and yet at the end their morale was higher than that of the Germans, who had moved from one aggressive triumph to another. During that war we repeatedly asked ourselves the question, "How are we going to win?" and no one was able ever to answer it with much precision, until at the end, quite suddenly, quite unexpectedly, our terrible foe collapsed before us, and we were so glutted with victory that in our folly we cast it away. . . .

What General Weygand called the "Battle of France" is over. I expect that the battle of Britain is about to begin. Upon this battle depends the survival of Christian civilisation. Upon it depends our own British life and the long continuity of our institutions and our Empire. The whole fury and might of the enemy must very soon be turned on us. Hitler knows that he will have to break us in this island or lose the war. If we can stand up to him all Europe may be free, and the life of the world may move forward into broad, sunlit uplands; but if we fail then the whole world, including the United States, and all that we have known and cared for, will sink into the abyss of a new dark age made more sinister, and perhaps more prolonged, by the lights of a perverted science. Let us therefore brace ourselves to our duty and so bear ourselves that if the British Commonwealth and Empire lasts for a thousand years men will still say, "This was their finest hour."

102. THE BEVERIDGE REPORT

by WILLIAM BEVERIDGE

Few English "bluebooks" (i.e., government reports) have ever become best sellers. But *Social Insurance and Allied Services: Report by Sir William Beveridge* (1942) won that distinction during the War. The *Report* captured the imagination of a generation to which some comprehensive scheme of social security seemed the only safeguard against the conditions they had suffered in the 1930s. Sir William Beveridge (later Lord Beveridge), 1879–1963, was a Liberal who had long studied unemployment and social problems, and who had been Director of the London School of Economics from 1919 to 1937. These extracts are from pp. 9–11, 120–125, 153–170 of the *Report*.

17. THE main feature of the Plan for Social Security is a scheme of social insurance against interruption and destruction of earning power and for special expenditure arising at birth, marriage or death. . . .

. . . .

20. Under the scheme of social insurance, which forms the main feature of this plan, every citizen of working age will contribute in his appropriate class according to the security that he needs, or as a married woman will have contributions made by the husband. Each will be covered for all his needs by a single weekly contribution on one insurance document. All the principal cash payments—for unemployment, disability and retirement will continue so long as the need lasts, without means test, and will be paid from a Social Insurance Fund built up by contributions from the insured persons, from their employers, if any, and from the State. . . .

. . . . . .

300. *Scope of Social Security:* The term "social security" is used here to denote the securing of an income to take the place of earnings when they are interrupted by unemployment, sickness or accident, to provide for retirement through age, to provide against loss of support by the death of another person, and to meet exceptional expenditures, such as those connected with birth, death and marriage. Primarily social security means security of income up to a minimum, but the provision of an income should be associated with treatment designed to bring the interruption of earnings to an end as soon as possible.

301. *Three Assumptions:* No satisfactory scheme of social security can be devised except on the following assumptions:—
 (A) Children's allowances for children up to the age of 15 or if in full-time education up to the age of 16;
 (B) Comprehensive health and re-habilitation services for prevention and cure of disease and restoration of capacity for work, available to all members of the community;
 (C) Maintenance of employment, that is to say avoidance of mass unemployment.

The grounds for making these three assumptions, the methods of satisfying them and their relation to the social security scheme are discussed in Part VI. Children's allowances will be added to all the insurance benefits and pensions described below. . . .

302. *Three Methods of Security:* On these three assumptions, a Plan

for Social Security is outlined below, combining three distinct methods: social insurance for basic needs; national assistance for special cases; voluntary insurance for additions to the basic provision. Social insurance means the providing of cash payments conditional upon compulsory contributions previously made by, or on behalf of, the insured persons, irrespective of the resources of the individual at the time of the claim. Social insurance is much the most important of the three methods and is proposed here in a form as comprehensive as possible. But while social insurance can, and should, be the main instrument for guaranteeing income security, it cannot be the only one. It needs to be supplemented both by national assistance and by voluntary insurance. National assistance means the giving of cash payments conditional upon proved need at the time of the claim, irrespective of previous contributions but adjusted by consideration of individual circumstances and paid from the national exchequer. Assistance is an indispensable supplement to social insurance, however the scope of the latter may be widened. In addition to both of these there is place for voluntary insurance. Social insurance and national assistance organised by the State are designed to guarantee, on condition of service, a basic income for subsistence. The actual incomes and by consequence the normal standards of expenditure of different sections of the population differ greatly. Making provision for these higher standards is primarily the function of the individual, that is to say, it is a matter for free choice and voluntary insurance. But the State should make sure that its measures leave room and encouragement for such voluntary insurance. The social insurance scheme is the greater part of the Plan for Social Security and its description occupies most of this Part of the Report. But the plan includes national assistance and voluntary insurance as well.

303. *Six Principles of Social Insurance:* The social insurance scheme set out below as the chief method of social security embodies six fundamental principles:

> Flat rate of subsistence benefit
> Flat rate of contribution
> Unification of administrative responsibility
> Adequacy of benefit
> Comprehensiveness
> Classification

304. *Flat Rate of Subsistence Benefit:* The first fundamental principle of the social insurance scheme is provision of a flat rate of in-

surance benefit, irrespective of the amount of the earnings which have been interrupted by unemployment or disability or ended by retirement; exception is made only where prolonged disability has resulted from an industrial accident or disease. This principle follows from the recognition of the place and importance of voluntary insurance in social security and distinguishes the scheme proposed for Britain from the security schemes of Germany, the Soviet Union, the United States and most other countries with the exception of New Zealand. The flat rate is the same for all the principal forms of cessation of earning—unemployment, disability, retirement; for maternity and for widowhood there is a temporary benefit at a higher rate.

305. *Flat Rate of Contribution:* The second fundamental principle of the scheme is that the compulsory contribution required of each insured person or his employer is at a flat rate, irrespective of his means. All insured persons, rich or poor, will pay the same contributions for the same security; those with larger means will pay more only to the extent that as tax-payers they pay more to the National Exchequer and so to the State share of the Social Insurance Fund. This feature distinguishes the scheme proposed for Britain from the scheme recently established in New Zealand under which the contributions are graduated by income, and are in effect an income-tax assigned to a particular service. Subject moreover to one exception, the contribution will be the same irrespective of the assumed degree of risk affecting particular individuals or forms of employment. The exception is the raising of a proportion of the special cost of benefits and pensions for industrial disability in occupations of high risk by a levy on employers proportionate to risk and pay-roll.

306. *Unification of Administrative Responsibility:* The third fundamental principle is unification of administrative responsibility in the interests of efficiency and economy. For each insured person there will be a single weekly contribution, in respect of all his benefits. There will be in each locality a Security Office able to deal with claims of every kind and all sides of security. The methods of paying different kinds of cash benefit will be different and will take account of the circumstances of insured persons, providing for payment at the home or elsewhere, as is necessary. All contributions will be paid into a single Social Insurance Fund and all benefits and other insurance payments will be paid from that fund.

307. *Adequacy of Benefit:* The fourth fundamental principle is adequacy of benefit in amount and in time. The flat rate of benefit pro-

posed is intended in itself to be sufficient without further resources to provide the minimum income needed for subsistence in all normal cases. It gives room and a basis for additional voluntary provision, but does not assume that in any case. The benefits are adequate also in time, that is to say except for contingencies of a temporary nature, they will continue indefinitely without means test, so long as the need continues, though subject to any change of conditions and treatment required by prolongation of the interruption in earning and occupation.

308. *Comprehensiveness:* The fifth fundamental principle is that social insurance should be comprehensive, in respect both of the persons covered and of their needs. It should not leave either to national assistance or to voluntary insurance any risk so general or so uniform that social insurance can be justified. For national assistance involves a means test which may discourage voluntary insurance or personal saving. And voluntary insurance can never be sure of covering the ground. For any need moreover which, like direct funeral expenses, is so general and so uniform as to be a fit subject for insurance by compulsion, social insurance is much cheaper to administer than voluntary insurance.

309. *Classification:* The sixth fundamental principle is that social insurance, while unified and comprehensive, must take account of the different ways of life of different sections of the community: of those dependent on earnings by employment under contract of service, of those earning in other ways, of those rendering vital unpaid service as housewives, of those not yet of age to earn and of those past earning. The term "classification" is used here to denote adjustment of insurance to the differing circumstances of each of these classes and to many varieties of need and circumstance within each insurance class. But the insurance classes are not economic or social classes in the ordinary sense; the insurance scheme is one for all citizens irrespective of their means. . . .

. . . .

311. *Eight Primary Causes of Need:* The primary needs for social security are of eight kinds, reckoning the composite needs of a married woman as one and including also the needs of childhood (Assumption A) and the need for universal comprehensive medical treatment and rehabilitation (Assumption B). These needs are set out below; to each there is attached in the security scheme a distinct insurance benefit

or benefits. Assistance may enter to deal with any kind of need, where insurance benefit for any reason is inadequate or absent.

Unemployment: that is to say, inability to obtain employment by a person dependent on it and physically fit for it, met by unemployment benefit with removal and lodging grants.

Disability: that is to say, inability of a person of working age, through illness or accident, to pursue a gainful occupation, met by disability benefit and industrial pension.

Loss of Livelihood by person not dependent on paid employment, met by training benefit.

Retirement from occupation, paid or unpaid, through age, met by retirement pension.

Marriage needs of a woman, met by Housewives' Policy including provision for:—

(1) Marriage, met by marriage grant.

(2) Maternity, met by maternity grant in all cases, and, in the case of a married woman in gainful occupation, also by maternity benefit for a period before and after confinement.

(3) Interruption or cessation of husband's earnings by his unemployment, disability or retirement, met by share of benefit or pension with husband.

(4) Widowhood, met by provision varying according to circumstances including temporary widow's benefit for readjustment, guardian benefit while caring for children and training benefit if and when there are no children in need of care.

(5) Separation, i.e., end of husband's maintenance by legal separation, or established desertion, met by adaptation of widowhood provisions, including separation benefit, guardian benefit and training benefit.

(6) Incapacity for household duties, met by provision of paid help in illness as part of treatment.

Funeral Expenses of self or any person for whom responsible, met by funeral grant.

Childhood, provided for by children's allowances if in full-time education, till sixteen.

Physical Disease or *Incapacity,* met by medical treatment, domiciliary and institutional, for self and dependants in comprehensive health service and by post-medical rehabilitation. . . .

. . . . . .

409. Social security as used in this Report means assurance of a certain income. The Plan for Social Security set out in the Report is a plan to win freedom from want by maintaining incomes. But sufficiency of income is not sufficient in itself. Freedom from want is only one of the essential freedoms of mankind. Any Plan for Social Security in the narrow sense assumes a concerted social policy in many fields, most of which it would be inappropriate to discuss in this Report. The plan proposed here involves three particular assumptions so closely related to it that brief discussion is essential for understanding of the plan itself. These are the assumptions of children's allowances, of comprehensive health and rehabilitation services, and of maintenance of employment. . . .

. . . . . .

455. There are some to whom pursuit of security appears to be a wrong aim. They think of security as something inconsistent with initiative, adventure, personal responsibility. That is not a just view of social security as planned in this Report. The plan is not one for giving to everybody something for nothing and without trouble, or something that will free the recipients for ever thereafter from personal responsibilities. The plan is one to secure income for subsistence on condition of service and contribution and in order to make and keep men fit for service. It cannot be got without thought and effort. It can be carried through only by a concentrated determination of the British democracy to free itself once for all of the scandal of physical want for which there is no economic or moral justification. When that effort has been made, the plan leaves room and encouragement to all individuals to win for themselves something above the national minimum, to find and to satisfy and to produce the means of satisfying new and higher needs than bare physical needs.

456. There are some who will say that pursuit of security as defined in this Report, that is to say income security, is a wholly inadequate aim. Their view is not merely admitted but asserted in the Report itself. The Plan for Social Security is put forward as part of a general programme of social policy. It is one part only of an attack upon five giant evils: upon the physical Want with which it is directly concerned, upon Disease which often causes that Want and brings many other troubles in its train, upon Ignorance which no democracy can afford among its citizens, upon the Squalor which arises mainly through haphazard distribution of industry and population, and upon

the Idleness which destroys wealth and corrupts men, whether they are well fed or not, when they are idle. In seeking security not merely against physical want, but against all these evils in all their forms, and in showing that security can be combined with freedom and enterprise and responsibility of the individual for his own life, the British community and those who in other lands have inherited the British tradition have a vital service to render to human progress. . . .

103. THE 1944 EDUCATION ACT

Not all the enthusiastic schemes for reconstruction could be translated into legislation during the War, nor was there complete unanimity on some of the measures within the government itself. The most far-reaching social reform enacted by the Coalition Government was the Education Act of 1944, which ranks in importance with the Education Acts of 1870 and 1902. By up-grading the service to a Ministry of Education, raising the minimum school-leaving age, and providing secondary schools for all, the Act made possible a new era of development in public education. Indeed, so comprehensive was the Act that its implementation seemed likely to take several decades, given the pace of change in the 1950s. The following paragraphs are from pp. 1–56 of the *Education Act, 1944: 7 and 8 Geo. 6 chap. 31.*

1.—(1) IT shall be lawful for His Majesty to appoint a Minister (hereinafter referred to as "the Minister"), whose duty it shall be to promote the education of the people of England and Wales and the progressive development of institutions devoted to that purpose, and to secure the effective execution by local authorities, under his control and direction, of the national policy for providing a varied and comprehensive educational service in every area. . . .

. . . . . .

THE THREE STAGES OF THE SYSTEM

7. The statutory system of public education shall be organised in three progressive stages to be known as primary education, secondary

education, and further education; and it shall be the duty of the local education authority for every area, so far as their powers extend, to contribute towards the spiritual, moral, mental, and physical development of the community by securing that efficient education throughout those stages shall be available to meet the needs of the population of their area. . . .

. . . .

9.—(1) For the purpose of fulfilling their duties under this Act, a local education authority shall have power to establish primary and secondary schools, to maintain such schools whether established by them or otherwise, and, so far as may be authorised by arrangements approved by the Minister, to assist any such school which is not maintained by them.

(2) Primary and secondary schools maintained by a local education authority, not being nursery schools or special schools, shall, if established by a local education authority or by a former authority, be known as county schools and, if established otherwise than by such an authority, be known as voluntary schools. . . .

. . . .

11.—(1) As soon as may be after the date of the commencement of this Part of this Act, every local education authority shall estimate the immediate and prospective needs of their area, having regard to the provisions of this Act and of any regulations made thereunder and to the functions relating to primary and secondary education thereby conferred on them, and shall, within one year after that date or within such extended period as the Minister may in any particular case allow, prepare and submit to the Minister a plan (in this Act referred to as a "development plan") in such form as the Minister may direct showing the action which the authority propose should be taken for securing that there shall be sufficient primary and secondary schools available for their area and the successive measures by which it is proposed to accomplish that purpose. . . .

. . . .

RELIGIOUS EDUCATION IN COUNTY AND VOLUNTARY SCHOOLS

25.—(1) Subject to the provisions of this section, the school day in every county school and in every voluntary school shall begin with collective worship on the part of all pupils in attendance at the school, and the arrangements made therefor shall provide for a single act of worship attended by all such pupils unless, in the opinion of the local education authority or, in the case of a voluntary school, of the managers or governors thereof, the school premises are such as to make it impracticable to assemble them for that purpose.

(2) Subject to the provisions of this section, religious instruction shall be given in every county school and in every voluntary school.

(3) It shall not be required, as a condition of any pupil attending any county school or any voluntary school, that he shall attend or abstain from attending any Sunday school or any place of religious worship.

(4) If the parent of any pupil in attendance at any county school or any voluntary school requests that he be wholly or partly excused from attendance at religious worship in the school, or from attendance at religious instruction in the school, or from attendance at both religious worship and religious instruction in the school, then, until the request is withdrawn, the pupil shall be excused from such attendance accordingly. . . .

26. Subject as hereinafter provided, the collective worship required by subsection (1) of the last foregoing section shall not, in any county school, be distinctive of any particular religious denomination, and the religious instruction given to any pupils in attendance at a county school in conformity with the requirements of subsection (2) of the said section shall be given in accordance with an agreed syllabus adopted for the school or for those pupils and shall not include any catechism or formulary which is distinctive of any particular religious denomination. . . .

. . . . . .

29.—(1) The provisions of the Fifth Schedule to this Act shall have effect with respect to the preparation, adoption, and reconsideration, of an agreed syllabus of religious instruction.

(2) A local education authority shall have power to constitute a standing advisory council on religious education to advise the authority upon matters connected with the religious instruction to be given in accordance with an agreed syllabus and, in particular, as to methods of teaching, the choice of books, and the provision of lectures for teachers.

(3) The method of appointment of the members of any council constituted under the last foregoing subsection and the term of office

and conditions of retirement of the members thereof shall be such as may be determined by the local education authority. . . .

. . . . . .

COMPULSORY ATTENDANCE AT PRIMARY AND SECONDARY SCHOOLS

35. In this Act the expression "compulsory school age" means any age between five years and fifteen years, and accordingly a person shall be deemed to be of compulsory school age if he has attained the age of five years and has not attained the age of fifteen years and a person shall be deemed to be over compulsory school age as soon as he has attained the age of fifteen years:

Provided that, as soon as the Minister is satisfied that it has become practicable to raise to sixteen the upper limit of the compulsory school age, he shall lay before Parliament the draft of an Order in Council directing that the foregoing provisions of this section shall have effect as if for references therein to the age of fifteen years there were substituted references to the age of sixteen years . . .

. . . . . .

FURTHER EDUCATION

41. Subject as hereinafter provided, it shall be the duty of every local education authority to secure the provision for their area of adequate facilities for further education, that is to say:—

(a) full-time and part-time education for persons over compulsory school age; and

(b) leisure-time occupation, in such organized cultural training and recreative activities as are suited to their requirements, for any persons over compulsory school age who are able and willing to profit by the facilities provided for that purpose. . . .

. . . . . .

GENERAL PRINCIPLE TO BE OBSERVED BY MINISTER
AND LOCAL EDUCATION AUTHORITIES

76. In the exercise and performance of all powers and duties conferred and imposed on them by this Act the Minister and local education authorities shall have regard to the general principle that, so far as is compatible with the provision of efficient instruction and training and the avoidance of unreasonable public expenditure, pupils are to be educated in accordance with the wishes of their parents. . . .

Chapter 23.

The Labour Government, 1945-1951

The Labour victory at the election in 1945 was a landslide. For the first time a Labour government had an overall majority in the House of Commons—393 members against 189 Conservatives and 12 Liberals. Not even the great prestige of Winston Churchill was sufficient to rescue the Conservative Party from the odium of their prewar policies; the country voted clearly and decisively for a change.

The circumstances in which the Labour Party came to power were very unlike anything which had been foreseen in the prewar years. Following a great world war, in which they had striven wholeheartedly for national victory, the Labour Party found itself in an era of full employment, with restrictions, rationing, and shortages of all kinds, given an overwhelming electoral mandate, and faced with a weak and demoralized opposition. Moreover, Britain's world position was greatly changed as a result of the war. In international affairs the polarization of world power in two giant nations, the U.S.A. and the U.S.S.R., altered radically the role which Britain could expect to play; though this was not immediately apparent, and, indeed, was only reluctantly accepted later. The economic difficulties which had plagued her in the interwar years were also now accentuated: the loss of British investments abroad, the destruction of much of her shipping, and the run-down state of her industry and capital equipment were the price of six years of total war. The need to accept American help between 1947 and 1950 made England much more dependent economically on the United States; and the development of the Cold War reinforced this close association in the field of foreign policy. These objective factors forced upon the Labour Party, with its memories and slogans of the 1930s, the necessity of fundamental reorientation. The achievement of the Labour government was to implement and yet adapt a considerable part of its traditional program in this new environment.

Three main groups of measures were effected. First, there was a great extension of the social services, resulting in a type of society which became known as the Welfare State. Second, certain basic industries and utilities were nationalized, thus increasing the public sector of the economy; and at the same time planning control over the private sector of industry was developed. Third, by means of redistributive taxation an attempt was made to create a more equalitarian society.

104. LET US FACE THE FUTURE

by THE LABOUR PARTY

Socialists of all shades had long been committed to public ownership, in some form, of "the means of production, distribution, and exchange." For the Labour Party this meant a program of nationalization. Much was hoped for from these measures by Labour supporters, and conversely the opponents argued against each case bitterly. In fact the concerns actually nationalized were the Bank of England, the coal industry, transport (railroads, canals, and trucking), electricity and gas. An Act to nationalize the iron and steel industry was passed too late in the life of the government to be effective, and was subsequently repealed by the Conservatives. Nationalization proved to be neither the cure-all that some socialists had believed, nor the bogey that conservatives had pretended. The following section on public ownership was headed "Industry in the service of the nation" in the Labour Party program, *Let us Face the Future* (1945), pp. 5–7.

BY the test of war some industries have shown themselves capable of rising to new heights of efficiency and expansion. Others, including some of our older industries fundamental to our economic structure, have wholly or partly failed.

To-day we live alongside economic giants—countries where science and technology take leaping strides year by year. Britain must match those strides—and we must take no chances about it. Britain needs an industry organised to enable it to yield the best that human knowledge and skill can provide. Only so can our people reap the full benefits of this age of discovery and Britain keep her place as a Great Power.

The Labour Party intends to link the skill of British craftsmen and designers to the skill of British scientists in the service of our fellow men. The genius of British scientists and technicians who have produced radio-location, jet propulsion, penicillin, and the Mulberry Harbours in wartime, must be given full rein in peacetime too.

Each industry must have applied to it the test of national service. If it serves the nation, well and good; if it is inefficient and falls down on its job, the nation must see that things are put right.

These propositions seem indisputable, but for years before the war anti-Labour Governments set them aside, so that British industry over a large field fell into a state of depression, muddle and decay. Millions of working and middle-class people went through the horrors of unemployment and insecurity. It is not enough to sympathise with these victims: we must develop an acute feeling of national shame—and act.

The Labour Party is a Socialist Party, and proud of it. Its ultimate purpose at home is the establishment of the Socialist Commonwealth of Great Britain—free, democratic, efficient, progressive, public-spirited, its material resources organised in the service of the British people.

But Socialism cannot come overnight, as the product of a week-end revolution. The members of the Labour Party, like the British people, are practical-minded men and women.

There are basic industries ripe and over-ripe for public ownership and management in the direct service of the nation. There are many smaller businesses rendering good service which can be left to go on with their useful work.

There are big industries not yet ripe for public ownership which must nevertheless be required by constructive supervision to further the nation's needs and not to prejudice national interests by restrictive anti-social monopoly or cartel agreements—caring for their own capital structures and profits at the cost of a lower standard of living for all.

In the light of these considerations, the Labour Party submits to the nation the following industrial programme:

1. *Public ownership of the fuel and power industries.*—For a quarter of a century the coal industry, producing Britain's most precious na-

tional raw material, has been floundering chaotically under the ownership of many hundreds of independent companies. Amalgamation under public ownership will bring great economies in operation and
make it possible to modernise production methods and to raise safety
standards in every colliery in the country. Public ownership of gas and
electricity undertakings will lower charges, prevent competitive waste,
open the way for co-ordinated research and development, and lead to
the reforming of uneconomic areas of distribution. Other industries
will benefit.

2. *Public ownership of inland transport.*—Co-ordination of transport
services by rail, road, air and canal cannot be achieved without unification. And unification without public ownership means a steady
struggle with sectional interests or the enthronement of a private
monopoly, which would be a menace to the rest of industry.

3. *Public ownership of iron and steel.*—Private monopoly has maintained high prices and kept inefficient high-cost plants in existence.
Only if public ownership replaces private monopoly can the industry
become efficient.

These socialised industries, taken over on a basis of fair compensation, to be conducted efficiently in the interests of consumers, coupled with proper status and conditions for the workers employed in
them.

4. *Public supervision of monopolies and cartels* with the aim of
advancing industrial efficiency in the service of the nation. Anti-social
restrictive practices will be prohibited.

5. *A firm and clear-cut programme for the export trade.*—We would
give State help in any necessary form to get our export trade on its
feet and enable it to pay for the food and raw materials without which
Britain must decay and die. But State help on conditions—conditions
that industry is efficient and go-ahead. Laggards and obstructionists
must be led or directed into better ways. Here we dare not fail.

6. *The shaping of suitable economic and price controls* to secure
that first things shall come first in the transition from war to peace and
that every citizen (including the demobilised Service men and women)
shall get fair play. There must be priorities in the use of raw materials,
food prices must be held, homes for the people must come before
mansions, necessities for all before luxuries for the few. We do not
want a short boom followed by collapse as after the last war; we do
not want a wild rise in prices and inflation, followed by a smash and

widespread unemployment. It is either sound economic controls—or smash.

7. *The better organisation of Government departments* and the Civil Service for work in relation to these ends. The economic purpose of government must be to spur industry forward and not to choke it with red tape. . . .

105. [A FREE HEALTH SERVICE]

by ANEURIN BEVAN

The Beveridge Report (see Reading No. 102) provided a magnificent blueprint for a scheme of social security and also indicated the need for wider measures of social legislation. From 1946 the Labour government proceeded to put these plans into effect. The creation of a National Health Service was the most impressive—and expensive—of all the achievements of the Welfare State. Under the 1946 Act a free medical service for all, with doctors and dentists receiving capitation fees based on the number of patients they accepted for treatment, was established. Public clinics, ophthalmic services, drugs and appliances were included in the Service, and the various types of voluntary and public hospitals were coordinated under regional boards. The scheme was at first resisted by the medical profession, but their opposition was overcome by the skill and toughness of the Minister of Health, Aneurin Bevan (1897–1960). He had been a coal miner in South Wales, and M.P. for Ebbw Vale since 1929. On most issues he was identified with the left wing of the party. This account of the health service is from his book, *In Place of Fear* (1952), pp. 73–91.

THE field in which the claims of individual commercialism come into most immediate conflict with reputable notions of social values is that of health. That is true both for curative and preventive medicine. The preventive health services of modern society fight the battle over a wider front and therefore less dramatically than is the case with personal medicine.

Yet the victories won by preventive medicine are much the most important for mankind. This is so not only because it is obviously preferable to prevent suffering than to alleviate it. Preventive medicine, which is merely another way of saying health by collective action, builds up a system of social habits which constitute an indispensable part of what we mean by civilisation. In this sphere values that are in essence Socialist, challenge and win victory after victory against the assertions and practice of the Competitive Society.

Modern communities have been made tolerable by the behaviour patterns imposed upon them by the activities of the sanitary inspector and the medical officer of health. It is true, these rarely work out what they do in terms of Socialist philosophy; but that does not alter the fact that the whole significance of their contribution is its insistence that the claims of the individual shall subordinate themselves to social codes that have the collective well-being for their aim, irrespective of the extent to which this frustrates individual greed. . . .

When I was engaged in formulating the main principles of the British Health Service, I had to give careful study to various proposals for financing it. . . .

One thing the community cannot do is insure against itself. What it can and must do is to set aside an agreed proportion of the national revenues for the creation and maintenance of the service it has pledged itself to provide. This is not so much insurance as a prudent policy of capital investment. . . .

The means of collecting the revenues for the health service are already in the possession of most modern states, and that is the normal system of taxation.

This was the course which commended itself to me and it is the basis of the finance of the British Health Service. Its revenues are provided by the Exchequer in the same way as other forms of public expenditure. I am afraid this is not yet fully understood. Many people still think they pay for the National Health Service by way of their contribution to the National Insurance Scheme. The confusion arose because the new service sounded so much like the old National Health Insurance, and it was launched on the same date as the National Insurance Scheme. Some part of the misunderstanding was caused by the propaganda of the B.M.A., which warned the people at one time that, although they would be paying their contributions, the Health Service would not be there to meet their needs. There was a certain irony about this, because when the time came for enrolment in the Health Service more than ninety per cent of the population hastened to get their names in; some under the impression, helped by the B.M.A. itself, that they had started paying for it. This gave me some quiet satisfaction. . . .

The hardest task for any public representative charged with the duty of making a free Health Service available to the community, is overcoming the fears, real and imaginary, of the medical profession. His task is to reconcile the general public interest with their sectional claims. No pressure groups are more highly organised in Britain than the professions, and among these the medical professions are the strongest.

I was anxious to ensure that the General Practitioner should be able to earn a reasonable living without having to aim at a register which would be too large to admit of good doctoring. To accomplish this I suggested a graduated system of capitation payments which would be highest in the medium ranges and lower in the higher. This would have discouraged big lists by lessening the financial inducement. The B.M.A. refused this, though now I am told they are ready to re-open the question. Had they agreed at the time the position of doctors in the over-doctored areas of the country would have been made easier as re-distribution over the country as a whole gradually took place.

I have a warm spot for the General Practitioner despite his tempestuousness. There is a sound case for providing a little more money to help the doctor with a medium list who wants to make a decent living and yet be a good doctor. The injection of several million pounds here would refresh the Service at its most vulnerable point; that is, the family doctor relationship. The family doctor is in many ways the most important person in the Service. He comes into the most immediate and continuous touch with the members of the community. He is also the gateway to all the other branches of the Service. If more is required than he can provide, it is he who puts the patient in touch with the specialist services.

He is also the most highly individualistic member of the medical world. As soon as he leaves medicine he seems to think in slogans. These are shot through with political animus of the most violent description—usually Conservative. I speak here primarily of the British Medical Association. The Medical Practitioners' Union on the other hand is a progressive body, affiliated to the Trades Union Congress and more up-to-date in its views. But it was with the B.M.A. I had to negotiate. I usually met its representatives when they had come hot from a conference at which the wildest speeches had been made, frequently by the very men who then had to try to come to terms with the people they had been so immoderately denouncing.

I enjoyed the challenge. My trade union experience had taught me to distinguish between the atmosphere of the mass demonstration and the quite different mood of the negotiating table. I was therefore able to discount a great deal of what had been said from the rostrum. Also it was easy for me to enable them to win victories, for they had usually worked themselves up into a fever of protest against proposals which had never been made. Thus they would "never be made into civil servants." As I never intended they should, I was able to concede the point without difficulty.

Then there must be "free choice of doctor." I myself was most anxious to insist on this, for I saw in it one of the most important safeguards for the public. The right of the patient to leave his doctor and choose another whenever he liked, had a double edge that the B.M.A. spokesmen did not fully appreciate until later. Then there was the demand for full rights of free expression of opinion, both about the Health Service and anything else. To this again I was most ready to respond, as it had never occurred to me that anything otherwise had been intended.

And so it went on from one blown out slogan to another. Indeed, I warned the leaders of the profession that they were making a fundamental mistake in strategy. They were mobilising their forces to fight a battle that was never likely to begin. When later I was able to make a considered statement in Parliament giving a solemn undertaking to abide by principles that were my own from the very start, the B.M.A. found its forces leaving the field just when the crucial stage in the struggle was reached. . . .

In dealing with the medical profession it is wise to make a distinction between three main causes of opposition to the establishment of a Free National Health Service. There is the opposition which springs from political opinion as such. This is part of the general opposition of Conservative ideas, and it is strong in the medical profession, though the expression of it tends to be supercharged with the emotions borrowed from other fears and ambitions. Second, there is the defence of professional status and material reward. The latter, of course, they share with other pressure groups. Then, thirdly, there is the opposition which springs from the fear that lay interference might affect academic freedom and come between the doctor and his patient. The third group is the most legitimate and will unite all the members of the medical world, from the self-seeking to the truly idealistic. Any health service which hopes to win the consent of the doctors must allay these fears. The fear of State interference in academic matters is very strong in the Western world, although it tends to ignore the power that patronage already has to influence the pattern of medical investigation. Nevertheless, entitlement to advancement on grounds of merit alone, free from any tinge of political nepotism, must be jealously guarded by any self-respecting profession. Nor should less informed opinion be allowed to influence the medical curriculum. Here there is no substitute for the refreshment of renovating influences within the profession itself. Freedom of discussion and a readiness to add to, and receive from, the corpus of accepted knowledge, are the only ways we have yet discovered to safeguard what we have gained, and to open ways to new discoveries. . . .

There is no alternative to self-government by the medical profession in all matters affecting the content of its academic life, although there is every justification in lay co-operation in the economy in which that is carried out. The distinction between the two is real. It is for the community to provide the apparatus of medicine for the doctor. It is for him to use it freely in accordance with the standards of his profession and the requirements of his oath.

This is also the case with respect to the relations between the doctor and his patient. A great deal of nonsense has been talked about this. There never has been any danger that socialised medicine would destroy the privacy of doctor-patient relationship. Such a danger would indeed rupture a health service from the start. The privacy rightly accorded a patient under a health service is much more than is often the case in, for example, private insurance. The consulting room is inviolable and no sensible person would have it otherwise. . . .

106. SOCIALISM AND THE WELFARE STATE

by KINGSLEY MARTIN

For socialists the building of a welfare state created a dilemma. They could not but approve of the various social reforms which removed the want, insecurity and denial of opportunity that they had always fought against. At the same time they were uneasy about the society which was the outcome of the measures, for it was still far short of anything they had thought of as socialism. At most it was a "mixed economy," with the private sector of industry still dominant. Moreover, it was apparent that a majority of working-class electors were quite content with a welfare-state and the prospect of steady progress towards higher standards of living under capitalism. Full employment and social security seemed to have seriously undermined the dynamic of socialism. This problem was clearly posed by Kingsley Martin (b. 1897), editor of the socialist weekly, *The New Statesman,* in his Fabian tract, *Socialism and the Welfare State* (1951), pp. 8-11.

WHEN the war ended, . . . Marxist theory had been largely forgotten. The Soviet Union had been our ally, and the hopes of social change arising out of the war were everywhere encouraged by the spectacle of Resistance movements taking charge throughout the war-weary countries of Europe and Asia. Hatred of Conservatism, now inseparably associated with war, unemployment and misery, gave us the Labour Party victory of 1945. There was a large body of agreement to carry out measures which were primarily reforms to remove grievances, elements in the Welfare State, if you like, but not what used to be thought of as Socialism. Where this Socialist ideal prevailed it was mainly among the older type of Fabian. It was a theoretician like Dalton who was most bellicose in the nationalisation of steel. Policy was based partly, it is true, on the Fabian belief that a social revolution could be gradually carried out through the nationalisation of industry. But in the background, . . . there stood the dominating figure of John Maynard Keynes whose voice was heard with ever greater authority urging that, through the technique of a managed currency and a deliberate redistribution of income, capitalism could be induced to end its own contradictions. . . .

Given financial control, in short, a Labour government could achieve a really substantial change in society by shifting the balance of income so that the surplus savings of capitalism were not left to accumulate in a few hands but spread more evenly throughout society, with a result that poverty was abolished, the booms and slumps of capitalism ironed out, and the constant urge of capitalism to find new overseas markets in backward areas where a higher rate of profit could be obtained would disappear. The result would not be a Socialist omelette, but the eggs would be so far scrambled that it would be impossible to go back to Capitalist ham and eggs. . . .

Keynes quite consciously offered a rational and ingenious alternative to Socialism. I would go so far as to say that if Keynesism will work, the middle-class Social Democrat cannot really desire what used to be called the Workers' State. Most of us became ardent Socialists between the first two World Wars because our consciences were torn by the facts of unemployment and social misery. If it were really possible to abolish the booms and slumps of capitalism, to see that there were guaranteed a good minimum standard of life, then very few would want to upset so good a society because it did not come up to some ethical norm of equality and substitute co-operation for the profit motive. I think that the members of the last Government who believe that they have really produced a Welfare State can quite logically say, as some of them indeed do, that they see no merit in nationalisation except in so far as it increases efficiency, that they have no reason to end capitalism if its intolerable evils are removed and that they certainly do not believe in workers' control. They do not find themselves worried by the prospect that there may still in the Welfare State be wide discrepancies of comfort between the rich (who will not be able to be millionaires) and the poor (who will all have at least a *petit bourgeois* standard of living).

Any of you who are shocked at my saying this should frankly face this question. If the economic and social system of Norway, Denmark, or even Sweden, where the class basis of society is still much more evident than it is in other Scandinavian countries, can be attained in Britain, would any sane person really say that on some ground of doctrine he or she would still demand a social revolution? Would they say that they preferred the Socialist system of the Soviet Union to the Welfare State of Scandinavia? Would they say so even if some of the worst features of Socialism in Russia can be excluded from the picture on the ground of the special circumstances and inheritance of Soviet Communism? If everybody were guaranteed a minimum standard of life, if the main features of political democracy were safeguarded, and, in addition to the rights of free speech and all the other civil rights won by the bourgeoisie, there were added the new guaranteed rights of social security, adequate leisure, and adequate employment, would it not be idiotic to denounce such a system as Keynesian, reformist, Kautskyist, or any other phrase from the vocabulary of Marxist controversy, and to demand, in order to produce something called Socialism, that we should fight class war to the bitter end with all that that implies? . . .

What we have to consider is not whether the Welfare State is good (which in comparison with unrestricted capitalism it clearly is) but whether it is a *possible* alternative to Socialism, whether it can be sustained in a climate such as England, whether there is any escape from the class war which is now being fought out all over the world. To make myself quite clear, let me say that the more I can hear of it, the system now at work in the Soviet Union is bad and not good. According to my definition it is perverted Socialism. For those who have lived in a Western bourgeois democracy it would be altogether intolerable. By way of contrast, I think of Norway. A small country, still classified as capitalist in Marxist terms, but containing in itself a near equality, a freedom, and a happiness of life which I think more close to the ideal than that of any other country that the world has known. But it is no use making such comparisons if the conditions of this happy Scandinavian backwater are not present for large industrial countries such as ours. . . .

107. THE RIGHT ROAD FOR BRITAIN

by THE CONSERVATIVE PARTY

The overwhelming defeat of the Conservative Party at the election in 1945 left them stunned and bewildered. From this state they were rescued by the leadership of the party chairman, Lord Woolton, who put in hand a thorough reorganization of the party machinery and finance. The policy problem for the Conservatives was how to adopt sufficient of the Labour Party's program and achievements to undermine their opponents, without taking over so much socialism as to alarm their supporters. (It was what Disraeli had done in 1867 when he "dished the Whigs" over the Second Reform Bill.) In 1949 the Conservative statement of policy was issued as a pamphlet under the title, *The Right Road for Britain,* and in a foreword Winston Churchill, as leader of the party, wrote that he felt they were "reviving the Tory democracy of Lord Beaconsfield and after him of Lord Randolph Churchill." The following passages are from pp. 6–10.

THE CHALLENGE OF TODAY

FIRST we must earn our own livelihood. Unless we can sell our products in foreign markets at competitive prices, we shall suffer unemployment and will not be able to sustain our standard of living or our Social Services. Until we re-establish once again our economic independence, our way of life and the possibility of defending it will remain precarious.

We must maintain our moral independence and the form of society through which individuality is expressed and safeguarded. There may have been a time in the last century when it was plausible to argue that there was a danger of too much freedom, of too many large private fortunes, of too little planning and control, of too parsimonious Government expenditure. But, if that were ever the principal danger of our society, we are at the opposite extreme today. Now the fear is not that we have too much freedom or enterprise, but too little. We have too much planning and control, too much centralisation, too little money in the private purses of individual citizens, and a top-heavy administrative machine too heavy and costly for the people to carry.

Abroad we must face the world problem of the Twentieth Century —whether a Communist society on the principles of Marxist Socialism is to be establishd by gradual but inescapable pressure all over the world, or whether a rival and superior ideology can be developed and armed with sufficient inspiration to organise resistance and to win back lost ground. Britain, from her central position as the heart of the British Empire and Commonwealth, one of the leaders of Europe and the founder and centre of the English-speaking world, has a unique opportunity and a special responsibility.

By the organisation of her own social and economic life at home and by maintaining her position as a world power, Britain must assume the responsibilities of her greatness. . . .

These problems are not to be solved by proclaiming a belief in Britain. Such a belief is common ground and is not the issue between the major political parties. The country will support the Party which can show that it has a firm faith and a practical policy to match the stern tests of the hour.

THE SOCIALIST PLAN

The Labour Party is trying to create a completely Socialist Britain. The vast State monopolies which are being set up are but one aspect of a society in which all forms of power are to be centralised in the Government, and the interference of Government will pervade and dominate the private life of the citizen.

In practice Socialism is proving to be restrictive and negative. It would create a uniform and standard society in which the best is levelled down and success is the target of envious attacks.

Britain's experience is that, even in its earliest stages, Socialism is cumbersome and inefficient. It has made no contribution to regaining our economic independence. Indeed the disturbance of our basic industries has greatly aggravated our difficulties. Some Socialist leaders have fomented social strife by attacking whole classes of the community, although they have been only too ready to seek the services of these same classes in carrying out the nation's economic policy. If present policies are pursued to their logical conclusion, property with its rights and duties will be destroyed, management will be left without initiative, the trade unions will cease to be independent and local government will become a rubber stamp.

Experience abroad shows that, however democratic at heart some Socialist leaders may be, the creation of a Socialist State prepares the way for Communism. To attempt to disarm the Communists by doing peacefully and slowly the things which they want to do quickly and by force is appeasement in the worst sense of the word. So far from Socialism being a barrier to Communism, it has proved itself in other lands, by its concentration of authority, to be the stepping stone of the Communist to power.

CONSERVATIVE POLICY

We Conservatives would lead the nation through the present dark hours to a form of society centred upon the importance, the dignity and the ultimate value of the individual human being. Wherever modern life tends to dwarf the individual in comparison with the economic, political or social unit, the need is to humanise organisation, not to organise humanity. Today we insist on individual liberty not in order to proclaim anarchy, but because we fear to see freedom crushed out and human personality forgotten altogether. An individual is an end in himself and the final justification of Government is that it makes possible the fullest development of personality and enables all men and women to lead their own lives in their own way within the limits of law and social justice.

We believe that only by the release of personal energy and endeavour can our present economic difficulties be surmounted. Only by strengthening Britain's traditional way of life can the forces of totalitarianism be repelled.

Our policy, therefore, is to build a society in which all men and women will have the chance of developing their special talents and using them for their own and the community's benefit. In leisure and in work, at home and abroad, men and women find their fulfilment in a small group, in their own family, among their neighbours in the street and at the work-bench, with their fellow members in their union branches, in their clubs and in all the many voluntary organisations which enrich our national life. People find satisfaction and stability in the ownership of property, especially of their own homes and gardens. By fostering the life of communities and the variety of property we shall strengthen the independence of the individual. Power must not be concentrated in the Government; it must be diffused throughout the whole democratic community.

We believe that free enterprise is necessary to ensure independence and efficiency, and that public organisation of the social services is required in the interests of social justice.

We put forward proposals for releasing enterprise and initiative in the economic field and for encouraging private thrift and house-ownership. In industry and agriculture we shall encourage the small enterprise which depends directly on individual character and skill. We shall seek to develop personal interest in a common undertaking. Where nationalisation cannot be undone, we shall introduce some of the merits of free enterprise into the administration of nationalised industry by greater decentralization and wider opportunities for management and men. We shall safeguard the independence of the trade unions and enable them to make their special contribution to national policy. We shall restore confidence and authority to local democratic government. Through the social services we shall maintain a basic minimum below which none shall fall. Through education we shall promote equality of opportunity. We shall restore the House of Commons to its rightful place as the guardian of the individual against the

Executive. Abroad we intend to strengthen the bonds of the British Empire and Commonwealth of Nations and to fortify the ties between the freedom-loving democracies throughout the world.

Conservatives see the Britain of the future as a family of free and energetic individuals helping one another in misfortune, spiritually alive, rich in the infinite variety of social organisms and communities —a nation in which town and country, professions and unions, localities, free associations and individuals all have their own characteristic parts to play. Thus, inspired by our glorious history, shall we create a national solidarity which binds all together.

THE NATION'S CHOICE

The choice before the electorate is clear. It is the choice between the Socialist illusion that wealth can be legislated into existence and the Conservative belief that greater production and careful saving are the only ways of improving the nation's standard of life and making the social services safe; between a plan which rests on multiplying restraints and a policy which puts the emphasis on freedom; between the view that the worker is most satisfied when he is the servant of a national monopoly, and the conception of industrial reform as something which starts in the factory and with the individual; between the abolition of personal property and the extension of ownership; between social conflict and social unity; between a community in which nothing stands between the Government and the individual, and a community in which there are many centres of vigorous and independent group life. Only a society, decentralised, diversified, neighbourly, resourceful and resolute can have the idealism and vitality required to meet and defeat the challenge of the pessimist or the materialist wherever he is found.

Chapter 24.
England in the 1950s

In 1945 it was confidently assumed that Labour was likely to be in power for a long period. But after the election in 1950 the Labour majority was so small that it proved unworkable; and from 1951 the Conservatives won three elections in succession. The 1950s were thus a Conservative decade.

For the most part the issues in English society and politics during this period were a continuation from the 1940s, and fall into two broad categories. First, there was the dominant theme of Britain's external difficulties, resulting from her new—and greatly reduced—role in world relationships. This was expressed in constant economic uncertainties (resulting in a "stop-go" economic policy) and in painful readjustments to changes within the Commonwealth. There was reluctance to accept the finality of a new role in general world affairs; but events such as the fiasco of intervention in Suez in 1956 relentlessly hammered home the realities of the situation.

The second category of problems was concerned with the nature and quality of life to be attained in the welfare state. Both political parties were committed to maintaining a high level of welfare services, and indeed at elections tried to outbid each other on this score. The Conservative slogan at the 1959 election was, "you never had it so good"; and compared with the 1930s this was true for a majority of the electorate. There was a danger of complacency in this situation, and in certain important respects English society seemed to lack some of the dynamic qualities which had been present in the past. The rate of economic growth lagged behind that of Russia, America and West Germany; and the rigidities of the English class structure remained extremely tenacious. It was clear that in the 1950s social change in England was still a slow process.

108. [THE DECLINE OF THE CHURCHES]

by B. SEEBOHM ROWNTREE *and*
G. R. LAVERS

The changing attitude towards organized religion was clearly documented by Seebohm Rowntree (for whom see Reading No. 81) in the material he collected over a half century in York. By the 1950s only a minority of Englishmen were actively associated with any religious body, though a vestigial form of Christianity was more widely diffused. Within the churches the awareness that they were such a relatively weak minority led to serious self-examination, particularly over their unhappy divisions; and the ecumenical movement for reunion of the churches made considerable headway. The following reading is from B. Seebohm Rowntree and G. R. Lavers, *English Life and Leisure* (1951), pp. 342–367.

. . . THE number of places of worship of the different denominations in York in 1948 was:

Anglican	. . . .	29
Nonconformist:		
Methodist	 18	
Congregationalist	 2	
Other sects	 11	
	—	31
Roman Catholic	. . . .	5
Salvation Army	. . . .	2
Missions	. . . .	2

This total of 69 places of worship is equivalent to one for every 1,137 adults. In 1935 there was one for every 1,032 adults and in 1901 one for every 941.

The three censuses of church attendance in York were made in October, March and November respectively. From the point of view of the weather, there was nothing to render a comparison of the results of the censuses unreliable. All figures are the averages of censuses taken on two Sundays, and in each case the term "adults" has been taken to mean 17 years of age or over.

Number of Attendances at Places of Worship in York by
Adults in 1901, 1935 and 1948

	1901	1935	1948
Anglican	7,453	5,395	3,384
Nonconformist	6,447	3,883	3,514
Roman Catholic	2,360	2,989	3,073
Salvation Army (indoor services)	800	503	249
Totals	17,060	12,770	10,220

The first striking fact disclosed by this table is the steady decline in church attendances, notwithstanding the fact that the adult population of York increased from 48,000 in 1901, to 72,248 in 1935 and to 78,500 in 1948. In other words the attendances which represented 35.5 per cent of the adult population in 1901, fell to 17.7 per cent in 1935 and to 13.0 per cent in 1948. This means that the proportion of attendances at church by adults in 1948 was only a little over one-third of the proportion of attendances in 1901.

The total attendances were divided between the various denominations in the following proportions:

	1901 %	1935 %	1948 %
Anglican	43.7	42.2	33.1
Nonconformist	37.8	30.4	34.4
Roman Catholic	13.8	23.4	30.1
Salvation Army (indoor services)	4.7	4.0	2.4

To be fully significant this table should be read in conjunction with the previous one, which shows the total numbers of attendances. If this is done, it will be seen that in the thirteen years from 1935 to 1948 the Roman Catholic Church improved its position substantially relative to the other churches, but the attendances in 1948 represented a somewhat smaller proportion of the adult population of the city in 1948 than in 1935, and thus its real position is slightly less favourable than in 1935. The Anglican Church has lost ground sadly in the same years, both relatively and absolutely. It is indeed startling that in an archiepiscopal city the total attendances at Anglican Churches is less

than that at the Free Churches, and only 10% more than the attendances at the Roman Catholic Churches. Nor can the relatively
improved position of the Free Churches since 1935 be a great source
of consolation to their members, for they too have lost ground in terms
of total attendances. . . .

Quite apart from any question of belief or disbelief of the Christian
religion, which is a separate matter . . . we have found so widespread
a dislike of the ministers of religion of the Anglican and Free Churches
that it can only be described as anti-clericalism. . . .

One of the strongest criticisms of the clergy is that they are parsons
"just for a job," as another man might be a bank manager. In a remote village with which one of us is acquainted, a new vicar stopped
a man in the village street with a friendly greeting and said brightly,
"I'm the new vicar." He received the reply, "Ah, tha' has a right good
job. Stick to 'un, lad."

We have come across many other examples of this distrust of the
motives of the clergy of which we quote three as typical:

(*a*) A working-class man in early middle age. "Nobody believes all the
nonsense they read out in church. The parsons just do it to earn their
living."

(*b*) A middle-class man in middle age describes the attitude of both
church-goers and clergy as a "mixture of superstition, sentimentality, hypocrisy and—in the case of the parsons—pure chicanery."

(*c*) A working-class widow in late middle age. "Don't talk to me about
parsons! They've got a pretty soft job, if you ask me. Telling decent working
folk how to behave! What do they know about it? Never done an honest
day's work in their life, most of them." . . .

Quite apart . . . from any question of sincerity of purpose, another
factor which has tended to lower the esteem in which Protestant, and
particularly Anglican, clergy are held, is the reduction in the difference between their degree of learning and social position and those
of the average member of their congregations. This has come about in
two ways. First, the general standard of education in the country has
risen to a marked extent over the last half-century, and the economic
position of wage earners has improved even more strikingly. Second,
because of the difficulty of getting enough men of university education and high culture, a great many individuals have been accepted
for ordination whose educational standard (apart from a period of
intense but specialized study at a theological college) is not above

secondary school standard, while the economic position of the clergy —not generally too favourable at the beginning of the century—has become desperate through sharply rising costs, and stipends that have either remained stationary or at best have increased proportionately less than the cost of living, so that a curate is often paid scarcely more than an errand boy, and a vicar less than an artisan. . . .

Most people in Britain do not believe that the *Churches* are relevant to life in a scientific age because they observe that the Churches are in a double strait-jacket of clerical domination and rigid dogma. Since a considerable proportion of the clergy are respected neither for their learning nor for their personal qualities, and since much of the dogmatic belief is considered to be simply untrue, and since persons outside the Church consider that, in general, laymen within the Church do not live up to the ideals that they profess, there is a deep and widespread conviction that the Churches are of little practical account in modern life notwithstanding the fact that most children are baptized, many people are married in Church, and in most cases clergy conduct funeral services. At the same time there are three favourable factors. First, spiritual hunger. Many men and women feel the need of a supernatural religion that will reconcile the contradictions inherent in a purely secular and material conception of life. Second, vestigial Christianity. The time when open renunciation of the Church was so shocking as to be almost unthinkable is still sufficiently recent for the idea to linger at the back of people's minds that, whatever the state of the Churches, and however much the dogma may be disbelieved, there is still "something in Christianity." Third, the fact that people have a vivid sense of right and wrong, a deep sense of decency, ideals about what the pattern of family life should be, and how their country and the world should be organized. Speaking generally, the standards are Christian. . . .

109. EDUCATION 15 TO 18

by THE CROWTHER COMMITTEE

One of the least satisfactory aspects of the postwar years was the slowness with which the 1944 Education Act (see Reading No. 103) was acted upon. Unlike the Beveridge Report on social security, the 1944 educational blueprint was not accorded a very high priority, with the result that changes in public education were slow and uneven. The 1944 Act set up a Central Advisory Council for Education in England, and in 1956 this body, under the chairmanship of Sir Geoffrey Crowther (b. 1907), was given the task of investigating the education of boys and girls between 15 and 18. The following passages are from his report, *15 to 18* (1959), pp. 3, 447–473, and summarize some of the main conclusions.

13. THIS report is about the education of English boys and girls aged from 15 to 18. Most of them are not being educated. But they are all at a highly impressionable age, with their characters still being formed and, except in rare instances, with their minds still capable of considerable development. It seems to us clear—to anticipate our conclusions—that it is both necessary and practicable greatly to extend in the next few years the provison made for the education of boys and girls in their later teens . . .

* * * * * *

660. *Chapter 1. Sixty Years of Growth*

(*a*) In 1894 it is probable that 4 per cent of all boys and girls aged 14 or 15 were in school and only 1 per cent of those aged 16 and 17. It was not until 1918 that full-time education until 14 became binding on everybody. By 1938 there were roughly six times as many pupils over the age of 14 as in 1894.

(*b*) About two-fifths of all boys and girls aged 15 to 17 inclusive get education either full-time or for one day a week. The proportions of boys and of girls getting full-time education are about the same, but only 6 per cent of the girls (compared with 22 per cent of the boys) get day release.

(*c*) Part-time education by day did not begin to develop on a large scale until the end of the last war.

661. *Chapter 2. The Pattern of Secondary Education*

(*a*) There are over 2,550,000 boys and girls in maintained secondary schools; only 320,000 of them are aged 15 or over.

(*b*) Most pupils of secondary school age are in modern schools, the successors to the old senior elementary schools. The course that most pupils take is now between three and four years in duration instead of between two and three as it was until 1947.

(*c*) About half the modern schools and under 30 per cent of the grammar schools are co-educational. A varied national provision, however, does not ensure varied local opportunities.

(*d*) Fee-paying in maintained grammar schools was abolished by the Education Act of 1944 which rounded off a process already well advanced. By 1938 the majority of pupils admitted to secondary schools paid no fees.

(*e*) Secondary Technical Schools have been created since 1944 out of the old, more restricted, Junior Technical schools, but over 40 per cent of the local education authorities have no technical schools. In much of England the "tripartite" system of grammar, technical and modern schools has never come into existence.

(*f*) New types of secondary schools are being developed in many districts to provide within the same institution for pupils of the whole range of ability. In 1956 they provided for some 2 per cent of the pupils in maintained secondary schools; in 1959 for 6 per cent; the Association of Chief Education Officers estimate that by 1965 they may well contain 11 per cent.

662. *Chapter 3. Population Changes and their Educational Consequences*

(*a*) It seems clear that most families can now support their children throughout a longer school education than would formerly have been practicable. This is a consequence of earlier marriage, earlier childbearing within marriage, smaller families, longer expectation of life and more opportunities of paid employment for married women.

(*b*) But there is evidence that children in unusually large families are less likely to get a long education than other children.

(*c*) Child-bearing and child-care now represent a break in employment for married women rather than an end to it. This has important consequences for teaching as well as other careers. It points to the need for an education which encourages girls to qualify before marriage for careers and to develop interests which they can resume in later life.

(*d*) The early age of marriage points to a radically different concept of how girls of this age should be treated and educated. Over 4 per cent of the girls with whom this report is concerned are married women.

663. *Chapter 4. Changing Social Needs*

(*a*) If the family is to be as secure in the future as it has been in the past (and we can be content with nothing less), there will have to be a conscious effort to prepare the way for it through the educational system on a much greater scale than has yet been envisaged.

(*b*) The problem of sexual ethics is wider than marriage. Young people enjoy a freedom of unsupervised association which is quite new and brings both gain and loss. At the same time there is much public indecision over what is right and wrong. Disaster often results for the young.

(*c*) Juvenile delinquency and other social problems are especially marked in certain areas in which, more even than elsewhere, the teacher has to be a social worker. A quick turnover of teachers is to be especially avoided in these areas, but is commonly to be found in them.

(*d*) The fact that the peak age for juvenile delinquency is the last year at school suggests that more thought ought to be given to the conditions of boys' and girls' life, both in and out of school, during the last year or so before they reach the leaving age.

(*e*) Teen-agers are especially exposed to the influence of the "mass media" of communication. The duty to see that this power is used responsibly is one for the whole community, but there is a specific educational responsibility to see that the young learn how to approach the mass media with discrimination.

664. *Chapter 5. The Pressure of Economic Change*

(*a*) The community is about one-third richer in material wealth than it was in 1938.

(*b*) The larger part of the rise in the national standard of consumption has been in the lower income groups—those who knew the schools twenty years ago can see the revolution in the faces of the children.

(*c*) The earnings of young people have risen faster in proportion than those of adults. Those who stay at school have to resist the lure of a high immediate wage and to reconcile themselves to a lower earning capacity, until they are over 20 years of age, than that enjoyed by those who leave at 15. But it is evident that they do then catch up and go well ahead. On balance, the effects of prosperity have been beneficial to education.

(*d*) There is a growing stress on the need for special qualifications and for a good general education to secure entry into an increasing number of occupations. This tendency may be reinforced by the fact that the proportion of young people to the whole population of working age is going to rise again after a long period of decline.

(*e*) The rapidity of technological change presents an exciting challenge for those who can qualify themselves as scientists, technologists and technicians. The numbers of these produced by the schools have risen rapidly and will continue to do so. But they will remain a minority of the working population. For the remainder, the advent of a technological age creates different needs—to be able to comprehend something of the language of science and technology; to be at home in a world of machines; and to be able to adjust to a rapidly changing environment. There may be less need in the future of "skill" in the old fashioned sense of the word; what will be needed in ever-growing volume will be the quality that can perhaps be described as "general mechanical intelligence."

665. *Chapter 6. Burdens and Benefits*

(*a*) Education can be regarded in two ways—either as a duty that the state owes to its citizens, and therefore as part of the "welfare state"; or as a means of increasing the economic efficiency of the whole community, and therefore as a form of productive national capital investment. The cost of education must therefore be compared both with the other forms of welfare expenditure and with other forms of capital investment. We have not attempted to disentangle these two purposes.

(*b*) So far as can be ascertained, expenditure on the central purposes of education in schools (as distinct from school health and nutrition programmes on the one hand and from expenditure on university and other forms of higher education on the other) has in the last twenty years been doing little more than keep up with the general expansion of the national income.

(*c*) The cost of our recommendations would not be very large when set against such other items of national capital investment as expenditure on dwellings or plant and machinery, or alternatively against such items of consumption expenditure as drink and tobacco. . . .

. . . . . .

669. *Chapter 10. The Act of 1944*

Both the unfulfilled provisions of the Education Act of 1944 affecting older children—the raising of the school-leaving age to 16, and the creation of county colleges for compulsory part-time day education to 18—should be re-affirmed as objectives of national policy.

670. *Chapter 11. Why the School-Leaving Age should be Raised:*
     (1) The Benefit to the Individual

(*a*) Throughout the period, not only of physical puberty, but of emotional and social adolescence, the welfare of the individual ought to come before any marginal contribution that he or she can make to the national income.

(*b*) Many of the things that the schools can do for boys and girls can be carried much nearer completion by 16 than by 15. The secondary education for all promised in the Education Act of 1944 cannot be effectively provided unless it is continued for all to 16.

(*c*) The additional year should offer new and challenging courses and not be simply a continuation of what has gone before. These should be so devised that they satisfy the adolescent's intensified interest in the real world and recognize his rapidly growing need for independence.

671. *Chapter 12. Why the School-Leaving Age should be Raised:*
(*2*) *The National Interest*

(*a*) The country is a long way from tapping all the available supply of talent by present methods—half the National Service recruits to the Army who were rated in the two highest ability groups had left school at 15.

(*b*) It is most unlikely that this waste of talent can be remedied within a reasonable period without compulsion, because leaving at 15 is so deeply embedded in certain parts of the social structure. Among National Service recruits to the Army coming from families of manual workers, two-thirds of those rated in the two highest ability groups had left school at 15.

(*c*) The part-time route, even with day release, is not an efficient substitute for longer full-time education.

(*d*) While the number staying on at school voluntarily is increasing, this trend provides only a precarious basis for a national system, and may depend to a considerable extent on the continuation of general prosperity and, in particular, a plentiful supply of good jobs for young workers.

(*e*) The demand both for more educated workers and for more deeply educated workers is growing at almost all levels in industry—raising the school-leaving age to 16 would give those near the bottom a better foundation, and would be reflected in larger numbers receiving full-time education to 18 or beyond.

(*f*) The strongest part of the case is the general need for secondary education for all to 16 extending through the difficult and important period of adolescence. . . .

. . . . . .

694. . . . Already there is some danger, we think, of English education lagging behind the times. Even in the education of our brightest children—which is what the English system does best—there is still a grave waste of talent through too early an abandonment of formal education. We do not think that the figure of about 12 per cent of the age-group still in full-time education at the age of 17, and of 6 per cent at 20, is nearly good enough. The education that is provided for the great mass of children is inadequate both in its quality and in its duration. In the middle, between the brightest quarter and the great mass of ordinary children, the deficiencies, relatively to the need, are greatest of all, for it is in this "second quartile" that the richest vein of untapped human resources lies, which will have to be exploited if this country is to keep a place among the nations that are in the van of spiritual and material progress. . . .

. . . . . .

696. We do not believe that there is any hope of carrying out the measures we have outlined—or any other list of proposals adequate to the needs—unless they are worked out and adopted as a coherent, properly phased development programme, extending by timed and calculated steps a long way into the future. Nothing of this sort has ever hitherto been possible in English education. There has been no lack of aspiration, or of definition of objectives; but the attainment of them has been left to the mercies of the parliamentary time-table and of financial exigencies. Nothing more than this has been possible because there has not been support in public opinion for anything more. We believe this situation may be changing. Public interest in educational policies is steadily rising, and we think it should not be difficult to convince the public that there is as much need for a twenty-year programme of educational development as there is for similar programmes of railway modernisation or of atomic generation of electric power.

697. For any such programme the primary need is a public determination to will it. But when this is forthcoming, attention will have to be paid to the inadequacy of the tools that lie to the hand of the educational planner in this country. There are the most extraordinary gaps in our knowledge of what goes on in the schools and technical colleges we have today, let alone in the minds of their pupils. The Ministry's statisticians are constantly in the position of being asked to make bricks without straw. Other countries are wrestling with the same problems as ourselves and, some of them, finding interesting

solutions to them; but our knowledge of what they are doing rests far too much on the subjective basis of returning travellers' tales. When one moves from what is to what might be—the proper field of research—the absence of information is even greater. In view of the very large sums of money that are spent on education every year, the expenditure on educational research can only be regarded as pitiable. If there is to be a consistent programme of educational development, almost the first step should be to review the provision for statistics and research.

698. We plead, then, for a forward plan for education. Just as with similar plans for transport or for power, there need be nothing immutable; the money will have to be voted every year, and the details can be subject to constant modification. But if the objectives are to be attained, there will have to be a programme, with dates fixed in the future for the execution of its various component parts. Education, after all, should be peculiarly susceptible to forward planning. Teachers, once trained, practise their profession for up to forty years. The processes of institutional change, of educational fashion and practice, are necessarily slow-moving. And though the children, the objects and beneficiaries of the whole apparatus, flash through the schools in a few brief years, we know, within close limits, how many of them there will be, at least in the secondary schools, for a long way ahead. The problem is to make sure that an instrument requiring many years to prepare will be ready for opportunities that must be seized at once or they are gone for ever. Only by the most careful planning can we make sure that most of them are taken. . . .

110. ["GIVING THE PUBLIC WHAT IT WANTS"]

by THE PILKINGTON COMMITTEE

The very great influence of sound and television broadcasting in a modern society was widely assumed in England. Until the 1950s all broadcasting in the United Kingdom was undertaken by the British Broadcasting Corporation, a public body incorporated by Royal Charter. But in 1954, as a result of a campaign for commercial television conducted by a small group of Conservative backbenchers, the B.B.C.'s monopoly was broken through the establishment of another public corporation, the Independent Television Authority. This body (ITA), unlike the B.B.C., did not itself produce programs, but contracted with commercial organizations (known as "programme contractors") to provide them. These programs relied upon advertising revenue, and were therefore "commercial TV." In 1964 both the B.B.C.'s charter and the ITA's powers were due for review, and so in 1960 a committee under the chairmanship of Sir Harry Pilkington (b. 1905) was appointed to consider the future of broadcasting in the United Kingdom. The committee was critical of ITA, and considered the B.B.C. was doing a good job. The following passage deals with the controversial topic of "giving the public what it wants" and is from the *Report of the Committee on Broadcasting, 1960* (1962), pp. 14–19.

41. AS we have already noted, the disquiet about television derived from the view that the power of the medium to influence and persuade is immense. This assessment is widely regarded as being self-evident; but, since it lies at the root of much that is said and thought about the conduct of the television services, we examined it closely. Some found a striking expression of their views in the assertion of the Beveridge Committee ten years before that "broadcasting is the most pervasive, and therefore one of the most powerful of agents for influencing men's thoughts and actions." Many drew attention to the special characteristics of television: to its capacity for dramatic presentation and so for exemplifying in a specially effective way the thoughts and actions of living people, to the transience of its pictorial statements, and to the consequent difficulty of analysing and criticising them. If the medium has unique characteristics, so too have television audiences. Many submissions drew attention to the vast size of the audiences for many programme items; audiences of over eighteen millions are not unusual and of twelve millions relatively common. Another characteristic often attributed to television audiences was, in the words of the Workers' Educational Association, their vulnerability. "Going to a cinema or a theatre, buying or borrowing a book or a magazine involve a conscious critical approach," said the Association; by contrast, "The television audience is vulnerable to influence in a way that readers of newspapers and cinema audiences are not." Sitting at home, people are relaxed, less consciously critical and, therefore, more exposed. Further, audi-

ences are often family groups and include children who are normally protected from outside influences, and therefore especially vulnerable. Many submissions emphasized how the power of television was due largely to the unique way in which it brought actuality, or the appearance of actuality, into the home. This point was most effectively made by a spokesman of the Proprietary Association of Great Britain, who said this to us: "The best way to sell the goods is to put a man in the home. The nearest you can get to that is television."

42. We cannot say that this assessment of the power of the medium is proved. So far, there is little conclusive evidence on the effects of television on values and moral attitudes. But those who work professionally in this sphere told us that what evidence there was, showed that there was an effect. We were told that this effect, good or bad, need not be sudden or spectacular. Rather it was to be compared with that of water dripping on a stone: persistent, apparently imperceptible, but in the end prevailing. It may be that in this sphere cause and effect can never be absolutely demonstrable. But there must be a presumption one way or the other on which to found policies for the conduct of the services, and against which to measure the responsibilities of those who provide them. The strong tide of opinion, explicit or implicit, in the submissions to us, leaves no doubt whatsoever what, in their authors' views, the presumption should be. Our own judgment, after weighing such evidence as is available to us, leads us to a clear conclusion. It is that, unless and until there is unmistakable proof to the contrary, the presumption must be that television is and will be a main factor in influencing the values and moral standards of our society. We strongly refute the argument that because an effect has not been conclusively proved the broadcasting authorities need not concern themselves with it. The measure of their responsibility is this: that by its nature, broadcasting must be in a constant and sensitive relationship with the moral condition of society. Broadcasters are, and must be, involved; this gives them a responsibility they cannot evade.

43. Whereas the disquiet about television arose from "sins of commission"—from the conviction that its capacity to influence people was often misused—the dissatisfaction, the other main element in the submissions made to us, arose from "sins of omission"—from the conviction that many of the best potentialities of television were simply not being realised. The theme common to nearly all those submissions which expressed dissatisfaction was that programme items were far too often devised with the object of seeking, at whatever cost in quality

or variety, the largest possible audience; and that, to attain this object, the items nearly always appealed to a low level of public taste. This was not, of course, to say that all items which attracted large audiences were poor. But in far too many the effect was to produce a passively acquiescent or even indifferent audience rather than an actively interested one. There was a lack of variety and originality, an adherence to what was "safe"; and an unwillingness to try challenging, demanding and, still less, uncomfortable subject matter. It was put to us that, in television as elsewhere, one man's meat ought to be another man's poison; that too often viewers were offered neither meat nor poison but pap—because, presumably, though no-one much likes it, at least no-one will get indigestion. Against this, it has been said that in fact people watch these items; that the justification lies precisely in the fact that they are mass-appeal items. In a free society, this is what people freely choose; they do not have to watch; they can switch off. In short, by these tests, these items are "what the public wants," and to provide anything else is to impose on people what someone thinks they ought to like. Indeed, it has been held that, for this reason, it is not of great relevance to criticise television at all. We found this last a deflating thought.

44. We were bound to examine these alternative and opposing views. "To give the public what it wants" seems at first sight unexceptionable. But when applied to broadcasting it is difficult to analyse. The public is not an amorphous, uniform mass; however much it is counted and classified under this or that heading, it is composed of individual people; and "what the public wants" is what individual people want. They share some of their wants and interests with all or most of their fellows; and it is necessary that a service of broadcasting should cater for these wants and interests. There is in short a considerable place for items which all or most enjoy. To say, however, that the only way of giving people what they want is to give them these items is to imply that all individuals are alike. But no two are. Each is composed of a different pattern of tastes, abilities and possibilities; and even within each person the emphasis on this or that part of the pattern is not always the same. Some of our tastes and needs we share with virtually everybody; but most—and they are often those which engage us most intensely—we share with different minorities. A service which caters only for majorities can never satisfy all, or even most, of the needs of any individual. It cannot, therefore, satisfy all the needs of the public.

45. Television has not of course the time to cater for all tastes. If all programmes excited in us an equal intensity of interest it might, therefore, be wrong to use its limited time to appeal to interests shared only by a few, at the expense of those common to most. But they do not. A television viewer may be acquiescent or indifferent; he may be enthusiastic. It is by no means obvious that a vast audience watching television all the evening will derive a greater sum of enjoyment from it than will several small audiences each of which watches for part of the evening only. For the first may barely tolerate what it sees; while the second might enjoy it intensely.

46. No one can say he is giving the public what it wants, unless the public knows the whole range of possibilities which television can offer and, from this range, chooses what it wants to see. For a choice is only free if the field of choice is not unnecessarily restricted. The subject matter of televison is to be found in the whole scope and variety of human awareness and experience. If viewers—"the public" —are thought of as "the mass audience," or "the majority," they will be offered only the average of common experience and awareness; the "ordinary"; the commonplace—for what all know and do is, by definition, commonplace. They will be kept unaware of what lies beyond the average of experience; their field of choice will be limited. In time they may come to like only what they know. But it will always be true that, had they been offered a wider range from which to choose, they might and often would have chosen otherwise, and with greater enjoyment.

47. It might be said that this is a theoretical argument; that in fact there is no point in offering the public the whole range of experience from which to choose. For much of it will not be understood, far less enjoyed, by more than a very few; and, though television is to cater for minorities, the line must be drawn somewhere. There is of course some truth in this; and those who draw the line have to make a judgment of the public's capacity for interest and enjoyment. No one can claim to know what this is; and it would be presumptuous to make the claim. We have seen in the past thirty years the development of a widespread interest in symphony concerts which could never have been predicted: competitive swimming, both as a pursuit and as a spectacle, has captured the public's interest in an even shorter time: where interest in classical literature was all but dead, now there has been a sudden demand for pocket translations of the classics. In each instance, to have denied the public the chance to develop the taste

would have deprived many of pleasures—in short, would have deprived them of "what they want." The point was neatly made to us as follows: "Those who say they give the public what it wants begin by under-estimating public taste, and end by debauching it."

48. In summary, it seems to us that "to give the public what it wants" is a misleading phrase: misleading because as commonly used it has the appearance of an appeal to democratic principle but the appearance is deceptive. It is in fact patronising and arrogant, in that it claims to know what the public is, but defines it as no more than the mass audience; and in that it claims to know what it wants, but limits its choice to the average of experience. In this sense we reject it utterly. If there is a sense in which it should be used, it is this: what the public wants and what it has the right to get is the freedom to choose from the widest possible range of programme matter. Anything less than that is deprivation.

49. The alternative is often presented as this; that the broadcaster should "give the public what he thinks is good for it." This philosophy too we would reject as patronising and arrogant. But it was never advocated to us in evidence; and it is not, as is sometimes suggested, the only alternative. The choice is not between *either* "giving the public what it wants," *or* "giving the public what someone thinks is good for it," and nothing else. There is an area of possibility between the two; and it is within this area that the choice lies. The broadcasting authorities have certainly a duty to keep sensitively aware of the public's tastes and attitudes as they now are and in all their variety; and to care about them. But if they do more than that, this is not to give the public "what someone thinks is good for it." It is to respect the public's right to choose from the widest possible range of subject matter and so to enlarge worthwhile experience. Because, in principle, the possible range of subject matter is inexhaustible, all of it can never be presented, nor can the public know what the range is. So, the broadcaster must explore it, and choose from it first. This might be called "giving a lead": but it is not the lead of the autocratic or arrogant. It is the proper exercise of responsibility by public authorities duly constituted as trustees for the public interest.

50. The antithesis: "broadcasting should give the public what it wants, and not what someone thinks is good for the public" is, then, a gross over-simplification of a complex and continuing problem; a statement which presents unreal extremes of view as though they were the only choice. That they have become the usual expression of two

alleged and opposing philosophies is unfortunate: and for this reason we cannot escape using them. But they should be recognised for what they are: slogans which are largely deceptive. . . .

51. To sum up: from our preliminary study of the representations put to us, it seemed to us that there was ground for supposing that in television the purposes of broadcasting were to a material extent not being realised. . . .

FURTHER READING: Part Six

Churchill, Winston S., *The Second World War*, 6 vols. (1948–1953).

Hoggart, Richard, *The Uses of Literacy* (1957).

Marsh, David C., *The Changing Social Structure of England and Wales, 1871–1951* (1958).

Titmuss, R. M., *Essays on "The Welfare State"* (1958).

Watkins, Ernest, *The Cautious Revolution* (1950).

Worswick, G. D. N. and P. H. Ady, *The British Economy, 1945–1950* (1952).

Worswick, G. D. N. and P. H. Ady, *The British Economy in the Nineteen Fifties* (1963).